Innocent
Abroad

Innocent Abroad

Charles Dickens's American Engagements

JEROME MECKIER

THE UNIVERSITY PRESS OF KENTUCKY

Library of Congress Cataloging-in-Publication Data

Meckier, Jerome.
    Innocent abroad : Charles Dickens's American engagements / Jerome
Meckier.
        p.   cm.
    Bibliography: p.
    Includes index.
    ISBN 0-8131-1707-0 :
    1. Dickens, Charles, 1812-1870—Journeys—United States.
2. United States—Description and travel. I. Title.
PR4581.M48   1989
823'.8—dc20
[B]   89-16530

For my mother and father,
and for my daughter, Alison

Contents

"Don't be so dreadfully regardless of yourself. Don't go to America!"

—Tom Pinch to Martin Chuzzlewit

Preface

Charles Dickens visited America—unsuccessfully—twice. In 1842, the overly expectant novelist discovered his fundamental Englishness, becoming more British and less equalitarian each day he spent in the United States. The new country, as yet rough hewn, did not just fall short of the ideal democratic republic; it also displeased by demanding unqualified praise, as if these United States had already implemented the perfect social contract. Such perfection, Dickens sadly perceived, was foreign to the nature of things.

American Notes, his first travel book, and *Martin Chuzzlewit*, his sixth novel, reveal a major disappointment that adversely affected his worldview for the remainder of his career. The letdown in 1842 was ideological, not just monetary; the would-be utopist suffered a more serious blow than did the commerical novelist, despite the celebrated embroilment with an informal confederacy of American publishers determined to continue pirating his work.

A quarter of a century later, Dickens failed to exercise shrewd management: he compounded several misjudgments prior to the start of the reading tour by proving insufficiently flexible during it when profits were threatened. Had the ticket speculators been thwarted, receipts could easily have swelled into the bonanza that this venture is wrongly assumed to have been. Collectively, scalpers made more from Dickens's performances in 1867-68 than he did—an ironic reprise of the success American publishers enjoyed by reprinting his work without compensating him.

Noel C. Peyrouton, founding editor of *Dickens Studies* and an authority on Dickens in America, once confided that he considered *American Notes* conclusive proof that Boz had been too British to understand us. Thirteen years later, in 1980, I retrieved this remarkable insight as the basis for a Gallery Series lecture at the University of Ken-

tucky's M.I. King Library. Revised for delivery to the Victorian Association of the Five Colleges, a meeting held at the University of Massachusetts in Amherst, it then became a paper in the *Modern Language
Review*; that paper, revised again and enlarged, is now chapter 1.

The second chapter began as a review essay (for *Dickens Quarterly*)
of Sidney P. Moss's partisan book on Dickens's "quarrel" with America.
This monograph was the culmination of an unfortunate revaluation process: the credulous reviving of allegations first lodged against the visiting novelist (and then against *Martin Chuzzlewit*) nearly a century and
a half ago. Conspiratorial editors of America's newspapers, however,
were more successful than either Moss or Alexander Welsh (in *From
Copyright to Copperfield*) at putting Dickens undeservedly in the
wrong, not just on the copyright question, but as the ungentlemanly
party in that controversy, which I show to have been insidious.

Revaluators of Dickens's first visit forget that it was the last of a
marvelous cluster, each trip inspiring a famous travel book. Looking
back at investigative tours by Basil Hall (1827-28), Mrs. Trollope (1828-
31), Alexis de Tocqueville (1831-32), and Harriet Martineau (1834-36),
Dickens considered his 1842 trip climactic; it gave him an opportunity
to utter cautionary words about the chimerical efficacy of fresh starts;
that is, it alerted him to the unregenerative nature of the social process
and the limited prospects for any substantial renovation of human nature. In both *American Notes* and *Martin Chuzzlewit*, Dickens focused
on Tocqueville, Fanny Trollope, and especially Miss Martineau just as
steadily as he looked at America: he challenged prior judgments that
seemed too favorable and magnified reservations in what is depicted in
chapter 3 as a revisional battle royal.

Treating the overlapping themes of Love, Health, and Money,
chapters 4 and 5 correct existing interpretations of Dickens's second
visit; it should be presented as an ironic second coming that raised new
problems instead of allowing him to settle old scores. Chapter 4 relies
heavily on new information from the diaries of Annie Adams Fields, the
thirty-three-year-old wife of Dickens's American publisher (the diaries
are housed in the Massachusetts Historical Society). She was strongly
drawn to the fifty-five-year-old novelist and he to her. Besides preferring George Dolby's account of the Chief's health problems during the
readings over those given by John Forster and Edgar Johnson, chapter
5 uses correspondence in the James T. Fields Collection at the Huntington Library and the account books of Ticknor and Fields (in Harvard's Houghton Library) to revaluate business arrangements with the

firm Dickens called his "only authorized representatives in America."
They did not treat him more liberally than good business sense dictated; indeed, he and Fields argued twice: in the beginning over the
performer's plan to commence touring in New York and at the end over
the extent to which the publisher had acquired rights to *The Mystery
of Edwin Drood.*

Three patterns are thus charted and compared in two successive
chapters: Dickens's hold on Annie Fields's heart strengthened in spite
of his physical ups and downs caused by influenza and regardless of the
string of humiliating defeats his manager suffered trying to outflank a
legion of ticket speculators.

One can demonstrate how much more rewarding the reading tour
could have been if Dickens, often denigrated as an opportunist, had
been more mercenary. Given the extent to which he captivated Annie
Fields, however, the novelist was not in extremely poor health by winter 1868, not ill to the point where he can be said already to have begun
working himself to death—if, in fact, he ever did. Nor was he sorely
missing Ellen Ternan: since an infatuated Annie Fields was willing to
imagine herself occupying Georgina Hogarth's position in the Gad's
Hill household, it remains uncertain whether Dickens's American
sponsors knew all about Ellen.

Finally, chapter 6 reexamines Dickens's parting comments at the
1868 New York press dinner; they bear a strong resemblance to the
good-natured copyright speech delivered in Boston a quarter of a century earlier with unexpected inflammatory effects. Such similarity not-
withstanding, it was impossible to apologize to Americans for treating
them so unfavorably in *American Notes* and *Martin Chuzzlewit.* Even
if an apology had been possible, the country could never have refunded
the vast sums it had denied Dickens, nor could it have retracted the
bleaker outlook on social progress and human nature that he had begun
to acquire there.

I am grateful for fellowship support twice from the Huntington Library
and on two occasions also from the Travel to the Collections Program
of the National Endowment for the Humanities. Librarians at the Huntington Library, Widener Library, the Houghton Library, the Free Library of Philadelphia, and the Massachusetts Historical Society—all
excellent places to work—were unfailingly helpful. Excerpts from Annie Fields's diary and from documents in the Fields Collection appear
by permission of the Massachusetts Historical Society and the Hun-

tington Library. A paragraph from Dickens's letter for 16 October 1867 is quoted with the permission of the Rare Book Department of the Free Library and the editors of the Pilgrim edition of Dickens's *Letters*.

Grants from the University of Kentucky Research Foundation made possible extended stays in Cambridge and Boston and financed a swing duplicating Dickens's in 1842 (by car this time, not boat) from Cincinnati through Louisville to Cairo and St. Louis and then north again as far as "The Golden Lamb" in Lebanon, Ohio. Jerome Hamilton Buckley's comments over lunch at the Harvard Faculty Club were instructive as well as supportive. Also helpful were conversations with my former colleagues at the University of Massachusetts, Thomas Ashton and David Paroissien. At the University of Kentucky, Joseph Bryant, Donald Ringe, and John Clubbe have always listened patiently and offered excellent advice. Finally, my thanks go to the staff of Harvard's Dunster House, where I was once resident tutor, for continued demonstrations of hospitality.

Abbreviations

A   Arthur A. Adrian, *Georgina Hogarth and the Dickens Circle* (London: Oxford Univ. Press, 1957)

AN   Charles Dickens, *American Notes*, ed. John S. Whitley and Arthur Goldman (Baltimore, Md.: Penguin, 1972)

AW   Alexander Welsh, *From Copyright to Copperfield: The Identity of Dickens* (Cambridge: Harvard Univ. Press, 1987)

B   James J. Barnes, *Authors, Publishers, and Politicians: The Quest for an Anglo-American Copyright Agreement, 1815-1854* (Columbus: Ohio Univ. Press, 1974)

BH   Charles Dickens, *Bleak House*, ed. Duane DeVries (New York: Crowell, 1971)

CD   Gilbert Keith Chesterton, *Charles Dickens* (New York: Schocken, 1965)

CD-TF   Sidney P. Moss, "Charles Dickens and Frederick Chapman's Agreement with Ticknor and Fields," *Papers of the Bibliographical Society of America* 75 (1981), 35-38

D   George Dolby, *Charles Dickens As I Knew Him: The Story of the Reading Tours in Great Britain and America* (New York: Haskell House, 1970)

DA   Alexis de Tocqueville, *Democracy in America*, ed. Richard D. Heffner (New York: Mentor, 1965)

DAF   Diaries of Annie Adams Fields, Massachusetts Historical Society, Boston

DC   Charles Dickens, *David Copperfield*, ed. George H. Ford (Boston: Houghton Mifflin, 1958)

DM   Frances Trollope, *Domestic Manners of the Americans* (Oxford: Oxford Univ. Press, 1984)

E   Hebe Elsna, *Unwanted Wife: A Defense of Mrs. Charles Dickens* (London: Jarrolds, 1963)

EP	Edward F. Payne, *Dickens Days in Boston* (Boston: Houghton Mifflin, 1927)
EW	Edward Wagenknecht, *Dickens and the Scandalmongers* (Norman: Univ. of Oklahoma Press, 1965)
F	John Forster, *Life of Charles Dickens*, ed. Andrew Lang (New York: Charles Scribner's Sons, 1899)
FC	James T. Fields Collection, Huntington Library, San Marino, California
GC	George Curry, *Charles Dickens and Annie Fields* (San Marino, Calif.: Huntington Library, 1988)
GF	George Ford, *Dickens and His Readers* (New York: Norton, 1965)
HD	Joseph Conrad, *Heart of Darkness*, ed. Robert Kimbrough (New York: Norton, 1971)
IA	Mark Twain, *The Innocents Abroad or The New Pilgrims Progress* (New York: Signet, 1980)
J	Edgar Johnson, *Charles Dickens: His Tragedy and Triumph* (New York: Simon and Schuster, 1952)
JA	James C. Austin, *Fields of the Atlantic Monthly: Letters to an Editor, 1861-70* (San Marino, Calif.: Huntington Library, 1953)
JP	Aldous Huxley, *Jesting Pilate* (London: Chatto and Windus, 1926)
JW	James Grant Wilson, *Thackeray in the United States, 1852-3, 1855-6* (New York: Dodd, Mead, 1909)
K	Fred Kaplan, *Dickens: A Biography* (New York: Morrow, 1988)
KF	Kate Field, *Pen Photographs of Charles Dickens's Readings* (Boston: Osgood, 1871)
KP	Andrew J. Kappel and Robert L. Patten, "Dickens' Second American Tour and His 'Utterly Worthless and Profitless' American Rights," *Dickens Studies Annual* 7 (Carbondale: Southern Illinois Univ. Press, 1978)
L	John Lauber, *The Making of Mark Twain: A Biography* (New York: American Heritage, 1985)
M	Sidney P. Moss, *Charles Dickens' Quarrel with America* (Troy, N.Y.: Whitston, 1984)
MC	Charles Dickens, *Martin Chuzzlewit*, ed. Margaret Cardwell (Oxford: Clarendon Press, 1982)
MH	M.A. De Wolfe Howe, *Memories of a Hostess* (Boston: Atlantic Monthly Press, 1922)

MM	George Eliot, *Middlemarch*, ed. Gordon Haight (Boston: Houghton Mifflin, 1958)
N	Ada Nisbet, *Dickens and Ellen Ternan* (Berkeley: Univ. of California Press, 1952)
NFD	Houston A. Baker, Jr., *Narrative of the Life of Frederick Douglass, an American Slave* (Harmondsworth, Eng.: Penguin, 1987)
NL	Walter Dexter, ed., *The Letters of Charles Dickens* (Bloomsbury, Eng.: Nonesuch, 1938)
NP	Noel Peyrouton, "Bozmania vs. Bozphobia: A Yankee Pot-Pourri," *Dickens Studies* 4 (1968), 78-94
OMF	Charles Dickens, *Our Mutual Friend* (New York: Modern Library, 1960)
P	Robert L. Patten, *Charles Dickens and His Publishers* (Oxford: Clarendon Press, 1978)
PD	Paul B. Davis, "Dickens and the American Press, 1842," *Dickens Studies* 4 (1968), 32-77
PL	*The Letters of Charles Dickens: The Pilgrim Edition*, ed. Madeline House et al. (Oxford: Clarendon Press, 1974)
PS	Paul Schlicke, *Dickens and Popular Entertainment* (London: Allen and Unwin, 1985)
RF	Raymund Fitzsimons, *Garish Lights: The Public Readings of Charles Dickens* (Philadelphia, Pa.: Lippincott, 1970)
RS	Ralph Straus, *Charles Dickens: A Biography from New Sources* (New York: Grosset and Dunlap, 1928)
S	Michael Slater, *Dickens on America and the Americans* (Austin: Univ. of Texas Press, 1978)
SA	Harriet Martineau, *Society in America*, ed. Seymour Martin Lipset (New Brunswick, N.J.: Transaction, 1981)
SM	Sylvère Monod, *Martin Chuzzlewit* (London: Allen and Unwin, 1985)
SN	Philip Collins, *Sikes and Nancy and Other Public Readings* (Oxford: Oxford Univ. Press, 1983)
T	W.S. Tryon, *Parnassus Corner: A Life of James T. Fields, Publisher to the Victorians* (Boston: Houghton Mifflin, 1963)
TAJ	T.A. Jackson, *Charles Dickens: The Progress of a Radical* (New York: International Publishers, 1987)
W	William Glyde Wilkins, *Charles Dickens in America* (New York: Haskell House, 1970)
Y	James T. Fields, *Yesterdays with Authors* (Boston: James Osgood, 1872)

1

Dickens Discovers Dickens

When Dickens discovered America in 1842, he was world famous, universally beloved, and profoundly unhappy with social conditions in the Old World. America had been haunting his dreams: did this democratic republic coincide with his utopian fantasies?[1] Not long after arriving, he began to realize that it did not and could not. In place of El Dorado, Dickens found a self-centered society that seemed militantly materialistic, many of its dollar-serving citizens not just brazen in their acquisitiveness but so unrefined and uncivil by British standards as to appear savage, without a trace or prospect of nobility.

As grandiose expectations collided with frontier habits, the first visit became a nasty formative experience—a blow to innocence on a par with the stint in Warren's Blacking Warehouse or the shock of Mary Hogarth's death. Dickens's unfavorable comments have less to do with America than with the revelations he had about himself—about his bedrock Englishness—while preparing them; his projected triumphal tour turned out to be a voyage of self-discovery.

The voyage had three stages, during only the first of which Dickens was physically traveling. (1) The novelist underwent a change of heart while still in the New World; this shift in attitude is reflected in the negative reports he sent home, which culminated in *American Notes* (1842), an anti-American travel book based on his letters to such privileged correspondents as John Forster and William Macready. (2) Undeceived and feeling defrauded, Dickens could not keep a gnawing sense of disappointment from depressing his heretofore largely comic vision of society and human nature. *Martin Chuzzlewit* (1843-44) registered the onset of a bleaker outlook; after he introduced eight American episodes, the subsequent British chapters became noticeably more satirical. (3) Reconsideration of man's allegedly Edenic past in terms of America's present led to humbler expectations for society's future;

it was foolish, Dickens decided, to pretend that man had been perfect or ever could be. In short, America failed to corroborate Rousseau's idea of a more innocent past and Victorian forecasts of a glittering tomorrow; this double letdown was largely responsible for Dickens's increasing negativity, which turned the later fictions, except for *David Copperfield*,[2] into ever gloomier dystopian pronouncements.

The quondam republican, disgusted with America, and the creator of despicable Englishmen such as Jonas Chuzzlewit, Pecksniff, and Montague Tigg appear to be traveling in opposite directions during the years 1842-44—unless the modern revaluator discerns a dual process informing the three stages just enumerated. The novelist elevated his newly cherished Englishness while using America to devalue human nature's capacity for new starts—that is, for significant and lasting betterment. One process did not rule out the other; instead they coexisted until the latter eventually prevailed as a painful and more encompassing truth.

The farther the Englishman distanced himself from Jefferson Brick and General Choke, the more strongly the disappointed utopian was compelled to acknowledge a fraternity no longer desired. Man's perennial flaws, writ absurdly large in America and thus unmistakably visible, brought the two countries together in a counterpoint yoking elements that were, ironically, both similar and dissimilar. England's customs and traditions put America's bad manners to shame, but imperfection, a core of selfishness and deceit, developed into an ironic synonym for the common humanity in all men.

Paradoxically, Dickens grew increasingly English and superior at the moment his revised estimate made all men, at home or abroad, equally unqualified candidates for the ideal society. The middle-class Englishman's opinion of what it meant to be British rose in *American Notes* and again more insistently in *Martin Chuzzlewit*, while the satirical novelist's view of human nature sharply declined, particularly throughout the latter. Since America was neither a return to Eden nor the promised land, England became a better place than before; with the cancellation of utopia past and future, however, the world's prospects worsened.

Greater self-awareness was offset by darker hues, both of which Dickens's newly complicated artistic personality imparted to subsequent work. The consolations of identity were accompanied by the crystallization of a nonroseate philosophy that extracted much of the pleasure from self-realization. Instead of supplying an alternative social system, the New World was a detour that rerouted Dickens permanently: obliged to say goodbye to exalted sentiments and romantic dreams, he began expanding and coordinating the stringent social criticisms already mounting in his first five novels.

Madeline House and the other editors of the Pilgrim edition of *The Letters of Charles Dickens* sensed as much when they contended that the "American visit has never been thoroughly examined."[3] America's role as both catalyst and contributing cause in the shaping of Victorian England's foremost writer has been underestimated, one may insist, because the process of epiphany was unique: it was sudden and dramatic in 1842 and yet prolonged, a political and philosophical watershed growing in size and extent from one year to the next; in other words, Dickens's traumatic disillusionment, his loss of an alternative vision when it was needed most, changed the course of his career and kept right on changing it. The 1842 visit does not just confirm the division of Dickens's works into two phases, the early comic novels yielding to an increasingly satirical social realism; it also separates a pre-America Dickens, who coincided with the first phase, from a post-America Dickens for the second.

After nearly fifty pages devoted to the New World, Edgar Johnson's conclusion that Boz was "an Englishman after all" will not do (J, 1:405); Dickens behaved in America like an Englishman *from the start.* The biographer ignores the steps by which Dickens himself came to realize this fact and then resolved to capitalize upon it artistically. Johnson's statement sounds accurate at first reading, as does Forster's choice of "*Chuzzlewit* Disappointments" as the heading for 1843-44 (F, 1:327), but the implication in both is that disenchantment had mainly local effects, as if one could treat an ordeal's long-term consequences as an interruption.

"The significance of Dickens's American journey in his career," editors of the recent Penguin edition of *American Notes* cautiously speculate, "is quite possibly greater than is commonly thought. He left England one kind of reformer and he returned another" (AN, 35). Actually, he returned as committed to radical reform as he had been when he departed, possibly more so, but his estimate of man's capacity for reform, of the extent to which individuals and institutions could be improved, had changed. One could say that Dickens went out an *innocent* reformer, a young Marlow or untested Kurtz, and returned more experienced but less sanguine: gone prematurely—that is, well before the critical cultural transitions of the 1850s and 1860s—was the confident meliorist soon to become one of the archetypal, indeed stereotypic, personas of many Victorian progressives. This persona became a former self to whom the more skeptical, more satirical Dickens would give offense whenever he encountered it as part of the makeup of a rival novelist.

The Penguin editors add that the American trip "appears to have given Dickens further insight into the nature of evil. Depths of hypocrisy, malice, duplicity appear to have been unveiled to him" (AN, 35). This comment inadequately suggests the Conradian coloring with which one may imbue the first visit. The journey influenced the rest of Dickens's career by obliging him to expunge from his mind any secular political philosophy or semiscientific sociology reluctant to acknowledge the full extent of man's innate imperfectibility; this basic flaw, an irreparable consequence of original sin, made constant struggles to rehabilitate communities mandatory but ruled out steady, inevitable progress toward earthly utopia.

Consequently, Alexander Welsh ought not to question the prominence biographical criticism has traditionally given to eye-opening encounters (AW, 2). One must revise not just the number of Dickens's life-shaping experiences (from two to three) but their nature. He drew great strength from early disappointments, enormous amounts of personal resolve and creative energy; it is almost as if these setbacks had been the wellsprings of his art. When Welsh tones down the Blacking Warehouse episode as an excuse for also palliating the political and personal turnabouts that America caused, Dickens's life becomes deceptively smoother, forfeiting the fateful days and untoward events characteristic of his sensational realism and doubtless among its sources; his art comes to seem less fully funded, the Swiftian satire curiously underfueled.

Welsh's idea that Dickens's personality coalesced in midlife (at age thirty) mainly through playful engagements with the work of Milton and Molière (AW, viii) is tame and misleading. It confuses the re-finement of an artistic identity with the starker re-formation process with which it was concurrent but which it ultimately capped, thereby adding spice to redirection. First, Dickens found out who he was and learned that the world is always and everywhere defective. Disenfranchised, he discarded his misjudgments by attacking the delusions of previous thinkers, especially nineteenth-century visitors to America, as chapter 3 will show. Only then was he ready to bolster his discovery of the depths of hypocrisy in man's fallen nature with allusions to Tartuffe for Pecksniff and to Paradise Lost in the American chapters. In short, Dickens relied on Milton and Molière to separate himself further from rival philosophies, but American Notes and Martin Chuzzlewit extensively contradicted earlier travelogues to effect that separation forcefully. The way in which they did so is the real story.

Along with Warren's Blacking and Mary Hogarth's death, American disappointments deserve to be paramount—if only because the self-conscious novelist learned to employ them that way: that is, as epiphanic persons and places, palpable yet so diaphanous that he believed they had helped him see into the heart of things and explain his life to himself. The conclusion that Dickens "did not suffer an 'identity crisis' of debilitating proportions" in 1842 (AW, 12) is accurate only if one italicizes *debilitating*. Dickens's losses—whether of self-esteem, an idolized sister-in-law, or utopian anticipations—were necessarily depressing; the last sharpened his comedy to a satiric edge. But they were never enfeebling or impairing. On the contrary, they deepened and enriched his art, besides specifically inspiring David Copperfield, Little Nell, and *Martin Chuzzlewit*. Paradoxically, each jolt to a maturing mind and high-strung nervous system provided an artistic windfall, in America's case simultaneously with the consternations it brought.

From 22 January 1842, when he landed in Boston, until April, when he headed west "through the wilds of Kentucky" (F, 1:230) for St. Louis and a glimpse of American prairie, Dickens spent the bulk of his time in New England and New York; he also visited Philadelphia, Washington, Richmond, Baltimore, Harrisburg, and Pittsburgh. On the return from St. Louis, he went north to Montreal before repairing to New York for the voyage home. Dickens toured businesses, schools, hospitals, and prisons, and one gathers from *American Notes* that some of these institutions impressed him favorably as models of enlightened reform;[4] but he soon began to wonder whether he had come to see America or to enable America to see him: he had traveled across the Atlantic to be a spectator and honored guest, not the spectacle he immediately became. As a result, although *American Notes* tries to record what Dickens saw, the American chapters of *Martin Chuzzlewit* are often about being seen and the discomforts steady scrutiny brings.

Public dinners, receptions formal and informal, even a Boz Ball in New York (14 February) turned the visiting novelist into a public exhibit. In Philadelphia during one of the worst of these debacles (8 March), Dickens became a hand-shaking machine: he reports being kept standing for hours by 500 total strangers; acquainted with him in print, they felt entitled to treat his person with importunate familiarity (PL, 3:75n). At the two-hour levee held each day of his stopover in Hartford (8-10 February), he was mobbed by between 200 and 300 people, an average of at least one new face every thirty-six seconds (F, 1:221). Afterward, the novelist needed only to combine Philadelphia and Hartford impertinences to create the ultimate "occular inspection." This comic traffic jam at Captain Kedgick's, featuring every species of hand and hand shaker, is so phantasmagoric it becomes a daytime nightmare for Martin Chuzzlewit, proof that hell is other people:

Up they came with a rush. Up they came until the room was full, and, through the open door, a dismal perspective of more to come was shown upon the stairs. One after another, one after another, dozen after dozen, score after score, more, more, more, up they came: all shaking hands with Martin. Such varieties of hands, the thick, the thin, the short, the long, the fat, the lean, the coarse, the fine; such differences of temperature, the hot, the cold, the dry, the moist, the flabby; such diversities of grasp, the tight, the loose, the short-lived, and the lingering! Still up, up, up, more, more, more: and ever and anon the captain's voice was heard above the crowd—"There's more below! There's more below. . . . Will you clear? Will you be so good as clear, gentlemen, and make a little room for more?" (*MC*, 365)[5]

Nor were orchestrated, ceremonial incivilities the extent of Dickens's difficulties with American inquisitiveness. The boat carrying the novelist and his wife from Sandusky to Buffalo stopped overnight at Cleveland (24 April). The next morning, "a party of 'gentlemen,'" Dickens wrote in italics to Forster, planted themselves outside the cabin window and stared in "while I was washing and Kate lay in bed" (J, 1:418).

Compared with these intrusions, constant demands for his autograph and several hundred requests for a lock of his hair seemed minor inconveniences. The New York barber who cut Dickens's hair and then offered the clippings as premiums to attract female customers deserves a prize for ingenuity (PD, 74). In London, Dickens had walked the streets at will, but gaping Americans taught him the meaning of dehumanization. Perhaps as a consequence, the dramatic readings later done for money, both in England and during the second American visit (1867-68), were designed to afford the kind of author-reader contact that he discovered he really desired: controlled periods of performance and intoxicating applause followed by a return to sobriety in private.

Initially, Dickens viewed his reception as an outpouring from hearts his writings had touched. An early letter home registers hysterical approval of "crowds that pour in and out" of his hotel, "people that line the streets" whenever he goes out, the "cheering" for him at the theater—in short, "the cry that runs through the whole country!" (PL, 3:34) But outbursts of unsolicited attention soon struck a slightly paranoid Dickens as vulgar curiosity. By the end of February, having changed his mind about becoming a cynosure, he was relating the same facts in a different light: "I can do nothing that I want to do, go nowhere where I want to go, and see nothing that I want to see. If I turn into the street, I am followed by a multitude. If I stay at home, the house becomes, with callers, like a fair. . . . I take my seat in a railroad car, and the very conductor won't leave me alone. I get out at a station, and can't drink a glass of water, without having a hundred people looking down my throat when I open my mouth to swallow" (PL, 3:87). The frustrated tourist hyperbolized because, having come to see utopia, he must spend his time watching himself being watched.

Martin Chuzzlewit consistently duplicates the worst aspects of Dickens's visit: a mob inspects Martin as "if he had been a figure of stone, purchased, and paid for, and set up there, for their delight" (MC, 366) just as a Baltimore crowd lowered the windows of Dickens's railroad carriage "and fell to comparing notes on the subject of [his] personal appearance, with as much indifference as if [he] were a stuffed figure" (AN, 161). Martin's plight transmutes into effective satire Dickens's full-fledged outrage as a violated man. To the levee sponsored by Captain Kedgick,

Two gentlemen connected with the Watertoast Gazette had come express to get the matter for an article on Martin. They had agreed to divide the labour. One of them took him below the waistcoat; one above. Each stood directly in front of his subject with his head a little on one side, intent on his department. If Martin put one boot before the other, the lower gentleman was down upon him; he rubbed a pimple on his nose, and the upper gentleman booked it. He opened his mouth to speak, and the same gentleman was on one knee before him, looking in at his teeth, with the nice scrutiny of a dentist. Amateurs in the physiognomical and phrenological sciences roved about him with watchful eyes and itching fingers, and sometimes one, more daring than the rest, made a mad grasp at the back of his head, and vanished in the crowd. . . . Those who were not professional or scientific, audibly exchanged opinions on his looks. New lights shone in upon him, in respect of his nose. Contradictory rumours were abroad on the subject of his hair. [MC, 366]

Newspapers are being hawked at dockside when young Chuzzlewit reaches the United States. This detail establishes the tone for the hero's subsequent encounters, such as the examination at Kedgick's; the papers include the New York Private Listener, the New York Peeper, the New York Family Spy, and the New York Keyhole Reporter, tabloids whose contents Martin finds "horribly personal" (MC, 255).

Conventional views of the 1842 visit attribute Dickens's increasingly negative reactions to inadequate copyright protection and the existence of slavery.[6] His stand on these issues explains the country's dwindling enthusiasm for its famous guest but fails to account for the breakdown of his love affair with America; he did not come to lobby for an international copyright, and he expected to encounter slaves. Outcroppings of vulgar curiosity that became a virtual persecution make a better cause. Overbearing Americans who disregarded an Englishman's person could not be expected to worry about his royalties or to treat Negroes fairly; indeed, Dickens has the correspondents inspect Martin as callously as slaveowners contemplating a purchase. Thus when Colonel Diver dignifies the slander-prone American press as one of the country's "ennobling institutions," Jefferson Brick adds that it is as ennobling "as nigger slavery itself" (*MC*, 265). The presence of slavery and the absence of copyright, although seemingly unrelated, stemmed from a disrespect for individual integrity which the novelist felt he had experienced from the outset of his visit.

In America Dickens discovered how fundamentally English he was: Americans, he felt, desecrated a Britisher's cherished conceptions of proper reserve. He could not dwell on this point in *American Notes;* as a visiting intelligence, he had to report on major cities and prominent individuals. So the travel book is generally straightforward and, for Dickens, quite flat, a judgment Forster makes even clearer, preferring the "instant impression" in the letters home to "eloquent recollection" (F, 1:270). Swiftian procedures in the eight American chapters, however, designate *Martin Chuzzlewit* a masterful product of further consideration which dramatized the negative reactions of a dyed-in-the-wool Englishman to a country everywhere crass and provincial. Martin is an innocent who can be bitingly perceptive: each new American is introduced by his predecessor as "one of the most remarkable men in [the] country" (*MC*, 268), and Chuzzlewit resembles Gulliver among the Lilliputians. When the boarders at Mrs. Pawkins's stuff themselves as if "famine" were imminent (*MC*, 271), he is Gulliver in a land of Yahoos, which became Dickens's implicit analogy for the plight of the British subject in a rude, countrified America.[7]

During dinner aboard the riverboat returning from Eden, the swampy hell where Martin and his servant-companion, Mark Tapley, nearly perish from fever, "a gentleman in a high state of tobacco"— "overflowings of that weed . . . had dried about his mouth and chin" (*MC*, 535)—sucks his knife before making a "cut" at the butter. Sickened, young Chuzzlewit loses his appetite, much to Elijah Pogram's delight. Pogram attributes Martin's disgust to "the morbid hatred of you British to the Institutions of our country," a view, objected Dickens, that puts matters the wrong way round: the knife sucker's atrocious manners place the value of America's ideals and institutions in jeopardy. "A man deliberately makes a hog of himself," Martin exclaims, and his fellow countryman calls it "an Institution!" (MC, 535) Having come to praise America, Dickens ended by conferring institutional status on the prevailing vulgarities: selfishness, crassness, hoggishness, he suggested, were America's real institutions, the governing factors in business, politics, and human relationships generally.

The bad manners of many Americans angered the republican in Dickens because they ran counter to democratic principles, which should assure the rights of all, but vulgar insensitivity also offended against British taste, a unique blend of moral restraint, social awareness, and hygienic concern. The tobacco fancier's breach of decorum and Martin's consequent indictment of an entire social system stand as a history in miniature of Dickens's reaction to America: he concluded that larger shortcomings were the effect of poor manners rather than their cause; distasteful behavior, especially the liberties taken with Dickens personally, led to reservations concerning the New World's democratic postulates. Since each of Martin's steamboat companions "appeared to have had a difference with his laundress, and to have left off washing himself in early youth" (MC, 530), a fastidious Dickens was inclined to forget the Bill of Rights and the Declaration of Independence.

On the basis of a five-month visit to America, Dickens determined that civilization depends upon civility: the chief drawback in the typical American, Martin maintains, is that he is no better than "a brute in small matters" (MC, 536). The "mass of your countrymen," he informs Pogram, "begin by stubbornly neglecting little social observances, which have nothing to do with gentility, custom, usage, government, or country, but are acts of common, decent, natural, human politeness. . . . From disregarding small obligations," the argument continues, Americans "come in regular course to disregard great ones," including, one presumes, a Negro's right to freedom or an author's to copyright protection. Bad manners, in short, make for bad government by "natural succession" because an uncouth society is "rotten at the root."

The exchange between Martin and Pogram is the crux of the American sequence. Most Americans, the former insists, lack "that instinctive good-breeding which admonishes one man not to offend and disgust another" (MC, 536). When young Chuzzlewit delivers his onslaught, the outburst defeats oratorical Americans at their own game,[8] especially Pogram, the "celebrated" but unwashed Congressman who vocalizes their point of view. Martin complains that the New World elevates "social offenses" into "a beautiful national feature" (*MC*, 536). "We have no time to ac-quire forms, sir," is one of Pogram's prompt rejoinders. But Martin, schooled in Rousseau, contends that "it's not a question of acquiring anything"; the point is not to lose "the natural politeness" even savages supposedly possess.

Dickens struggled in this discussion scene to reconcile his allegiance to the revolutionary theories of Rousseau with a growing awareness of himself as a middle-class Englishman: America's inhabitants, ignoble as well as savage, forced him to reconsider his assumption that a Brave New World would be less corrupt than the old. Martin's insistence that major crimes and the pervasive appetite for violence originate from a neglect of small "social observances" has validity, even if this gentleman's perspective, which finds well-mannered criminals inconceivable, was corrected in later fictions where white-collar villainies also abound. Less convincing is the contention that "small obligations," which Dickens now realized he prized highly, "have nothing to do with" such products of advanced civilization as "gentility, custom, [and] usage."

In America Dickens discovered that man in his natural state—in a country at an earlier phase of development than England—was not necessarily preferable to the average European. Although never improving as steadily or to the extent that rival novelists such as Mrs. Gaskell and George Eliot would proclaim, Englishmen were the product of a limited but beneficial social evolution, not a massive deterioration from primitive times and Romantic models. Pogram is wrong to dismiss "forms" cavalierly but is more correct than Martin—and closer to Dickens's true feelings—in presupposing that they are gradually acquired, not innate.

From Americans Dickens learned that innocence (that is, not knowing how one appears in the eyes of one's peers) can be a particularly objectionable form of vulgarity that tells heavily against Rousseau's respect for simpler kinds of social organization. The author of "The Pogram Defiance" has no more idea of the ludicrous figure he cuts internationally than the knife sucker of the disgust he inspires in Martin: Pogram's boast that America is unbeatable "on any hook," ridiculously colloquial for a warning to foreigners, becomes another sign of the speaker's vulgarity.

In *Martin Chuzzlewit* Dickens criticized America for not corroborating the theories of Rousseau; he also satirized the French Romantic for offering an estimate of human nature having little relation to hard realities.[9] "Natural politeness" could not compete with a reawakening Victorian respect for "gentility" by accrual, the thrust of Dickens's anti-Romantic satire being that nothing seems more unnatural—unpleasant and unacceptable—than man in his natural state. The most natural thing for man to do, Dickens discovered, was to become more and more civilized as quickly as possible.[10]

Mr. Norris Junior invokes Rousseau when he dubs his fellow Americans "nature's noblemen," members of a society allegedly "based on one broad level of brotherly love and natural equality" (*MC*, 288). This characteristic should preclude the competition, acquisitiveness, jealousy, and crooked practices that Rousseau naively contended were inevitable products of forced cohabitation by men with conflicting interests. Unfortunately, Martin and Mark are addressed as "Aristocrats of Natur" (*MC*, 353) by Zephaniah Scadder, devious agent for the Eden Land Corporation, before he sells them a choice piece of swamp. The fledgling republic contravenes the reclaimability of Nature and the regeneracy of Man: greed, shallowness, sharp practice (fraud), and a concomitant talent for boasting in inflated language are the un-English hallmarks of the American character.[11]

Moral optimists such as David Hume and Adam Smith, Dickens discovered, had deceived him as badly as Rousseau had. In *The Theory of Moral Sentiments* (1759), Adam Smith argued that when Nature formed man for society, she endowed him with the desire to please and instilled in him an original aversion to offend his brethren. Newly molded Americans, however, exhibited neither of these endowments; they had no desire to please or to behave inoffensively, a realization which Dickens used the knife-sucking incident to place beyond doubt. Thus if Americans sprang "quite fresh from Natur's mould!" as Pogram exclaims (*MC*, 533), Dickens had to face the possibility that the mold, not a surfeit of civilization, was at fault.

In England, social institutions had acquired undesirable characteristics over centuries; consequently, they did not manifest themselves as clear-cut externalizations of inherent shortsightedness. It seemed plausible to assume that if corrupt agencies were swept away, man's better self, if not his innate goodness, might reassert itself. But once Dickens saw flaws crudely similar to those in England quickly emerging in the American character, he was bound to decide that *all* social orders are extensions of men's characters and personalities, hence defective; they constitute a rein on the individual's fallen nature but are also an indication of it, possibly an exacerbation.

When Martin accuses Pogram of converting deficiencies into national features and the latter complains of the English propensity to calumniate his country's institutions (*MC*, 535), the anti-American satire is actually multiedged. Unlike the English, Americans lack well-established institutions but exhibit no shortage of vices as old as Adam, to whose postlapsarian self they appear to stand even closer in time than does Pecksniff. Latent in Dickens's attack on Americans, however, is his discovery that human nature's perennial shortcomings are obligatory flaws in any society's building materials: whether one points to the Eden Land Corporation, Negro servitude, or the pirating of English authors' books, institutions are rapacious because selfishness—hoggishness, greed—is necessarily part of the permanent foundation on which they were raised.

This is the ultimate ironic burden of Dickens's most architectural novel, in which Pecksniff's former pupil has come to Eden hoping to build magnificent structures. The irony extends to the novelist's own architectonics: keeping a better watch on the design of the whole as he added each new part meant expressing graver reservations about whatever men design. Chuzzlewit's castigation of Pogram for institutionalizing human failings as if they were strengths is tantamount to conceding permanent limitations in the temporal order itself. This side of paradise, Eden is always a mockery because social process remains at the mercy of deficiencies within those presuming to regulate its course.

Having been schooled in America, Martin returns to the port from which he sailed so that an English chapter can build upon the discoveries just made: he sets foot "on native ground" (*MC*, 546) in time to discern more clearly the way institutions incorporate human flaws. During the hero's year-long absence, Pecksniff appropriated one of his designs but "spoilt" the symmetry by adding four windows. Nevertheless, his stolen, faulty plan wins the "First Premium" from a community's prize givers, who are surely as incompetent and pompous as he. When the "Corporation" celebrates Pecksniff and prepares to erect his building, a school no less, the awards ceremony institutionalizes sharp practice and imperfection in a way that Dickens conceded must be called human, not simply American.

By 1843-44, Dickens was primed to realize that referring to the faults responsible for flawed institutions as institutions themselves is compulsory metonymy: one substitutes causes for effects that have hitherto been mistaken for causes. In the interval between *American Notes* and *Martin Chuzzlewit*, the novelist came to repent his ignorance in journeying to America to study its institutions, something Martin does little of, scrutinizing American characters instead. Comparative institutionalism, the basis for many travel books, including Dickens's, appears quixotic once the same error-prone human nature is discovered to have produced the new institutions being compared with more familiar ones back home.

Martin attracts attention in America by being conspicuous in the way that Dickens thought he himself had been: as a man of keen sensibilities stranded on barbarian shores. Despite reiterated insults, young Chuzzlewit struggles never to appear "ungentlemanly," that is, un-English (*MC*, 349). Although Martin's steamboat is headed for a "flat morass" (*MC*, 375) from which no colonist returns, the journey delights him once he discovers "several gentlemen passengers" aboard (*MC*, 372). Traveling toward New York, Dickens was similarly elated to encounter "a Mr. Felton," whom he had met previously in Boston. A professor of Greek at Harvard, C.C. Felton became a lifelong friend; he was American born and educated but possessed excellent manners and a kind heart, which justified Dickens's description of him to Forster as "quite an Englishman of the best sort" (*PL*, 3:69).

The personality of the only American who sincerely befriends Martin Chuzzlewit resembles Felton's. Mr. Bevan has a well-developed moral sense, like Fielding's Heartfree of Squire Allworthy: neither overly curious nor impertinent, he is invariably "open-hearted, unaffected, and good-natured" (*MC*, 279); in short, virtually an English gentleman. Only he can liberate Martin from the penury of Eden by sending money for a return passage to New York. To impress Dickens, Americans had to possess the Christian benevolence and critical intelligence that the Victorian novelist had learned to admire by reading eighteenth-century fiction.

Bevan endears himself further by "plain-speaking" about his country's faults. Equally outspoken, Dickens considered being critical of one's country the mark of a patriot. Bevan does not consider America "a model of wisdom, and an example to the world, and the perfection of human reason" (*MC*, 279); this self-satisfied attitude, a bogus, unfounded utopianism, surfaces in the discussion scene at the Norrises' when General Fladdock laments "the limited diffusion of a moral sense" in Europe, which he calls a "country" (*MC*, 290). Martin's conversations with Bevan should be placed alongside his subsequent argument with Pogram, whose unlicensed patriotism is merely an extension of his vulgarity.

Unfortunately, Bevan, intending to promote Martin's architectural prospects, gives him a letter of recommendation to General Choke, who directs him to Eden. Yet Dickens never intended to compromise Bevan;[12] on the contrary, the point was to show why, like Martin, the novelist had not been better protected from disillusionment by the handful of superior personalities he met in America. Whether English or American, the implied argument runs, the well-bred individual's main strength—a good-hearted, unaffected nature—keeps him vulnerable in a given instance to the cunning he is sagacious enough to condemn en masse. Bevan becomes a dangerous ally in America, an inadequate guide to the crooked dealing afoot, precisely because he is almost English, just as the testimonials of Dickens's confederates (such as Felton and Washington Irving) proved insufficient when stacked up against the boisterous outcries of impolite newspaper editors; having made public opinion a slave to the press, they crudely denounced Dickens's request for copyright legislation.

Money given Martin for return passage not just to New York but back to England entitles the nonpracticing physician to remain a healer insofar as kindness can atone for the error in judgment it originally caused. Nor should one overlook Bevan's apology for having been "unwittingly, the original cause" of Chuzzlewit's "misfortunes" (MC, 543). Too trusting (that is, English) himself, Bevan has also excusably underestimated the extent of Martin's innocence: "I no more supposed," he explains, that "you would go to Eden on such representations as you received; or, indeed, that you would do anything but be dispossessed, by the readiest means, of your idea that fortunes were so easily made here; than I thought of going to Eden myself" (MC, 543).

Were Bevan accountable for Martin's fiasco, the same criterion would sooner condemn John Westlock, an English gentleman and Ruth Pinch's future husband; he first puts the notion of "going abroad" in the hero's head (MC, 201). Bill Simmons would also be culpable: the van driver carrying Martin to London tells him about Lummy Ned, who quit as guard on the Light Salisbury coach and "made his fortune" in "the U-nited States" (MC, 217). Dickens's ultimate target is Dickens, both for coming to America "on such representations" as those offered by thinkers like Rousseau and for not being immediately "dispossessed" of the idea that a perfect society was under way ("fortunes . . . easily made").

The belligerent Hannibal Chollop, a first-rate parody of Davy

Crockett, Daniel Boone, and the backwoodsmen whom James Fenimore Cooper's Natty Bumpo had made famous, supplies Bevan's antithesis. Armed with his swordstick "Tickler," his knife "Ripper," and a set of revolving pistols, Chollop seems impervious to the fever that causes effete colonists to drop all around him, but he riles murderously at the slightest insult. Dickens wrote Forster about "noble specimens . . . out of the West . . . Splendid men to look at" (PL, 3:133), yet he expected readers to extol kindhearted Bevan, an honorary Englishman, and despise the violence-prone Chollop, denizen of the great outdoors. Bevan epitomizes Dickens's fantasy of Americans as Englishmen of the best sort; an equally necessary figure, Chollop caricatures the uncultured brute that Dickens felt the New World considered an exemplary naturalized American. To friends, Chollop is "a splendid sample of our na-tive raw material," but he strikes Dickens as "a violent vagabond" (MC, 520) who confuses lawlessness with liberty, thereby vulgarizing the latter. Dickens's satire, however, was based on a city-dweller's misunderstanding of how wildernesses are cleared and by whom: a cosmopolite who professes to be a quiet New Englander visiting New York, Bevan could not venture west of the Mississippi until men like Chollop made it safe to do so.[13]

Throughout *Martin Chuzzlewit* the main trouble with Americans is that they are not English. An English virtue exists for every American failing catalogued: for sharp practice substitute good sportsmanship; for oratorical bragging, reticence and modesty; for neglect of one's toilette, the fastidiousness that motivated sanitary reform. Even Dickens's undue emphasis on "salivatory phenomena"—the Americans' habit of spitting tobacco juice and their "universal disregard of the spittoon" (AN, 144, 169)—can be explained by his fear that well-bred Europeans would not believe so offensive a practice could be so widespread. If you "drop anything" indoors in America, he advised his countrymen, even if it is a purse filled with money, do "not . . . pick it up with an ungloved hand" (AN, 169). Repeatedly, he underscored the Americans' poor marksmanship when using what he inelegantly termed the "spit-box" (F, 1: 239). Despite the country's so-called general proficiency with the rifle, one gentleman missed the spittoon "at five paces" (half the proverbial dueling distance), while another "mistook the closed sash for the open window, at three" (AN, 169).

T.A. Jackson preserved his picture of a radical socialist by transferring the novelist's niceness to Mrs. Dickens, "a very genteel person, one not at all easy to please," whose "petulant fault-finding attitude" her husband allegedly "adopted" (TAJ, 50-51). Going against his "*revo lutionary* Republicanism," he "submitted . . . from mistaken chivalry" to his wife's "exaggerated over-emphasis upon tobacco chewing . . . and all those complaints about dirtiness . . . and lack of gentility, which spoil the *American Notes.*" Ironically, this suggestion of a refinement that was feminine rather than English overlooked Dickens's determination to ridicule women travelers, such as Frances Trollope and Harriet Martineau; both declared themselves horrified by spitting yet self-consciously preserved a womanly reticence in their accounts. Dickens's facetiousness in America was often his fastidiousness at work. His amusing but unkind description of Kate's "propensity . . . to fall into, or out of" every coach and boat, to scrape skin off her legs, chip fragments out of her ankle bones, and cover herself with bruises (J, 1:414) marked the beginning of their separation. To a novelist whose sense of absurdity as an object of curiosity to Americans augmented his petulance, a pratfall-prone wife proved another source of embarrassment; Dickens estimated her total number of falls in the New World at 743.[14] Upon their return from America, Kate's sister, Georgina, moved into the family circle to manage the household.

Nevertheless, Dickens was the one foreign author whom Americans "claimed equally for their own," seeing in him an "embodied protest against what was believed to be worst in the institutions of England" (F, 1:211). The first visit was to be "a triumph over the mother-country," with America lavishing on Dickens's "genius" the adulation that Europe reserved for titles and wealth. Readers this side of the Atlantic regarded Dickens as a congenital democrat. Shortly after his arrival, the New York *Herald* proclaimed: "His mind is American— his soul is republican—his heart is democratic" (PL, 3:xii), extravagant sentiments that probably seemed accurate to Dickens at the time. Such a man was not supposed to rail about America's shortcomings as warmly as he had vented his wrath against imprisonment for debt and the New Poor Law.

When Dickens spoke unkindly of partisan politics as a reflection of American manners, therefore, the criticism was not just unanticipated but constituted betrayal by a man whom the natives regarded as one of themselves.[15] Negative remarks in *American Notes* cut deeper than Mrs. Trollope's in *Domestic Manners of the Americans* (1832) or Miss Martineau's in *Society in America* (1837) because Dickens made them; in *Martin Chuzzlewit*, his treachery seemed enormous. Thus Dickens discovered that he was not American enough to please his hosts, just as they were insufficiently British to gratify him.

Despite an improvident father, Dickens clung tenaciously to his origins in the middle class; by 1842 he had worked his way into its stratosphere. More conditioned by a class-conscious culture than he realized, he expected a nation of immigrants to be cultivated, lively, and genteel. Disappointed, he objected to the general lack of sophistication among the populace, where, as a would-be republican, he had anticipated that democracy would have its greatest effects. After America, Dickens was never again an enthusiastic egalitarian: his conviction that Britian's institutions were antiquated and reforms too slow in coming remained unshaken, but he realized that he was more English in thought and deed than he was American, French, or European, and although he became increasingly disgruntled, he was more Victorian— a man of his time and place—than Romantic or utopian. In *American Notes* and more insistently in *Martin Chuzzlewit*, Dickens tightened his hold on his hard-won identity as a member of England's upper middle class whenever he judged frontier society by drawing-room standards.

Democracy, Dickens feared, creates its own aristocracy, not of worth and intelligence but of dollars.[16] As Colonel Diver proclaims when haranguing Martin, America's "aristocracy" of "intelligence and virtue" has "dollars, sir" as its "necessary consequence" (*MC*, 258)— that is, as its sole goal and standard of measurement. Dickens charged that Americans used equality as an excuse to disregard what Bevan calls the "humanizing conventionalities of manner and social custom" (*MC*, 278). That conventions humanize is again a Victorian concept, at odds with Rousseau and contrary to the impression America gave of wanting to break with the past. Like the more conservative Carlyle, who would later agree, Dickens found democracy a leveling downward, a movement away from intellect and social grace toward a vulgar, greedy mediocrity, an uncouth sameness.[17] Martin's fellow customers in the bar of the National Hotel, Dickens observes, "did the same things; said the same things; judged all subjects by, and reduced all subjects to, the same standard" (*MC*, 349).

After one month in America, an alarmed Dickens felt himself moving back toward the political center. Pangs of self-discovery beset him in a letter to Forster: "I tremble for a radical coming here," he wrote, "unless he is a radical on principle, by reason and reflection, and from a sense of right. I fear that if he were anything else, he would return home a tory" (PL, 3:90).[18] In England Dickens had criticized a do-nothing aristocracy, a cumbersome Parliament, and a class system indifferent to the tribulations of the poor; he rightly saw himself, in that fixed context, as a fire-breathing reformer. More volatile and formless, America taught him that he was an exclusively English radical with Romantic enthusiasms that needed toning down. Disappointments in America separated him permanently not just from thinkers like Rousseau but from Marx, Engels, and other indiscriminate admirers of the proletariat.

After 1842, even when spontaneous combustion of the entire British system seemed not only inevitable but desirable, Dickens invoked extreme measures mainly as a scare tactic; utopian counterproposals were never offered, and the American trip best explains their absence.[19] Having seen the situation this side of the Atlantic, he gave up hope for a new sociopolitical arrangement to substitute for England's. The first truly foreign country (more so, for example, than France or Belgium) that the thirty-year-old novelist visited was the only one that might have suited his needs; instead of writing a utopia, he went to visit one. Disillusioned, the would-be utopist complained that America had "put in hazard the rights of nations yet unborn, and the very progress of the human race" (MC, 369), for he believed that a context as favorable for testing democracy was unlikely to present itself again.[20]

Although Dickens did not return home a Tory, he abandoned as Romantic foolishness the notion of sweeping social change and a totally transformed society. The mood of his novels from *Martin Chuzzlewit* onward began to darken as he resumed the uphill task, no doubt Sisyphean, of transforming an unsatisfactory England into the best of all possible worlds he had naively expected to discover in America. After *Chuzzlewit*, Dickens proceeded to denounce the business mentality in *Dombey and Son* (1846-48) and *A Christmas Carol* (1843); he pleaded for fairer courts and greater social responsibility in *Bleak House* (1852-53); while demanding safer factories in *Hard Times* (1854), he foresaw the technological revolution as a threat to the poetic imagination, not to mention the shriveling impact he expected the worship of machinery to have on the bonds between men and masters, brothers and sisters, husbands and wives;[21] he called for less bureaucracy in *Little Dorrit* (1855-57), and in *A Tale of Two Cities* (1859) invoked the French Revolution in support of his argument that kindlier interpersonal relationships within and between classes keep countries from tearing themselves apart. These warnings and admonitions anticipate the severity of his satires in the 1860s against the accelerating Victorian practice of putting faith in wealth and possessions (*Great Expectations, Our Mutual Friend*) in that their tone was not cautionary but Cassandra-like, motivated by the novelist's desire to ward off catastrophe. Collectively, the post-*Chuzzlewit* novels share a dystopian or antiperfectibilitarian bias—none was issued in anticipation of a greatly improved society, much less a perfect one.

From Baltimore Dickens wrote to his actor-friend Macready the saddest traveler's letter ever penned: "This is not the Republic I came to see. This is not the Republic of my imagination" (PL, 3:156). Extravagant expectations and ingrained English prejudices made it impossible for him to be pleased. "What are the Great United States for, sir," demands General Choke, "if not for the regeneration of man?" (*MC*, 348). This had been Dickens's position before leaving England. Shattered hopes lie behind the transfer of so important a question to a scoundrel like Choke: America might not be able to return man to the Garden, but a resentful Dickens would show one of its unregenerate citizens absurdly boasting that it could.

Although morals were bad in America because manners were, Dickens could not show the moral sense triumphant in Britain, where manners had perceptibly improved. Instead, the more he ruminated in the interval between *American Notes* and *Martin Chuzzlewit*, the more he felt obliged to sketch damaging parallels: the Anglo-Bengalee Disinterested Loan and Life Assurance Company and the Eden Land Corporation, for example, each as much "a light-hearted little fiction" (*MC*, 432) as the other. An unscrupulous Montague Tigg and his partner, the murderous Jonas Chuzzlewit, have primitive prototypes in Zephaniah Scadder, the swamp salesman, and the menacing frontiersman, Hannibal Chollop. To match the blatant hypocrisy in Colonel Diver, Jefferson Brick, and General Fladdock, incompetent rascals all, England features the pretended disinterestedness of John Jobling and the smooth and oily selfishness of Mr. Pecksniff.

American Notes is a travel book about a nation whose principles and declarations distressed Dickens as so much forged currency, but *Martin Chuzzlewit* developed into a tale of two countries, not just an anti-American tract. Through reciprocal exposure, Britain threw into high relief the crudities of savage America, while America revealed what cultured societies are still like beneath the surface; an outlook that anticipated Conrad displaced a worldview derived from Rousseau. America starts out to be a land of opportunity for Martin and Mark, but as it becomes more like England—only worse—it furnishes a key to the latter's essence, which Dickens discovered he now saw with a major satirist's perspicacity. If America is a country of caricatures and hence a caricature of a country, the country being caricatured is England.

Thanks to America, Dickens began to suspect that it might be impossible to balance the perils of too little civilization against the stultifying effects of too much: in the United States, the first situation left man's natural ferocity unrestrained, but many time-honored inequalities and outmoded procedures for redressing them had virtually solidified into immovable objects in Europe. The seemingly indispensable "conventionalities" that Bevan and Chuzzlewit extol—that is, the proprieties by another name—grow increasingly irksome in the later novels when supported by grotesques such as Mrs. General (*Little Dorrit*) and the Podsnaps (*Our Mutual Friend*).

Since prescribed manners and artificial observances do not humanize indefinitely and Dickens had been shorn of belief in fresh, uninhibited starts predicated on man's innate goodness, he arrived at a dilemma no other Victorian social realist would reach as clearly: he was fated to decide that civilization initially promotes good breeding by enjoining its citizens from disgusting each other; as societies evolve, however, they bury the fundamentally bestial nature in man deeper and deeper under artifice and deceit, thus creating the potential for an eruption of savage monstrosity.[22] Society's rituals remain preferable to barbarism but eventually generate subtler forms of hypocrisy that foster an unhealthy self-repression. These detriments were scheduled to reach their climax nine novels later in John Jasper (*The Mystery of Edwin Drood* [1870]). Cloisterham's outwardly respectable choirmaster harbors within him a violent-erotic second self, a veritable Mr. Hyde, but neither the two-faced Mr. Scadder nor the unbridled Major Chollop, essentially comic though each is, would consider this secret sharer, who is a recrudescence of man's fallen nature, an embarrassment to one's public personality.

In 1843-44, however, parallels between England and America, no matter how compromising, persuaded Dickens that he had furthered his case against the New World. If good manners are a prerequisite for better morals, Britain was further along than America, though not yet commendable. In the meantime, better the polish of an economically unfair and politically hypocritical Britannia than Columbia's crasser renditions of the same human failings: when fresh starts are placed alongside established civilizations—the strategy in *Martin Chuzzlewit*—"England, even England," as Dickens wrote Macready, "bad and faulty as the old land is, and miserable as millions of her people are, rises in the comparison" (PL, 3:156), if only as the lesser of two evils.

Touring India in 1925, Aldous Huxley, who found postwar hedonism futile in England, began to praise good roads and clean sheets

(Henry Ford and modern technology) because he had been taken aback by the mixture of spirituality and squalor in Bombay and Lahore (*JP*, 109-10). Upon returning home, he immediately resumed his critique of a rudderless British society that had not improved during his absence. Similarly, indeed prototypically, Dickens became the only major Victorian debunker of America whom the loss of an alternative vision did not deter from later stepping up his attacks on his own country.

One finds in both satirists a contrapuntist's frame of mind fatal to the would-be utopist. Given such a mind's discovery that all things are related and yet limited by each other, it develops an extraordinary alertness to the need for contrasts, parallels, and juxtapositionings to elicit life's meaning; this awareness prevents any one place from becoming self-sufficient; it rules out an incomparable society. When confronted with men in their natural state in America and a more civilized England where millions are miserable, Dickens unblinkingly chose the latter, but like the contrapuntist weighing East against West in *Jesting Pilate*, he also discovered the lack of ideal choices, or as Huxley would later phrase it: "to travel is to discover that everybody is wrong" (*JP*, 214).

Dickens nevertheless resented the fierce national pride that expected visitors to rank America above their homelands. The worst he could say about such a "boastful, vain-glorious spirit" was that it was "*not English*" (PL, 3:176). Repeatedly angered by America's chauvinism, young Chuzzlewit discovers an upstart nation of braggadocios. Lafayette Kettle rudely inquires about the Mother Country: "how's the unnat'ral old parent by this time?" (*MC*, 345), and General Choke hopes that the British Lion will "have his talons eradicated by the noble bill of the American Eagle"; "the Lion," he boasts, "shall be roasted whole" (*MC*, 346, 362). After several chapters of such talk, Martin's cockney servant-companion wants to repaint the American Eagle "like a Bat, for its short-sightedness; like a Bantam, for its bragging; like a Magpie, for its honesty; like a Peacock, for its vanity; like a Ostrich, for its putting its head in the mud" (*MC*, 545). Speaking through Mark Tapley, the deep-seated Englishman in Dickens sounds as biased as Kettle and Choke.

That a social critic at home quickly became a British supporter when abroad is even clearer from the Anglophilia in Dickens's letter to Macready announcing his demise as a utopian dreamer; it balances the loss of republican hopes against a recovery of one's senses. The epistle speaks of Dickens's resolve to take England to his heart again "for better or worse, and reject this new love" for America "without a pang or moment's hesitation." The marital metaphor, a reaffirmation of vows, discloses the depth of his feelings and emphasizes the wiser man he believed a few months in America had made him: his homeland assumed the attraction of an enduring relationship, whereas America came to resemble an adulterous infatuation. Dickens felt like a husband who had deserted his marriage for a younger mistress whose enticing beauty disappeared upon closer inspection. The letter writer presents himself as an unfaithful lover breaking off an unpromising entanglement to go home to his wife.[23] Dickens was proclaiming the end of his affair not only with America but with radical utopianism and all hypothetical, untested tenets of Romanticism; when he voiced his displeasure with America in *Martin Chuzzlewit*, he was simultaneously punishing himself for infidelity to England.

Sending Martin to America to suffer, Dickens owned up in print to having entertained mistaken notions about the nature of man and the process by which civilized societies grow. Like *Great Expectations* rather than *David Copperfield*—that is, indirectly, as an indication of a changed attitude or new state of mind—Dickens's sixth novel is a remarkable autobiographical document. Satiric exposure of American pretensions does double duty as a revelation, not always completely intentional, of an author's prejudices and as a confession, this time more deliberate, of his errors in philosophy. While still in America, Dickens spoke publicly only about infringements upon his works, but one detects in this channeling a preliminary outlet, a vaguely realized metaphor, for the more serious assault he felt America was making upon his republicanism. In *Martin Chuzzlewit* he came to terms with his deeper dissatisfactions but without always fully realizing that they dovetailed with his Victorian biases and middle-class limitations in a manner that must seem inevitable to the modern revaluator.

Dickens's disappointment with America began almost at once, came to a head in April toward the end of his visit, and went on working itself out, in a series of aftermaths, at least until July 1844, when the last installment of *Martin Chuzzlewit* appeared. The nadir of Dickens's trip and the climax for his fermenting discontent coincide at the point where resemblances between author and eponymous hero are closest: the final stages of the journey to Eden (chapters 22-23) are basically the trip Dickens took down the Ohio from Cincinnati to St. Louis. One must restore this journey to prominence because it consolidated his impressions; it provided the satiric symbol for America that the novelist needed to make his personal misadventure pertinent for all readers.

Edgar Johnson crams Dickens's passage through three states into one paragraph (J, 1:383), but the southwestern excursion, not longer stays in Boston or New York, embedded itself in Dickens's mind as an encounter with America's essence. Had it not been for Ohio, Kentucky, and Illinois, *Martin Chuzzlewit* would have been vastly different and would perhaps not even have mentioned the New World.

Ohio and Kentucky aggravated Dickens's displeasure, presenting in reprise all the vulgar failings he regretted in Americans. One must mention the oppressive delegates to a temperance convention among whom he found himself when en route from Pittsburgh to Cincinnati; the party at Judge Timothy Walker's in the Queen City, during which he felt suffocated by "one hundred fifty first-rate bores"; the landlord of the Galt House in Louisville, a mere publican, who volunteered to acquaint his guest with the best families in Kentucky; Porter, the "Kentucky giant," who reportedly mistook the dandyish Dickens for a riverboat gambler; and, finally, the hours of "changeless," "monotonous" scenery along the Ohio's riverbanks.[24] These combined to ensure that when Dickens steamed past Cairo, Illinois (9 April 1842), he would regard himself as a parody of a pilgrim, a hoodwinked Englishman on a fool's errand in search of a fool's paradise.

The quick trip from Cincinnati to the prairies crystallized the entire American expedition as a movement away from civilization, which is how Dickens represented the first visit in *Martin Chuzzlewit*; it was a journey not toward perfection but from England through New York to a pestilential backwater. Having decided that America was a step backward, he ignored the established cities he had written about in *American Notes*; the America of his sixth novel is almost all frontier. Martin and Mark travel to Eden the way Conrad's Marlow moves toward Kurtz, for Dickens decided to emphasize the ubiquity of uncivilized and unscrupulous behavior in America by turning "This dismal Cairo" (*AN*, 216)[25] into a disillusioned Englishman's anti-Romantic microcosm not only for the New World but for the unsavory origin (that is, initial phase) and abiding core of all civilizations.

An enterprise known as the Cairo City and Canal Company, the model for the Eden Land Corporation, struck Dickens as a business of facades: it was like America itself, a land of false promise. Buildings in Cairo were poorly constructed by unprincipled developers who touted the new settlement to prospective British colonists and investors "as a mine of Golden Hope" (*AN*, 215). Dickens turned Cairo into an inverted Eden to epitomize the intellectual and political fraud he felt America had perpetrated against him and the Old World. His satirical image, inspired by the Cairo Company, depicted the new nation as an enormous real estate swindle, an ideological bubble of continental proportions, and a symbol for reality's failure to satisfy the expectations of the mind.

Although Dickens was not a victim of the Cairo City and Canal Company, the once popular view that he lost money in the venture reveals how strongly the novelist identified with deceived investors.[26] Dickens found America a bad buy for the political philosopher but had already thrown all of his utopist's capital into the speculation; his political disillusionment can thus be likened in severity to the financial losses sustained by Englishmen actually taken in. Dickens was duped by a theory of human nature garnered from Wordsworth and Rousseau, by the promulgated ideals of American democracy, and, above all, by misconceptions about himself. When Dickens saw Cairo, the novelist in him realized that he had found a source to which he could trace all the inflated rhetoric, vulgar pretense, and complacent pomposity that had thwarted his utopian hopes and irked his pride as an Englishman.

The rapid sweep past Cairo made it the mandatory choice, upon reflection, as the locale for an epiphany. Dickens subsequently recognized that he had experienced the definitive breakdown of his American dream on the morning of 9 April; at that point, the country became a dead issue for the utopist but had only begun to come alive in the brain of the satirical novelist. If Dickens underwent "psychic collapse,"[27] an untoward eye opening about the origins of man and society, it seemed, in retrospect, to have culminated at the juncture of the Ohio and Mississippi.

After completing *American Notes*, he realized that he still had not worked off his climactic moment of painful awareness; a travel book could not denigrate without mercy the Romantic philosophy behind Choke's contention that Americans, being in "a more primeval state," had not, like the English, "lapsed in the slow course of time into degenerate practices" (*MC*, 348). When Dickens grasped what he believed to be the truth about civilizations, he spelled out the relationship between New World and Old; in the sixth installment of *Martin Chuzzlewit*, he sent Martin and Mark to America to make these discoveries evident, not just to boost his novel's sagging sales. Fortunately, *Chuzzlewit* was already unfolding as a story about pretense and hypocrisy, failings its young hero was uncovering in others and was also exhibiting, so Dickens could enhance the scope of his novel by introducing the findings he had made about society and himself in America. Specifically, the creative artist condensed his own many-sided, multiphased disillusionment into young Chuzzlewit's climactic negative epiphany.

Martin's story proceeds like the parable of the Prodigal Son, into which Dickens has read a lesson for British travelers to America.[28] A swindled Martin cries from disappointment and barely survives his bout with fever, but symbolic death and resurrection clarify his moral vision and redirect his life as sharply as Dickens's visit altered his political and philosophical perspective. To be forever outside Eden and inescapably imperfect, Dickens has Martin realize, is the human condition, not just the glaring state of affairs in America. Chastened, Chuzzlewit ceases to be a snob who overvalues genteel company; instead he personifies the only combination of gentleman and democrat that Dickens discovered he approved of: discreet, sensitive, and fair-minded, he will be an active humanist but with few surviving illusions.

Dickens described Martin's increasing self-awareness as a "curtain" that "slowly rose" until the mirage of integrity, equality, and fraternity disappeared and "Self, Self, Self, dilated on the scene" (MC, 525). Like Dickens, who expected to find in the democratic future the uncorrupted individuals who allegedly existed in the Edenic past, Martin travels to the home of the free to discover that man's enslavement to his deficiencies, especially to his selfish ego, is timeless and universal; thus he learns how limited a prospect freedom itself is in a fallen world and descries that man is always confined to the prison house of self-interest at all stages of society's development.

Martin's stint as the Prodigal Son—that is, as another version of the original innocent abroad—fits his American adventures better than the Unfaithful Husband suited Dickens's view of himself foolishly searching for utopia, nor is it at odds with the novelist's mounting sense of temporal existence as a "wale of grief" (MC, 320). Sairey Gamp's confusing of whale/wail/vale is hilariously yet sadly apropos: an eagerly anticipated forward step had carried Dickens backward from a seemingly refined but incommodious society to an ostensibly wide open civilization where unwanted attentions and sharp practices nevertheless hemmed him in to the point of suffocation. Mrs. Gamp's first allusion to the "wale" cannot occur in the American episodes but was positioned to seem inspired by Dickens's dystopian experiences. The nurse delivers her unforgettable line in installment 8, an interlude between two monthly numbers given over entirely to American events. Three of the novel's eight American chapters precede it and three more follow, neatly bracketing Mrs. Gamp's utterance by illustrating its truth.

Four hundred pages later, the loquacious nurse embellishes her favorite conceit: "He was born into a wale, . . . and he lived in a wale; and he must take the consequences of sech a sitiwation."[29] Besides being Dickens's post-America sentiments on mankind exactly, this rendition of Keats's "Vale of Soul-making," wherein sufferings fashion one's identity, serves as a eulogy for young Bailey, a promising lad who has incorrectly been reported killed when his employers, Jonas Chuzzlewit and Montague Tigg, are "upset on a journey" (*MC*, 745). Mr. Sweedlepipes's account of the carriage accident goes on to assert, accurately, that Tigg's Assurance Company is an even bigger "smash," having been found out as "a swindle altogether."

Easily interpreted as a parodic parallel for young Martin, Bailey Junior reenacts the latter's involvement in a crooked scheme and certifies the need for near death and resurrection because of it. The collapse of Tigg's insurance fraud echoes Martin's almost fatal discovery of the Eden real estate boondoggle in that the disastrous participation of young innocents in both swindles signifies young Dickens's growing lack of confidence in life's benevolence. A mere boy who dresses like a swell and affects to know a great deal, Bailey Junior incarnates the youthful novelist's awareness of what had been his own naiveté. Thanks to Mrs. Gamp's eulogy, the concept of earthly existence as a "wale" overtakes the image of life as "Eden" (a potential utopia) or as "Assurance" (the steady appearance a process has if developing purposefully). Indeed, Mrs. Gamp promulgates the novel's controlling metaphor, perhaps the most pessimistic satirical image for life that Dickens coined prior to his concept, ten years later, of the diurnal round as an endless law case (*Bleak House*).

Martin Chuzzlewit contains a strong antitravel, antiutopia component because Dickens envisioned Martin and himself as prodigals originally too innocent to comprehend man's Jonah-like predicament: entrapment within an innately imperfect self renders goings abroad futile; expatriation is impossible because there is no escaping the sin of one's first parent.[30] Regardless of the consoling superiority of England to America in letters to Macready and Forster, Dickens realized by 1843-44 that he could have discovered nothing in the New World to exempt him from the whale's-belly existence that life is everywhere.

Yet this, too, is a discovery America helped him to make. Her prisons contributed to it—especially Dickens's dismay, in back-to-back chapters of *American Notes*, with "the Tombs" in New York and Philadelphia's Eastern Penitentiary, the latter having implemented a lamentably "rigid, strict, and hopeless solitary confinement" (*AN*, 131-33, 146). Ironically, a novel taking place on two continents, incorporating

eight chapters of travel episodes, and exploring the worldwide disten-
tion of "Self" or selfishness in all its variant forms adopts a claus-
trophobic worldview. Confinement imagery for life in society, so
prevalent in *Bleak House* and *Little Dorrit*, is previewed in *Martin Chuzzlewit* when Martin and Mark, having virtually been swallowed by
America, disappear into the bowels of anti-Eden.

Insofar as Martin is both the Prodigal Son who returns and Jonah
inside the whale, Dickens may have sensed that he had experienced
a curious homecoming in 1842—one that marked the commencement
of a lifelong uneasiness, repatriation and alienation simultaneously. He
was never able to stabilize his marriage to England despite having broken off with mistress America. The eleven exclamation points of relief
he felt when about to leave the New World—"Oh home-home-home-
home-home-home-HOME!!!!!!!!!!!! (F, 1:296)—were therefore insufficient. By 1843-44 he had begun to discover that, unlike the Prodigal,
he could never go home again completely because, more so than Jonah
following confinement in "the belly of hell" (*The Prophecy of Jonas*,
2:3), he was no longer the person he had been when he left.

Over several months during his own illness and slow recovery and
again when Mark is stricken, young Martin endures an elongated epiphany. Although it exceeds Kurtz's momentary eye-opener in Conrad's
Heart of Darkness, its termination, which comes after a depressing
stint virtually in solitary confinement, is no less painful or climactic and
seems to have transformed Dickens for life: "It was long before he
fixed the knowledge of himself so firmly in his mind that he could thoroughly discern the truth; but in the hideous solitude of that most hideous place, with Hope so far removed, Ambition quenched, and Death
beside him rattling at the very door, reflection came, as in a plague-
beleaguered town; and so he felt and knew the failing of his life, and
saw distinctly what an ugly spot it was" (*MC*, 525). The beginnings of
wisdom lie in Martin's "solemn resolution . . . not to dispute" these
"established" facts once he has recovered his strength.

The forcefulness of the writing suggests that Dickens reached some
similar resolution to face hard facts.[31] Why else inflict upon one's prodigal hero a proto-Conradian epiphany under conditions no better than
a Philadelphia penitentiary's yet no less conducive to moral resurrection than "three days and three nights" in a fish's belly? The novelist
wanted to emphasize that he would never forget "the failing of his life,"
his ideal republic's refusal to materialize; it led to increased awareness
of man's intrinsic imperfection: "what an ugly spot it was," an inner
state no healthier than "a plague-beleaguered town." Dickens was

speaking for himself when Martin conceded that America is "a hard school" to "learn so hard a lesson in," but the novelist and his hero both appear thankful for "teachers" (swamp, thicket, "pestilent" air) who possess "a searching method" all their own.

Dickens's repetition of "hideous" foreshadows the modern novelist's stress upon "The horror! The horror!" With that outburst, Conrad's ivory trader, disgusted by omnipresent greed, connects the West's exploitation of Africa with savage drives that an absence of restraints has unleashed within himself.[32] Similarly, Martin recognizes the speculators who swindled him as brazen personifications of selfishness, the deplorable tendency to defraud and enslave others that can be found in all men, whether they be slaveowners and book pirates or Pecksniff duping Tom Pinch and Martin feeling superior to the more resourceful Mark Tapley.

In Dickens the tendency manifested itself as presumption: he had expected to come to the fore as England's finest analyst of America by discrediting Mrs. Trollope's many complaints and eclipsing Harriet Martineau's many encomiums with an unrivaled paean to the new democracy; it was to be based on his sounder grasp of politics, Rousseau, and republican principles. To his chagrin, he found himself forced to undo one woman's praise and outdo the other's severity. Thus the Victorian novelist and young Chuzzlewit both took a fall: it occurred during the Conradian inner journey Martin underwent while traveling down the Ohio and Mississippi in Dickens's wake.[33]

The ultimate failure in colonization from which all others spring was Adam and Eve's, as Dickens showed he knew by substituting the biblical name "Eden" for the Egyptian-sounding "Cairo." But Conrad's Kurtz and Dickens's Martin both see through a modern colonial enterprise and into the rapacious darkness of men's hearts, their own included. For Dickens it marked the beginning of an investigation into the deepening interiority of evil; this inquiry would lead to a lustful murderer's full-fledged emergence from within Cloisterham's outwardly commendable choirmaster, which would have made the final scenes in *Drood* more sensational than Kurtz's deterioration from Europe's Christian emissary in the Congo to the orchestrator of "unspeakable" native rites.

There could have been no John Jasper without Jonas Chuzzlewit, however, and no Jonas without Martin's American epiphany. When Jonas prepares to ambush and murder Montague Tigg, an uncivilized, antisocial self rises from the darkness within him; it assumes control of the insurance company director's daylight personality in a manner confirming Martin's introspective moments at Eden and foreshadowing the transformation Jasper undergoes. As night falls, "another dark shade emerging from within him [Jonas] seemed to overspread his face, and slowly change it. Slowly, slowly; darker and darker; more and more haggard; creeping over him by little and little; until it was black night within him and without" (*MC*, 716).

The ascendancy of Jonas's dark side or nighttime self would be unexpected and thus implausible were it not preceded by Martin's discovery of America's most "ugly spot," or essence, and of man's internal darkness, both of which that "spot" symbolizes. Since Jonas's emergent "dark shade" is Martin's Conradian epiphany made good at home, one can see Dickens's disappointments in the New World starting to "overspread" the English chapters of *Chuzzlewit*, the key pejorative insights discovered abroad repeating themselves in an English context. The "hideous place" and "ugly spot" that Martin reflects upon, both an actual location and an inner state, lead to the "dark, dark stain that dyed and scented the whole summer night from earth to Heaven" (*MC*, 722); this "stain" from the murdered Tigg's blood soaking into the leaves connotes man's damaged soul, the mark of Adam (and Cain) he carries with him everywhere.

Jonas's transformation into a "dark shade," his public personality succumbing to an inner one until the novelist cannot distinguish the "black night within" his villain from the same pigmentation "without," is an early instance of that late Victorian/early modern cultural detriment, the split man or dual personality. In Jasper, whose public personality is more deceiving than Jonas's, such duality would be final proof that an inextricable evil component prevents man's nature from evolving to perfection. In Jonas, the modern revaluator sees the origin of Dickens's argument that evil evolves along with good, assuming new and increasingly complicated shapes as society becomes more complex.[34]

Whether in the hold as an unlucky presence for the ship's company or subsequently trapped in the whale's belly, Jonah exemplified dilemmas that blacken Dickens's novel the more they illuminate the human situation. Mired in Eden, America's plague-spot, young Martin perceives his own deficiencies and comprehends mankind's; similarly, a darker self inside Jonas Chuzzlewit reveals that he personifies the principle of imperfection that, unfortunately, is latent in all communities. Analogically stated, *within* relates to *without* the way Eden stands to America, Self to Martin, Martin to mankind, Jonas's secret sharer to his outward self, Jonas to Martin and to the community at large.

The transmogrification that Jonas engineers, summoning forth his meaner self as if changing into a werewolf or vampire bat, can be pinpointed as the post-America passage in which Dickens gave the tone of his thinking and writing about human nature an irreversibly darker, more serious turn. From this juncture onward, *Dickens is Dickens*; that is, he increasingly resembled the modern-sounding, satirical novelist whom most critics of the last forty-five years have ranked above the equally talented comic genius who wrote *Pickwick Papers*.

Although shorter and sharper than Martin's and despite being set in a village near Salisbury, Tom Pinch's long-overdue moment of negative awareness is an immediate consequence of the dystopian tenor steadily more audible in Dickens's philosophy after the first visit. Once Martin has espied man's interior darkness, Pinch's innocence is also doomed; indeed, after the American episodes begin, Tom's reverence for Pecksniff is presented ever more strongly as a singular obtuseness in the way of his reaching maturity.

While Martin and Mark are still homeward bound, Mary Graham complains about Pecksniff's lubricity, which rivals Tartuffe's, and "the full agitation and misery of the disclosure, came rushing upon Tom indeed. The star of his whole life from boyhood, had become, in a moment, putrid vapour. It was not that Pecksniff: Tom's Pecksniff: had ceased to exist, but that he never had existed" (*MC*, 491). "Putrid vapour" is harsh language, as was Martin's view of himself as an "ugly spot"; in short, a foul-smelling gas is all that remains of Tom's idol. If one substitutes Dickens's romantic notion of utopian America for "Tom's Pecksniff," *Martin Chuzzlewit* becomes doubly disillusioning as a novel about the author's realization that a young man's ideals not only break down but are generally discovered to have been gaseous illusions all along.

Just as the "star" by which Pinch has regulated his course "from boyhood" has constantly misled him, Dickens acknowledged that he had squandered time and effort not just thinking about but actually trying to reach a lodestone rock that was always a figment of his imagination. His rancor is more understandable if one grasps that America, like Pinch's Pecksniff, did not simply fall from grace; it was never in a sanctified condition, because such a temporal state was impossible. Believing in it politically came to seem no less naive and ultimately self-serving than the crudest form of hero worship that meretriciously brightens the hero worshiper's days.

Thus even the selfless Pinch is made to understand that he has been selfish, holding fast to his unreal vision of Pecksniff as a paragon when neither John Westlock nor young Martin was able to substantiate it. For years Tom has deluded himself into thinking his life and life-in-general better than they are or can be, a utopist's error not unlike Dickens's in coming to an imagined republic that some of the previous Victorian visitors had not reported finding, as if he, like Tom, was entitled to an ideal that others were denied. Dickens burdened Tom with "the anguish of recollecting what he [Pecksniff] never was" (*MC*, 491), which is a way of saying that one of the most painful things about losing one's innocence in 1842 was having to recall it not as a lost condition, the way Adam could, but as a nonexistent state, a sort of trance not real even when one was in it.

As Dickens recorded Tom's growing awareness that a glory had passed away from this earth, he confessed that, for him, too, much of the visionary gleam was gone; things seen delightedly heretofore would be seen so no more. After expulsion from Pecksniff's, Pinch cannot reexperience the excitement of his previous expedition to Salisbury, just as Dickens discovered he had to treat not only England but the world less kindly after seeing the truth about civilization at Cairo/Eden. Such is the novelist's indirect but souring import when relating a former innocent's exclamation: "Oh! what a different town Salisbury was in Tom Pinch's eyes to be sure, when the substantial Pecksniff of his heart melted away into an idle dream!" (*MC*, 555).

That the novelist would depict humanity differently from 1843-44 onward is as evident from Pinch's epiphany as from Martin's, on which it seems contingent. Disabused about Pecksniff, Tom soon discovers that Mercy, his former master's younger daughter, is so unhappily married that her nickname, "Merry," no longer applies. Upon meeting Jonas's crestfallen wife at Mrs. Todgers's, the ex-innocent has "a shadowy misgiving that the altered relations between himself and Pecksniff, were somehow to involve an altered knowledge on his part of other people, and were to give him an insight into much of which he had had no previous suspicion" (*MC*, 580). An "altered knowledge . . . of other people" translates into a less cheerful perspective regarding the human comedy—such clearly was also Dickens's American legacy.

In short, as a former innocent now abroad in Salisbury and London following the collapse of his Pecksniffian paradise, Tom Pinch is a variation on Martin after Eden and Dickens after Cairo. The triple parallelism does not simply draw England and America closer; it goes on to show that Dickens, having seen through the latter, decided that he could also see through the former more incisively—indeed, that he was obliged to, just as disclosure of a "putrid" Pecksniff follows narrowly on the discovery that America is a "pestilent" Eden.

Welsh's observation that Martin's achievement of self-awareness is an ineffective turning point that Dickens "scampers away from as fast as he can" (AW, 72) is simply not tenable; Pinch's changed perspective, Jonas transformed, and Dickens's gloomier outlook are among the results of Martin's eye-opening disappointment at Eden and the novelist's at Cairo. Indeed, Dickens considered it hypocritical *not* to see things differently after such a catastrophe: thus Pecksniff, having unfairly expelled Tom from his household for defending Mary Graham, can still exclaim: "I shall endeavour not to think the worse of my fellow-creatures in general, for what has passed between us" (*MC*, 497). The so-called "Emperor of Cheerfulness"[35] would have emulated Tartuffe if, despite America, he had continued as a predominantly comic novelist.

Martin has a Kurtz-like epiphany and then, like Marlow, suffers through a fever that is both a nervous breakdown and a purgation, an experience of death and rebirth. But unlike Oliver Twist and Little Nell, young Chuzzlewit must reenter the same difficult world out of which he seems to pass—neither the Brownlow-Maylie world, nor the next world, nor Tom's sinecure cataloguing the library of an unnamed wealthy employer awaits him. Subsequently, while ministering to Mark and aiding other distressed settlers, Martin begins to love his neighbor as himself, provided the neighbor is English and not like Pecksniff. These provisos work because Dickens maintains a distinction between the hero's legitimate standoffishness in the face of vulgarity and the denial of brotherhood that would result from neglecting genuine unfortunates. Throughout the return from Eden, Martin's fastidiousness, like Dickens's, retains barometric powers for determining the sociopolitical climate; nevertheless, it is no substitute for the self-forgetfulness necessary to expand one's moral consciousness. As a repentant Martin, back from America, says in apology to his grandfather for their previous quarrels: "I should have best remembered myself in forgetting myself" (*MC*, 667).

The closer one presses connections between Dickens's sixth novel and the first visit, the more selfishness, self-discovery, and self-forgetfulness become intertwined themes. Dickens's determination to vent his displeasure with America in a novel whose hero improves in self-awareness by becoming less mindful of himself while there is largely responsible for this. Martin must discover the prevalence of

Selfishness in order to have the satisfaction that goes with overcoming it. For such an operation, America, land of greed and self-interest, provided the ideal theater, a place where the "curtain" of self-ignorance was most likely to rise.[36] In one sense, Dickens ruled out goings-abroad because no one escapes his imperfect self; in another, only by going abroad as an innocent and prodigal does one confront this depressing fact and begin to cope with it.

Ironies and paradoxes of the sort just mentioned characterize the first visit from start to close, carrying over into Dickens's writings about it. For example, the travel book he wrote to defray expenses sold wildly in America but is not among his better efforts. In contrast, skillful incorporation of American episodes into his sixth of fifteen novels failed to reverse slumping sales at home but resulted in a pivotal performance: as the last of Dickens's early comic novels and the first of his later, better-constructed but increasingly satiric productions, *Martin Chuzzlewit* is simultaneously the harbinger and first instance of that general downgrading of expectations for which the so-called darkness of the later multiplot novels has been the popular term.

Having jettisoned the Romantic myth of a pristine society existing in a simpler, still recoverable past, Dickens found himself in a quandary because he was unable to replace it—certainly not with the soon-to-be-dominant Victorian myth of steady progress toward a not-so-distant millennium. Utopia, Dickens discovered, was not across the sea, having come to fruition rapidly there, nor was perfection arriving daily by inches at home, a surmise that his trip's disclosure of perennial flaws in human nature had converted into fact. Having completed the circuit from England to America and back, Dickens suspected that he had seen civilization's entire cycle: from primitive unscrupulousness in its beginnings (America) to a less febrific state of imperfection (England) featuring smoother scoundrels who were cunning refinements of the vices and viciousness Martin condemns as American institutions.

Thus Myron Magnet was being unduly precocious in contending that Dickens discovered the New World's "primary meaning . . . in its powerful confirmation of precisely those conservative beliefs about human nature and the nature of society which form the imaginative center of *Barnaby Rudge*," his fifth and last pre-America novel.[37] Were this statement valid, Dickens's identity crisis would not just evaporate as it does in Welsh's argument; it would become a trauma of corroboration, an orgy of self-justification. But the tone of growing disappointment in letters home and throughout *American Notes* militates against an

I-told-you-so experience. For Magnet's explanation to work, young Chuzzlewit's traumatic insight into men's hearts ought not to precede Pinch's disillusionment with Pecksniff and the emergence of Jonas's secret sharer, a veritable visualization of the "dark spot" discovered at Eden and within all men. In short, English developments bear out and build upon American discoveries, not vice versa, as Magnet would have it.

Civilization gives man his soul through a process of socialization, during which he internalizes the values, qualities, and attributes that render him fully human—Magnet's "panoply of . . . rituals, celebrations, and myths." For this theory of communalization Dickens supposedly found additional evidence in America.[38] But the counterpoint pitting that barbaric country against civilized England does not stop there: it goes on to compare unbridled duplicity resulting from a lack of social restraints with those refinements in the art of double-dealing for which, as Dickens's subsequent novels would make even clearer, a society's confining customs, laws, and traditions act as subtle forms of coercion, virtual stimulants. That civilization is humanization is both an anti-Romantic theorem and a Victorian half-truth. The newly reconstituted Englishman in Dickens accepted it willingly, but the satirist also explored the other half of what then became a paradox— namely, that although civilization makes man human, a major threat to both is always civilization itself.

Although Martin departs for the New World hoping to accomplish splendid things as an architect, Dickens's novel is about collapse, not corroboration: (1) Pecksniff's richly deserved downfall at home—proof well in advance of Darwin that retribution (not evolution) keeps things straight—and (2) the disintegration while abroad of the novelist's republican spirit,[39] which should be taken to include all essentially comic solutions to the world's ills and to novels addressing them.

Consequently, the novel that brought the first half of Dickens's career to a close has difficulty ending. The strain of attaining comic resolution is apparent when Dickens requires the entire double number (chapters 51-54) yet seems to be struggling. Such a drawn-out conclusion becomes an obstacle for the concept of life as gradual betterment; it demonstrates that providential comeuppances for individuals arrive slowly, albeit inevitably, and societal improvements are even harder to identify. The resolution, therefore, is not a tribute to social process as a self-perfecting operation; instead, it is only self-correcting, the final chapters suggesting Judgment Day despite the marital matters they also contain. A revived Old Martin, having feigned subservience to Pecksniff as Boffin will feign miserliness in *Our Mutual Friend*, is virtually Dickens's deus ex machina: holding court in his London rooms by the authority that age and wealth bestow, the Chuzzlewit clan's patriarch concludes the novel by dispensing rewards and punishments.

One is struck by Manichean fluctuations, light laboriously breaking in upon darkness or happiness kept from becoming complete. In chapter 51, Jonas is acquitted of poisoning Anthony Chuzzlewit, his father, but apprehended for the murder of Tigg, his partner; then both Martin and Mary and Mark and Mrs. Lupin plight their troths in chapter 52, but only after Old Martin has cast off Pecksniff. In chapter 53, John Westlock is accepted by Ruth Pinch only to have the salutary pattern of pairings off interrupted in chapter 54 when Augustus Moddle abandons Charity Pecksniff on their wedding day and Tom Pinch must be consigned to a life of single blessedness.

For Tom and Ruth, Dickens forecasts a heavenly afterlife that "shuts out the grosser prospect of an earthly parting" (*MC*, 832). But his purgative double number achieves no such uniformity of content or tone. In the midst of favorable events, one is reminded of the worst when the "neighbours" who helped Martin and Mark in Eden show up in London: husband and wife have sustained losses; in Tapley's words, they have "come a strugglin back, without a single child for their consolation" (*MC*, 825). Dickens's description of the cornered Jonas emphasizes "grosser" aspects, thus denying him the modicum of sympathy awarded to Sikes after Nancy's murder in *Oliver Twist*: "struggling with his cowardice, and shame, and guilt," Jonas is "so detestable" that his captors, even Chevy Slyme, "turned away from him, as if he were some obscene and filthy animal, repugnant to the sight" (*MC*, 782).

Like Dickens, Martin returns home less innocent, with a lower estimate of social process and mankind's potential but a higher sense of personal prestige as a cultivated European newly appreciative of England's traditions and restraints. Dickens's concern for others was already legendary by 1843-44, so only Martin needs to combine a commendable personal delicacy with greater social awareness. Dickens's alter ego in most other respects is thus also employed prescriptively for his country's national character. The would-be colonist and apprentice American is then born again, not only as a wiser, less selfish man, but, like Dickens, as a bona fide Englishman, henceforth a grateful subject for Victoria's England.[40]

This conclusion rings true even though the novelist's deep insight into recalcitrant human nature—the unregenerativeness of his fellow men typified alike by a scoundrelly Scadder and the abject Jonas— proved increasingly detrimental to convictions of added worth. That America made England look good by comparison but also made everything seem worse than before was a costly irony. But seeing one's respect for Englishmen rise at the expense of devaluing human nature in general was even costlier.

Just as Dickens discarded Rousseau in 1842, he would also be eternally skeptical of the kind of thinking that culminated in a rival novelist's enthusiasm for the "wonderfully slow-growing system of things." In 1866, Felix Holt, George Eliot's idea of a radical—but one who, like her, had never been to America—exhorted the English to pin their hopes for a brighter future on a systematic gradualism built into the nature of the social process; it supposedly ensured that "the structure of the old" will be "gradually altered,"[41] as if Darwin's theory of evolution could be applied benevolently as a promise of constant amelioration for the Victorian community. Dickens had, in effect, decided against Holt's ideas as early as 1844.

Throughout the 1850s and 1860s, therefore, perhaps *the* decades of scientific and sociological change in Victorian England, the post-*Chuzzlewit* novels became stumbling blocks for most of Dickens's emerging competition. They not only pointed to persistent problems and underlined stoppages in the reform process; their author also implied that change was not necessarily synonymous with progress toward eventual perfection, any more than he had considered equality in America automatic proof of that society's superior quality. No matter how thankfully English Dickens felt he had become, self-styled social realists, as different from each other as each was from him, detected insufficient gratitude in the bleaker, more satirical fictions of his maturity; they were dismayed by the core of antiperfectibilitarian sentiment on which the post-*Chuzzlewit* novels implicitly rest. Throughout the 1850s and 1860s, in works as diverse as *The Warden, North and South,* and *Felix Holt,* they voiced their displeasure by redoing Dickens in order to tone down, repair, or discredit altogether his damaging observations.[42]

In a slaveholding country, Martin discovers that self-awareness commences with the recognition that every person is a slave to Self. This disconcerting glimpse of man's dark heart drove Dickens homeward yet left him nearly as estranged from the Victorian ethos emerging there as Gulliver was from his fellows or as Marlow would be. By the time Conrad's sailor resents "the sight of people hurrying though the streets to filch a little money from each other" and ridicules "their insignificant and silly dreams" (*HD*, 72-73), his depiction of the "sepulchral city" has been strongly prefigured in *Bleak House, Little Dorrit,* and *Our Mutual Friend.*

Although Dickens was more English and Victorian after visiting America, more tied to his own time and place, he also became singular the more central he began to seem. As a network of evils took shape from the specific abuses his novels deplored, the acutely disappointed novelist, persuaded that humanity was not steadily on the rise, could be neither conservative nor liberal in the accepted sense of the time. As a result, he frequently became persona non grata to all sides. He still demanded extensive reform, which sounded too radical for most conservatives; at the same time, however, he was too satirical, hence too pessimistic, for other progressives, many of whom chose to remain more sanguine about England's situation and mankind's in general. Paradoxically, the more Dickens developed into the voice of his era, the more his main rivals—Anthony Trollope, Mrs. Gaskell, and especially George Eliot—took exception to his darkening worldview and tried to make him seem exceptional, that is, eccentric and inconsequential, although he was their attack's focal point.

Having visited a land where he alleged that democracy meant sameness, the paramount practitioner of the nineteenth-century novel was destined to become an anomaly: in a category by himself as the period's most radical pessimist or pessimistic radical. This is one implication of considering Dickens modern. Of all the major Victorians and especially among novelists, none seems as proreform ideologically on a daily case-to-case basis and yet by temperament as dystopian in his or her prognosis. The more desperately he demanded certain improvements but did not witness them, the greater his doubts grew that significant, lasting changes—fundamental alterations in the minds and hearts of men—were imminent or could ever prove totally efficacious.

Essentially an increasing sombreness, Dickens's "*Radical* pessimism" never "stiffened" into the "positive Socialism or Communism" that Marxists like T.A. Jackson, who coined the term, wanted to consider its inevitable outcome (TAJ, 32,6). Convinced of the ineradicable evil in man, that hint of the aboriginal beneath society's foundations new or old, Dickens went to the roots, not to extremes: after 1842, he could never have countenanced revolution or foreseen utopia because he was dismayed by man's insurmountable Selfishness, not just by the results of it, such as the class divisions based on money even in America's so-called classless society, results which Jackson mistook for causes.

Dickens discovered his real self in 1842 and proceeded to elaborate, but rival novelists soon objected: they tried to make his increasingly satirical worldview seem as unrealistic as he had found the republic of his imagination. The first trip's crowning irony is that, because of the long-term consequences of American disillusionments, Dickens was accused of treating England as unfairly as transatlantic readers had claimed *American Notes* and *Martin Chuzzlewit* treated America.

2

The Newspaper Conspiracy of 1842

At no point during the first visit ought one to perceive Dickens as a scalawag who mistakenly thought himself at large among the inexperienced. On both excursions he was more of an innocent abroad, a victim of what he himself called the national penchant for " 'smart' dealing" (AN, 286).[1] America's newspapers prejudiced public opinion against the novelist's call for a copyright law in 1842; ticket speculators took unmerciful advantage of the public reader twenty-five years later.

The two occasions have a common denominator: each time, persons not legitimately connected with Dickens—pirates in 1842, scalpers in 1867-68—refused to stop making money from his talent at his expense. Although one depredation was as unwarranted as the other, this crucial difference is noteworthy: newspapers that later complained about scalpers extorting outrageous prices from the public supported the "bookaneers" against Dickens. The reprinting of his works without remuneration proved costlier than the sharing of profits with ticket speculators; indeed, had Dickens fared better in 1842, the second visit, viewed strictly as a financial transaction, would have been unnecessary.

Dickens first broached the matter at the "great dinner . . . of February 1st," which has been called the "climax" of his reception in Boston (J, 1:374). Since he had arrived on 22 January, Sidney P. Moss's assertion that he began "at once" to agitate for copyright reform creates a false impression of preordination (M, 3). The pertinent remarks came at the end of a short speech devoted primarily to other concerns: "But before I sit down," Dickens added, "there is one topic on which I am desirous to lay particular stress" (W, 33); his initial mention of the need for copyright legislation thus has the appearance of an afterthought.

Nothing could have been more tactful than Dickens's roundabout pressing of his claims; if he erred initially, it was in being unctuous. He began by acknowledging the presence of great writers in America. "I hope," he went on, "the time is not far distant when they, in America, will receive of right some substantial profit and return in England from their labours; and when we, in England, shall receive some substantial profit and return in America from ours" (J, 1:375). Carefully balanced syntax underscores the theme of reciprocity running throughout this short speech: the visiting novelist expressed a hope; he made no demands; nor did he insist on a timetable, although periphrasis ("not far distant") could be construed as urgency. Also, he declined to suggest rates at which royalties were to be paid. While firm, "some substantial profit" is flexible enough to apply to pirated articles as well as books and still not mean an actual percentage from every copy sold.

The elaborate turn Dickens gave his sentence should not rule out extemporization; he always thought well on his feet. Whatever the extent of preparation involved, however, he could not have planned these remarks at home or on the high seas, even though he received an invitation from "The Young Men of Boston" while still in England. Before arriving in Boston, he hardly foresaw the likelihood of several heavily advertised public dinners, and so he could not have resolved upon using them as forums. Had he been so inclined, he would not have discouraged several cities from scheduling banquets; instead, as he informed Angela Burdett Coutts on 22 March, he had had to tell their deputations how much he regretted "having only mortal powers of digestion" (PL, 3:146).

By resisting copyright, Dickens pointed out, America was failing to protect the interests not just of British authors such as himself but of its own budding literary establishment. This argument seems as compelling today as it ought to have sounded 147 years ago. Dickens appealed to the country's enlightened self-interest with his own welfare in mind; nevertheless, a nation anxious to have its writers recognized as international figures was obliged to shield them, he argued, from the losses he and his brother authors had suffered. This friendly advice tied in with another argument that should have prevailed despite the subsequent uproar: like Dickens, many Americans questioned whether the country could spawn a great national literature as long as publishers found it cheaper to steal the works of foreign writers.[2]

"Pray do not misunderstand me," Dickens went on, "I would

rather have the affectionate regard of my fellowmen than I would have heaps and mines of gold." On the other hand, as he noted later in Hartford, there was no reason not to have both. His prayer for understanding is hyperbolic yet not unduly so for Dickens and not hypocritical. It seems clear from the pacific tone of the first copyright speech that he had not crossed the Atlantic spoiling for a fight. His immediate audience was even less belligerent: applause following the Boston speech was "tumultuous" (J, 1:375). As Dickens resumed his seat the night of 1 February 1842, he must have felt confident of having brought the "not far distant" day of Anglo-American copyright agreement closer.

Confidence in that modest millennium quickly evaporated "next day" (not "a week later" [PD, 66]) as one newspaper after another accused him of "bad taste": he had mixed business with pleasure by mentioning money during dinner (J, 1:375-76). Moss resurrects this absurd charge and then bolsters it: Dickens was guilty of impropriety in that he petitioned for personal gain on "state occasions" (M, 3). But a banquet at Papanti's, superintended by a hotel proprietor whose prices ("fifteen dollars a head") caused grumbling (J, 1:374), scarcely qualifies as an affair of state; inasmuch as Dickens was not officially representing the British government, he had every right to speak up. To contend otherwise, as Moss does, only revives accusations that were false and self-serving when originally made. Conductors of America's newspapers were just as piratical as book publishers, possibly more so, and thus even less likely to find this request for copyright enactment congenial.

Far from being an agitator, Dickens became, somewhat gullibly, the victim of an informal conspiracy: within days, he was summarily put in the wrong by the powerful and often unprincipled American press. Since newspapers often reprinted each other's stories, one Boston or New York editor need not have consulted another. The rapidity with which similar outcries were picked up in cities that Dickens had not yet visited or never would suggests that it was logical for publishers and their editors to hit upon the same defensive strategy: they would defame the visitor by ascribing to him motives more monetary than their own; they would protect their own greed by depicting an even greedier Dickens. This was a brilliant propaganda ploy, which a more artful man would have foreseen.

American publishers easily won the battle for the public's sympathy: they claimed they were pirating the novelist's work to make a living, whereas he, already flourishing, had come expressly to take this major source of income away. After being feted in a lavish and unprecedented manner, Dickens, they protested, had had the bad manners to ask his hosts for money; it was to be subtracted from the earnings of publishers whose presses had purportedly made the writer famous enough to be received as America's guest.

Three weeks after the dinner at Papanti's, Dickens wrote to Boston's mayor to protest against unjust imputations in "your newspapers." The city's journalists, he objected, used "such terms of vagabond scurrility as they would denounce no murderer with" (PL, 3:76-77). Dickens's letter was addressed to Jonathan Chapman rather than Boston's newspaper editors because, as an Englishman who had been the city's guest, he was complaining to his host about uncivilized treatment. Underlying the exchange, indeed fueling the entire controversy, was the crucial issue of who was being impolite to whom. The American press strove to compete with Dickens for the privilege of appearing aggrieved. But Dickens reminded Chapman that he had committed no crime, violated no etiquette, offered no insult; his speech had merely expressed "hope" for a day "when Writers will be justly treated." Such a statement could not offend against decorum because it had been delivered "in perfect good humour and disinterestedness," the speaker having been neither angry nor selfish.[3]

The letter of 22 February contained the first of Dickens's famous references to himself as "the greatest loser by the existing Law alive," but it occurred within dashes, virtually as an aside. He liked the phrase well enough to repeat it in a letter to Forster for 24 February (F, 1:224-25). The novelist is often criticized for issuing this declaration, but his point appears to be that he would have been justified in making such a claim at the Boston dinner but had refrained from a sense of good form. Dickens tried to impress upon Chapman just how diplomatic his speech had been: of all who might have complained personally, said Dickens, he felt most entitled yet had spoken generously of the plight of *all* writers, not of himself as the world's most ill used.

Instead of expatiating on the financial losses he had sustained in America since 1837, the letter concentrated on the blow that Boston had dealt to the pride of an English gentleman: "I vow to Heaven that the scorn and indignation I have felt under this unmanly and ungenerous treatment has been to me an amount of agony such as I never experienced since my birth." Here, assuredly, is Dickensian hyperbole: unfair treatment in America, Dickens insisted, surpassed any insult or embarrassment inflicted upon him in thirty years in England.

Throughout the copyright controversy, one realizes yet again from the Chapman missive, the un-Englishness of the experience bothered Dickens most. But the "amount of agony" suffered when indifferent parents sent young Charles to Warren's Blacking must have been greater than having his motives in coming to America impugned by Boston's newspapers. On the other hand, had he conceived of the autobiographical fragment before 1842, he could hardly have called being libeled his worst humiliation but one and then have recounted his degrading stint as a label paster.

Rather than condemn the letter as an "excess of outrage," which is Moss's response (M, 10), one should underline a parallel that Dickens seems to have sensed: similarities between the fiery tone of the "vow to Heaven" and the resentment later imperfectly suppressed throughout the autobiographical fragment connect events he found equally traumatic. Coming to America to be subjected to obloquy resembled banishment to the warehouse in that both were perceived, if only subconsciously, as virtual reenactments of the Fall and of man's consequent expulsion from the Garden; that is, both were seen as devastating losses of innocence and dignity. Constant scrutiny from the nation's press was as bad as being forced to exhibit one's dexterity in a shop window in Chandos Street; as lionization increasingly gave way to ridicule, such scrutiny became more unbearable.

In other words, mistreatment in America was as disillusioning to Dickens's utopian expectations of being received into an ideal republic as relegation from a schoolboy of promise to a manual laborer had been to his hopes for a splendid academic future. Both catastrophes threatened his fragile conception of himself as an English gentleman. Suddenly in 1842, within a month of arrival in America, Dickens went from adulation as a genius superior to visiting royalty to "a mere mercenary scoundrel"; he was "no gentleman," just a "contemptible Cockney," a "penny-a-line loafer" asking his betters for money.[4] Welsh's caveats against "arranging" life stories around their traumatic incidents to the contrary (AW, 2), these were especially telling insults—more cutting, conceivably, than was realized or intended—to a man who felt he had narrowly escaped the debasements of poverty.

Not surprisingly if one posits a newspaper conspiracy, the public dinner in Hartford on 8 February was followed by greater unpleasantness in the press. Otherwise, taken per se, Dickens's second public reference to copyright is a subtler model of indirection than the Boston speech with its reciprocity theme. Dickens asked his listeners to imagine Sir Walter Scott's final moments as, having written himself to death while clearing off financial obligations, he sank "beneath the mighty pressure on his brain" (J, 1:381), a line that scans as nicely as Wordsworth's blank verse.

Listening from his deathbed to the rippling Tweed, Scott was doubtless attended by Jeanie Deans, Rob Roy, Caleb Balderstone, and Dominee Sampson. But these phantoms of his imagination, Dickens complained, could not bring him "one grateful dollar" in royalties from the United States "to buy a garland for his grave" despite the pleasure the novelist who created them had given millions of Americans.

Scott was always a lesson to Dickens in what professional authors should do and avoid.[5] In the Hartford speech, the Great Unknown perished by proxy for the Inimitable, whose recurrent fears of a penurious end were assuredly present, if not uppermost, in his mind. But when Dickens entreated Americans to look with remorse on Scott's tomb in Dryburgh Abbey, he found what his illustrious predecessor also frequently sought: a historical incident to clarify the present by showing the way things change (in this case, how they should be changed). In a manner sentimental, lachrymose, and probably not without guile, Dickens suggested that lack of proper recompense killed his famous antecedent as surely as traversing the Black Country had just recently done in Little Nell.

Whether appealing to America's enlightened self-interest in Boston or to the country's reverence for Scott at Hartford, Dickens deserved better marks for diplomacy and restraint than the press was disposed to award him. Having failed to sway the minds of his hearers in Massachusetts, he tried to win their hearts in Connecticut. To Forster he later boasted of feeling twelve feet tall as he "thrust" Scott "down their throats" (F, 1:225), but the real assault seems to have been on the audience's tear ducts.

The bellicose description of his conduct in Hartford occurs in a letter for 24 February, one week after his observations at the New York dinner brought the copyright controversy to a peak; that explains the letter's militancy. "I had no sooner made that second speech," Dickens's report from New York to Forster about Hartford continued, "than such an outcry began (for the purpose of deterring me from doing the like in this city) as an Englishman can form no notion of" (PL, 3:83). The un-Englishness of the continuing outcries against him, one should emphasize, did more than confirm the blow his pride had suffered in Boston; it coincided with a myriad of unfavorable impressions he was forming of a raw, unfinished country, the process culminating in a conviction, unanticipated and unwelcome, that the insufficiently progressive civilization from which he had come was superior to the barbaric one he was visiting.

Even so, Dickens had not embarked on a "collision course" (M, 11) with the New York press as a result of unfair treatment by New England newspapers; in the midst of mounting disillusionment, he refused to be deterred in New York and tried to sound warlike to Forster but actually remained polite. If in Hartford he had begged leave to "whisper" in the audience's ear "two words: *International Copyright*" (J, 1:381), he made in New York what Edgar Johnson accurately describes as "only a brief and mild allusion to the theme" (J, 1:389), presumably out of deference to his hosts, whose pleas for caution seem to have registered.

Of the three copyright speeches, the one in New York is certainly the most direct; yet it sounds just as moderate as Dickens's previous utterances, despite the visiting novelist's admission that he resented being pressured to desist: "I claim . . . for the last time, my right in reason, in truth and in justice, to approach as I have done on two former occasions, a question of literary interest. I claim that justice be done, and I prefer this claim as one who has a right to speak and be heard" (J, 1:389). One may note that Dickens still casts himself in a suppliant's role. The petitioner to the court of public opinion sought to do society a favor by correcting an injustice, of which his own case happened to be a specific example; that is, the general wrong served as Dickens's starting point, while the personal grievance became a secondary motivation, a handy illustration of the larger problem. The speech at "the great Dickens Dinner" (J, 1:387) of 18 February in New York's City Hotel differed from the earlier ones mainly in its defensiveness. That the press had already carried the day seems clear inasmuch as Dickens was forced to retreat from a call for copyright to an assertion of his "right" to have issued such a call.

Upon reconsideration, Edgar Johnson's verdict—that "much of the anger" against Dickens "was no doubt whipped up by the newspapers, who were themselves often among the worst offenders against the rights of authors" (J, 1:376)—is not harsh enough. Dickens foolishly came to America "expecting greater things" (AN, 300) than he could possibly have found, but the biggest mistake he made here lay in underestimating the ferocity of the press. As an Englishman and guest of honor, he naively anticipated fairer play.

Dickens ought to have realized that newspapers not only had a vested interest in thwarting the change he had in mind; they also controlled his only access to the public. As long as he remained in America, he could address its citizens only through speeches that would be reported, commented on, even altered or omitted, by cohorts and employees of the parties from whom he sought redress. Conceivably, the American press helped Dickens to comprehend the plight of individuals who must ask for justice from institutions bent on denying it to them in the first place, the insidious process he subsequently anatomized when satirizing the courts (*Bleak House*) and bureaucracies (*Little Dorrit*) of his own country.

Had Dickens heeded Alexis de Tocqueville's *Democracy in America* (1835, 1840), he might have been forewarned: "When many organs of the press adopt the same line of conduct, their influence in the long run becomes irresistible; and public opinion, perpetually assailed from the same side, eventually yields to the attack. In the United States, each separate journal exercises but little authority; but the power of the periodical press is second only to that of the people" (*DA*, 95). Similarly, when discussing "Newspapers" in *Society in America* (1837), which Dickens certainly had read, Harriet Martineau cautioned: "Throughout the greater part of the Union, nothing is easier than to make the people know only one side of a question; few things are easier than to keep from them altogether the knowledge of any particular affair; and, worse than all, on them may easily be practised the discovery that lies may work their intended effect, before the truth can overtake them" (*SA*, 103).

In short, there was ultimately only one American press, no matter how many cities Dickens traveled to—a fact of modern life he does not seem to have realized fully until too late. Thus Hartford was bound to be worse than Boston, the rebuff in New York more resounding than Hartford's because Dickens never received a fresh hearing before a new judge and jury; instead, he was always pitted against a megapower, its mind already made up to prejudice the public from the outset against proposals that he could only futilely reiterate. If the press could be "irresistible" whenever its many organs adopted "the same line," even greater invincibility was to be expected in 1842 because the line adopted, the defense of pirating, was inseparable from their cherished interests as pirates. Newspapers were eager to stir up the copyright controversy because they could expect to dictate public reaction to the furor they created. Before Dickens could muster adequate support among the intelligentsia, newspapers had turned the average reader against him, thus eliminating any widespread clamoring for congressmen to introduce new laws.

Dickens's first prandial allusion to copyright was intended mainly for the elite and influential. Doubtless he envisioned press coverage, but this speech was not designed to generate a groundswell; he hoped to spur those in power to act expeditiously in their country's best interest. A few carefully chosen words, followed by a petition and climaxing in an act of Congress—that was to have been sufficient, with no need for a referendum. Ironically, Dickens's British approach, as if he had Parliament's key members to deal with, was thwarted by a republican press eager to carry its case to the populace because it knew how to enslave public opinion.

Once an apparently general disdain for copyright had been orchestrated by the newspapers, it became difficult for the general reader to identify *them* as the real special-interest group: although Dickens was urging America to abide by internationally accredited rules, he was doomed to sound like a minority voice pleading for special consideration. Villified in nearly all the papers for having made a civil request of a select few, Dickens recognized too late that he had aroused what Forster says he sneeringly called "the sacred wrath of the newspapers" (F, 1:244); as Dickens would accurately write to his subsequent biographer, a broader, cruder struggle had begun, a "war to the knife" (F, 1:234).

Throughout the ensuing exchange of barbed words, however, Dickens's belated efforts to outdo the press at its own game—at lobbying the public, at bombarding it with propaganda—were ill advised and Sisyphean. Regardless of the merits of his appeals, he was at a disadvantage metaphorically, surely a unique situation for a master of figures of speech. When the press portrayed him as a money-hungry, ungrateful guest, Dickens countered by calling himself a robbery victim, piratical publishers being the "robbers." Deserved though this retaliatory name-calling was, only Horace Greeley of the New York *Tribune*, one of Dickens's few friends in editorial office, had also used it: "who," he asked on 14 February 1842, "shall protest against robbery if those who are robbed may not?" (M, 10).

Robbery imagery failed dismally because few persons who have been mistreated by brigands can afford to travel thousands of miles in style to point a finger at the transgressors. Having steamed across the ocean in a stateroom of the Cunard's *Britannia*, Dickens was warmly greeted upon arrival as if he were a royal visitor; then he had the temerity to speak of royalties. Inevitably, he found his circumstances conducive to distortion, especially to Colonel James Watson Webb's charge in the New York *Courier and Enquirer* that he had come solely for "pecuniary considerations"[6] and was therefore accepting American hospitality under false pretenses.

Remarkable at first glance is the failure of American authors to rally round the outspoken visitor. Dickens groaned to Forster that Washington Irving, William Cullen Bryant, R.H. Dana, and others had consoled him, "yet not one of them dares to raise his voice and complain" (W, 248). On second thought, however, vociferous American support would not have done either Dickens or the supporters much good: American authors, unlike Boz, would have been biting the hands that fed them. Ironically, they were more vulnerable, hence hamstrung, than the beleaguered Dickens, who received hardly anything from their publishers and so had less to lose. The more openly American writers seconded Dickens, the more threatened their publishers would have felt, and the level of vituperation would have risen. Actually, Dickens received stronger encouragement than recent biographers elect to emphasize; such oversight allows critics like Moss to portray the visiting novelist as an isolated complainer, whose taking up of the cudgels on behalf of America's writers was uncalled for and unappreciated.

To Washington Irving's credit, he spoke out as president of the New York dinner, proposing for a toast the sentiment: "International Copyright" (W, 241). Cornelius Matthews, editor of the *Arcturus*, defended an author's right to the benefits from his labor by enumerating the damage being done to the cause of American literature from the lack of a copyright law (J, 1:389-90). Irving's toast and Matthews's speech, especially the latter, a marvel of economy and spirit, should not be minimized on grounds that both were given only after the failure of efforts to dissuade Dickens from bringing up a touchy subject (J, 1:388).

In addition, by 27 February, the authors whose alleged reticence Dickens criticized had signed a memorial in favor of a copyright law, and he planned to submit it to Henry Clay, who was to present it to the Senate (F, 1:232). This, however, was merely the sort of high-level, largely ceremonial campaigning that the newspapers had already circumvented by disposing the public mind against Dickens. By the time James Fenimore Cooper declared his support, Dickens had lost the press war and gone home. But even this belated sally, which Moss never mentions, does not confirm Dickens's lack of seasonable allies; on the contrary, it puts Bryant, "the American Dickens had wanted

most to meet" (NP, 91), in a favorable light and makes more understandable the caution shown by Irving and Dana.

Although Cooper denied a need for international legislation and
so had not affixed his signature to the February memorial, he defended
Dickens in a letter to Bryant's New York *Evening Post* (dated 6 August,
but published 11 August). Simple justice, Cooper wrote, demanded
that Dickens's novels and the works of other Englishmen be protected
in the United States.[7] Bryant had printed a favorable review of Dickens's copyright activities in his paper for 2 August, while politely ex-
onerating some of his fellow editors from the English novelist's blanket
condemnations. This article probably prompted Cooper's letter.

On the other hand, the American writer's motives were not entirely disinterested. Park Benjamin of the New York *World* and Colonel
James Watson Webb of the *Enquirer*—two of Dickens's most vocal
critics—were prominent among several Whig editors whom Cooper
had sued for libel in 1837. His tardy letter, therefore, had a timely
aspect—the libel suits were still in the courts. In effect, Cooper cited
the mistreatment of Dickens as further evidence that he had been
abused by parties one could regard as habitual offenders. Nevertheless, the only American novelist with a truly international reputation
could afford to plead Dickens's case in public chiefly because Bryant's
columns offered a friendly forum and because, unlike Irving and Dana,
he was already anathema to several New York papers.

One should appreciate the difficulty an Englishman unfamiliar
with America's partisan politics must have had in distinguishing friend
from foe. Did Dickens comprehend, even in retrospect, how often arguments over copyright had split on party lines—some Democrats
(Bryant, for example) in favor and many Whigs, including Webb and
Benjamin, vehemently opposed? If the novelist was alert to this split,
ought he to have entrusted his main chance in the nation's capital to
Henry Clay, the Whig party chief? Although a Whig (John Tyler) occupied the White House, Clay's petition to the Senate was quickly referred to committee.

Dickens was not abandoned by America's authors, but he may have
been misled by the country's politicians, from whom he seems to have
expected wonders despite their tergiversations. Kentucky's most famous legislator was not the only Whig to offer sparkling assurances:
"When Clay retires, as he does this month," Dickens wrote Forster from Washington in March, "[William Campbell] Preston [from
South Carolina] will become the leader of the Whig party. He so sol-

emnly assures me that the international copyright shall and will be passed, that I almost begin to hope" (F, 1:247). By March, however, Dickens had already been pilloried countless times in the press; he could only have meant that he could "almost begin to hope" *again*—that is, for a congressional fiat reversing the newspapers' victories.

Besides being none too strong, Dickens's March optimism was predicated on insufficient awareness of the Whig party as an unstable alliance: Westerners (Clay), Virginia planters, South Carolinian pro-slavers (Preston), and Eastern magnates numbering anticopyright publishers (Benjamin, Webb) in their front ranks. Conceivably, Clay and Preston sincerely backed a copyright law, thereby disagreeing with their party's powerful eastern wing. (Clay had worked for copyright with Captain Marryat in 1837.) But their encouragement mollified Dickens unrealistically on more than one occasion, while the New York press continued demolishing his credibility. Letters to Forster never mentioned that two professed advocates and two declared enemies had common political affiliations.

Dickens's description of Clay as a "perfectly enchanting; an irresistible man" (F, 1:247) seems unintentionally ironic; the novelist was enchanted but copyright's many opponents easily resisted Clay's efforts. Indeed, he was retiring from the Senate in frustration at not getting bills passed. Although he ran for president in 1845, failure to carry New York, the hotbed of anti-copyright sentiment in 1842, ruined his bid. With Preston, Dickens's bad luck persisted: having alienated his constituents by opposing Van Buren's financial policies, the Philadelphia-born southern legislator resigned in January 1843, just ten months after reassuring Dickens.

Looking back, the novelist must have marveled at the quandary into which he had stumbled, assuming he ever fathomed it: during and after his stay, he was criticized incessantly everywhere but defended well only sporadically in one or two places, notably Bryant's *Post* and Greeley's *Tribune*. Unfortunately, these organs were not aligned with each other closely enough to succor him coordinately; their help usually came after he had been effectively calumniated by a rowdy chorus of Whig-run papers. Dickens had received Clay's unsolicited offers of assistance immediately following the New York copyright speech (F, 1:228), but the worst of the newspaper conspirators, such as Benjamin and Webb, were doubly foes, acting from motives simultaneously political and piratical.

While still in America, Dickens also produced an endorsement from Carlyle and a petition in support of his stand on copyright bearing the signatures of several prominent British authors, such as Edward Bulwer-Lytton, Thomas Hood, and Tennyson. At issue is whether the testimonials were voluntered, as Dickens claimed, or commissioned. Dickens asked Professor C.C. Felton, his best friend in America, if it would be advisable to distribute copies to the country's leading papers and magazines, where these documents could appear more or less at once. The novelist wanted to create a sort of media blitz, not unlike the one America's press had just used against him; he fondly hoped that saturation might turn the tide of public feeling in his favor.

Did the novelist mislead Felton and America in general by not explicitly disclosing that he had summoned the supportive materials into existence? If he did, as Moss takes pains to assert (M, 6-8), the deception seems minor, hardly grounds for condemning his conduct during the entire controversy; it ranks as a veritable misdemeanor when measured against the liberties that journalists took with his speeches and those of his allies. After the New York dinner, for example, many local papers "simply dropped" Matthews's procopyright speech "out of their reports" (J, 1:390). To have announced that the signatures had been solicited by Forster would have given the press a reason to discount them automatically.

Insofar as Forster deputized for Dickens, the latter's boast of receiving voluntary reinforcements was technically correct. The package was rushed to him on 28 March, but more than a month had already elapsed since the New York dinner and nearly two since the one at Papanti's, during which interval unfriendly newspapers had addressed the controversy almost daily. The testimonials were not published until 9 May (J, 1:420); by that time they constituted little more than a parting shot from a novelist soon to retreat to England.

Journalists repeatedly claimed in 1842 that Dickens had laid out his campaign for copyright before leaving England. Moss, who agrees, resurrects the charge by insisting that the petition Forster sent is evidence of a conspiracy of less-than-forthright Britishers against unsuspecting Americans. According to this view, Dickens was no avid tourist but the "hired agent" of "money-minded" Englishmen, who sponsored his travels because they were "interested in profiting from the American literary market" and expected his prestige to gain the desired access (M, 5, 7).

Actually, the newspapers again encumbered Dickens with a deviousness better illustrated by their own behavior. Conspiracy to profiteer was their specialty, not his. To accuse Dickens of coming to America in hopes of singlehandedly taking advantage of piratical publishers not only sounds absurd; it also perpetuates the stratagem newspapers employed when laboring to transfer their grasping, unethical activities to the man they were corporately and systematically robbing. A novelist who was the prearranged spokesman for a confederacy of British publishing and authorial interests would surely have fortified himself for emergencies prior to departing; instead, one finds him outnumbered, unarmed, and writing home desperately for ammunition.

Dickens never imagined such a need developing. Polite allusions to the absence of copyright protection were to have sufficed, particularly when addressed to a democratic audience uniquely sensitive to individual rights. Naively, the British novelist mistook piracy for the result of administrative oversight, which could easily be rectified by a single piece of legislation. He did not anticipate the vigor with which this deeply entrenched, highly lucrative mispractice would be defended not only by the publishers themselves but, thanks to their exertions, by the general public in a country that, ironically, had come into existence in opposition to unjustified levies. When the press implied that Dickens desired Congress to pass laws "for his particular protection,"[8] it became exigent to show that he was standing up for his countrymen with their consent, if not, strictly speaking, at their request.

When Dickens claimed voluntary support from Bulwer-Lytton and others, he meant that their sentiments genuinely coincided with his; some of these authors had put their names to previous documents of a similar sort, one of them sponsored by Harriet Martineau. The American newspapers, in contrast, tried to foment anti-Dickens (that is, anticopyright) sentiment in a readership much of which probably had had no strongly chauvinistic feelings on the matter to start with.

Either way Dickens turned in the winter-spring of 1842, the press contrived to manipulate popular opinion in order to frustrate him: if he he spoke on his own behalf, he was a self-aggrandizer; if he represented the general feeling of England's literary establishment, he was a mercenary in its pay. Given this bind, the tardy propaganda counteroffensive launched in late March must be judged too little too late; William Glyde Wilkins to the contrary, it does not show the novelist "equally as adept in the means by which public sentiment is created . . . as any press agent" (W, 249). On this occasion, "Mr. Popular Sentiment," as Anthony Trollope later christened the crusading journalist he disliked,[9] became the victim of a consensus manufactured by his opponents to prevent the reform he advocated.

Throughout *Martin Chuzzlewit*, Dickens satirized Americans for turning each other's vices into virtues. Whenever critics take Moss's approach by substituting a conniving novelist for the esurient publishers who outsmarted him, they sound embarrassingly American in the manner Dickens criticized; ignoring actual monies involved, they convert avarice into Yankee ingenuity: the practice of plundering Dickens, transformed into a contest against the clock, shows America's resourcefulness to advantage. Copies of *American Notes*, for example, reached New York on 6 November, a Sunday. So "competitive" (that is, (greedy) were the "reprint houses" (that is, pirates), marvels Moss, that two weeklies had editions out in newspaper form on Monday, while Harper and Row issued it in pamphlet form on Tuesday, "winning by a day its race" with publishers in Philadelphia (M, 37).

Whether speaking in Boston or writing to that city's mayor, Dickens played down his financial losses; literary historians should not. In New York, *Brother Jonathan* and the *New World* both issued the entire text of *American Notes* on 7 November for $0.125.[10] The *New World* boasted of printing 24,000 copies in twenty-four hours, expecting to gross $2,880 from one run of one Dickens book done in one day. At 0.0001 cents' royalty an issue, Dickens would have made $2.40; at 0.001 cents, a more realistic computation, his share comes to $24, or $1 an hour. For *Pickwick Papers*, Dickens finally averaged £100 a part, which means that he earned roughly 0.01 cents a copy when sales reached 40,000 toward the end of the serial run. Figured in Pickwickian dollars and cents, that is, at the rate of 1 percent of the profits, since profit-sharing was a more common arrangement in the nineteenth century than royalties, Dickens lost $240 during the first twenty-four hours his travelogue was available in America.

The New York *Herald* also reprinted *American Notes*, selling 50,000 copies in two days (P, 131; but see chapter 4, footnote 2). In Philadelphia, according to one story, 3,000 copies changed hands in thirty minutes. There Lea and Blanchard found a market for 5,000 copies at 0.25 cents each with a picture of Dickens, or at the Harper's price of 0.125 cents without one. By 12 November, in less than a week, *Brother Jonathan* reported 60,000 copies had been sold, and sales figures by the end of the month were estimated at 100,000, which sounds conservative. Still, if he had been granted 0.0001 cents a copy, Dickens would have earned $6 in a week and $10 for November, whereas at 0.001 cents the rate jumps to $60 a week and $100 for the month. Assuming that Dickens might have obtained 0.01 cents apiece, one may conclude that he could have been $1,000 richer.

These calculations pertain to only one of the six major works Dickens had published by 1842. Park Benjamin's statement that he distributed 20,000 copies of Dickens's books every week throughout America in the pages of the *New World* is probably exaggeration (M, 103). If it was true, however, Dickens lost $2 a week at 0.0001 cents a copy, and $20 a week a 0.001 cents, from one newspaper alone.

To the extent that money was a factor in Dickens's disillusionment with America, it was because the heretofore innocent author realized, for the first time, the constantly expanding size of the New World's market, the proliferation of newspapers in consequence, and thus the steadily increasing magnitude of the injustice being done him. When Dickens referred to the "enormous sale" (PL, 3:407) of his travel book in America, he must have considered it a mixed blessing: thousands would read his critique of a nation whose publishers were habitually cheating him, but the book enabled the pirates to capitalize on his prose to an unprecedented extent.

From *Pickwick Papers* Dickens netted £2,000, while Chapman and Hall cleared £14,000 from the monthly numbers alone (P, 70,68). If Dickens felt like an indentured servant in 1837, he was no better than a slave to *Brother Jonathan* and the *New World* five years later; by then arguably the best-known and most widely read contemporary author in the Western world, he was publishable without the risks that Chapman and Hall had taken with an untried talent.

To offset the obscene profits American publishers reaped, their defenders traditionally credit the robbers with having made an "ungrateful" Boz popular in the United States. Ironically, Dickens smoothed the way for this tactic when he elevated having the "affectionate regard" of Americans over owning "mines of gold"; subsequently, however, he found the suggestion that he was indebted to the pirates contemptible.[11] The cue for Moss's revival of this notion comes from Wilkins, who was merely repeating American claims when he doubted "whether Dickens would have had so many readers in the United States if it had not been for those cheap reprints" (W, 238). Yet Dickens more than returned the favor, while the pirates kept all the money. The rejoinder that the novelist craved American dollars to refurbish Devonshire Terrace and give "lavish" entertainments there is flimsier still (M, 63). If the novelist deserved compensation, speculation as to how he might have spent it seems irrelevant. No one has suggested that the book pirates donated emoluments held back from Dickens to libraries and orphanages.

Moss's references to proposed expenditures in the Dickens household differ only slightly from the position taken by Boston's envious *American Traveller:* inasmuch as he received 40,000 guineas per annum for his works in England, the paper decreed, he had no right to ask Americans "to double the sum out of [their] own pockets" (M, 102). Instead of Moss's luxury-crazed Dickens feasting on gains from austere Americans, the Boston paper chastised him for asking to be paid twice—in this way it refused to pay him at all. It also tacitly confessed that America was picking Dickens's pockets of more than £40,000 yearly, or, in other words, was denying him the chance to double his income. If one believes these figures, he was being denied $200,000 a year in 1842, more per year than his profit ($140,000) from the subsequent American reading tour, which many think overtaxed his health. Were sums the *Traveller* used ten times too high, the $20,000 a year remaining, taken as a constant, would still have amounted to $500,000 between 1842 and 1867, a bonanza nearly four times greater than the net from seventy-six American readings.

Not surprisingly, apologists for a profiteering American press tend to misread *Martin Chuzzlewit.* Sylvère Monod's euphemism for the American chapters—prolonged "extemporization"—seems mild-mannered once Moss condemns one-seventh of the novel as an "obvious" excrescence (SM, 34; M,115). As sequences about hypocrisy in England alternate with descriptions of its starker transatlantic manifestations, Monod concedes that the procedure foreshadows bolder experiments with multiplotting in *Bleak House,* if only "faintly and indirectly" (SM, 34). But in Moss's opinion, the American episodes constitute "A Libel," a malicious exaggeration of "the worst aspects of the United States" (M, 115). Obeying an entirely nonartistic compulsion, Dickens decided "to interpolate suddenly episodes so offensive to Americans—publishers, booksellers, and readers alike—that one or another of the installments would force the 'Robbers' to halt their piracy in mid-career and prevent their republication of the serial, upon its completion, as a book" (M, 131).

On the contrary, it was not beyond a multifaceted genius to outfox American pirates while simultaneously broadening his novel's satiric scope in hopes of boosting sales as well. (Critics of the decision to send Martin Chuzzlewit and Mark Tapley to America naively assume that inspiration cannot be commercial and aesthetic simultaneously.) The case for unpremeditated interpolation would carry more conviction if the American chapters occurred consecutively; instead of becoming a huge stumbling block for the pirates, they are introduced at intervals as contrapuntal variations on established themes.

Dickens's resolve, as stated in the 1844 preface, "to keep a steadier eye upon the general purpose and design" refers primarily to the enumeration of variant forms of selfishness, his sixth novel's core idea or main target. If the cataloguing includes American as well as English examples, Dickens's narrative strategy does not preclude capitalizing on the American reprinters' greed as a de facto illustration of his novel's satiric outlook. That the book appeared at all in America became a self-validating act, vindication for the satirist. Dickens hit upon a way to wrest ultimate control of his product from the pirates, even though he was unable to prevent them from receiving unauthorized benefits from it. Existing in America in spite of itself, that is, through the complicity of some of its targets, the first of Dickens's increasingly satirical novels acquired an additional ironic dimension; this gamelike quality behind the actual telling now seems protomodern.

The same fascination-aversion that compelled readers to continue with *American Notes* no matter how upsetting it became would work, Dickens assumed, for *Martin Chuzzlewit*; persisting demand would prevent American publishers from breaking off. They would not "want to halt their piracy in mid-career" because doing so would involve slitting their own throats melodramatically before all the world, a punishment Dickens considered too good for them. Instead, they were to be driven by popular demand and their own covetousness to go on stealing the very text they would have to denounce as slanderous in other parts (or issues) of their magazines and in countless newspaper editorials.

No tactic, however Swiftian, could have exposed the hypocrisy and duplicity of the newspaper conspiracy more resoundingly or shown more clearly in whose mind "pecuniary" motivations were foremost. Seizing moments of opportunity without regard for customs and common courtesy—that, said *Chuzzlewit*, was the American way; if this critique was unfounded, the argument continued by implication, pirates should refuse to make money by reprinting the novel containing it.

Champions of the American episodes as an integral part of *Martin Chuzzlewit* cannot afford to minimize the newspaper conspiracy either, as Edward J. Evans does when arguing for the primacy of Martin and Mark's American sojourn. He suggests that America's "national disease," violent self-assertion, brought the theme of selfishness glaringly to Dickens's attention; in short, the first visit inspired the entire novel.[12] But the New World is not simply "the Old World carried to an extreme" as Evans says—that is, a nineteenth-century phenomenon or brand-new calamity. Granted, America adds to "the number and variety of humours and vices that have their root in selfishness," Forster's definition of the novel's scope (F, 1:314); yet *new,* paradoxically, was also *old.* Dickens found that the new country was Europe carried backward, not forward; it exhibited human nature and society stripped again to basics, deprived of the patina of form and usage that time's passage supplies.

Every American is greed personified because Dickens makes him as ambitious to outwit his fellows as each publisher was to outstrip rival reprinters of *American Notes.* That is how violent self-assertion taught Dickens about selfishness. Collectively, all but Mr. Bevan take advantage of Martin and Mark just as the robbers, except for a minority voice such as Horace Greeley's, supported one another against Dickens, their common prey. Warlike among themselves but hostile to outsiders, Americans in *Martin Chuzzlewit* ape the country's newspaper editors and book publishers; they behave like the primitives and predators Dickens had begun to suspect that all human beings essentially are, no matter how sophisticated they may seem.

According to the experts, Dickens's attempts to discredit America in *Chuzzlewit* backfired. Ada Nisbet contends that the general disapproval of *American Notes* ruined the novel's sales, lowered Dickens's prestige, and disillusioned his public.[13] Moss merely expands such criticism when he asserts that *Chuzzlewit* hurt Dickens's profits worldwide (M, 121). But the modern revaluator must deal cautiously with the "period of comparative coolness, indifference, and disfavor" that George Ford, drawing on Forster's chapter about "*Chuzzlewit* Disappointments" (F, 1:327-48), locates "between *American Notes* and *Dombey and Son*" (GF, 54): it was too complicated to be blamed solely on the first American visit. *Martin Chuzzlewit* ought not to be made the scapegoat novel in the Dickens canon, nor should the first visit and his satiric treatment of it take full responsibility for the novel's so-called failure because English factors, more than American ones, caused most of Dickens's monetary and artistic troubles in the mid-1840s.

Serial novelists depend greatly on momentum, the popularity of the previous publication being relied upon to sell the current venture. Nisbet notes that *Barnaby Rudge* sank from 70,000 copies a week to 30,000, so that the 20,000 with which *Chuzzlewit* began continued a downward slide. Switching from a weekly serial to a monthly publication did not help either. If the opening number is "slow, uneven, and unfocused" (P, 133), readers already disappointed with *Barnaby Rudge* had to languish for three weeks between January and February 1843 before Dickens could correct unfavorable first impressions.

Martin Chuzzlewit brought to six the number of novels Dickens had published in as many years. Also, *American Notes* had appeared just three months earlier, and *A Christmas Carol* came out in December 1843, when *Chuzzlewit*, already running for nearly a year, had six months still to go. A public surfeited with Dickens sounds implausible to moderns, especially to those who have read about dockside queues of Americans awaiting the next installment of *The Old Curiosity Shop* for news of Little Nell; it was not as unthinkable in 1843. Dickens forecasted the impending overexposure to Forster two years earlier: "Scott's life warns me that let me never write so well, if I keep on writing, without cessation, it is in the very nature of things that the sale will be unsteady, and the circulation will fall" (P, 121).

Before contracting for *Chuzzlewit*, Dickens wisely demanded a year's sabbatical, living expenses for which were to be met by an advance from Chapman and Hall, whom he already owed money. Although Dickens spent a large portion of his time off in America, the visit was intended as a cure for financial and emotional difficulties already extant or correctly foreseen prior to 1842. After giving details of "The *Chuzzlewit* Agreement" that Dickens signed with his publishers in 1841, Robert L. Patten summarizes the novelist's state: he was "broke, tired, restless, and heavily in debt" (P, 125).

Consequently, Dickens's sixth novel would have to have been phenomenally successful to extricate him, much less enrich him. He needed to realize enough from the profits to repay his publishers for an £1,800 advance and £5,019 9s. 5d. in loans; until he liquidated these debts, he would receive only his £200 per part (P, 126). America thus aggravated Dickens's sense of his English problems: in bondage to publishers at home, tired and overextended artistically, he could see American pirates grossing more for themselves than he required to get clear.

This irony grew more painful when *American Notes* sold widely in the United States, netting Dickens little, while *Chuzzlewit*, on which he and his publishers were betting heavily, fared only moderately well in England, bringing him less than expected. He was entitled to three-fourths of *Chuzzlewit*'s profits, a handsome arrangement, but only after advances and loans were repaid. Prescient in other ways, neither the novelist nor Chapman and Hall could have anticipated in 1841 the extent and duration of the "general depression" that had sent

British and American publishers into "the doldrums" by 1843 (P, 133-34).

Regardless of *Chuzzlewit*'s plummeting sales (due in part to its author's overexposure) and despite a depression in the book trade, the idea of an 1843-44 decline in Dickens's reputation as a result of *American Notes* and a novel's American episodes must be dismissed as a popular myth. It has been nurtured by eminent critics who, coincidentally, are also American. Nisbet called *American Notes* Dickens's "Dunkirk," while George Ford said *Chuzzlewit* gave him "his first real taste of failure" (GF, 43). Although not untrue, these observations become sensational when Moss enlarges upon the climate they create to rewrite Dunkirk as Waterloo. Overemphasizing difficulties with "ebbing reputation" and "poor sales," he creates a Dickens outraged at America for compromising him internationally, making him unsure of his talents, and then leaving him with a growing "sense of financial doom" (M, 149).

But reviewers passed largely "favorable" verdicts on *Martin Chuzzlewit*,[14] and Forster concluded that "it was felt generally to be an advance upon [Dickens's] previous stories" (F, 1:335). According to Ford, again echoing Forster, *Chuzzlewit* "eventually gained proper recognition when it appeared in book form" (GF, 43). By July 1844, when that happened, the novel had outlasted the glut of Dickensian productions that, along with depressed markets, makes the early 1840s unique in Dickens's career.[15] From the 1850s onward, his sixth novel ranked third among his most popular works.[16] It disappointed as a serial but never failed, either monthly or in book form; any other Victorian novelist—Thackeray for example—would have been gratified by its success.

Ford wisely stresses how "comparative" the so-called "coolness" to Dickens's sixth novel was, pointing out that it seemed serious only by comparison with the runaway sales of *Pickwick Papers* and *The Old Curiosity Shop*. Less would be made of "*Chuzzlewit* Difficulties" had Dickens and Chapman and Hall not been hoping, unrealistically, for a repetition of spectacular sales to put their financial arrangements with each other on a surer footing. Ironically, exaggerated hopes, shared alike by author and publisher, and not resentment over American disappointments, as Moss charges (M, 146), were primarily responsible for driving Dickens into the arms of Bradbury and Evans, a rival publishing firm.

Chapman and Hall were making a profit of £400 a number after printing expenses but before paying Dickens £200 (P, 136). The panicky publishers incurred his wrath by suggesting that this monthly payment be reduced £50 in accordance with a clause in the *"Chuzzlewit* Agreement" regarding slumping sales.[17] Already angered by the extent to which he was being pirated abroad, Dickens was in no mood to accept a pay cut at home. But America was only partially responsible for the switch in publishers, because the collapse of utopian expectations was inconveniently followed by a decline in circulation for the novel attesting to that collapse. The one seemingly underscored the other. When the pay cut was suggested, it was as though Dickens was being warned twice over that no one, including his publishers, wanted to hear about one of the severest disillusionments of his life, which he believed held grave consequences for all Victorians intent on computing man's chances of creating a better society. Dickens may have felt he was being told that his reduced estimate of human potential would earn him less sympathy from British audiences thereafter than his pleas for copyright had just obtained from Americans.

Unfavorable reviews of Dickens's travel book were not chiefly responsible for his serial's sales slump either. Little basis in fact or logic exists for the accepted picture, which Moss has grossly exaggerated, of a justly chastened Dickens: he was allegedly being repaid for the anti-Americanism of *American Notes* by the decreasing popularity of *Chuzzlewit* yet was resorting to slander of America again in order to salvage his novel. A need to improve sales is still widely regarded as the only rationale for the introduction of American scenes. Could Dickens have hoped for such improvement by sending Martin and Mark to disparage America if milder reservations about the country in *American Notes* caused the decline?

Had Dickens managed to secure copyright protection in February 1842 or cajoled American publishers into offering reasonable terms, his travel book and sixth novel would have become his best money makers up to that time. In 1843-44, he would have received monies rightly his from transatlantic reprintings; far from declining like the stick of a rocket, his annual income would have risen dramatically despite the depression.

Nowhere else in Forster's biography does Dickens insist so vehemently that his current effort exceeds its predecessors: he called *Martin Chuzzlewit* "in a hundred points immeasurably the best of my stories" (F, 1:331-32). Nor was he as certain elsewhere that his creative powers have not declined: "I have greater confidence in myself than I ever had," his letter for 2 November 1843 continues; "I could sustain my place in the minds of thinking men, though fifty writers started up tomorrow." Unless one feels that Dickens protests overmuch in a desperate search for self-reassurance, it seems wisest to believe him. Not before the mid-1850s and into the 1860s would outbreaks of new talent—Trollope, Mrs. Gaskell, and especially George Eliot—challenge him to make good his determination to sustain his place at the front of the first rank.

Forster, it follows, should be taken more seriously when he implies that the "depression of sale" in Dickens's writings, "grave" albeit "very temporary," was a fluke, "unaccompanied by any falling off" in the quality of the work itself "or in the writer's reputation" (F, 1:327). Instead of suggesting a loss of self-confidence, the nearly four-year delay between *Chuzzlewit* and *Dombey and Son* should be reinterpreted as an attempt to ride out the slump in the publishing business and rekindle reader interest, which, if it had been hurt, had been damaged not by *American Notes* but by the bad timing of publishing too many items in rapid succession (that is, by Dickens's prolificness).[18]

The success of the opening number of *Dombey and Son* indicates that Dickens worried needlessly that his career might end prematurely: 32,000 copies were sold, 12,000 more than the first number of *Chuzzlewit*. If a serial is indebted to its predecessor, one must attribute some of this boom to headway made by *Chuzzlewit* itself; it can be said to have smoothed the path for the less comical, less sentimental, more satirical Dickens it previewed. Forster recognized this trend when he observed that characters in the pre-*Chuzzlewit*—that is, pre-America—novels "had been more agreeable" (F, 1:336). Put more positively, he meant that the Jonsonian satirist in Dickens, aiming at "something much more pestiferous," had "never shown the imaginative insight with which he now sent his humor and his art into the core of the vices of the time" (F, 1:340,336).

George Ford observed that Dickens "shifted his satire away from remote institutions such as the Yorkshire schools and directed it upon the Victorian sanctuary: the home and family" (GF, 48). At first glance, calling a novel with eight American chapters less "remote" seems ridiculous, but Ford and Forster are equally correct. Indeed, as a precursor of the bitterer satirical novels to come, *Martin Chuzzlewit* contains one of Dickens's finest comic creations (Mrs. Gamp) and yet is considerably sterner than either Ford or Forster thought.

Dickens's sixth novel proposes a number of satirical metaphors for existence, viewing life on earth not just as confinement in a whale's belly, as the previous chapter of this study maintained, but also as an arduous, quixotic pilgrimage even for those resolved to overcome their innate selfishness en route. At the end of the journey, the reformed individual must attempt to go home again because no promised lands await, at least not within the *temporal* order. Dickens aimed his satire not only at the popular myth of the Victorian home as a sanctuary but, given man's fallen nature, at the very possibility of a newly consecrated place existing within the secular dispensation; he exploded the myth both of the home as a refuge or holy place and of Eden or some promised land as an alternative haven to be found abroad.

One may conclude that *Martin Chuzzlewit* was hurt by poor timing mainly in that it was ahead of its time in the Dickens canon. Later additions by a writer whose vision of man's inner nature was darkened by American disappointments have put his sixth novel in clearer perspective: it is the most Swiftian of the serials prior to *Bleak House* and the first of the later works as well as the last of the early fictions, a fact Forster assimilated more readily than Edmund Wilson did.[19] *Chuzzlewit* is the novel in which one can actually see a bleaker social vision beginning to encroach upon Dickens's comedic talents.

It seems wrong, therefore, to perceive *Dombey and Son* as atoning for Dickens's alteration of his "formula" in *Martin Chuzzlewit*. Dickens did not finally accede to requests from Francis Jeffrey and others for another Nell, that is, for a story that would arouse equivalent feelings of tender compassion. With Tiny Tim in *A Christmas Carol* (1843) and little Paul in *Dombey* (1846-48), Dickens was not "attempting . . . a repeat performance" of earlier successes in hopes of wooing back his readership (GF, 59).

Granted, the opening number of *Dombey* contains a pathetic death scene, and George Ford rightly considers the fifth installment, in which Paul dies, "worthy to succeed that describing the last hours of Nell" (GF, 59). But Dickens was too skilled to repeat a success so blatantly; just as he could outsmart America's pirates without destroying the integrity of *Martin Chuzzlewit*, he could appease Jeffrey without abandoning the new directions for severer social satire mapped out in 1843-44.

The deaths of the first Mrs. Dombey and little Paul do not recycle old matter as an end in itself; Dickens lures readers into his novel so that, by the fifth number, he can proceed logically from the opening pathos to resume his investigation of faults in the national character, which, of course, is also human nature in general. Epitomized by Mr. Dombey, these failings, it becomes clear, were responsible for the deaths on which the novel focused at the outset. The world buffeted Pickwick, victimized Oliver, and smothered Nell; the difference is that

Dickens now feels better prepared to be both more specific and more satiric in accusing the antilife forces he found increasingly at large. This awareness of having become more suitably equipped to judge the age is what Forster sensed when he emphasized "the degree to which" Dickens felt "his mental power had been enlarged by the effect of his visit to America" (F, 1:335).

Pecksniff, Jonas Chuzzlewit, Americans who praise each other's greatness but swindle Martin, Scrooge, Dombey, Gradgrind, and Bounderby are successive exhibits in Dickens's full-scale revaluation of both man's nature and material progress in the oncoming secular-scientific age, a time of deceptively promising economic expansion and technological innovation. The novelist felt compelled to undertake this reassessment after recognizing that America had not furnished proof that innocence and uprightness were the rule at earlier, supposedly less corrupt stages of society, hence recoverable through reforms or, if need be, by revolution; instead, America supplied a cruel parody of all civilizations in that it revealed man's essential cupidity.

Subsequently, because Dickens had come to feel that some human failings, such as Selfishness, are virtually "irremediable" (F, 1:340), biological slippages in *Bleak House* combine with an abundance of animal imagery throughout the later fictions to suggest that society has not come very far; moreover, it remains prone to regress. Dickens's satirical zoology acquires additional teeth as *Chuzzlewit* proceeds. Before Martin has seen essential human nature in America, Jonas Chuzzlewit describes Pecksniff as "a sleek, sly . . . tom-cat" (*MC*, 173); in the post-America chapters, however, Jonas becomes a "Wolf" (*MC*, 643) and then a "filthy animal" too "repugnant" for zoological classification (*MC*, 782). Mary Graham finds the novel's archhypocrite's touch distasteful: she "would have preferred the caresses of a toad, an adder, or a serpent: nay, the hug of a bear" (*MC*, 482)— which makes Pecksniff a menagerie all by himself. When he attempts sexual blackmail, promising to restore Martin to his grandfather's favor in return for Mary's favors, he seems as charming as "an affectionate boa constrictor" (*MC*, 480).

Once Martin and Mark have verified the report that "there's lots of serpents" in the "Walley of Eden" (*MC*, 342) and England has capped that with a boa constrictor at large near Salisbury, nothing surprises. Even a Megalosaurus "waddling" up Holborn hill in the first paragraph of *Bleak House* will not sound implausible; nor will simian moneylenders and vampirelike members of the bar overtax one's credulity. London in *Bleak House* and again in *Our Mutual Friend* is both the capital city of Europe in the second half of the progressive nineteenth century and a darkening, prehistoric waste patrolled by predators and scavengers—"Birds of Prey" in the 1864-65 novel—now that the floods have seemingly just receded.

A pattern developed after 1844 of loosely scientific yet antievolutionary satires against ideas and movements Dickens found less conducive to genuine advancement than advertised, advancement itself being a process the satirical zoologist could only regretfully describe as one of fitful starts and stops, often with a minus for every plus. The list of targets in the 1850s included an insatiable legal system that devoured suppliants; inhumane manufactories that reduced workers to insects (a proto-Lawrentian illustration of the pitfalls of so-called technological progress); and unimaginative theories of education that demoted learning to what now seems a Pavlovian matter of stimulus and trained-animal response. Instead of conceding life's forward movement, the evolution of man and society, a dissenting Dickens often seemed to be anatomizing the later, more insidious stages of an untrustworthy life process he had begun to understand only after seeing it at its naked worst throughout America but especially in the un-Edenic swamp community patterned after the canal company's real estate bubble at Cairo, Illinois.

No contradiction exists between the seeker of copyright and the ill-fated utopist searching for the republic of his imagination: both were congruent parts, in 1842, of an innocent abroad. The first drove ever shrewder bargains with publishers thereafter; the second wrote progressively grimmer explorations of the dark places in British society and within man himself.

G.K. Chesterton to the contrary, "quarrel" is an inadequate term for the collision between the world's foremost novelist and the West's fastest-rising civilization.[20] Two curiously intertwined quests for fuller self-actualization led to mutual disenchantment. We must remember that a young author was visiting a very young nation and that each sought validation from the other. (Dickens turned thirty in America; as a nation, the country was only sixty-six.)

Dickens wanted reassurance that the superior social system still inchoate in his mind was a legitimate alternative to the England he knew. This is what Chesterton meant when he stated that Dickens "looked at England almost with the eyes of an American democrat" (*CD*, 134): the novelist came to see whether the internal standard against which he had been measuring his country's deficiencies had been approximated, perhaps achieved, by Americans. It was a fact-finding mission, like the trip to inspect a Yorkshire school or the later visit to Preston, except that Dickens sought to corroborate his fondest hopes, not confirm his worst fears. America wanted him to endorse its image of itself as the new paragon among nations; a celebrated social critic from the mother country was expected to acknowledge England's grown-up former colony as civilization's apex.

Clearly, in more than one sense, America got the best of it. The conflict between Dickens and the newspapers was lopsidedly in the latter's favor, and America also admonished the idealist-democrat in Dickens's makeup; it dealt a mortal blow to the utopist whose views were so adversely affected that the very idea of a model republic became untenable in his writings thereafter. In contrast, although America failed to obtain Boz's blessing, it escaped the trauma he underwent when he discovered his quintessential Englishness on American soil. Despite *American Notes* and *Martin Chuzzlewit*, the country emerged with a stronger sense of independence and identity: it discovered that it could survive a bad notice from a world-famous commentator because its self-confidence, which he found insufferable, turned out to be self-insulating.

Ironically, by the time Dickens made a return visit in 1867, that self-confidence had grown, and Mark Twain was at work on *The Innocents Abroad or The New Pilgrims Progress* (1869); this work attempted to reverse the process that had brought Tocqueville, Harriet Martineau, Mrs. Trollope, and Dickens to the New World. With America sitting in judgment, Twain gleefully varied the formula painfully discovered in Dickens's travel book and sixth novel; although he, too, described the dissipation of unfounded expectations, this time the high hopes pertained to traditional, allegedly superior cultures in the Old World. As the next chapter will explain further, the author and his party on the *Quaker City* looked forward to their tour of Europe and the Middle East as a gigantic "picnic" (*IA*, 17), but in the course of it, such sacred cows as cosmopolitan France, eternal Italy, and especially the epical Holy Land were found to be much smaller than anticipated, rather grimy, and extremely old.

Most of the recent complaints about Dickens's criticisms of America do not originate with Chesterton or Twain. James J. Barnes blamed Dickens for believing that literary popularity could be translated into political power and that Congress could be bullied into jeopardizing a "home industry" (that is, pirating) with the country in "the depths of a depression" (B, 75-76). Moss simply amplifies both indictments, doubly underlining what Barnes called Dickens's "naiveté about influencing America's literary and political life" until it appears morally reprehensible rather than inevitable and excusable. If no correlation existed between nineteenth-century social commentators and actual reforms, history would have determined by now that most Victorian novelists (and many of the best essayists, including Thomas Carlyle and John Ruskin) wasted their time. Also, Dickens hardly seemed ungracious to ask for justice during hard times when American publishers showed no inclination to be generous in periods of relative prosperity.

Moss's unique contribution to the lore surrounding Dickens's American engagements is his insistence that the novelist bore a monumental grudge against the New World: he allegedly spent the next quarter of a century scheming to obtain revenge. Having failed in his copyright mission because it was surreptitious and mismanaged, Dickens reportedly resumed the quarrel sneakily in spring 1842 once he was back on English soil. Lest the debacle of the first visit permanently damage his reputation at home as well as across America, he turned to the *Foreign Quarterly Review* for help. Four fulminations in that journal, none of which Moss can prove was actually penned by Dickens, were meant to discredit America, thus repaying the country for rejecting the visiting novelist's monetary demands. None of these pieces bore Dickens's signature, but Moss contends that they appeared disguised as independent testimony that would corroborate the anti-Americanism in *American Notes* and *Martin Chuzzlewit*.

"The Newspaper Literature of America" (22 October 1843) deemed American newspapers "execrable" but as yet the only national literature the country had produced. Although this assertion seems unfair to Irving, Longfellow, Cooper, Poe, and Hawthorne, it scarcely exceeded its probable source: Tocqueville's declaration that America has "no literature. The only authors I acknowledge as American are the journalists" (*DA*, 174). Even worse was Frances Trollope's nastier reference in 1832 to America's "insect authors"; it was based on her snobbish conclusion that "the higher graces of composition can hardly be looked for" whenever "newspapers are the principal vehicles of the wit and wisdom of a people" (*DM*, 268). America did have 1,631 newspapers in 1842, three times as many as Great Britain. Nevertheless, reviving accusations from American editors of the time, Moss brings in a "verdict of collusion," arguing that Forster, then in charge of the *Quarterly*, wrote the piece at Dickens's instigation (M, 19).

"The Newspaper Press of France" (January 1843) was written by John Frazer Corkran, yet Moss treats it as one of the "follow-up" articles (M, 59). The third diatribe in the series, "American Poetry," was allegedly "designed to make good *Martin Chuzzlewit*" (M, 144), but one fails to see why or how, especially since Tocqueville had already asseverated that "the Americans have no poets" (*DA*, 181). The final salvo, in October 1844, was a review of Featherstonhaugh's *Excursion Through the Slave States*, supposedly inserted to bolster antislavery pronouncements in Dickens's travel book and novel. Moss objects that a book based on a journey in 1834-35 could have no bearing on Dickens's veracity because it was ten years out of date when published, as if conditions in the South had improved in the interval (M, 186).

Rebuffed in his plotting to secure a copyright law, Dickens, Moss argues, went "underground" in the 1840s to "libel America" again, this time in a British journal (M, 16, 53). But it is difficult to understand the need for an additional outlet, given the impact of Dickens's travel book and sixth novel. Moss explains that Dickens "had trouble resisting" opportunities for "self-vindication" (M, 52). Actually, he shows him creating opportunities, not resisting them; and it is Forster, not the novelist, who comes off worse: he emerges from editorship of the *Foreign Quarterly Review* not only as an insular and parochial figure whose incipient "Podsnappery" Dickens encouraged but as his friend's willing drudge and underpaid assassin. Forster supposedly shared Dickens's paranoia that a "personal defeat" in America, if left unreversed, would ruin the novelist as a literary property profitable to them both (M, 61).

Logically, one cannot argue backward from four post-America essays to substantiate the thesis that Dickens went to the New World resolved to demand copyright protection. Even if he coauthored "The Newspaper Literature of America" in 1843, for instance, that fact does not provide an infallible index to his state of mind in December 1841, when he decided to cross the Atlantic.

If Dickens did contrive to give the American press a taste of its own medicine, one feels that he was entitled to the satisfaction; still, the expenditure of energy involved in creating such ephemeral stuff seems regrettable, hardly the wisest recourse for an already overworked author. Besides, Dickens seems to have lost much of his interest in copyright after 1842, and with it would have gone the need to get even. Although he served on several committees to secure protection for British authors, his efforts in 1852, for example, were less strenuous, if not half-hearted, compared to those in 1842 (B, 219-26). Working always in concert, Dickens never spearheaded another copyright campaign; his willingness to continue adding his voice to those of others, however, further obviated the need for a magazine outlet other than his own *Household Words*. During the second visit, he refused to join in at all: according to George Dolby, "some of the leading authors and publishers waited on Mr. Dickens in Boston" to enlist his support for the "establishment of an International Copyright Act"; they asked him "to attend a meeting, and to express his views on the matter, an invitation which Mr. Dickens declined," not because he feared a repetition of 1842 but "on the ground that he felt the case to be a hopeless one" (D, 271).

From the way Moss exploits Chesterton in order to elaborate upon negative hints in Wilkins, Nisbet, Barnes, and Ford and thus to incriminate Forster and Dickens, the modern revaluator might well feel as if *American Notes* and *Martin Chuzzlewit* had appeared only yesterday and *Charles Dickens' Quarrel with America* were the indignant response by a spokesman for the offended nation. Dickens's allegedly premeditated call for copyright becomes the root of all evil: it is blamed for bringing closer to war two countries already at loggerheads over the boundary between Maine and Canada and on "the Oregon question" (M, 83). Dickens, whom Johnson described as "a resolute abolitionist" (J, 1:402), even supposedly refrained from denouncing slavery while in America in order to appease southern legislators; he expected them to support a copyright law, since their constituencies had few book-publishing centers (M, 177).

It is not simply that these positions give every accusation ever made against Dickens during or following his first visit new life in exacerbated form; such comments are less discriminating in the 1980s than their sources in the 1840s, which frequently turn out to have been the very ringleaders in the newspaper conspiracy that thwarted Dickens. James Gordon Bennett of the New York *Herald*, Park Benjamin of the *New World*, and Colonel James Watson Webb, whose vituperative editorials assailed Dickens in the New York *Enquirer*,[21] do not deserve to speak again as if their veracity were beyond question or on a par with Dickens's or Forster's. On the contrary, not just their duplicity in accusing Dickens of greed and bad manners but their informal complicity in doing so ought to be underlined.

Ironically, a conspiracy theory that focuses on Dickens and his British backers, as Moss's does, overlooks the complementary nature of the attempts by Bennett, Benjamin, Webb, and others to discredit him but depends on the utterances of these men for evidence, thus inadvertently exposing the only real conspiracy operating in 1842. Just as the

American press called Dickens avaricious to conceal its own avarice, it fabulated a confederacy involving Dickens and other British authors to divert attention from its ability to create a consensus against copyright, one paper after another reprinting the same assertions.

Proponents of a conspiracy theory making Dickens the tool of foreign interests have forgotten similar defamations leveled against Captain Basil Hall, the most despised man in America until Dickens issued *American Notes*. Mrs. Trollope, who was living in Cincinnati when Hall's *Travels in North America* appeared, reported the widely held belief that the Englishman wrote so negatively because he "had been sent out by the British government expressly for the purpose of checking the growing admiration of England for the government of the United States" (*DM*, 314).

Since Tocqueville *was* commissioned by the French to investigate democracy in 1831-32, overly sensitive Americans had some anticipatory grounds for suspecting Hall in 1830. But they appear to have found conspiracy theories useful for protecting the national ego: harsh criticisms could be turned to advantage if they were seen as the work of jealous rivals unwittingly testifying to American superiority. Not surprisingly, the public ascribed similarly ignoble motives to Hall and Dickens, the difference being that attacks on the novelist were orchestrated by a press familiar with the country's reaction to the captain ten years before. Also, America owed Hall nothing, whereas the calumniation of Dickens was an expedient for refusing to pay royalties and began during his stay.

Partisans like Moss to the contrary, Dickens did not discuss a copyright campaign with Forster until the crucial letter of 24 February (PL, 3:81-90). By then he had already spoken in Boston, Hartford, and New York, each time more adamantly as opposition to his stand hardened and some supporters counseled restraint. In this letter Dickens sounds genuinely astonished that Americans should be so uncivil to someone raising only "one point" on which they were remiss (F, 1:225). He pictured himself as Horatius at the bridge: "a man alone by himself" yet forced to engage the shapers of public opinion in major cities across America. The letter then requested that Forster secure testimonials from British authors in support of his copyright speeches; they should be "expressive," Dickens advised, "of their sense that I have done my duty to the cause" (PL, 3:86-87).

Far from thinking he was sure to prevail, Dickens seems to have wanted the petition in commemoration of a valiant try: "As the gauntlet is down," he told Forster, "let us go on" (F, 1:228). He was not the challenger but one who had been challenged to validate his claim that *all* British authors felt badly treated.

Moss's contention that Dickens was already part of a plot with Forster prior to leaving England turns the letter of 24 February into a singular exercise in hypocrisy and self-deception for both sender and receiver; instead of writing as one conspirator to another, Dickens exudes a sense of surprise and outrage, both of which sound sincere. His need to convince Forster that he had stepped into a hornet's nest and required assistance eliminates the possibility that he had premeditated plans to manipulate his hosts. Were Dickens a secret agent reporting to his control, it would be not just dishonest but pointless to complain at length of "the most monstrous mis-representations relative to my design and purpose in visiting the United States" (F, 1:225).

A year later, with such misrepresentations still in the air courtesy of the American press, the London *Times* for 16 January 1843 carried a similar denial from Dickens, this time public, that he was ever a "missionary in the cause of International Copyright": "Upon my honour, the assertion is destitute of any futile aspect or colouring of truth" (W, 240). In consequence of this protest, a journal that had aroused Dickens's ire by relying on transatlantic reports to proclaim the "missionary" charge backed down; although James Spedding, its correspondent, had just spent four months in America and had presumably double-checked his sources, the *Edinburgh Review* printed a retraction. Alexander Welsh considers it a "careful" apology (that is, reluctant, insincere),[22] but that assessment hardly diminishes Dickens's right to it or rivals the bad grace America's journals exhibited when they were similarly questioned.

Since Forster declared on his own authority that Dickens "went to America with no express intention of starting this question [of copyright] in any way" (F, 1:219), one must either believe him or rank not just Dickens but also his biographer and the letters the former wrote the latter far above Pecksniff and his antics in the annals of self-conscious hypocrisy.

In effect, Welsh's book has done this very thing and has thus added one more American voice to the newspaper conspiracy. Unlike Moss's book, it initially mentions only the "possibility" that Dickens went to America in pursuit of an agreement; within a few pages, however, the argument is that "since Dickens spoke on behalf of copyright he *probably* intended to speak [italics added]," as if commission of a deed guaranteed premeditation. The novelist's clamorous defense of his motives has convinced Welsh that he not only expected the hypocrisy charge but was in fact culpable. Dickens's guilt feelings allegedly taught him personally what it was like to be two-sided and so facilitated the creation of Pecksniff, an assertion that negates the novelist's credentials as a moral realist and in the process rescinds negative capability (AW, 30, 37, 39, 45)[23].

What becomes of Dickens's credibility if one makes the satirist of hypocrisy not only hypocritical but a hypocrite who protested ever more loudly that he was not one because he feared that he was? The questionable method by which he acquired his materials—the means by which he gained insight into the vice he attacked yet repeatedly denied personifying—would seem to disqualify him from casting stones. Similarly, in 1842 the American press set out specifically to convict Dickens of the accusations he was leveling against others.

Welsh's idea that there was some of Pecksniff in Dickens and, therefore, some of Dickens in Pecksniff works well only if one fabricates a time scheme and eschews the historical context. Dickens did not feel slightly uneasy or moderately two-faced in America in 1842 and then go home to create Pecksniff in 1843-44. His fight to reverse the charge that he was a copyright conspirator continued *after* the new novel had been announced and production of it had begun, as the spirited reply to the *Edinburgh Review* indicates. Were Welsh correct, he would be obliged to pursue his point to its logical conclusion—that is, to maintain that the Dickens who denied being a copyright missionary actually kept getting more proficient at hypocrisy while executing his satire against it and that Forster, reemphasizing Dickens's disclaimers thirty years later in the official biography, was just as bad.

The letter of 24 February (F, 1:224-29) remains pivotal both to the discussion of Dickens's role in the copyright controversy and to any estimate of its contribution to his disillusionment with America. The reason is that it did four things: (1) it opened with Dickens's account of his surprise at the growing resistance to his call for copyright legislation; (2) it described with dismay rancorous attacks in the country's newspapers, in particular the charge that he was "no gentleman"; (3) it asked for a petition vindicating his claim to be representing a "cause," not lobbying for himself; (4) in one of the last and most important paragraphs, it lamented at length the manners of intrusive Americans who were persecuting him with unwanted attentions.

This "at last" paragraph revealed an especially sore point; it capped the letter and set the tone of mounting disenchantment heard more loudly in every letter thereafter, such as the famous one to Macready written in March from Baltimore (PL, 3:155-60), and subsequently throughout *Martin Chuzzlewit.*

Forster speaks of "the slowness with which [Dickens's] adverse impressions were formed" (F, 1:254), an observation true enough if slowness connotes reluctance; but in Dickens's mind by mid-February of 1842 at the latest, the incivilities of Americans, robbing him of privacy, had become the major complaint. What took longer to emerge was the connection between the problems enumerated in Dickens's pivotal letter. Such discourtesy, he figured out, was of a piece with the eagerness of journalists to deprive him of his say and the willingness of publishers to go on divesting him of royalties. Subsequently defined further as the result of a lack of worthwhile customs, traditions, and restraints, incivility became the root of the trouble in *Martin Chuzzlewit*; it was the general problem in America, which the absence of copyright, a specifically galling invasion of privacy, had helped to uncover.

One begins to savor the ironies of the first visit by noting again that newspapers in Boston and New York attempted to shift public opinion from the justness of Dickens's complaints to the alleged impropriety of voicing them at a public dinner. It was a matter of manners, they tried to argue, not of money; the satirist subsequently agreed. Throughout *Martin Chuzzlewit*, America's lack of manners is blamed for all other shortcomings, including the unbridled pursuit of money. Dickens answered the press that accused him of inordinate self-interest by portraying America as the abode of selfishness, one that was nationwide.[24] Insofar as the copyright controversy was a contest to show that one's opponent was more acquisitive and had worse manners, Dickens eventually won, belated and Pyrrhic though his victory was.

Politically, economically, and on the propaganda front, Dickens not only lost but set back the cause he championed. The book-publishing interests, writes Edgar Johnson, grew "alarmed" at the agitation Dickens had caused: they convened in Boston on 26 April, when Dickens was off to Canada, to memorialize Congress, "not only protesting against the passage of any international copyright law, but asking that a duty be imposed on foreign books" (J, 1:420). Furthermore, they wanted permission to continue altering British authors so that pirated books would suit American opinions and tastes. Instead of an alarm, this demand sounds like the follow-up on victory, a tallying of the spoils. The book publishers' petition to Congress not only displaced Dickens's but asked for greater freedom to take advantage of him and his ilk. The "bookaneers" were to do so for nearly another fifty years,[25] longer than they might have if Dickens had not fallen victim to their conspiracy and thus helped them strengthen their position.

To add to the irony, Thackeray later spoke out against copyright just as stoutly as Dickens had. The visiting lecturer claimed that he had "only found Englishmen" (that is, gentlemen) in America and declined to be so "imprudent" as to write a travel book, both statements palpable hits at Dickens (JW, pt. 1:15, 22). Nevertheless, when he agreed to supply a preface to the popular reprints of his writings being reissued in twelve volumes at fifty cents apiece, he chose an even more inauspicious occasion to castigate piracy than that upon which Dickens had seized at the Boston dinner.

Thackeray's opening reference to the "extreme liberality with which American publishers have printed the works of English authors" is wickedly misleading because only satirically polite; he was not complimenting their generosity but underscoring its absence, as the next paragraph explained: "It is, of course, not unnatural for the English writer to hope, that some day he may share a portion of the profits which his works bring at present to the persons who vend them in this country" (JW, pt. 1:62). This remark differs neither in tone nor in content from Dickens's first copyright speech, to which Thackeray seems to be alluding.

Protesting against being robbed in a preface to the stolen goods themselves seems nearly as audacious as compelling pirates to print the anti-American chapters of *Martin Chuzzlewit* while denying their veracity. Thackeray's observations failed to raise an outcry in the New York press but not merely because lesser sums were involved in 1852 than in Dickens's case; freedom to use the preface to a pirated edition to plead for copyright shows how unconcerned publishers had become during the decade since Dickens had made his plea and lost.

Having engaged in the copyright battle of the 1840s, however, Dickens was primed for the realism wars of the 1850s and 1860s. He had to let the pirates keep his American earnings but, as a consequence, was not about to permit additional usurpations, especially not at home. When one major Victorian realist after another—Trollope, Mrs. Gaskell, George Eliot, and even his protégé Wilkie Collins—tried to displace him as the era's most listened-to social critic, Dickens stubbornly fought back, parodically revising their themes, characters, and situations to corroborate his worldview as forcibly as they redid his to substantiate theirs. When Moss depicts Dickens coming home from America frantic "to regain reputation and income" and "feeling

a volcanic hatred of America" for sealing his "financial doom," therefore, he does so prematurely (M, 149). When a literary historian revises
favorably the imbroglio that newspapers created from Dickens's
speeches, he misrepresents more than the principal event with which
he is dealing: he overlooks the real calamity. Many of Dickens's best
days, creatively and financially, lay ahead of him in combats to come,
but the utopian optimism with which he set sail for America was gone
forever.

Charles Dickens' Quarrel with America and *From Copyright to
Copperfield* may seem like legitimate responses to Ada Nisbet's sensible plea for the "decanonization" of Dickens (N, 61), but each revives
too many false or dubious charges: "As the story of this quarrel unfolds," Moss's preface warns in an uncharacteristic understatement,
"the Dickens we admire does not appear as frequently as we would
like." How could he if revaluators regularly impute to the visiting novelist the worst possible motivation?

One must reassess Dickens's American engagements not just because they were more important to his development than has been
realized but as a way of holding the line for a reputation in danger of
being overly maligned. Yes, it seems likely that Dickens later took a
mistress young enough to be his daughter; nor was he incapable, while
away from Ellen Ternan during the second visit, of playing on Annie
Fields's sympathies toward a wifeless, womanless man of genius, as this
book's fourth chapter will show. But in 1842, when he was just about
to pass thirty, he did not come among unprepared Americans expressly
"to exploit" them (M, 4).[26]

3

The Battle of
the Travel Books

Captain Marryat, Mrs. Trollope, Isaac Fidler, Basil Hall—an uniden-
tified American journalist, calling at Devonshire Terrace in December
of 1841, found Dickens's study "piled high" with books by these travelers who had preceded him to America (J, 1:360).[1] Harriet Martineau's travelogue is not mentioned, although Dickens supposedly
considered it "the best book written on the United States."[2] More surprisingly, the reporter's short list omits Alexis de Tocqueville's *Democracy in America*, from which Sylvère Monod thinks it "not
unlikely" that Dickens derived some of his sanguine expectations (SM,
36).

What seems even likelier is that Dickens later repudiated his quondam hopefulness by writing to exterminate its sources: in *American
Notes* and again in *Martin Chuzzlewit*, he took a reviser's glance at the
travel literature that had sparked his interest in the New World. Thus
he began the decisive round in the battle of the travel books by straining to transfix the Victorian image of America once for all. He wanted
to oust from public esteem the texts whose laudatory observations had
misled him into expecting a facsimile of utopia; simultaneously, he
strove to outstrip travelogues in which the reporter's opinions, albeit
negative, now seemed kinder than his own.

Once the composing of travel books about America had developed
into "a minor industry,"[3] each author inevitably commented on his
predecessors. It was not just a furthering of consensus on such topics
as the vulgarity of spitting tobacco juice, the irresponsibility of the
American press, and the discomforts of bumping along a "corduroy"[4]
road; correcting a previous authority became the readiest means of assuming superior authority for oneself.[5]

Frances Trollope began this revaluative practice when *Domestic Manners of the Americans* (1832) contradicted Fanny Wright's *Views of Society and Manners in America* (1821). For the latter's enthusiastic account of the new republic's perfections, Mrs. Trollope substituted the graceless, ill-bred frontier of Louisiana, Tennessee, and Ohio; its culture was stifled by a proliferation of evangelical religious sects and by the inability of its subjugated women to exert a civilizing influence. Similarly, Harriet Martineau's *Society in America* (1837) took issue with Mrs. Trollope for failing to perceive that the insignificance imposed upon women generally and the enslavement of the Negro race in the South were interconnected phenomena; these analogous departures from civilized behavior made North and South equally detestable examples of the country's pervasive defection from its own first principles. Thus Miss Martineau corrected Mrs. Trollope on the woman question while combining with her against Tocqueville's judgment that the Americans' "singular prosperity and growing strength" stemmed from "the superiority of their women" (*DA*, 247).

Dickens was in an enviable position to bring the infighting between Victorian travelers to a climax: the famous visits of the 1830s—by Hall, Tocqueville, Mrs. Trollope, and Miss Martineau—were over by 1842, and Boz could review the decade of investigative journeys at his leisure, revising the entire canon whenever he chose. For Dickens especially, writing about America entailed writing about all of the best-known previous guidebooks.

Wherever Tocqueville entertained several reservations about the state of manners in a democracy, Dickens's objections increased tenfold. His deconversion from republicanism in America, a loss of innocence he considered by no means "comparable" to Mrs. Trollope's fickle switch to conservatism,[6] was meant to appear unique, strictly one of a kind, its painfulness and importance unrivaled. He depicted slavery as a wellspring for atrocities in order both to outclass the outraged Harriet Martineau and to remedy Fanny Trollope's sketchy treatment of a national disgrace; when the task was depicting a pervading social problem, Dickens brooked no competition.

The brunt of his displeasure, however, was reserved for Miss Martineau; her ignorance of the impact manners have on morals was more glaring in his opinion than either Tocqueville's or Mrs. Trollope's. Moreover, although she had written what was often a scathing abolitionist tract, the archetypal Victorian in her saw America as proof that life is constantly improving, presumably by some law of inevitable progress. Thus she spoke of social ills in utopian undertones as temporary setbacks, a point of view particularly galling to a disconcerted radical whose hopes of finding an existing model society had just been dashed.

So pronounced is the intertextuality between, on one hand, *American Notes* and *Martin Chuzzlewit* and, on the other, *Democracy in America*, *Domestic Manners of the Americans*, and *Society in America* that Dickens appears to be conducting several concurrent operations: (1) recording his own impressions; (2) measuring firsthand experience against books he has read; and (3) actively seeking situations that test a previous traveler's conclusions. On occasion, he seems to be responding as much to an existing target text (or texts) as to the subject it shares with his own work-in-progress, the reaction becoming a second way of treating the subject.

In other words, between 1842 and 1844, when Dickens's feelings about America coalesced into a negative, satiric rejection and he reused material from *American Notes* for *Chuzzlewit*, he also rewrote Tocqueville, Mrs. Trollope, and Harriet Martineau. This massive redoing he accomplished cleverly and imaginatively, going further than any forerunner who had previously commented mostly on an immediate antecedent.

Appearances to the contrary, Dickens was not entirely the instigator. Roseate reports of a staunchly progressive America, whether denied by Mrs. Trollope or confirmed by Miss Martineau, could be construed as a challenge to satirical elements already present in his 1841 worldview, such as the criticism of humbuggery in *Pickwick Papers* and the outrage in *Oliver Twist* at society's indifference to the poor. If America was solving some of the problems on which European nations had foundered, if others were proposing the new country as the wave of the future, then Dickens was duty bound to report the fact. He could not continue to be a timely social analyst by portraying goodness in *The Old Curiosity Shop* as a passive quality invariably overwhelmed by menacing evils, nor need he try to spur on reform by reviving threats of an English revolution, as he had done in *Barnaby Rudge*, a historical novel ultimately about Chartism (that is, labor unrest).

Either way the visit turned out, going to America became "imperative" (F, 1:197): if the new country was a utopist's dream, as he fondly hoped, it would not only justify satirical treatment of the old order at home but also furnish a model for change; should the exemplary republic he sought turn out to be illusory, then travelers preferring it were as subject to ridicule as those who overemphasized its inadequacies to do apologetics for the English system.

Domestic Manners of the Americans, the first of the travel-book cluster to have lasting literary value, appeared as debate raged over the Reform Bill of 1832.[7] Should there be a wider franchise? This was not only the specific question but a way of raising larger issues: to what extent, for example, should the further democratization of England be carried? How capable was human nature of self-governance, that is, of additional moral and intellectual enlightenment? Displeased with democracy, Mrs. Trollope wrote "to encourage her countrymen to hold fast by a constitution that ensures all the blessings which flow from established habits and solid principles" (*DM*, xxxiii). Inadvertently, she revealed that a travel book about America supplied an excellent means of writing about England by airing one's attitudes toward change, progress, and the future, for which three things Victorian travelers of the 1830s soon considered the United States virtually metonymic.

Shortly after midcentury, Victorian social realists began authoring rival fictions disputing each other's conclusions about England's prospects: they pondered the possibility that significant progress was practically inevitable, if not for the first time, then on a much greater scale than at any previous point in the history of Western civilization. In much the same fashion that the Spanish Civil War previewed World War II, the battle of the travel books in the 1830s and 1840s as to whether or not America was the "land of promises"[8] led to subsequent wars between competing realists about the chances that a secular-scientific England might become the promised land. America beckoned progressives and conservatives of all different hues, thus serving as a preliminary battleground for more heated discussions over the real nature and true extent of societal advancement.

Only in Dickens's case, however, was déjà vu close to cause and effect. In 1842 he confronted, on one side, sanguine expectations for Western man's future in works by Tocqueville and Miss Martineau and, on the other, Mrs. Trollope's support for England's status quo. Owing to his stated dislike for both of these positions, he later felt squeezed between what he saw as an unacceptably conservative approach to reform in moderates such as her youngest son, Anthony, and the equally unfounded optimism of social evolutionists such as Mrs. Gaskell (defender of Manchester's manufactures in *North and South*) and George Eliot (champion of an ameliorative gradualism in *Felix Holt* and *Middlemarch*).

Dickens, a "Utopian Radical" full of "the Utopianism inherent in the Radicalism" of his day (TAJ, 31, 27), set out for America thinking to distinguish the book he would write from the insufficiently approbatory travelogues of his forerunners, in particular his female English forerunners: Mrs. Trollope and Harriet Martineau. He "was convinced that he could understand, as neither of these ladies could, a democratic kingless country freed from the shackles of class rule" (J, 1:357); his report "would redress the balance of their disdainful praises and prevailing tone of depreciation." But the novelist discovered that Tocqueville had been too generous regarding democracy's strong points, while the ladies, even more reprehensibly, had not been stringent enough. Otherwise, how could his own anticipations have been so unrealistic? America thus marks the beginning of Dickens's conviction that women make inferior social commentators. Not surprisingly, his most formidable rivals both in the travel-book battles and in the subsequent realism wars of the 1850s and 1860s were female.

Chagrined at an unexpected turn of events that spelled disappointment with America, Dickens found himself in an artistic bind: he had to devise an alternative to discharge his agreement with Chapman and Hall. Already in *American Notes* but more resolutely as *Martin Chuzzlewit* progressed, he determined to convert his projected paean into the harshest account yet of manners and morals in the New World. Having come to fight one kind of battle, he ended by waging a very different campaign, but the goal remained the same: to demonstrate that he could evaluate a foreign country better than one Frenchman and two ladies had. The point was to add luster to his reputation as the newly begun Victorian era's emergent expert on social systems. Through criticizing America's new institutions more incisively than his predecessors had, he would enhance his qualifications as an observer of social progress and subsequently appear most entitled to address England's changing conditions as the century wore on.

The battle of the travel books proved a godsend to Dickens: to the extent that he triumphed, it was because he was able to disguise major acts of self-revision and redirection as reworkings of rival creations. Dickens's speculations about the relative merits of hypocritical Europe and barbaric America quickly burgeoned into a skeptical reconsideration of the progressive forward drive supposedly inherent in social process; in short, he had to reduce drastically his estimation of human nature's capacity to improve ethically. But changing one's attitudes could have been construed as a sign of uncertainty and hence no credential for the would-be comparer of social systems; fortunately, it seemed excusable, indeed, commendable, when presented as the expunging of mistakes imbibed from rival travelers. Dickens was not just recanting utopian fantasies, not just dismantling forever his assumptions that a perfect society might exist and that human nature might be made fit to inhabit it; he was not just changing his own mind but changing—one could say canceling—the sort of mentality responsible for creating his former outlook.

Despite good intentions, Dickens had less success than other visitors at discovering in America the best of possible worlds. Consequently, it was to be expected that he would regularly form darker impressions whenever he and his contemporaries surveyed the same sociological developments. Dickens learned that it was to be his role to see that things were seldom as good as reported or worse than others had perceived. This crucial bit of self-discovery is already implicit in a joking reference to those inns "mentioned—rather vaguely—by Miss Martineau, where they undercharge literary people for the love the landlords bear them" (F, 1:243); visiting her El Dorado, Dickens repeatedly felt *over*charged. When his plan to exonerate America turned into an obligation to be denigrating, he adopted for good the uncompromising satirical tone that makes the author of *Bleak House, Hard Times, Little Dorrit, Great Expectations,* and *Our Mutual Friend* sound so original and often protomodern amid the competing voices of less perturbed Victorian social realists.

Although no political scientist, Dickens was bent on showing that a middle-class Englishman was a more reliable judge of equalitarianism than a French aristocrat could be. After less than five months in America (January-June 1842), he consistently voiced stronger reservations about democracy than Tocqueville had entertained after nine (May 1831-February 1832). Thus if the Frenchman states: "I know of no country in which there is so little independence of mind and real freedom of discussion as in America" (DA, 117), Dickens writes: "I believe there is no country, on the face of the earth, where there is less freedom of opinion on any subject in reference to which there is a broad difference of opinion than in this" (F, 1:224-25). Adding "on the face of the earth" and replacing "so little independence" with "less freedom of opinion," Dickens upgraded his predecessor's severities; also, he usurped them for his own. Open-mindedness was not just missing in America, Dickens added; its absence seemed most noticeable on topics controversial and debatable everywhere else.

Tocqueville saw in "the sovereignty of the people" the potential for a new form of despotism: the "tyranny of the many over the few" (DA, 20-21); Dickens expressed a "fear that the heaviest blow ever dealt at liberty will be dealt by this country, in the failure of its example to the earth" (F, 1:231). This fear became a grimmer foreboding in *Martin Chuzzlewit* when the "very progress of the human race" and "the rights of nations yet unborn" are said to have been jeopardized by an America allegedly "senseless to the high principles on which [it] sprang into life" (*MC*, 369). The *Chuzzlewit* passage is more damning than Tocqueville's opinion that America, no longer pursuing "lofty" ambitions, has lost the "manly candor . . . which frequently distinguished" the country's founders (*DA*, 256, 120).

In the 1859 Library Edition of *American Notes*, as Dickens began to contemplate recrossing the Atlantic for a reading tour, his tone softened: "I hope and believe [America] will successfully work out a problem of the highest importance to the whole human race" (*AN*, 49). But both of the original condemnations and the warier admonishment fifteen years later exhibit a tendency to enlarge upon Tocqueville. Where the Frenchman "sought" in America "the image of democracy itself" (*DA*, 13), Dickens was after an "example to the earth," a lesson he could expound "to the whole human race."

Tocqueville arrived, hoping to reconcile democracy, the new political movement, with the best aspects of the old order. Initially more sanguine than Tocqueville, Dickens wanted a system different in substance and spirit. That he collided with an unvarnished reality instead of stepping into the utopian future revealed him to have been a starry-eyed idealist; yet throughout *Martin Chuzzlewit*, he concealed his innocence by deeming unrealistic the Frenchman's program of reconciliation.

First, Dickens elected his disillusioned self the better reconciler, if only ironically. Given startling affinities between the old and new orders because human nature is unfortunately the same everywhere, their respective inhabitants must turn out to be equally selfish; the new order, Dickens informed Tocqueville, combines more readily with the worst aspects of the old. Then, with greater irony, Dickens stamped himself more expert than Tocqueville on innocence abroad. The French traveler criticized America's naive pairings of equality with freedom and of majority rule with liberty. But acute innocence, Dickens explained, can more easily be found in travel literature about America, even in negative appraisals like his own, than in the new country's Constitution. Naiveté did not consist of fallacious American equations; rather, it underlay quixotic journeys by cultured Europeans who expected both a return to Eden and an ideal republic that would demonstrate progress as a natural law, as if one could recapture the past and experience the future simultaneously; they should have known better than to expect in the New World radical departures from the nature of things familiar to them at home.

Naive expectations, however, were precisely what Dickens under-stood himself to have entertained, more foolishly than any predeces-sor, by taking the new land at its own estimation: "No visitor can ever have set foot on those shores with a stronger faith in the Republic than I had, when I landed in America" (AN, 48).[9] Artfully, Dickens declared himself to be the most credible because he had been most credulous; that is, upon arriving with the strongest faith, he underwent the sharp-est disappointment, which entitled him to become the most censo-rious. Humility does not lie behind the admission of credulousness; one detects, instead, an oblique accreditation: gullibility is translated into authority, with hyperbole serving as a sort of character reference.

In other words, even when in error or, better yet, repenting of one, Dickens was apt to confess himself wrong in a bigger way or to a greater extent than persons of lesser capacity. Appropriately, several of his earliest references to himself as "the inimitable" occur in letters sent to Forster from America (F, 1:205). Since Dickens came as a be-liever rather than a scientific observer (Tocqueville's approach), his reservations about democracy had to be more convincing; they were allegedly acquired both more painfully and more reluctantly.

Three additional examples of Dickens's insistence on always being utmost, whether for good or ill, should be conclusive as a key to his strategy for supplanting previous travel books. First, compare Thack-eray's letter to Macready for 20 November 1852 with Dickens's missive to Forster for 24 February 1842, the point being the inability of the later to outdo the earlier. Lamenting that "there never *is* a day's quiet," Thackeray refused to detail the "day after day skurry and turmoil, friends calling, strangers calling, newspaper articles bawling out abuse" (JW, pt. 1:37). But Dickens, piling one specific example atop another, complained of being "followed by a multitude" when he went out or of having the house filled with callers "like a fair" if he remained at home; not only was he "inclosed and hemmed in" to the point of suf-focation at parties but he was unable even in private to "drink a glass of water, without having a hundred people looking down [his] throat" (PL, 3:87).

Dickens seems so set upon as to be deprived of oxygen and liquid nourishment, crises that seem life-threatening. Besides attacks in the newspapers, which form the extent of Thackeray's problems, "letters on letters arrive" for Dickens "by every post, . . . all demanding an immediate answer" (F, 1:229). The impression of a persecution spilling over from the public forum to become an importunate invasion of the victim's private life expands Dickens's sufferings beyond anything Thackeray could match.[10]

Second, place Mrs. Trollope's indictment of the calumnious American press alongside Dickens's personal sense of himself as every slanderer's favorite target. She began by doubting the truthfulness of newspapers generally. "If I am not greatly mistaken," the onslaught then continued, "there are more direct falsehoods circulated by the American newspapers than by all the others in the world, and the one great and never-failing source of these voluminous works of imagination is England and the English" (DM, 152). Having asked for copyright protection, Dickens was accused of having such "low purpose" in coming to America that "a notorious murderer named Colt was an angel" by comparison (J, 1:382). Even Mrs. Trollope's negative superlatives—American newspapers are the most calumniatory, and the English are their most dependable whipping boy—failed to deter Dickens. When he bridled at "such terms of vagabond scurrility as [newspapers] would denounce no murderer with," calling such abuse the most "ungenerous treatment" he had experienced in his life, the novelist crowned himself the most severely slandered member of the race most often slandered by the world's most slander-prone press (PL, 3:76-77).

Third, gauge the animadversions on tobacco chewing in *American Notes* against those in either *Society in America* or *Domestic Manners of the Americans*. "Of the tobacco and its consequences, I will say nothing," Miss Martineau began, "but that the practice is at too bad a pass to leave hope that anything that could be said in books would work a cure. If the floors of boarding-houses, and the decks of steam-boats, and the carpets of the Capitol, do not sicken the Americans into a reform; if the warnings of physicians are of no avail, what remains to be said? I dismiss the nauseous subject" (SA, 279).

Equally mortified, Mrs. Trollope had declared her ignorance of "any annoyance so deeply repugnant to English feelings, as the incessant remorseless spitting of Americans" (DM, 12). For her, exhibit A was the "well carpeted" ladies' compartment of the *Belvidere*, the steamboat on which she traveled to Memphis from New Orleans, yet even then she sounds singularly reluctant to reproduce it: "but oh! that carpet! I will not, I may not describe its condition." As Miss Martineau would also do, she threw up her hands in disgust and despair.

Not so Dickens. He was more than willing to furnish lengthy accounts of the tobacco-stained carpets that female modesty compelled Mrs. Trollope to forgo. Moreover, taking a hint from Miss Martineau, he located the worst examples of the nation's most disgusting habit in the national capital: his chapter on Washington, "headquarters of tobacco-tinctured saliva," announced that "the time is come when [he] must confess, without any disguise" how "sickening" he finds "those two odious practices of chewing and expectorating" (*AN*, 160). Indeed, he piled carpet upon carpet: "Both houses" of Congress, he continued, "are handsomely carpeted" but so "squirted and dabbled upon . . . in every direction" that the rugs' original patterns have become unrecognizable (*AN*, 169). There was no end to such sacrilege, for not even the carpet in the waiting room outside President Tyler's office, Dickens was horrified to discover, had been spared (*AN*, 172).

Since Dickens was grossly offended, the implied argument runs, he could correct the misimpression that only squeamish women are put off by American manners. Dickens condemned spitting and the use of spit-boxes without the "disguise" or reluctance that separated demure and defeatist reformers from the genuine article: unlike Miss Martineau, he would never "dismiss" a subject as a lost cause or feel as loath as Mrs. Trollope to describe vulgarity fully, no matter how "repugnant." It followed that he was the most forthright analyst of American manners, a claim that *Martin Chuzzlewit* substantiated when the hero's displeasure with a "gentleman in a high state of tobacco" (*MC*, 535) triggered a diatribe against the new nation's institutions.

In order to win the battle of the travel books, Dickens wrote to appear inimitable. Ironically, he came to the land of equalitarianism eager to defend what Mrs. Trollope had unkindly called its " 'I'm-as-good-as-you' population" (*DM*, 297); but he produced, instead, two works designed to certify himself a better traveler-commentator than any contemporary European, whether male or female, French or British.

Despite flaws and the need for safeguards against a tyrannical majority, America impressed Tocqueville as a manifestation of "the will of God" (*DA*, 30). The new country's ascendancy proved that "democratic revolution," worldwide, was "the whole future" (*DA*, 38), a truly providential development divinely ordained and superintended (*DA*, 26, 182). If one assumes a Dickens imbued with Tocqueville, the novelist's pilgrimage acquires a religious significance: the French sociologist crossed the Atlantic to discern democracy's strengths and weaknesses, thus making this new political religion safe for the world; but the English novelist came as the dedicated agent of providence, not just with a "stronger faith" than Tocqueville's but better equipped, because of it, to recognize and celebrate heaven's handiwork. Unlike Tocqueville, Dickens planned to worship in America, hence the sense of outrage and betrayal upon finding the tabernacle empty.

Oddly, Tocqueville and America, a Frenchman and a country teeming with Anglophobes, offered Dickens early subscription to what shortly became a leading tenet of Victorian optimism: if the transition from monarchies to republics was both the future without exception and God's will, then progressive change could be equated with divine intent or, easier yet, posited by secular-scientific humanists as a worthy substitute for it. Dickens's failure to verify a French aristocrat's prospectus for mankind's "whole future" was therefore monumental; it can be identified as one of the hitherto undetected first steps in the process that separated the foremost English novelist from many of his more hopeful peers—not just from Harriet Martineau, in whose travelogue Tocqueville's expectations were writ large, but from most subsequent Victorian meliorists. It is not just that America and man's perfectibility became interdependent in Dickens's thinking, so that disillusionment with the first mandated abandonment of the second; the interdependency was not entirely of Dickens's choosing but in large part an extension of what he took to be Tocqueville's vision of America's potential.

Eventually, the enormity of World War I demolished "the prevailing Meliorist myth" by seemingly reversing the Idea of Progress; it put an end to Victorian liberalism, the gradualistic, reform-minded progressiveness that addressed life with overconfidence.[11] Unequal as the events are, Dickens's first visit had the same modernizing impact on him personally that the world war, a trauma of international proportions, would exert on the Edwardians and on meliorism (or gradualism) itself.

Dickens's sense of America as a setback for civilization meant that linear progress—a steady, largely benevolent process of ascent—was not discernible as God's plan for the modern world. It also meant that Dickens could not imitate the ways of providence by writing non-melodramatic novels eschewing the reversals and upheavals that accompany rude shocks and negative epiphanies. He could not write, for example, a novel such as *Middlemarch* (1872), in which Dorothea Brooke's modest achievements are hailed as proof of "the growing good of the world" (*MM*, 613). There was to be scant evidence for such a proposition in the anti-Tocqueville, post-*Chuzzlewit* fictions; indeed, they seem to preclude the proposition, thereby obliging novelists of George Eliot's disposition to disparage them.

After 1842, predictions about the world's "growing good," as if this earth were a maturing organism or a ripening piece of fruit, could have no more validity for Dickens than the Americans' boast that their country was a new Garden of Eden expressly created for the regeneration of man. Each of these statements (had Dickens lived to read George Eliot's) would have sounded as hypocritical and utopian to him as the other. More pertinent was Tocqueville's warning that democratic countries are liable to "expand" the "scope of human perfectibility . . . beyond reason" (*DA*, 156, 158). In Dickens's opinion, the French aristocrat would not have misjudged God's intent had he perceived how clearly America symbolized the irrationality of utopianism. As the meliorist myth grew in an England more democratic after the First Reform Bill, Dickens came to feel that the American mistake— overestimation of man's "scope"—was also one of the cardinal miscalculations endangering Victorian humanism.

The novelist used Martin's first impressions of the new Eden to sabotage Tocqueville's disquisition on America as the coming age: the hero beholds a "hideous swamp" so "choked with slime and matted growth" that the "waters of the Deluge might have left it but a week before" (*MC*, 375). In 1852, the satirical social critic commenced *Bleak House* by transferring this conceit to Victorian London: that is, by depositing "as much mud in the streets" in the novel's fourth sentence "as if the waters had but newly retired from the face of the earth."

Although quoted less often, the 1843 passage is more emphatic, dating the watery recession precisely: figuratively speaking—in terms of receding water and consequent moral advancement—the world of *Martin Chuzzlewit* is barely seven days old. The earlier passage contains a reminder that corrupt societies have often had to begin the development process over again following a violent reform that seems heaven-sent. The "newly retired" waters in *Bleak House* refer to the story of creation when God "let the dry land appear" (Genesis, 1:9), but the thrust in both passages remains similar: the closer Dickens could push back the present day toward either the Deluge or the Creation, the more presumptuous it would be to think the modern age already well on the path to utopia, if not verging on arrival; even if gradualism proved to be scientifically and sociologically valid, it was going to involve a much longer haul, Dickens implied, than proponents pretended.

The exertions of the aqueously named Miss Brooke—her reformer's strength "spent itself in channels" (*MM*, 613)—seem intended to modify Dickens's allegedly unrealistic pessimism. But such "channels" are even less like a river than George Eliot conceded; the diffuse yet incremental improvements that rivulets of reform signify must offset two images of inundation, of which the seminal and antiutopian instance, thanks to Dickens's resolve to amplify Tocqueville's reservations, was also anti-American in origin and inspiration.

Tocqueville contended that "individualism" was a new form of "Self-ishness" originating in democratic countries (*DA*, 193). This idea furnishes an important clue to the inception of Dickens's novel; it bolsters arguments for the American episodes' thematic relevance to a work of fiction bent on anatomizing man's self-seeking ego. Throughout the American chapters, the novelist views democracy as a form of hypocrisy not unlike England's laissez-faire: it licenses greed under the guise of promoting equal opportunity for all. But *Democracy in America* did more than suggest a rationale for introducing American episodes; it also helped Dickens realize that he could exploit his extraordinary creative gifts to eclipse less talented traveler-commentators. In *American Notes* the novelist played his predecessors' game; by switching the contest to his own medium, however, he could dramatize Tocqueville's derogatory perceptions more unforgettably than *American Notes* had tried to magnify them.

"I know of no country," Tocqueville pontificated, "where the love of money has taken stronger hold on the affections of men" (*DA*, 52). Not uncommon in the French observer's tome, a generalization of this sort is already Dickensian, that is, in the superlative—America is the most money-minded of nations. The remark could be improved upon only by a satirical novelist able to caricature the national avarice: Dickens had to produce men whose only affection seems to be a love for dollars. He shows money-love operating supremely by recording the shady dealings of a despicable yet laughable pair, General Cyrus Choke and Zephaniah Scadder, who routinely bilk settlers and then send them to their deaths. The sale of lots in a place called Eden suggests "affections" so perversely monetized that nothing is considered beyond the dollar's purchasing power; even God's love—that is, places in Paradise—can be had for a price.

Going further still, Dickens forced the new republic to incriminate itself whenever its gentlemen-financiers speak. Wearing a "mixed expression of vulgar cunning and conceit," Colonel Diver declares that America's "aristocracy" is not merely one of "intelligence" but of that attribute's "necessary consequence": "dollars, sir" (*MC*, 256, 258). Tocqueville repeatedly pitted Europe's aristocracy against America's democracy, but *Martin Chuzzlewit* exposes the contrast as a false one because the New World has invented baser formulas for measuring worth and assigning privilege. Having proof issue from a boastful rogue such as Diver replaces accusation with comic confession, thus illustrating how readily the progress from travelogue to novel gave Dickens the advantage: freedom to make his points by manipulating his creative and linguistic skills, not just by logical argument. The French essayist-sociologist, who sounds Johnsonian when translated, was barred by professional ethics and a sense of stylistic decorum from taking similar liberties.

In a letter home or a travel book, Dickens could trace dishonesty to the national "love of trade" (*AN*, 287). Given a novel's format and a satirist's license, he could salute Major Perkins ironically for possessing "a most distinguished genius," if only "for swindling" (*MC*, 269). Similarly, Martin's contempt for American "smartness" (*MC*, 265) picks up Diver's equation of the aristocratic and the intelligent with the financial and extends it: to be smart in America means to be able to *out*smart one's fellows. If aristocrats in Europe claim to be better bred than the lower orders, America's nobility brags that it is made up of the most proficient thieves. Even as Dickens took advantage personally of the English language's richness, he showed America barbarizing the meaning of "smartness," "intelligence," and "aristocracy," a sure sign of a downward step for civilization.

It is as if Dickens had invented a penetrating caricature for every fault Tocqueville found in the national character. In *Martin Chuzzlewit* the satirist puts each shortcoming on a separate pair of legs, supplying living proofs in place of Tocqueville's general statements, which consequently become less trenchant. Enhancing the Frenchman's disdain for the "licentiousness" of the American Press (*DA*, 92), Dickens provides not only Colonel Diver of the *New York Rowdy Press* but also the newsboy who boards Martin's packetship to cry the merits of the *New York Sewer*. Instead of remarking that American writers regularly lapse into an "inflated" style (*DA*, 184), the novelist presents Mrs. Hominy ("the horrible Hominy") "talking deep truths . . . and pouring forth her mental endowments" (*MC*, 370), not to mention the "Transcendental" lady in a wig for whom

Howls the sublime, and softly sleeps the calm Ideal, in the whispering chambers of Imagination [*MC*, 541]

an outburst that scans nicely yet defies explication.

Tocqueville came down hardest on what he perceived to be the democratic paradox: on one hand, so much "leveling" downward, so much "uniformity" of mental and cultural acquirements—"the theory of equality . . . applied to the intellects of men"—and yet, on the other hand, more than enough irritating patriotism, a "national pride" rooted in each citizen's "personal vanity," to ensure that "the majority lives in the perpetual utterance of self-applause" (DA, 120, 113, 53, 105, 119). At Mrs. Pawkins's table, where self-touting mediocrity's egotism seems universal, the scene is virtually a tableau simultaneously illustrating and exceeding Tocqueville's charges: "there seemed to be no man there without a title: for those who had not attained to military honors were either doctors, professors, or reverends" (MC, 273). Yet the members of this motley group, Martin decides, were "strangely devoid of individual traits," so that "any one of them might have changed minds with the other, and nobody would have found it out" (MC, 273). Although titled and allegedly preeminent, these men are not just interchangeable; none is sufficiently perceptive, Dickens adds, to notice the substitution of a doctor for a professor or a reverend for a doctor, should it transpire.[12]

Performing as a novelist, Dickens outdistanced Tocqueville by portraying patriotic Americans who were not only incapable of self-criticism but whose "national vanity" (F, 1:289) was too strong to tolerate a negative word from visitors.[13] Colonel Diver demands to know "how do you like my Country?" before an embarrassed Martin, still aboard ship, has set foot on it. The colonel then interprets the hero's polite silence to mean that he was "not prepared . . . to behold such signs of National Prosperity" (MC, 257).

The Frenchman's Americans are strictly utilitarian, preferring "the useful to the beautiful" (DA, 169); citizens "are convinced that it is not for them that books are published." Dickens makes the identical point more compellingly when one of the many self-styled "captains" at Mrs. Pawkins's informs Martin that his countrymen are too "busy" a people to bother about books. A bad trait that Tocqueville ascribed to Americans becomes an attribute they recognize in themselves and boast about. The truth, Martin then decides, is worse then either Tocqueville or the unnamed captain thinks: Americans have "an inaptitude for social and domestic pleasure" (MC, 275), additional proof that a civilization in its beginning stages is too barbaric to set an example for the rest of mankind.

The difference of opinion is important. Tocqueville's view is closer to the captain's, which may be said to parody it; in place of an imbalance, an excess of one kind of positive energy driving out another, however, young Chuzzlewit discovers a void. Because Americans contend that dollars, cotton, and banks are their books, two negative ideas about democracy, which are stated separately in Tocqueville, coalesce in Dickens: it is both greedy and antiintellectual, the second deficiency being used by many self-satisfied Americans and one unobservant Frenchman to cover up the first.

Only on the subject of bores, especially if both patriotic and orotund, did Tocqueville come close to writing like a novelist:

> I have often remarked, in the United States, that it is not easy to make a man understand that his presence may be dispensed with; hints will not always suffice to shake him off. I contradict an American at every word he says, to show him that his conversation bores me; he instantly labors with fresh pertinacity to convince me: I preserve a dogged silence, and he thinks I am meditating deeply on the truths which he is uttering: at last, I rush from his company, and he supposes that some urgent business hurries me elsewhere. This man will never understand that he wearies me to death, unless I tell him so; and the only way to get rid of him is to make him my enemy for life. [*DA*, 224]

One must add to this passage Tocqueville's condemnation of the "garrulous" American patriot's propensity to "extort praise" or else praise his country himself; such a bore passes easily from discussion to "dissertation," often addressing the person with whom he is conversing as "Gentlemen" (*DA*, 252, 109). Once the addition is made, several of Dickens's cruelest caricatures appear in embryonic conglomeration. Think, for example, of Mr. Lafayette Kettle announcing his intention to have the British lion declawed or of Elijah Pogram's chauvinistic rantings that "defied the world" (*MC*, 346, 531).

In light of Tocqueville's dislike for self-centered, long-winded Americans, one must review the scene in which Martin, returning from "the salubrious air" of Eden, vanquishes Pogram in a debate about whether good manners are a prerequisite for good civilizations. This debate becomes even more important than it seemed in my opening chapter. Confounding one of the country's notorious noisemakers, Martin does not just state Dickens's renewed appreciation for the humanizing effects of established customs (*MC*, 536); he also shows Tocqueville how conclusively an English novelist can contradict, shake off, and dispense with an obnoxious type that the Frenchman's nameless "man" merely exemplified but Pogram epitomizes.

In the same scene, Tocqueville's apologetic explanation for America's lack of good manners is firmly disallowed. He feared that "the effect of democracy is not exactly to give men any particular manners, but to prevent them from having manners at all" (*DA*, 251); Dickens insisted, however, that the new democracy actively fostered the worst kinds of behavior. When Pogram tells Martin that industrious Americans have no time "to ac-quire forms" (*MC*, 536) and Martin replies that it is fairer to say that they have decided to dispense with them, Dickens caricatures and rejects Tocqueville's excusatory attitude.

Earlier, the novelist replaced the explanation that Americans were utilitarian, not antiintellectual, with Martin's sense of their ineptitude for pleasure. Similarly, he now contends that a concerted indifference to manners—not the inevitable blurring of distinctions in a democracy that Tocqueville cited—has resulted in an arrogant, aggressive vulgarity. Manners, Dickens corrected the Frenchman, are neither missing from America nor volatile; instead, as Chuzzlewit tells Pogram, they are almost uniformly atrocious. The visiting Englishman experienced them not as a loss or absence, as the less reliable French critic did, but as an ever-present insult and affliction.

Young Martin's decision that America's "gay flag in the distance" is "but sorry fustian" up close (*MC*, 362) keeps resonating throughout the debate with Congressman Pogram. The double reference to cheap cloth and mere bombast has obvious derogatory connotations: America is all noise and facade. Dickens makes it clear that, unlike Tocqueville, he is writing about changes in perspective; that is, about coming to observe change and then having to change his own outlook unexpectedly. Ideas that had seemed so admirable at a "distance," from across the ocean, looked as tawdry up close as do the American flag and the individual Americans whom Martin meets.

Martin's polemic against flag waving also implies that the closer one gets to details in America, to those all-important "small matters" of decency and decorum about which the hero lectures Pogram (*MC*, 536), the more specious the country's democratic principles begin to seem. In Dickens's opinion, neither Harriet Martineau nor Mrs. Trollope understood this point any better than Tocqueville did when he posited an absence of manners in America instead of the combination of missing civilities and ever-present *bad* manners that Dickens actually found. Consequently, any blows struck against Tocqueville's most grievous misjudgment fall on all three of Dickens's best-known predecessors; attempts to discredit Fanny Trollope and Miss Martineau can be read as elaborations of a middle-class Englishman's fundamental disagreement with a French aristocrat.

Mrs. Trollope stipulated her main concern in a preface to the first edition of *Domestic Manners of the Americans*: "the influence which the political system of the country has produced on the principles, tastes, and manners, of its domestic life" (*DM*, xxxiii). In like fashion, Harriet Martineau introduced *Society in America* by stating her mission: "to compare the existing state of society in America with the principles on which it is professedly founded" (*SA*, 48-49). Dickens objected that in both cases the commentators, no cleverer than Tocqueville, were obsessed with the effects of big on small. This approach was not only backward, large to small being the wrong way round; it also seemed similar to the Americans' willingness to unfurl a "gay flag," to concentrate on the high-sounding at the expense of honoring "small obligations," those all-important "little social observances" (*MC*, 536).

Dickens felt that Mrs. Trollope and Miss Martineau never progressed beyond the rudimentary methodology he reused more successfully in *American Notes*. Just as both women had found everyday life falling short of the founding fathers' belief in equality and the golden rule, Dickens was unable to corroborate Rousseau and never located the ideal republic he had been encouraged to envision. In *Martin Chuzzlewit*, however, the novelist proceeded to explain more fully how the vulgar manners and sharp dealings of everyday life were responsible for the erosion of America's first principles, which thus became suspect as unattainable, unrealistic ideals.

Although Mrs. Trollope had been forty-two months in America and Miss Martineau twenty-four, Dickens went on pondering his dissatisfactions longer after his return than they did: students of Boz's American engagements tend to forget that *Martin Chuzzlewit*, the final installment of which appeared in July 1844, represented the climax of more than two and one-half years of thinking and writing about the New World. *Society in America* was longer than *American Notes* and *Domestic Manners* was livelier because it featured an outspoken narrative rich in unabashedly personal anecdotes; but for verve and sagacity, Dickens considered his travel book, objectively told, and the extension of it in his satirical and autobiographical sixth novel the winning combination.

Mrs. Trollope and Miss Martineau stopped with consequences; Dickens claimed to be unearthing causes by tracing a "natural succession" from a true first principle (that is, greed) based not on the Constitution but on the very nature of things. The lady commentators exposed a country's departures from its premises, but the male novelist has young Chuzzlewit explain that Americans, "from disregarding small obligations . . . come in regular course to disregard great ones."

As Dickens's preface to the 1849 cheap edition phrased it, *Chuzzlewit* showed how selfishness, the "commonest" vice, "propagates itself; and to what a grim giant it may grow, from small beginnings." It was not a case of the abandonment of principles leading to incivilities but vice versa. Imperfect human beings, denied proper social restraints or, worse yet, encouraged in America to be indifferent to them, behaved abominably, much to the detriment of a democratic theory of government. Thus, continues Martin, the succession is always from small to great in countries as in crime: first one man offends another and then he and his countrymen "refuse to pay their debts" (*MC*, 536), whether these are loans from England, on which several states defaulted in the 1840s, or royalties publishers owed British authors.[14]

Mrs. Trollope and Miss Martineau were left with discrepancies between their conceptions of man and democracy, on one side, and American conduct on the other. But for Dickens, after registering the initial shock of disillusionment, American behavior revealed and confirmed the rules actually governing the country's daily life and, presumably, life-in-general, rules such as the selfish imperative to outsmart one's competition, an imperative which, ironically, Dickens himself then felt obliged to obey by exceeding the negativity in previous critiques of America.

At first glance, the examination of behavior in light of first principles does not seem drastically different from the evaluation of principles in view of behavior. But the disagreement is as enormous as the gap between utopian and dystopian thinking. In Dickens's method of assessing "natural succession" and the "regular course," two synonyms for social process, America's principles were found to be at odds with human nature; indeed, the new country's shortcomings suggested that most political ideals are impossible to achieve given man's fallen or natural state. In Miss Martineau's opinion, as in Tocqueville's, however, America's ideals were not implausible per se; instead, society was not yet prepared to live up to them. For the reactionary Mrs. Trollope, New World failures had no negative bearing on prospects for improvement of England's system of government because her dislike for the American character did not lower her regard for human nature; England rose by comparison for her, as it had for Dickens, but retained its elevated position. Utopia was still conceivable for Miss Martineau after visiting America; and Mrs. Trollope's England, measured against the fledgling republic, became a model for political maturation.

That Fanny Trollope inverted the connection between America's manners and first principles did not surprise Dickens once he decided she had entered the country from the wrong end: by steaming up the primeval Mississippi instead of landing at a sophisticated center such as Boston or New York. This miscalculation gave Dickens a perfect opening for a structural parody of *Domestic Manners*. He minimized Mrs. Trollope's deconversion from republicanism as a paler version of his own traumatic jolt and yet, paradoxically, presented it as a case of a woman overreacting.

Landing briefly at New Orleans, Mrs. Trollope proceeded directly to Nashoba, her Cairo or low point, but went on almost immediately to Cincinnati for a lengthy stay; eventually, her tour reached its climax in New York, which she called "one of the finest cities" she had ever seen (*DM*, 297). Having toured Boston, Hartford, and New York, Dickens sampled Cincinnati and Louisville before encountering pestilential Cairo while en route to St. Louis; he made the Illinois city the anti-paradise toward which Martin and Mark also journey after arriving in New York. Dickens thus revised Mrs. Trollope's journey *out* of the heart of darkness first by recounting his own plunge *into* it and again at length by dramatizing Martin's. Twice he stressed a contradiction between the disillusioning experience Mrs. Trollope claimed to have had and the progressive shape and positive direction that she was obliged to give her travels, the sense of improving conditions and movement upward rather than inward.

At the "entrance" to the Mississippi and for miles thereafter, Mrs. Trollope wrote, she "never beheld a scene so utterly desolate." She lamented the "total want of beauty" in one paragraph after another of nonstop deprecation: the omnipresent slime, mud banks, crocodiles, "monstrous bullrushes," and especially the uprooted trees floating downstream created an impression of a voyage back into prehistoric time; this was not a new or ideal place, she decided, but "a world in ruins" (*DM*, 1-3).

Then came Nashoba. Supposedly a utopian commune where blacks were to be educated as proof that their race was not inherently inferior, Fanny Wright's estate in the wilds of Tennessee turned out to consist of a few poorly constructed cabins and zigzag fences in a crudely cleared spot amid a dense, fever-ridden forest. "Desolation," Mrs. Trollope emphatically decided in a somber tone as Conradian as Marlow's, was the "only word" for it (*DM*, 23-24).

Undoubtedly, the Mississippi of *American Notes* is both the actual river down which Dickens traveled and the occasion for a more pejorative account than Mrs. Trollope's of sailing up it. Oxymoronic references to "an enormous ditch" of "liquid mud" (*AN*, 216) exaggerate the size of the waterway Dickens was in fact demeaning but suggest movement that is simultaneously stagnation. Arguably, the unwholesome Eden of *Martin Chuzzlewit* is based on the Nashoba that Dickens had read about in Mrs. Trollope as well as on the "dismal Cairo" he saw personally.

Although "desolation" was Mrs. Trollope's only description for Miss Wright's settlement, Dickens went on to perceive Cairo/Eden as "a spot so much more desolate than any we had yet beheld, that the forlornest places we had passed were, in comparison with it, full of interest" (*AN*, 215). Both travelers selected a disheartening, unhealthy locale as a symbol for the collapse of their American dreams in the face of ugly, primitive realities, but Dickens augmented as he borrowed, insisting that his nadir, which incorporated the horrors of hers and then some, caused even the most forlorn regions seen previously to appear cheerful and lively. That Dickens witnessed more dispiriting sights on the Mississippi than had Mrs. Trollope confirmed the difference in magnitude he proceeded to propose between his deconversion experience and hers.

Dickens's Mississippi is not simply muddier than Mrs. Trollope's and his Cairo/Eden more fever-inducing and dystopian than Nashoba; the more important difference is that, through hitting bottom prematurely, she employed a misplaced nadir. The miserable, "murky" Mississippi was succeeded by the "bright and clear" Ohio, truly "La Belle Rivière," the "beautiful" river (*DM*, 26-27),[15] whereas Dickens left the Ohio for the Mississippi. In the same manner, Nashoba yielded to Cincinnati and that city to Baltimore, Washington, and—the eventual high point—New York. Dickens implied that such a trip resembled a traditional pilgrim's progress past obstacles toward pleasanter experiences, unlike his, which had been anti-Bunyanesque, a true nightmare. When the novelist and Chuzzlewit, his fictional alter ego, descended into the belly and bowels of a continent at the climax of their respective travels, the negative momentum in both travel book and novel became twofold: besides encountering a selfishness not just rampant in frontier America but present in subtler forms as a common denominator in all men, Dickens and Martin parodically revised Mrs. Trollope's upward journey.

In view of that climb, Dickens found little logic in what Mrs. Trollope's modern editor calls her "rapid disillusionment."[16] Her book ought to have chronicled one long recovery. Nor was there merit in her declaration, as Mullen reports it, that she had gone to America "professing radical sentiments" but "had been converted to Toryism by her experience" (*DM*, xix). In Dickens's letter to Forster, the novelist carefully discriminated: returning home a Tory was a real danger confronting the British liberal after a visit to America (F, 1:231), but not necessary or desirable. So facile a transition from one extreme to the other must be avoided at all costs. The harder and more commendable course, Dickens rebuked Mrs. Trollope, was to shed one's enthusiasm for imaginary ideal republics without fatally compromising one's radicalism, which can be redefined as a determination to seek reforms without making their steady attainment the price for unflagging allegiance to the meliorist cause.

"Strong, indeed, must be the love of equality in an English breast, if it can survive a tour through the Union," Mrs. Trollope exclaimed, implying that the breast of at least one woman deserved credit for not being strong enough (*DM*, 101-2). But Dickens replied that America was an excellent test for the stouthearted male reformer not as easily swayed by emotion as women are. For Mrs. Trollope's "English breast," he substituted manlier attributes. Admittedly, only "a radical on principle, by reason and reflection, and from a sense of right" (PL, 3:90) could endure a visit to the United States, but Dickens claimed to be such a phenomenon; unlike America, he would never forsake his principles even if he had to modify them. Rational and reflective (that is, male) compared with the impulsive Mrs. Trollope, he could experience traumatic disappointment and still adhere to his "sense of right" despite the pressure to switch sides—a plus that made him the more responsible social analyst.

Equally reasonable and reflective after suffering in Eden, Chuzzlewit also undergoes a deconversion from republicanism but not all the way to conservatism. He develops into a more intelligent human being through a healthy moderating of lofty goals, a change that is not without paradox: Martin seems hardened by adversity yet is softened, or rather transformed, through disillusionment into a more sensitive, less abrupt individual. He becomes both more masculine and more feminine in America, whereas Dickens implied that Mrs. Trollope, tossing off lightly held Romantic illusions, seemed both superficial and inflexible as the easily adopted love of Toryism in her breast turned to stone.

Mrs. Trollope discarded most of her illusions in the first twenty-five pages of *Domestic Manners*, but Martin must stay several months in Eden until his purgation is complete. Dickens had an extended stay, too, in that he was still dealing with the Cairo letdown 500 pages into a novel not fully in print until more than two years after the fateful morning of 9 April 1842. Young Chuzzlewit's ordeal and Dickens's vicarious sharing of it long after his own return from America were used to distinguish Mrs. Trollope's relatively painless surrender of the republican faith not just from the novelist's sharper, traumatic loss but, consequently, from his arduous reconditioning of self and purpose. Symbolized by Martin's breakdown and virtual resurrection, Dickens's meticulous scaling down of false expectations without totally abandoning the radical cause was meant to contrast satirically with Mrs. Trollope's volte-face.

Recalling the journey by boat from New Orleans to Natchez, Mrs. Trollope bemoaned the "total want of all the usual courtesies" at table and the "voracious rapidity with which the viands were seized and devoured" (DM, 15). She was horrified by the men's "frightful manner of feeding with their knives" and "cleaning the teeth afterwards with a pocket-knife." Characteristically on these occasions, Mrs. Trollope's style becomes almost flowery; she appears determined to sound decorous, even literary, despite the incident's grossness, as if her words could both convey and counteract her content.[17] More important, since this scene occurs as a prelude to disappointments at Nashoba—that is, before the collapse of Mrs. Trollope's idealism—it remains an isolated instance of uncouth behavior, merely a personal affront to a Victorian traveler no less fastidious than Dickens was.

He clearly considered this critical anecdote badly misplaced. When the novelist dramatized a similar episode in Martin Chuzzlewit, it became the crucial event during the hero's return from Eden, the fitting climax of his disillusioning American sojourn. One of the "dirty feeders" on board Martin's steamboat, a gentleman besmirched "about his mouth and chin" with dried "overflowings" of tobacco juice, is "burning to assert his equality" at table; having "sucked his knife for some moments," he "made a cut with it at the butter," an action so repulsive that its "juicyness," reports Dickens, "might have sickened a scavenger" (MC, 535).[18] By comparison, Mrs. Trollope's reliance on "voracious rapidity," gobbled "viands," and "frightful manner of feeding" seems to disclose her artificiality as much as it exposes disgusting American behavior.

Did Dickens witness the knife-sucking, butter-cutting incident or develop it from suggestions in Domestic Manners or both?[19] It is impossible to tell. But his revision ridicules Mrs. Trollope's notion that one underscores and redeems life's vulgarities by treating low subject matter in an ornate style; such notions he finds hypocritical. For Martin, the incident is neither isolated nor prefatory but epiphanic; under its impetus, he discovers the "root" of the new country's problems. In light of Mrs. Trollope's democratic deconversion, Martin can be said to have two opponents in the critical debate with Pogram: he must not only overcome the uncouth congressman's defense of American vulgarities, thereby surpassing Mrs. Trollope as a condemner of New World manners; he must also show her readers that one can subscribe to many of European civilization's advantages—customs, traditions, usages—without sounding artificial or necessarily embracing the Tory faith.

One tobacco-stained ruffian, a case of a small event furnishing clues to larger issues, both elicits and illustrates Martin's thesis about the relationship of bad manners to unsuccessful institutions. By placing "dirty feeders" *after* the crucial Eden misadventures, Dickens substantiated his claim that systems depend on manners and morals more than these depend upon systems. Since one normally seeks causes for effects already seen, Martin is not a political philosopher approaching cause and effect the wrong way round. But Mrs. Trollope could not treat egregious eating habits as the product of inadequate institutions because she had yet to behold the desolation of Nashoba. Having done so, she could not review the cause-and-effect progression from missing courtesies to a utopia that was also nonexistent; to do so would have weakened her intention to study the influence that systems have on behavior.

As the author of a travel book, Mrs. Trollope could not tamper with chronology by shifting her knife-feeding incident to a later date. Similarly, having volunteered to accompany Fanny Wright to Nashoba, she had reason to land at New Orleans rather than New York. But for Dickens the novelist, these restrictions were so many invitations to parody. A lady traveler who entered the country from the bottom instead of the top, who allegedly underwent deconversion while proceeding from bad to better locations, and who positioned pivotal scenes wrongly— was such a person, Dickens asked, likely to comprehend the significance of ill breeding in America, not to mention the import of America itself?

Even as the issuer of *American Notes*, Dickens could build toward Cairo, although otherwise he was bound by many of the same limitations that impinged upon Mrs. Trollope. As a novelist, however, he could have Martin arrive at New York, thus reversing Mrs. Trollope regardless of his own landing at Boston. He could also reshape, perhaps relocate at will, episodes from such travel books as *Domestic Man-*

ners—and all to prove himself not only the expert on conduct, Mrs. Trollope's avowed forte, but a superior social analyst generally.

Mrs. Trollope devoted some of her most considered criticisms to the subservient role of American women. She blamed the country's male population for reducing the opposite sex to "habitual insignificance" (DM, 57). Men and women were segregated at dinners and parties, and the former pursued most of their major enjoyments in the absence of the latter; thus it was small wonder that American wives and mothers exerted no civilizing influence outside the home and very little within it (DM, 128, 244). But ironically, Mrs. Trollope's manipulation of her own femininity, repeated allusions to her own insignificance and lack of qualifications, gave Dickens his strongest invitation to supplant the ideas in her travel book with his.

Although Mrs. Trollope believed that the relationship between the sexes determines a society's quality of life, a notion as yet Greek to Dickens, she frequently pleaded her sex, using her womanhood as an excuse to refrain from severity or to retire from a subject altogether. Having reached Cincinnati, she deplored the loss of "the little elegances and refinements" that enrich the day-to-day lives of Europe's middle classes. But this anticipation of Martin's onslaught against uninhibited behavior is quickly vitiated by a confession: "it requires an abler pen than mine to trace the connection which I am persuaded exists between these deficiencies and the minds and manners of the people" (DM, 37). Surely Dickens felt that his abler pen could trace these deficiencies and atone for Mrs. Trollope's shortcomings as well.

Repeatedly, Mrs. Trollope singled out "want of refinement" as "the greatest difference between England and America," then invited her undoing by questioning her own competence: so "remarkable" is the "universal want of good, or even pleasing, manners" in America, she stated, that she "was constantly endeavoring to account for it" (DM, 37-39). Or again: "I will not pretend to decide whether man is better or worse off for requiring refinement in the manners and customs of the society that surrounds him" (DM, 39). And an admission even more damaging than such puzzlement: she is merely "a woman, who is apt to tell what her first impressions may be, but unapt to reason back from effects to their causes" (DM, 39).

Throughout American Notes and more persistently in Martin Chuzzlewit, Dickens resolved to account for America's lack of manners and decreed that a country is always worse off because of such a lack. Using Martin as his spokesman, he also worked back to small causes from larger effects; this is the very reasoning process that Mrs. Trollope seemed anxious to eschew, even if one credits her with speaking tongue-in-cheek.

Mrs. Trollope found American fundamentalists far more disgusting, improper, and hypocritical than England's Evangelicals. Outraged by the "atrocious wickedness" of a camp meeting at which young girls were tormented into confessing their faults and then consoled with caresses, she did some of her finest investigative reporting. Yet if "the convulsive movements" of these "poor maniacs" indicated a forgetfulness of their femininity, Mrs. Trollope remained ever mindful of her own: "Had I been a man, I am sure I should have been guilty of some rash act of interference" (DM, 143). Unfortunately, as she elsewhere allows, she is only "a feeble looker-on, with a needle for my spear" (DM, 89)—the precise status, even if mock-heroically assumed, to which Dickens strove to reduce her.

After a stay of three years and six months, Mrs. Trollope's needle-spear set down "Conclusions" showing her undecided on the principal issue that Dickens has young Martin settle: "Whether the government has made the people what they are, or whether the people have made the government what it is, to suit themselves, I know not" (DM, 359). Dickens believed he knew. Manners, the behavior of man to man in "small" things, shape new institutions or pervert already existing and imperfect ones because it is in "small" dealings that man's flawed nature, hypocritically inclined to take the high road on major issues, inevitably reveals itself. Thus the novelist wrote the debate scene between Martin and Elijah Pogram in *Chuzzlewit* to be more explicit than *American Notes* in the critical area where Tocqueville, a French aristocrat, had faltered and Mrs. Trollope, a woman, had defaulted.

Harriet Martineau subsequently criticized Mrs. Trollope as a justification for issuing *Society in America*, but the latter began the practice; besides correcting Fanny Wright, she promoted her travel book at the expense of Basil Hall's *Travels in North America*, which had presented the country "in full dress," not informally with its imperfections "unanointed," as *Domestic Manners* would (DM, 316). Immediately thereafter, however, Mrs. Trollope opened two doors for Dickens by virtually admitting not merely that she and her ilk were not up to a man's work but also that Hall's sanctions had been too mild: "I am deeply persuaded, that were a man of equal penetration to visit the United States with no other means of becoming acquainted with the national character than the ordinary working-day intercourse of life, he would conceive an infinitely lower idea of the moral atmosphere of the coun-try than Capt. Hall appears to have done" (*DM*, 317).

Coming first as himself, Dickens the celebrity found more fault with "full dress" America than any predecessor had; then, returning less conspicuously as young Chuzzlewit, he showed greater "penetra-tion" (a masculine strength) than Mrs. Trollope by entering America correctly at New York before falling upon "the moral atmosphere" of "the ordinary working-day intercourse of life" with a ferocity he con-sidered absent from Hall and beyond the capability of female social critics.

The frailty of her sex is not always mentioned but may be read be-tween the lines whenever Mrs. Trollope shuns a difficult task: "Were I to relate one-tenth part of the dishonest transactions recounted to me by Americans, of their fellow-citizens and friends, I am confident that no English reader would give me credit for veracity" (*DM*, 219). If one imagines Dickens's satire against the Eden Land Corporation as a sa-tirical response to Mrs. Trollope's feeble disclaimer, *Chuzzlewit*'s in-debtedness to *Domestic Manners* increases: the American chapters build toward, indeed revolve around, a dishonest transaction of the very sort Mrs. Trollope feared would ruin her credibility.

But Dickens added the Anglo-Bengalee Assurance Company to the Eden Corporation in order to correct Mrs. Trollope's English smug-ness, that sense of innate moral superiority which he, too, had dis-played in America; *Chuzzlewit*'s point was that England was superior to America but not as superior as the English thought. Dickens hoped to discredit a rival's veracity twice over: he implied that Mrs. Trollope was incapable of comprehending dishonest transactions whether at home or abroad; as a female, she averted her eyes from a detailed ac-counting of the duplicity polluting the world's working-day moral at-mosphere just as she shrank from describing the tobacco-stained carpet of a steamboat's ladies' cabin. It was as if she intuited that the grim com-petitions underlying the economics of so-called civilized life in New World or Old were too deeply rooted in selfishness to respond to a woman's mollifying influence.

Mrs. Trollope's concern for credibility was used both for and against her: Dickens encouraged readers to believe her when she pin-pointed Hall's deficiencies and admitted her own but not to believe her otherwise because the admissions of female inadequacy prevented her from remedying the captain's shortcomings. It followed that Dickens deserved a double recognition as the discerning critic whom Hall had merely foreshadowed and as Mrs. Trollope's replacement; he was the answer to a woman's prayer for a penetrating masculine intelligence that would redo Hall while filling in her omissions.

Michael Sadleir regards *Domestic Manners* as a "curiously prophetic" source for *American Notes* and *Martin Chuzzlewit*: the lesser-known female visitor's observations allegedly "anticipate" Dickens's; they "foreshadow" some of the novelist's scenes "almost to the smallest detail"—that is, "with a completeness so amazing as virtually to prove the authenticity of both."[20] Actually, the elements of anticipation and foreshadowing are Dickens's doing; they result from his conscientious reworking of Mrs. Trollope's ideas and incidents in order to promote his authenticity by detracting from hers.

Like Captain Marryat but less justifiably, Mrs. Trollope admired *American Notes* and wrote to tell Dickens that she felt vindicated by it (J, 1:443).[21] Dickens graciously replied: "I am convinced that there is no writer who has so well and accurately (I need not add so entertainingly) described [America] . . . as you have done" (NL, 1:494). This letter should be interpreted as an ironic instance of an Englishman's respect for the "politeness" and "good breeding" young Chuzzlewit extols; Dickens refused to be "a brute in small matters" (*MC*, 536), although he was preparing to disagree with Mrs. Trollope more extensively in *Martin Chuzzlewit* on all the larger issues, especially by arguing that bad manners are a manifestation of fallen man's imperfect state and thus a major cause of the imperfect states he invariably creates.

On numerous points, *Society in America* echoed previous assessments of New World conditions. "Of all newspaper presses," Harriet Martineau complained, America's was "the worst" (SA, 103). More so than Mrs. Trollope, she found the "Political Non-Existence of Women" perturbing; their plight, which she compared to a Negro slave's (SA, 125-28), merited a section all to itself. Also, she identified "money-getting," an excessive "regard for wealth," as the besetting American sin (SA, 241-42), just as Mrs. Trollope had condemned its "universal pursuit" for blunting the country's moral sense (*DM*, 258-59). Conformity in American thought and deed, Miss Martineau decided, was a more serious problem than her predecessors had realized: the "worship of [popular] Opinion," not Tocqueville's tyrannical majority, fostered a "fear of singularity" in the American breast (SA, 248, 250).

Nevertheless, contrary to Mrs. Trollope, Harriet Martineau approved of the United States: "the manners of Americans . . . are the best I ever saw," she generalized (SA, 272).[22] More specifically, she re-

jected all of the unfavorable impressions previous visitors had formed
of their behavior at table: "I do not think the Americans eat faster than
other people" (SA, 283). "The popular scandal against the people of the
United States, that they boast intolerably of their national institutions,"
she added, "appears to me untrue" (SA, 102). Ultimately, she had
fewer qualms about equalitarianism than either Tocqueville or Mrs.
Trollope had expressed. The "assumption of equality," Mrs. Trollope
maintained, although "empty" or unfounded, tinctured the manners of
the poor "with brutal insolence" (DM, 273), but instead of encountering the "insolence" of one class to another that polluted "the atmosphere of English daily life," Miss Martineau reported being
"struck . . . pleasurably" by "the invariable respect paid to man, as
man" (SA, 259).

In sum, Miss Martineau's conclusion that it was impossible to see
and know Americans "and fail to honour them as a nation" (SA, 257)
gave the lie direct to Mrs. Trollope's tight-lipped summation: "I do not
like them. I do not like their principles, I do not like their manners, I
do not like their opinions" (DM, 358).

Whenever Miss Martineau's travels took her to places subsequently on Dickens's itinerary, their impressions clashed dramatically.
For example, he idolized the Perkins Institute and Massachusetts Asylum for the Blind (AN, 79); she preferred its counterparts in Philadelphia, a city one can use to separate permanently the complaints in
American Notes from the paeans in Society in America.

Devoting an entire chapter to "Philadelphia, and its Solitary
Prison," Dickens railed against the solitary confinement of all its inmates: like Christ's crucifiers, the criminologists "who devised this system of Prison Discipline, and those benevolent gentlemen who carry
it into execution, do not know what it is that they are doing" (AN, 146).
As proof of the system's malignity, the novelist offered six telling examples, including one poor soul whose incessant labors at a loom foreshadow Dr. Manette's as a maker of shoes (AN, 149). But Miss
Martineau lauded what she called "absolute seclusion," hailing it as
"the best method of punishment which has yet been tried" (SA, 316-
17), an opinion she claimed was based on "the confidence" she received
from "a great number" of the prisoners themselves.

Such confidences resemble the one Dickens was honored with by
a burglar whose "time was nearly out," but the novelist dismissed as
"the most detestable cant . . . the unmitigated hypocrisy with which
he declared that he blessed the day on which he came into that prison,
and that he never would commit another robbery as long as he lived"

(*AN*, 150). Thus Dickens and Miss Martineau saw the same place in opposite terms, and each quoted the prison's inmates as references in support of his (or her) claim to superior accuracy. The prize, however, seems to go to Dickens: Miss Martineau is ridiculed for taking as gospel prisoners' testimonials of the sort he reused when David Copperfield reencountered Uriah Heep and Mr. Littimer in Creakle's model prison.[23]

Although far from Philadelphia, the Middlesex magistrate insists that "solitary confinement" is "the only unchallengable way of making sincere and lasting converts and penitents" (*DC*, 647), an advertisement in which Creakle blends Miss Martineau's paean to "the best method" with the hypocritical burglar's "detestable cant." Heep then extends the blessing the burglar conferred on his prison by making his own sequestration regenerative enough to be called utopian, so that "it would be better for everybody, if they got took up, and was brought here" (*DC*, 651).

The novels written after *Chuzzlewit* frequently indicate that Dickens only began to capitalize fully on his disheartening American experiences after 1849-50, when he stood on the threshold of *Bleak House* and the later masterworks. But *David Copperfield* clarifies *American Notes*: the earlier book implied that Miss Martineau could not distinguish a model institution, the Massachusetts Asylum, from an affront to humanity in the arrangements at the Philadelphia prison; this obtuseness discredited her and the sanguine political economists she typified as judges of societies. The Massachusetts Asylum and Philadelphia's prison were microcosms, scaled-down attempts at a perfect system, and Miss Martineau had failed to recognize a truly remarkable place in order to praise lavishly one that Dickens considered the opposite of ideal.

Tocqueville suspected democracies of putting too much faith in man's capacity for self-improvement. In the same vein, Mrs. Trollope found absurd a Fourth of July oration containing this glorious brag: "A frame of government, perfect in its principles, has been brought down from the airy regions of Utopia, and has found a local habitation and a name in our country" (*DM*, 275). But Miss Martineau encouraged Americans "to cherish their high democratic hope, their faith in man" (*SA*, 73). Contradicting both Tocqueville and Mrs. Trollope, she did more than reinstate perfectibilitarian possibilities; she augmented them. Not only did she stamp herself the most utopian of America's Victorian visitors, but her roseate views colored the subsequent thinking of midcentury progressives whether they cited America to prove

that radical advancement was already imminent politically or else foresaw signs in the new country that the secular order the world over was
destined to mature gradually into a New Jerusalem.

Throughout *Society in America*, Harriet Martineau suggested that
the United States had taken mankind a giant stride forward; indeed,
she often seems interested in the New World primarily as text and pretext for expounding previously formed euphoric convictions that society tends steadily to improve,[24] that the life process is by nature one
of continual betterment from age to age both for man and his communities. America, she proclaimed, signaled that "a new era of society
has begun"; the nineteenth century had been singled out as "the critical period out of which must arise a new organization for society" (*SA,*
215). Every "caterpillar" eventually becomes a "butterfly" in Miss
Martineau's evolutionary scheme, and England would too; but she decreed that America would reach perfection more easily than the mother
country because it was "less burdened with antique forms and institutions" (*SA,* 271, 215). This is precisely the point of view caricatured
relentlessly in *Martin Chuzzlewit*, where one American chauvinist after
another espouses it.

Miss Martineau's zoology—the turning of caterpillars into butterflies—is Romantic and affirmative, Faustian in fact. Goethe's would-be
superman repudiated worn-out values and long-term research in order
to strive upward, with all his heart, toward higher levels of being; he
exemplified the evolutionary thrust a farsighted deity has supposedly
placed in all things, a drive whereby even moles burrow upward and
worms turn themselves into lepidoptera.[25] Dickens made his Americans talk like tin-plate Fausts, every man the most "remarkable" in the
country, in order to challenge Miss Martineau's use of the New World
as proof that a transformation equaling that of Goethe's hero was in
store for entire communities, an improvement so inevitable or pre-
ordained as to seem to ensure an almost automatic millennium.

America, Miss Martineau maintained, had established "a true
theory of government, by reasoning from the principles of human nature" (*SA,* 58). Like Tocqueville and Mrs. Trollope, she approved of
working downward to specifics from generalizations and abstract
theory; that is, from large to small. To subvert conclusions reached
through this process of investigation, Martin and Mark redo it: ignoring
Franklin and Jefferson, they analyze American behavior by looking at
"small matters," beginning empirically with man's handling of "small
obligations" and reasoning from them to his management of "great
ones" (*MC,* 536). The basic characteristics to emerge from this inquiry

include a bat's "shortsightedness," a bantam's "bragging," a magpie's dishonesty, and a peacock's "vanity" (*MC*, 545). Given such traits, inherent even in members of brand-new societies, no realistic theory of government can hope to convert caterpillars into butterflies by assuming they are virtually butterflies to begin with.

The glory of human nature, Dickens informed Miss Martineau, had nothing to do with her overly confident meliorist's belief in "the profession, from age to age, of the same lofty something not yet attained," a profession of evolutionist faith that "may be taken as a clear prophecy of ultimate performance" (*SA*, 247). "Clear prophecy" about a "lofty something"—Dickens thought it folly to eulogize America so vaguely in order to predict one steady march toward "the days when mutual and self-perfection will be the prevalent idea which the civilization of the time will express" (*SA*, 269). Dickens remonstrated that human nature's strength lay not in its potential for utopian perfection but in its powers for endurance and recovery. Instead of fabricating a facile linear ascent toward an earthly paradise, one should proclaim man's capacity for surviving his perennially present flaws, his fitness for resuming the struggle no matter how often society must be rebuilt or reformed.

Martin Chuzzlewit says as much when its hero adds a coda to Mark's contemptuous, anti-Faustian zoological catalogue of human nature's principles: "Let us hope," says Martin, that man and society are ultimately "like a Phoenix, for its power of springing from the ashes of its faults and vices, and soaring up anew into the sky!" (*MC*, 546) Drastic revision of Miss Martineau's "high democratic hope" is all that Dickens will countenance; instead of caterpillars becoming butterflies, he has Martin hope for Phoenix-like recoveries closer to secular equivalents of the resurrection than to her benevolent prefiguration of Darwinian theories.

Clearly, Dickens felt that Miss Martineau overrated the reformer's authority as greatly as she overestimated human nature's potential. Martin and Mark personify reform's twofold aspect when, after the latter delineates shortcomings in the American national character,[26] the former rallies one's spirits with the possibility of improvement. This modest procedure countermands a lady Pangloss like Miss Martineau, who insisted that "mankind becomes more clear-sighted as time unfolds," so that "a transition in the morals and manners of nations is an inevitable consequence" (*SA*, 214). This, it bears repeating, is the theorem that America was being used to illustrate. Adumbrated throughout *Society in America* is the idea of modern history as a kind of mandatory evolution, or compulsory unfolding—one long yet marvelous process of gradual amelioration that Miss Martineau's successors later explored more painstakingly with greater reference to the new Victorian science of biology.

Such trust in the nature of things, such blind belief in the evolution of an ever-clearer-sighted humanity, convinced Dickens that Miss Martineau's experience of the world was not at all like his: she had returned from America more innocent about change, human nature, and the life process than when she ventured abroad. In her, then, he found his most irresistible contemporary target, a utopian thinker no less deluded than Rousseau had been and thus second on his list of dislikes only to that philosopher.[27]

Actually, because she looked to the future, Miss Martineau appears to be the opposite of Rousseau, who mythicized an allegedly less corrupt past, but they coalesced for Dickens: their writings had combined to mislead him, sending him several thousand miles on a fool's pilgrimage in quest of a perfect society. Dickens decided that one could no more invoke America to forecast the self-perfecting of mankind than one could encounter there proof of Rousseau's hypothesis that men are less imperfect the closer they are to the outset of a civilization. Tennyson's "Locksley Hall" (composed 1837-38, published 1842) echoed Miss Martineau's belief in a steadily unfolding historical process that enabled mankind to mature intellectually: "Yet I doubt not thro' the ages one increasing purpose runs, / And the thoughts of men are widen'd with the process of the suns" (lines 137-38). But for Dickens the Victorian myth of a future utopia—the notion in *In Memoriam* of "one far-off divine event, / To which the whole creation moves"—was no more plausible than the Romantic longing for a return to Eden, which it was rapidly replacing. Both were based on unrealistic conceptions of human nature and its potential for excellence. Not much better now than ever before, men were unlikely ever to be fundamentally much better than they were now, no matter how much better off they became—such was the unenviable twofold insight that Dickens's comparison of sophisticated England with frontier America had given him.

The modern revaluator concludes that Harriet Martineau's importance for Dickens's artistic and philosophical development has been as seriously underestimated as America's; she serves as both a nexus and a focal point. Her certainty that "a transition in the morals and manners of nations" was "inevitable" marked a transition from Romantic to Victorian. Variously, through recollection or anticipation, her attitude brought together interrelated connotations drawn from such places, ideas, and events as America, the French Revolution, democracy, and the perfectibilitarian impulse. It was largely by failing to discover Miss Martineau's American bridge from the first half of the century to the second that Dickens redefined himself as an antiutopian.

Romanticism and the nineteenth century began as a rebirth of wonder, a reawakening sense of limitless possibilities—a time when human nature itself, in Wordsworth's opinion, seemed about to be born again. This upsurge followed closely upon the republican experiment in France and the outburst of democracy in America. Thomas Paine hailed the French Revolution as a virtual blueprint for converting England into a democratic republic; William Godwin foresaw the peaceful evolution of society toward utopian conditions. In a work significantly titled *America: A Prophecy* (1793), William Blake proclaimed the advent of a brighter epoch by insisting that he was living during the fallen world's last days.

In *Society in America,* the Romantic myth of a golden age from the past being regained through revolutions like the one in France has begun yielding to the Victorian myth of a utopian future evolving into existence through the same natural law that has caterpillars straining to become butterflies. Samuel Taylor Coleridge and Robert Southey, both of whom sympathized with republican events in France, presaged this development when they planned an ideal democratic community in America, which Coleridge wanted to call "Pantisocracy," or equal rule by all. After Waterloo, reactionary despotisms were reinstalled throughout Europe. The idea behind the "Pantisocracy" scheme was to salvage gains from the French Revolution for an internal, spiritual evolution that Miss Martineau then externalized all over again as a gradual, inevitable unfolding for men and society, a process to which ideas culled from Darwin subsequently contributed scientific validity.

Miss Martineau's confidence in an oncoming "ultimate performance," during which individuals engage in "mutual and self-perfection," looks backward to "Pantisocracy" and forward through America to the evolutionary humanism informing many Victorian novels. It foreshadows that evolutionary intercourse of character whereby Mrs. Gaskell's Margaret Hale and Mr. Thornton in *North and South* (1855) or George Eliot's Felix Holt and Esther Lyon in *Felix Holt* (1866) and Dorothea Brooke and Will Ladislaw in *Middlemarch* (1872) are empowered to correct and enhance each other. Through a sort of natural selection even more promising in George Eliot's novels than in Mrs. Gaskell's, communities and nations go forward because their inhabitants improve and complete each other, remedying deficiencies and putting finishing touches on each other's viewpoint and personality.[28] With Miss Hale serving as a conduit, southern England's cultural graces are wedded to the north's progressive industrial vigor, symbolized by Mr. Thornton. Similarly, Ladislaw's interest in reform provides Dorothea in provincial Middlemarch with an outlet for the religious fervor Will needs to fuel the secular apostolate he offers her.

For Dickens, however, the Romantic and Victorian myths were essentially identical in their obtuseness even though the former had celebrated a new dawn and the latter promised a brighter tomorrow: both mistook or ignored life's cyclical nature, the pattern of rises and falls that was both a consequence of man's fallen nature and a repetition of its tendencies ad nauseam. Thus Dickens felt compelled to publish *A Tale of Two Cities* in the Darwinian year of 1859, when evolution rather than revolution was topical; using France as a reminder, he was simply restating the antievolutionary points about cycles, downfalls, and human nature's imperfections that he had scored against Miss Martineau while repudiating *Society in America*.

In *Martin Chuzzlewit,* Dickens substituted his dystopian version of America as a cruder rendition of England—those two places being the alpha and omega points of the social process—for Miss Martineau's utopian vision, her misuse of the New World as evidence of a uniquely Victorian acceleration in life's self-perfecting momentum. The tale of two countries in the 1840s and the consequent novel about two cities in the 1850s have a common thread: Dickens's disdain for utopian thinking as an aberration that continued unabated during the transitional 1830s, when Victorian replaced Romantic. Atrocities across the Channel in the 1790s were more repugnant than vulgarities across the Atlantic fifty years later, but whichever Dickens underlined, the sad truth remained: neither Paine and Godwin's model societies nor Miss Martineau's providential "transition" in "morals and manners" would ever totally materialize.

America was as crucial a stimulus to progressives in the 1840s, at the start of Victoria's reign, as France had been to Wordsworth, Coleridge, and Southey at the beginning of the century. Indeed, thanks to Tocqueville and Miss Martineau, America became both France's substitute and the continuation of its significance. Dickens considered an American visit mandatory in 1842 because, as a novel-writing comic spirit who was turning into a social realist increasingly interested in reform, he could not assess his country's chances for improvement otherwise. He hoped America would be a better beacon to Victorian optimists than France had been not just to the Romantics' political philosophy but to their revolutionary aesthetic. Having to downgrade his enthusiasm for democracy thus meant changing his mind about his Romantic heritage, the Victorian period's prospects, and the kind of novels he would have to write. The American-inspired idea that society should be seen as "one great growth" upward from "rotten" roots (that is, from man's incurable selfishness) was chiefly anti-Rousseauistic, but its parodic organicism also mounted to an antimeliorist satire on Victorian gradualism.

Disconcertingly, Dickens's satiric image for the life process reached forward as it looked back, just as *Society in America* proved to be a bridge from the republican fervor behind "Pantisocracy" to the evolutionary optimism underlying *Felix Holt* and continuing in the moderated tones of *Middlemarch*. George Eliot had to contest the emphasis Dickens placed on the cravings of man's ego because of Boz's prescience in fashioning an anti-Romantic image that also sounded antievolutionary: it precluded kindlier notions of society as a marvelously self-perfecting system illustrative of the steadily increasing amount of benevolence at work in the world.

Once Dickens's imaginary republic had collapsed, he must have recalled with disgust the utopianism audible in Miss Martineau's prose whenever she wrote about punishing crime, affording equal opportunity to women, obtaining copyright protection, or abolishing slavery. In the paragraphs praising the "absolute seclusion" of solitary confinement in the Philadelphia penitentiary that Dickens hated, she predicted even greater penological improvements. Americans had "far less superinduced misery than societies abroad" (*SA*, 316); in the "treatment of the guilty," they were already "beyond the rest of the world," thanks to "the superiority of [their] political principles." Admittedly, the country had "not yet arrived at the point at which all communities are destined to arrive, of perceiving guilt to be infirmity" and "of obviating punishment," but she implied that it was leading the rest of the world in the right direction.

On the one hand, there was no question in Dickens's mind that the Philadelphia system of solitary confinement for the length of the offender's sentence was a cruel punishment; it was ineffective both as a cure for criminality and a means of crime prevention. On the other hand, his sixth novel, going further than *American Notes*, challenged the lady reformer to prove that the violence-loving Chollop and the double-dealing Mr. Scadder—one "side of his face . . . seemed to listen to what the other side was doing" (*MC*, 352)—were *infirm*; that is, weak, physically ill, or insecure. Such attributes were reserved for any unfortunate who got into a scrape with the backwoodsman or settled in the swamp salesman's fever-inducing real estate development. In Dickens's opinion, which seems American-born, utopists such as Miss Martineau understood neither crime nor its punishments because their conception of human nature was far too lenient. Or one could put it the other way round: they glorified human nature because they misunderstood criminals and crime.

Although the plight of women vexed Miss Martineau throughout *Society in America*, it, too, was only a blemish, not a deformity. Deprived of equal rights in the land of equality, women were said to be as desperate for manumission as field slaves on a plantation. Yet the creator of this impression, herself doubly repugnant to many Americans in the South as a female abolitionist, contradicted Mrs. Trollope, who found manners hopelessly impaired by the subjugation of women. Instead, she eagerly forecasted an equal rights millennium: "the present" was merely an "interval between the feudal age and the coming time, when life and its occupations will be freely thrown open to women as to men" (*SA*, 307). Although Dickens said little about the women of America, his onslaught against two Victorian women's travel books suggests that he thought the occupation of social analyst should not be thrown open to the opposite sex.

On the copyright issue, destined to be Dickens's downfall, Miss Martineau sounded positively cheerful: "The present state of the law, by which the works of English authors are pirated, undefended against mutilation, and made to drive native works out of the market, is so conspicuously bad, that there is every prospect of a speedy alteration" (*SA*, 329). One could almost interpret Dickens's quest for copyright as Miss Martineau's handiwork; her outburst of optimism on the subject may have been an invitation alluring enough to persuade the novelist that a "speedy alteration" was his to effect.

Unfortunately, Miss Martineau was wrong about a copyright agreement, still half a century away when she wrote, just as she was too hopeful in predicting occupational parity for the sexes, which continues to be an issue 150 years later. But the first miscalculation was the one that fooled Dickens badly. If Tocqueville, Rousseau, and Miss Martineau collectively summoned him to both the Edenic past and the utopian future, only she did him an additional disservice: she held out "every prospect" of a personal El Dorado, where overdue royalties could easily be collected like so much gold in the streets.

Society, Harriet Martineau believed, always works eventually; sooner or later, reason peacefully prevails and life's forward movement continues as if there had been no interruption. Such thinking on crime, women's rights, and copyright protection made Miss Martineau the staunchest believer in the social organism's self-perfecting tendencies whom Dickens encountered prior to George Eliot; it also constituted her response to Tocqueville's fears of a tyrant majority. If the life process is more than just self-correcting, if the drive in things is toward betterment, thus ensuring the preponderance of good over evil, then Tocqueville's reservations evaporate: majority rule, rephrased positively as "the ultimate ascendancy of the will of the majority" (*SA*, 78), is virtually synonymous with progress in that it guarantees enactment of needed reforms once an injustice becomes "conspicuously bad," which injustice supposedly always does.

Miss Martineau had a Briton's penchant for seeing two nations— cautious Yankees up north and cavalier southerners farther down. But she was as reconciliatory as Mrs. Gaskell would be when imagining England's industrial north and the pastoral south coming together as harmoniously as husband and wife. Among the events Miss Martineau's vision of the future failed to include was the Civil War. Although slavery presented the biggest obstacle to her use of America to illustrate life's quick removal of intolerable conditions, she predicted the problem would soon be "rectified, probably, without bloodshed" (*SA*, 250, 228).

Because of its stand on slavery, *Society in America* seemed to Dickens more self-refuting than *Domestic Manners* had been. The earlier book's upward movement from the swampy Mississippi to cosmopolitan New York contradicted its author's growing disillusionment. *Society in America* showed slavery pervading and thus perverting every sector of American life—"The curse of slavery lies heavy on the land"; yet Miss Martineau's trust in nonviolent, self-correcting social processes compelled her to dismiss the plight of the Negro race and the South's slavocracy as an "anomaly" (*SA*, 90, 93, 356).

No matter the ostensible subject, Miss Martineau invariably resumed writing what might almost be called a series of antislavery pamphlets disguised as a travel book. Discussions of the "Morals of Politics" boil down to "Citizenship of People of Colour." Moving on to the "Political Non-Existence of Women," she immediately returns to the slavery issue because one form of nonexistence suggests the other. The section on "Morals of Economy" opens with the "Morals of Slavery" and never really leaves the topic. But the more Miss Martineau indulged her reformer's zeal as an ardent abolitionist outraged by the multiple miseries slavery caused, the weaker Dickens felt she made her case for a world in steady transition from feudalism to perfection.

Normally flat and unimaginative, Miss Martineau's prose only rose above the writing in Victorian religious tracts when it blamed slavery for the "process of demoralization" overspreading America. Even the pun in "demoralization" is unusual for her: she maintained that the loss of moral integrity, the country's violation of its own first principles, had produced not only uneasy consciences up north but a lassitude throughout the southern states, a spiritual lethargy that translated into rundown plantations and a general impression of inefficiency and decay.

Enlivened prose aside, however, the urge to speechify about resplendent progress was never stronger in Miss Martineau than it became over the slavery issue. This institution's "duration," she moralized, "is now merely a question of time," for it is "rocking to its foundations," thanks to abolitionists (SA, 93, 356): "The world has heard and seen enough of the reproach incurred by America, on account of her coloured population. It is now time to look for the fairer side. Already is the world beyond the sea beginning to think of America, less as the country of the double-faced pretender to the name of Liberty, than as the home of the single-hearted, clear-eyed Presence which, under the name of Abolitionism, is majestically passing through the land which is soon to be her throne" (SA, 124). As this blend of apologetics and oratory indicates, the rise of abolitionism in America gave Miss Martineau proof positive of an ameliorative energy, not simply corrective but perfectibilitarian, running through all things; it was a "Presence" or godlike immanence and it was feminine ("her throne").

First, Miss Martineau drew a depressing picture of the devastating effects of slavery, an "anomaly" that was nevertheless "ruinous" nationwide (SA, 171); then she heralded the triumphal march toward queenship of a "clear-eyed" agency she called Abolition but considered identical with Progress. Not only does the enthronement metaphor seem incongruous in a democratic context, but the vision of Progress "majestically passing through the land" approaches sacrilege, suggesting a Messianic procession or Second Coming.

Consequently, whenever Dickens emphasized Selfishness in *Martin Chuzzlewit* as society's bedrock principle and made America its special domicile, he contradicted the connotations of self-sacrifice and self-effacement in Miss Martineau's concept of abolition. America disclosed the essence of human nature by standing for aggrandizement, the enslavement of men and materials, not for manumission or release. Instead of an enthroned salvationary "Presence" with an almost mystical aura, the abstraction with which young Chuzzlewit must do battle—"and Self, Self, Self, dilated on the scene" (*MC*, 525)—sounds like a many-armed or multiheaded monstrosity out of Bunyan's *The Pilgrim's Progress* (it may be "single-hearted" but is not "clear-eyed"). Miss Martineau foretold the decline of double-faced pretenders, but Dickens presented, besides Pecksniffian duplicity, the prosperous American realtor, Mr. Scadder, who is physically two-faced, and Jonas's curious courting of Charity, during which he address all of his attentions to her sister Mercy.

It was not just Miss Martineau's "annoying moralizing"[29] that exasperated Dickens; he detested her sermons about accentuating life's "fairer side," which he saw as a way of ignoring the darker. Slavery in the United States had to be an exception to the rule for Miss Martineau; otherwise, her long view, an anticipation of secular evolutionary humanism in the 1850s and 1860s, would collapse. Intermittent war, working-class unrest, natural disasters, and persistent social abuses such as slavery, this philosophy argued, were terrible up close but ultimately irrelevant to life's subterranean progressive rhythms; they continue unabated or else quickly reinstate themselves. Dickens seized upon slavery to put forward the less melioristic overview that periodic upheavals, civil wars, collapsing social institutions, and the disintegration of formerly powerful nations prohibit any notion of a triumphal march toward earthly utopia; for such an idea to work, too many things had to be smoothed out along the way, as happened when Miss Martineau reduced enormity to anomaly.

In neither *American Notes* nor *Martin Chuzzlewit* did Dickens desire to discredit abolitionists and justify slavery; he sympathized with the former and lambasted the latter. But to embarrass Miss Martineau and rebuff *Society in America*, he cited the debasement of the Negro race as evidence for the recurrence throughout history of serious setbacks for man's moral evolution. The spread of slavery in a country simultaneously dedicated to liberty for all was not inconsistent with the way he thought the real world worked; on the contrary, although regrettable, it typified the manifold ups and downs of the social process, which always proceeds both well and badly at the same time; that is, for the worse in many cases rather than always or ultimately for the general betterment, as Miss Martineau wanted to believe.

In a preface to the fifth edition of *Domestic Manners* (1839), Mrs. Trollope realized that *Society in America* had eclipsed her travel book in at least one regard; she conceded that she ought to have devoted "a much larger portion" of her attention "to the great national feature— negro slavery." By reserving "Slavery" for the penultimate chapter in *American Notes*, therefore, Dickens accomplished four things: (1) he repaired Mrs. Trollope's omission more dramatically than Miss Martineau had; (2) he ridiculed the latter's reduction of a national feature, indeed a national disgrace, to a temporary irregularity; (3) he quashed the idea of America as a democratic utopia open to all; and (4) he disputed the philosophy that life was a process of constant amelioration.

Slavery and the Civil War to which it was leading must have seemed tailor-made as a refutation of "virtuous revolution," the pacific recipe for change that Miss Martineau foresaw being adopted (*SA*, 212)—her cure-all for what Dickens considered man's perennial backsliding. How could life progress "from age to age" toward "the same lofty something" (*SA*, 247), Dickens inquired of Miss Martineau, if the New World refused to relinquish a shameful practice already outlawed in the Old? Does mankind become "more clear-sighted as time unfolds," the quizzing tacitly continued, if slavery, a problem in ancient civilizations, has been reinstituted in a particularly nasty form by a modern one?

The slavery chapter can easily be recognized as an intentionally ironic use of anomaly because it is as conspicuous in *American Notes* as the sorest of thumbs: each of the previous sixteen chapters is named for an action ("Going Away") or place ("Boston," "New York"); none is consecrated to a single idea, institution, or social abuse. Occurring out of place *after* an account titled "The Passage Home," chapter 17 shows how starkly the woes of blacks stood out in the novelist's recollections; even after his return, he was unable to put the problem behind him either by duplicating Miss Martineau's prognosis that it must come to an end "before very long" (*SA*, 171) or by reserving his misgivings for the "Concluding Remarks" in chapter 18.

Dickens deliberately made his discussion of America's "national feature" a serious joke at Miss Martineau's expense, a structural parody of *Society in America*. On one hand, he demonstrated what a genuine anomaly looks like: it does not pervade every section the way the slavery issue repeatedly crops up in Harriet Martineau's travelogue. On the other hand, he emphasized that enslavement of the Negro was an anomaly so grossly outstanding, so contrary to the enlightenment of human nature, that it forced him to disrupt chronology and vary his pattern for naming chapters, just as it distorted the quality of American life and made Miss Martineau's progressive tone sound inconsonant with her theme.

That Dickens's accounts of slaves with notched ears and branded flesh were gleaned from America's own newspapers must have been especially gratifying to a novelist whose work had been pirated in them and whose claim to be a gentleman had been rejected there as well. More important, such accounts allowed Dickens to respond to Miss Martineau's examples of cruel treatment for "runaways" (*SA*, 224-25) with a voluminous compilation of maimings and torturings.

Her generalizations about the "Morals of Slavery" have a Utilitarian statistician's objectivity, whereas Dickens's concentration on specifics was truly incriminating. As a novelist well versed in sensational realism, he pointed angrily to individual cases, real victims: Mary, Ben, Ned, Josiah, Edward, Ellie, Randal, Bob, Tom, and so on (*AN*, 274-76). The "liveries of mutilation," his list of "disfigured persons," supplied irrefutable evidence that "upholders of slavery" were condoners of "atrocities" (*AN*, 284, 283, 269).[30] Thus Edward has "the letter E [carved] on his arm," Randal "has one ear cropped," Bob "has lost one eye," Tom "has one jaw broken" (*AN*, 275).[31]

Following this catalogue of inhumane punishments, six pages of clippings enumerate violent quarrels, impromptu combats, duels, murders, and assassinations to show "how the slave-owners" and the class of society to which they belong behave basely "not to their slaves but to each other" (*AN*, 277). These incidents are not an anomaly in a chapter on "Slavery." Dickens wanted to outdo Miss Martineau: her largely intellectual approach merely talked of "demoralization," but he substantiated in detail charges that the country had been "brutalized by slave customs"; license to mistreat the slaves resulted in a general disregard for decent behavior, the sort of progression from one brutality to savagery on a larger scale that Martin Chuzzlewit points out to Pogram (*MC*, 536). If members of the slaveowning class shoot and stab one another as vehemently as they lash their slaves, human nature's reputation for progress also suffers, and the oft-heard argument that Negroes were an inferior race that slavery had raised from barbarism quickly collapses.[32]

The same examples that outclassed Miss Martineau also made Mrs. Trollope's treatment of blacks seem supercilious as well as insufficient. Consider her reference in the fifth edition's preface to "our darkskinned fellow-creatures"; they may be her brothers and sisters, but she seems astounded by differences the more she emphasizes similarities. On Broadway she met "a young negress in the extreme of fashion, . . . accompanied by a black *beau*, whose toilet was equally studied" (*DM*, 310). As Mrs. Trollope continued to observe the "air of the most tender devotion" between the "elegantly dressed" man and his "sable goddess," she might as well have been describing cockneys aping aristocrats. In contrast, Dickens's tormented blacks arouse the same outrage and compassion the novelist had exhibited when describing denizens of the Fleet or paupers in England's workhouses.[33]

In the 1850s, when the issue was whether manufacturers like Mr. Bounderby "were quite justified in chopping people up with their machinery,"[34] Harriet Martineau (and Mrs. Gaskell) sided with the industrialists, who were exonerated as progressives implementing the new technology. Figures on the number of factory accidents were grossly inflated, Miss Martineau maintained. Besides addressing such charges directly,[35] Dickens adopted the same tactics used so effectively to make Mary, Ben, and Ned more real than her unnamed "runaways" or Mrs. Trollope's "sable goddess"; he depicted individual victims of the protomodern technological system, that nefarious combination of laissez-faire economics and Utilitarian educational theory. *Hard Times* described stunted and deformed workers, including Blackpool's drunken wife, and presented several of Coketown's imaginatively starved children peeping into a circus tent as if through a magic casement opened onto fairy land.

Rethinking the slavery question in *Martin Chuzzlewit* enabled Dickens to expand his revaluative parody of Miss Martineau: he promoted what William Lloyd Garrison called "that crime of crimes— making man the property of his fellow-man" (*NFD*, 39)—from a vanishing aberration to an American "Institution" (*MC*, 535), as if it had been established by the Constitution. Going further, he filled the British chapters of his sixth novel with a variety of relationships that seem virtually master-slave. His argument was that subjugation, defined broadly as the subordination of one person's will and energy to the needs of another's greedy or grasping Self, was rampant everywhere, fundamental to the human condition; the American scene, he insisted, was no anomaly.

Tom Pinch serves Pecksniff honestly but blindly and thanklessly; the latter in turn fawns hypocritically over Old Martin, eager to do his bidding as a way of gaining control of the senior Chuzzlewit's life and fortune. A very demanding Old Martin is dutifully served by Mary Graham, just as Mark Tapley looks after a self-centered young Martin. The last two arrangements mentioned, however, mature, the first into a father-daughter relationship, the second into partnership and camaraderie akin to brotherly love. Nevertheless, growth from a master-slave situation into something more commendable remains an exception to the rule.

Mrs. Harris's serviceableness to Mrs. Gamp introduces a comic variation on the enslavement theme, and Mercy Pecksniff, who makes Jonas Chuzzlewit "a perfect slave" (*MC*, 398) during their engagement, finds their positions suddenly reversed after marriage. Similarly, an alarmed Montague Tigg realizes that "instead of Jonas being his tool and instrument, their places seemed to be reversed" (*MC*, 645) when the deceived investor threatens the swindler. A recently betrothed Charity Pecksniff has "the air of having taken the unhappy Moddle captive" (*MC*, 695). That gentleman's mournful writhings under impending marriage bonds serve as Dickens's reminder that *any* institution, including matrimony, can inflict a kind of slavery if it is wrongly used. But the ascendancy of Jonas, first over Mercy and then over Tigg, is also a sharp rejoinder to facile meliorists like Miss Martineau; it supports the moral one must draw from the subordination of Chuzzlewit's external self to the darker, internal self who comes forth to commit murder: not only can goodness not enslave badness in the scheme of things, but lesser evils are always required to serve greater.

One can argue that Dickens, having seen slavery in the New World, felt qualified to unveil its subtler forms in older, allegedly more civilized societies like his own. He chose to locate the more insidious instances of victimization at home; they put to rest decisively Miss Martineau's daydream of life as an essentially ameliorative process: from age to age, Dickens showed, evil refines itself as effectively as good does. Master-slave arrangements in the English chapters of *Chuzzlewit* are worse than slavery in America insofar as they seem highly unstable, liable to reverse themselves at any moment. Paradoxically, Dickens concluded that less brazen types of enslavement in England's more settled society were actually more volatile than their equivalents in the American South: contrary to Elijah Pogram's contention that his countrymen have no leisure for developing "forms," owner stands to chattel there in a fixed hierarchy, a matter of hard-and-fast custom or tradition.

Much of the negative coloring in the early, strictly British chapters about the Chuzzlewit clan's origin and composition seems inexplicable unless attributed both to Dickens's New World disappointments and to Miss Martineau's alleged mishandling of major problems as minor obstacles to civilization's progress. It is not simply that the Chuzzlewit family is a Dickensian synecdoche for the family of man or that Seth

Pecksniff epitomizes "all the self-seeking hypocrisy of Victorian England."[36] His cousin, Old Martin, the Lear-like patriarch of the clan, is Dickens's idea of a disgruntled deity, a sign of the godlike novelist's own post-America desire to retreat from this world's unlikable inhabitants. So disgusted has Old Martin become with the selfish creatures on whom he would confer his all that he, too, personifies one of "the numerous vices that have their roots in self": self-pity.[37] "I have never found one nature, no, not one," Old Martin laments, "in which, being wealthy and alone, I was not forced to detect *the latent corruption* that lay hid within it, waiting for such as I to bring it forth" (*MC*, 39; italics added).

Instead of Diogenes searching with his lamp for a wise man, Old Martin has sought with his purse someone neither selfish nor hypocritical; but his travels have been as fruitless as Dickens's quest for an American El Dorado. Statements about detection and corruption would have sounded jarringly out of place in the pre-America novels, in *Pickwick Papers* or *The Old Curiosity Shop*, for instance, before Dickens had seen the self-seeking ego writ large, unmistakable evidence of the multiple imperfections innate in all men. One cannot imagine Old Martin's Swiftian expression of repulsion—his sense of himself and everyone he meets as partners in the activation of "corruption"—escaping from Miss Martineau; nor could it issue from George Eliot's characters, whose beneficial interactions frequently become advertisements for the coalescence of the human community.

"The curse of our house," says Old Martin near the novel's end, "has been the love of self; has ever been the love of self," which Dickens condemns as "the vile tree" in the Garden (*MC*, 800, 791). Old Martin could be speaking in a Greek tragedy about the House of Atreus or paraphrasing *Genesis*. In either case, he presides over the novel's English chapters not as a "single-hearted, clear-eyed Presence" who Miss Martineau said was to be enthroned and venerated but as a disagreeable divinity eager to resign because he fears he will be unable to find any "fairer side" (*SA*, 124) to his subjects.

That Old Martin's low estimate of human nature approximates Dickens's post-America point of view is clear from what happens to young Martin *before* he ventures on the journey the novelist had just completed: having parted from Pecksniff and feeling down and out in London while seeking passage to America, the hero deteriorates in five short weeks; he goes from a self-confident gentleman-architect of fastidious deportment to a lounger pawning items of his wardrobe for sustenance. Dickens's letdown in America best explains why he seized this early opportunity to rail against extravagant meliorists such as Miss Martineau, calling them "moralists" who behold "happiness and self-respect, innate in . . . every grain of dust in God's highway" (*MC*, 225).

Waxing nearly as angry over Martin's degeneration as he later became with "Right Reverends and Wrong Reverends of every order" (*BH*, 611), Dickens administered a tongue-lashing to all "Pharisees of the nineteen hundredth year of Christian Knowledge": whether erecting utopian castles in the air by imagining slaveholding America as "that regenerated land" (*MC*, 266) or justifying society's blindness to remediable ills at home, these distorters of the human situation were seldom merely "mistaken philanthropists," as Mrs. Trollope had called them (*DM*, 318); instead, they do man the greatest disservice by overestimating his internal fortitude in the face of life's trials. They "soundingly appeal to human nature" as if it were incapable of being "transformed . . . into the nature of the Beasts" (*MC*, 226).

The modern revaluator is impressed by the cominatory tone of an irate novelist who has just recently discovered how limited a progress civilizations have made: after nearly 2,000 years, there is still no shortage of Pharisees, Western Europe's Christian hypocrites having replaced Jerusalem's. The modern Pharisees see too little evil in man, whereas their ancient counterparts found fault even with the Messiah. One course of conduct, Dickens insisted, is as absurd as the other, and both run contrary to true "Christian Knowledge," which is obviously in short supply. Christ's accusers failed to recognize their invitation to paradise, but Victorian hypocrites of Miss Martineau's idealistic stamp err by seeing no obstacles for themselves along "God's highway." In both cases, the longed-for kingdom comes no closer to reality.

Young Martin's rapid-fire "transition" downward in "morals and manners" is anti-Martineau in nature yet hardly exceptional, Dickens implied; on the contrary, this reversion, as if from butterfly to caterpillar, suggests that the debasement of the enslaved Negro, far from being a phenomenon in America's social system, illustrates man's lack of sufficient grace when pressured. It shows how fragile is the "happiness and self-respect" in all men, even an English gentleman, as Dickens had discovered when his own claims to honesty and gentilty were reviled in American newspapers. Self-respect, it follows, is so perishable that it can be neither "innate" nor all that readily procured and guaranteed by what Miss Martineau called a social process of "mutual and self-perfection."

"Demoralization" was Miss Martineau's vicious epithet for slavery's impact on plantation life. Yet well before Martin reaches America to head south from New York and not long after Dickens had returned, the term is made to seem descriptive of the stronger tendency in all things, which is down, not up; that is, "into the nature of the Beasts" rather than away from it.

Foreshadowings of young Martin's London decline appear in two remarkably zoological passages at the conclusion of *Chuzzlewit's* first chapter. Reducing men to apes and pigs, the budding satirical novelist set the tone for his next nine novels: he replaced the ideal of universal brotherhood as a realistic product of a supposedly self-perfecting social intercourse with some highly questionable, pseudo-scientific theories of human behavior. To the quondam believer in America, however, these outdated theorems still made sense as moral judgments.

"Without implying any direct participation in the Monboddo doctrine touching the probability of the human race having once been monkeys," Dickens observed that "men do play very strange and extraordinary tricks" (*MC*, 6); and *Martin Chuzzlewit* proceeds to show some of them. "Without trenching on the Blumenbach theory as to the descendants of Adam having a vast number of qualities which belong more particularly to swine," Dickens concluded that "some men certainly are remarkable for taking uncommon good care of themselves." The recently returned author of *Martin Chuzzlewit* was not as cynical as the repatriated Gulliver, who saw his fellow men only as subhuman Yahoos, but he did set out to write a satirical alternative to Miss Martineau's hubristic overconfidence. The result is a Swiftian anatomy of simian and swinish tendencies in men who are seen not as heirs to the future but as "descendants of Adam" (*MC*, 6).

Obviously, Dickens put no more faith in Lord Monboddo's evolutionary theories as formulated in *Of the Origin and Progress of Language* (six volumes, 1773-92) or in Johann Friedrich Blumenbach's jokingly serious eighteenth-century paper "On Human and Porcine Races" than he later placed in Guiseppe Bianchini's investigations of spontaneous combustion (1731).[38] In September of 1853 Dickens might well have written in his *Bleak House* preface: one need not subscribe to the Veronese prebendary's reports to realize that internally corrupt societies and diseased individuals frequently collapse from within, as if exploding into flames spontaneously like Mr. Krook. Dickens laid the groundwork in *Martin Chuzzlewit* for his subsequent borrowings from popular science: he invoked it poetically, that is, by analogy, for the purpose of reaching a realistic moral verdict. He also demonstrated that a rival's conception of Progress "passing through the land" like a monarch on parade was poetry too, not an instance of scientific sociology.

The disillusioned utopist cites Blumenbach and Monboddo while still insisting on the necessity of reforms but only appears to flirt with contradiction. His original belief in America had been greater than either Mrs. Trollope's or Harriet Martineau's, hence the unrivaled traumatic severity of its extinction. Nevertheless, although badly shaken and less naive in 1843-44, he would not overreact; instead, he held to at least a modicum of his former faith in social activism. At the same time, he used the mistakes of two women travelers as evidence that he had retained his balance while passing successfully between Scylla and Charybdis. In short, Dickens did not revert to Toryism, the wrong move Mrs. Trollope made in becoming militantly rightwing; nor did he remain a hopelessly deluded "left-wing" meliorist the way Miss Martineau had.[39]

Compared to Mrs. Trollope, Miss Martineau was the greater danger, a conduit for intellectual currents whereby the Romantic idea of the universe as God creating and perfecting Himself became the Victorian secular humanist's mandate to continue the job on his own. Miss Martineau made Dickens feel entitled to take pride in being male, moderate, and realistic, for as he put it himself, "there never was such a wrong-headed woman born—such a vain one—or such a Humbug" (J, 2:855).[40] This magniloquent crescendo of pejoratives he might also have applied subsequently to all evolutionary humanists, Mrs. Gaskell and George Eliot included; in light of the battles of the travel books, both can be seen as Miss Martineau's intellectual heirs on a number of points that Dickens considered untenable.

The irony of Dickens traveling to America in order to discover utopia but having to write instead that human nature is flawed at all known stages of society's development is the crowning but not the ultimate irony stemming from the 1842 visit; the novelist's transformation from a would-be eulogist to America's staunchest detractor is not the final ironic turnabout.

In 1869, after Dickens had completed his American reading tour, the last skirmish in the battle of the travel books was fought: Mark Twain published *Innocents Abroad or the New Pilgrims Progress*, an Americanization of the format, techniques, and themes of the anti-America travel book that Boz, contrary to his original intentions, had seemingly perfected in the 1840s. *Innocents Abroad* could not exist without *American Notes* and *Martin Chuzzlewit* both as targets to discredit and models to surpass.

Besides turning letters written home into a travel book while combining the formats of travelogue and novel,[41] Twain devised more than half a dozen ways of redoing Dickens in order to outdo him. (1) Unabashedly chauvinistic, he evinced no qualms about judging another culture solely in terms of his own. (2) He bolstered his veracity by demeaning previous travelers more openly than Dickens had, even if he transcended his specific examples. (3) Repeatedly, he reversed Dickens's value system, exalting novelty over tradition or American brashness over so-called European sophistication. (4) Thus he redeemed innocence or naiveté by making the lack of cultivated tastes an asset for the traveler and the possession of pedigrees a liability for the persons and places being visited. (5) On the one hand, he claimed to have suffered a severer blow to his expectations than Dickens had; yet (6) on the other, he reclaimed the future for America by consigning Europe to the moldy past. (7) While doing all this, however, the American agnostic ruled out a promised land in the temporal *or any other order*, thereby canceling the idea more extensively than the British skeptic of secular humanism's worldly orientations probably intended.

"In going to the New World," Dickens stipulated, "one must . . . put out of sight the Old one and bring none of its customs or observations into comparison" (J, 1:357). In *American Notes* and *Martin Chuzzlewit*, however, the novelist's inability to obey this stricture gradually yielded to the conviction that it was inadvisable to do so. Benefiting from Dickens's experience, Twain automatically measured Europe and Asia by American standards.[42] He fashioned his book's finest satirical ploy by adopting from the outset a technique his predecessor had been unable to resist once he discovered his ingrained Englishness.

If Dickens considered the Mississippi a massive but shallow puddle, Twain countered that Gibraltar "is suggestive of a 'gob' of mud on the end of a shingle" (*IA*, 50). The Arno, he said, "would be a very plausible river if they would pump some water into it" (*IA*, 176). Lake Tahoe, he continued, was "much finer" than either Lake Como or the Tiber (*IA*, 144). Vesuvius he dismissed as a mere "ditch" (*IA*, 233). The mosque of St. Sophia was "the rustiest old barn in heathendom," while even St. Peter's seemed "not . . . nearly so large as the Capitol" and not as beautiful from the outside (*IA*, 260, 194). Architecturally or in matters of natural scenery, areas in which Victorian travelers regularly awarded the prizes to England, Twain promoted America to Europe's detriment.

The American humorist reversed the initially cautious Britisher of

American Notes by finding Europe and Asia immediately disappointing; more so than for the hero in *Martin Chuzzlewit*, Twain's trip got worse the farther he went. The oldness and dirtiness throughout Europe and Asia were hardly virtues, their art seemed overestimated if not outright humbug, their pride in the past amounted to a hypocritical covering up of present-day deficiencies, an excuse for pervasive backwardness. If Americans spat incessantly and washed themselves infrequently, as Dickens charged, they were at least spared the narrowness and filthiness of foreign streets, which were similarly revolting, whether in Florence or Damascus. On some of the unfortunate souls in the East, Twain complained, "the dirt had caked . . . till it amounted to bark" (*IA*, 340), such dirt being symbolic of the area's accumulation of a burdensome, unhealthy culture that literally sealed one's pores.

Promenading in the galleries of France and Italy, Twain kept noticing "how superior the copies" of paintings and statues he had seen at home "were to the original" (*IA*, 137); it was often symbolically faded, damaged, or falling apart, just as the Old World seemed to be when compared with the newer, cleaner, American version of it. The very proliferation of antiquities suggested a lack of discrimination and blunted their effectiveness—there were "acres" of paintings by Tintoretto and more "weary miles of picture galleries" across Europe than Dickens had traveled down the monotonous Mississippi. Furthermore, these galleries were generally crammed with portraits of "historical cutthroats" (*IA*, 175), each more detestable yet less useful than pioneers like Hannibal Chollop.

If every man in America prided himself on being exceptional, as Dickens had maintained, then every church in every European community claimed to own a piece of the true cross: Twain reported having seen at least "a keg" of nails allegedly used for the Crucifixion (*IA*, 120). "Little insect governments" in Capri and Naples and the "puppy kingdoms" of Greece (*IA*, 231, 255) boasted of oldness and venerability, but these were inferior qualities to America's newness, a resourcefulness bristling with unexpended energy. Whereas Dickens called America a real estate swindle, a fraudulent promised land, Europe and Asia, having declined in the scheme of things, struck Twain as an overrated, undersized, and thoroughly insignificant reliquary, whose contents were mostly a hoax.

The chicanery of the guides, whether in Paris or Turkey, easily exceeded the boastfulness and self-pride Dickens disliked in Americans. Constantly inveigling for "baksheesh" (tips) while inviting tourists to be awestruck before famous sights, these guides were aptly named only because they typified the shortsightednesses of their respective cultures. In Italy, "the heart and home of priestcraft," they never noticed what Twain called the consequent "ignorance, superstition, degradation, [and] poverty" of the general populace (IA, 149); similarly, Naples had "more princes than policemen" (IA, 229), while Florence, the American decided, needed more turnpikes, railways, and depots but fewer priceless art treasures (IA, 182).

Florence or Naples, in Twain's opinion, could be Italy in microcosm, and Italy could stand for the whole of Europe: country and continent were both "one vast museum of magnificence and misery" (IA, 185) with riches stockpiled but millions of neglected poor. This imbalance seemed worse to the American pilgrim than Dickens and Miss Martineau had found the contrast between the principle of equality and the reality of Negro slavery.

Moving eastward, Twain saw the pattern in Italy repeating itself. The fabled city of Constantinople, the "very heart and home" of penury and disease, harbored the continent's most persistent beggars, its most hideous cripples (IA, 259); they made a mockery of the much-heralded attractions in the former Rome of the East. The ultimate difference between America and Europe and the Near East, Twain concluded, was that the New World was dedicated to progress, while the Old had chosen to stand still: because of the lack of time-honored customs and usages that young Chuzzlewit deplored, people in the United States could strive to be wiser than their grandfathers (IA, 193-94).

Enlarging upon Dickens's short-term sojourn during the winter/ spring of 1842, Twain and the other passengers aboard the Quaker City undertook a colossal voyage in the spring of 1867 to Gibraltar, Marseille, Genoa, Naples, Athens, Constantinople, the Crimea, Smyrna, Ephesus, Beirut, Joppa, Alexandria, Malta, Sardinia, Majorca, Spain, Madeira, and Bermuda—plus overland excursions: one to Paris, another through Italy, a third trip across the Holy Land, and a visit to the pyramids. Admittedly, the hard-to-hoodwink American saw more of the world than Dickens could in America, but he purposely became more American the more he saw and prouder of it, achieving fuller self-definition much faster. Thus he surpassed Dickens's accidental discovery that travel, instead of broadening one's horizons, brings increased self-awareness: exposing the traveler to a challenge from otherness, it tests his mettle as a critic, thereby enhancing his self-esteem while crystallizing the personality he had when he started out.

The most grievous of Twain's disillusionments took place in the

East. "How I have been swindled by books of Oriental travel" (*IA*, 270), he exclaimed—an outburst that virtually echoed Dickens's dislike for Victorian books on American travel, not to mention his dissatisfaction with America itself as a real estate swindle or false land of promise. For both travelers, exposing the unreliability of predecessors justified adding yet another travelogue to those already in existence because such demonstrations of superior realism made extant volumes superfluous. The difference is that Twain actually cited allegedly typical passages from several travelers whose overly approving, highly romantic outlooks had misinformed him.

Journeying through Palestine, Twain realized that he had to "unlearn a great many things" that he had "somehow absorbed" during his upbringing; he was forced to "begin a system of reduction" (*IA*, 349), a ruthless curtailing of preconceptions. Although he pretends to be dissenting from a triumvirate of liars—"Thompson and Robinson and Grimes" (*IA*, 369), authors of such wildly-fanciful studies as *Life in the Holy Land* and *Nomadic Life in Palestine*—his major targets (besides Dickens) are classic books and dreamed-of places he dared not loudly name: not just the Orient of *The Arabian Nights* but the Jerusalem of the Bible. In short, he had to bid goodbye to all remnants of the romance and religion of his youth, things that the outwardly skeptical humorist was surprised to discover still had meaning for him. Similarly, Dickens's unspecified culprits included both Tocqueville (equalitarianism) and Rousseau (Romantic republicanism), the latter an embodiment of the young social realist's naive belief in the possibility of finding a perfect place.

Twain's insistence that he was "swindled" suggests how keenly he felt his failure to locate the Holy Land he had read about since boyhood. As the list of Eastern disappointments lengthened, he tried to make Dickens's disillusionment with America seem scarcely newsworthy by comparison: if a republican democracy was an imposture America had gotten away with for sixty years or more, Europe (especially Italy and Rome) and the Holy Land, arguably the two major sources of Western culture, were crueler impostures that had been going on for centuries.

Contrary to Dickens, it was not America that persistently exaggerated its size and importance; Europe and Asia were literally—that is, geographically—miniature versions of the status they enjoyed in the popular imagination. Thanks to a "reduction" process more systematic than Dickens's, the smaller these venerated biblical locales turned out to be, the more extravagant a disappointed Twain found the case that had been made for them. With a mixture of delight and chagrin, he saw "the empire of King Solomon diminish to the size of the state of Pennsylvania" (*IA*, 433). The entire New Testament, he was maliciously resigned to discover, took place in a neighborhood no larger than an American "county" (*IA*, 361).

Like Europe's reputation but to a far greater extent, Asia's virtues had been grossly inflated. The Turkish empire, in which "everybody lies and cheats" (*IA*, 265) on a scale beyond the smartness of General Choke and Zephaniah Scadder, contained too many mosques, churches, and graveyards but not enough fine whiskey or good morals (*IA*, 263). Smyrna's "Muhamadan stenches" (*IA*, 292) were an outrage to the olfactories second only to the offense a Syrian village gave to the eye: it was "the sorriest sight in the world" (*IA*, 336), more dismal than Dickens's insalubrious Cairo/Eden.

Every stream in Palestine, Twain complained, had been promoted to a river, Galilee was "dreary," the "cross-legged Grand Turk smoking his narghile" was a "shameless humbug," Turkish coffee tasted "the worst" of "all the unchristian beverages," and Jerusalem—"how small it is"—had streets that reminded Twain of chicken coops (*IA*, 356, 366, 272-73, 403). More so than the European sections, those on Asia and the Holy Land are a compendium of insults presented as insights: the grotto said to be Christ's birthplace was obviously "an imposture," Lazarus's tomb at Bethany appeared to be a dwelling superior to "any house in the town," and the great pyramid of Cheops, upon closer examination, shrank to a "corrugated, unsightly mountain of stone" (*IA*, 381, 427, 451). Phoniness, filthiness, and smallness reduced Asia a step below Europe, which had exhibited mainly the first two of these deficiencies and thus was only an aesthetic disappointment and not also a religious one.

One look at a real dromedary was sufficient "to take the romance out of [that animal] forever" (*IA*, 394) inasmuch as both the Bible and engravings of its scenes omit the dirt, rags, fleas, and stench that accompany camels and donkeys. By the time Twain has dismissed Palestine as "a hopeless, dreary, heartbroken land" (*IA*, 441), his lament that "another dream, another cherished hope, had failed" (*IA*, 430) sounds like a doubly Dickensian refrain, the trip to America and the misery of Warren's Blacking combined: "travel and experience," he keeps reiterating, had robbed him of "the grandest pictures" and "the most cherished traditions" of his childhood (*IA*, 433).

Nevertheless, saying farewell to his "old dreams of Eastern luxury" (*IA*, 273), although painful for Twain the adult, was doubly advantageous for the neophyte novelist responding to Dickens. On the one hand, he could claim to have suffered a severer wrench: the Victorian had repudiated utopian fantasies in order to return home, but every American was now compelled to stand on his own since he was cut off from the religious and cultural origins Twain had just learned to see through. On the other hand, the humorist and his fellow citizens were newly liberated, not just from the Mother Country but from tiresome Old World customs and beliefs that Dickens mistakenly thought should be imposed on America's rawness as civilizing influences. Paradoxically, the worse things grew for Twain as he proceeded from Europe to Asia, the better they ultimately became, so that the *New Pilgrims Progress* was an accurate subtitle as well as a comic and allusive one.

Mrs. Trollope was obliged to conclude that America was not "the land of promise" she had heard it called in Paris (*DM*, 196), just as Dickens conceded the new country was not truly "a land of resort" (*AN*, 290). When it came to showing that there were no promised lands, however, Twain's efforts outstripped Dickens, from whose contempt for secular, temporal utopias the Bible's stories were implicitly excluded. For Twain, "disillusionment with the present led to disillusionment with the past" (L, 211)—but, fortunately, mainly with the past. Biblical lands and their peoples "were exactly what they had always been," savages now as in former days (L, 211); but Americans, Twain could still suggest, were better, even if, like him, they must forgo once for all the religious orientations of their childhood.

Twain and Dickens agreed that pilgrimages were henceforth impractical inasmuch as promised lands do not exist. But the American's way of stating this fact—namely, that there never has been such a land despite what the Bible says—swept away a spiritual heritage as well as a material prospect. Cairo/Eden was a cruel parody of the biblical Garden, but now that garden and the Old Testament's Land of Promise were themselves deftly relegated to oblivion in *Innocents Abroad*; they were just as mythical as Rousseau's noble state, which Dickens had demolished.

Twain could dismiss Palestine and the ever-uncouth Palestinians as distinctly other, a cultural fount and ancestral people easily disowned by an American agnostic. His country had left the backwardness of biblical times behind more surely than Dickens could designate English gentlemen an improvement upon America's frontiersmen. In the squalor of Cairo/Eden, in contrast, Dickens believed he had encountered a sort of Magwitch or undesirable point of origin for all civilizations; in the not-so-noble savagery of the American West, he beheld a gross reincarnation of the fallen Adam in all men, a painful reminder that everyone must "do a little bit of Adam still" (*MC*, 384), as Pecksniff says in defense of his gardening.

Having made his American pilgrimage, Dickens ultimately concluded that the temporal order was deficient at both ends: in the beginning and at present. But Twain returned from the Holy Land to pronounce pilgrimages unnecessary for a less disturbing reason: because Americans would be foolish to form themselves on detestable Old World models. A New Jerusalem remained unlikely for both writers, but whatever Americans chose to do with their energies was bound to turn out preferable to the mishmash of inexplicably famous artifacts and untold human misery Twain had found everywhere abroad.

After a few weeks in America, Dickens lost interest in being considered an honorary equalitarian and regretted the loss. But Americans in *Innocents Abroad* are at their silliest when they put on European airs, trying to be like the French and Italians (*IA*, 168) or pretending they are "connoisseurs" who know "the difference between a fresco and a fireplug" (*IA*, 261). Indeed, the term "pilgrim," or tourist, becomes inseparable from the ignorance, imbecility, bigotry, and dotage that the pious majority aboard the *Quaker City* see over and over, often mistaking such cultural liabilities for a superior antiquity. "Sinners," reluctant skeptics such as Twain himself, are obviously disappointed not to find the Holy Land they learned about in Sunday school, yet had their quest been successful, they might have reaffirmed their former beliefs and ceased to be rambunctious, a quality for which America was to become famous and that civilization needs to avoid ossification. Ironically, Twain and his coterie of fellow sinners on the *Quaker City* are redeemed by a new kind of innocence peculiarly American: it adds to the inexperienced person's naiveté a vigorous or saving freshness, a brash and blissful irreverence for anything old, well known, or overly sophisticated (that is unduly polite and pompous).

When Twain reported that the "depth" of Raphael's "Transfiguration" is "profound, and the width . . . about four and a half feet" (*IA*, 218), he was not simply indulging in "lowbrow tourism."[43] The American satirist was reacting against Victorian abusers of his country, Dickens and Mrs. Trollope in particular,[44] who had unwisely objected to "the crude newness of everything" (*DM*, 133). Europeans, Twain replied, remain blind to what Mrs. Trollope only grudgingly called their "old-fashioned attachments to things obsolete" (*DM*, 133). Rephrased as *newness* versus *oldness*, Dickens's contrast of formlessness with tradition took on a positive coloring.

An innocent abroad, Dickens fell prey to the crude salvos of American newspapers when he petitioned for copyright protection. Disgusted to find such bad manners a national trademark, he fell back upon Victorian England's "humanizing conventionalities" (MC, 278); Twain retorted by using crudity and newness to expose artificiality and obsoleteness. Thus Odessa rose in his healthy, Philistine estimation because it "looked just like an American city" and contained "only . . . two pieces of statuary" (IA, 278-79). Also, he was "fervently thankful" to learn that Michelangelo, who seemed to have sculptured everything in outmoded, priest-ridden Italy, if not the very country itself, "was dead" (IA, 208).

In 1869, the battle of the travel books was only a memory for Dickens; he was about to become increasingly preoccupied with *The Mystery of Edwin Drood,* an attempt to repulse competition from Wilkie Collins by investing melodramatic realism with a stronger psychological component. The Inimitable believed this advance would also challenge George Eliot, whose concern for the inner lives of her characters ignored such tragic possibilities as Jasper's second or antisocial self. Striving to retain mastery of sensational realism at home must have seemed more important than resuming an argument nearly thirty years old. Consequently, *Innocents Abroad* escaped Dickens's notice, and Twain receives only two short mentions in Johnson's biography.[45]

Although the British novelist had no time for American humorists, the modern revaluator should still relish an engagement that prolonged the battle of the travel books into a thirty years' war. Twain's attempt to show that Europe looked as fraudulent through American eyes as the New World's democratic ideals had appeared from a British perspective was not a reaction "against the overwhelming, incomprehensible past" (L, 204). Nor was it an assertion of its author's American identity, an effort to help his readers "find out who we Americans are."[46] The point of the question Twain and his cohorts repeatedly ask about the subject or sculptor of every broken-legged statue they are shown—"Is he dead?"—was to render the past not only comprehensible but dispensable, something over and done with. Their goal was the *reassertion* of America's identity, not quite as the promised land that Dickens had come to see, but as a promising land nonetheless. If not exactly the country of the future—utopia was *not* imminent there—it was arguably the only place primarily with a future; that is, contrary to Europe and Asia, it had more of a future than a past.

Unlike Rome, Greece, and Palestine, America was not only new and alive but full of commendable individuals like Twain, who refused to be humbugged; seemingly less prepared, they were actually harder to fool than the gullible settlers in Eden. Twain reworked techniques from *American Notes* and *Martin Chuzzlewit* expressly to maintain that the rest of the nineteenth century and the years beyond still belonged to the America that Victorian excursionists of the 1830s and 1840s had misrepresented; Europe and Asia, he added, could keep the past. This redoing of Dickens amounted to a peculiarly American reinstatement of sanguineness about things-to-come, the very idea Dickens had used his disillusionment with the New World to discredit when he got back home.

Despite some effective satire against American tourists for aping Europeans or for wanting souvenir pieces of everything, including the pyramids, Twain's main goal was to restate his country's persisting significance. Consequently, *Innocents Abroad* is a landmark in the development of American literature, which the battle of the travel books can be seen to have influenced greatly. Although less seminal than *The Adventures of Huckleberry Finn* (1884), Twain's travelnovel ventured beyond a successful reuse of Dickens's stratagems to become a literature's declaration of independence. Its implicit and un-Jamesian position was that America's democratic values and a literature premised upon them could turn the tables on the English, depriving them of their vaunted cultural supremacy.[47] Such a literature, it followed, would continue to develop, even though naysayers like Dickens had once tried to tie its birth and survival to an Anglo-American royalty agreement.

Mark Twain was little more than a regional humorist until this redoing of Dickens, his first major work, earned him the beginnings of a national reputation. The success of *Innocents Abroad* surpassed its author's fondest expectations, selling 70,000 copies in 1869 and reaching 100,000 within three years. Twain received an average of $1,200 to $1,500 a month in royalties, or between $14,400 and $18,000 the first year, from a book that, during his lifetime, remained "his most popular work" (L, 256). In England, Dickens was allegedly hastening his own end with a final series of demanding readings to make his financial security irreversible, yet Twain was earning as much every month by disagreeing with *American Notes* as Dickens had probably lost in American royalties every month during 1842-44 and every month thereafter.

By reversing Dickens, by debunking the stale, run-down Old

World as smartly as the English novelist had ridiculed a barbarous and inchoate new one, a popular journalist began his rise to fortune and fame. Thus Twain pirated Dickens more imaginatively than any reprint house had—this was the last shot fired in the battle of the travel books as well as the first visit's final irony.[48]

4

An Ironic Second Coming

Learning of Dickens's inclination to perform in America, James Gordon Bennett referred to the proposed reading tour as "the second coming of Dickens" (RF, 107; D, 123). This editor-publisher was the novelist's archenemy among newspapermen: throughout the copyright controversy of 1842, he had misused the New York *Herald* as an Anglophobe's trumpet. Not surprisingly, therefore, Bennett's 1867 pleasantry contained nasty implications, even if likening Dickens's return to the Messiah's was an advance in subtlety over his customary billingsgate. Dickens had been welcomed as a god once already, Bennett wished to remind his countrymen, and he had repaid his worshipers with unflattering criticisms in *American Notes* and *Martin Chuzzlewit.* Furthermore, Dickens did not deserve to be idolized again, because his reappearance would constitute a financially motivated parody of Christ's: he would settle old scores not by sitting in judgment—he had done that inappropriately after the first visit—but by carting off large receipts from a country he felt still owed him money.

Facetiousness, not blasphemy, was Bennett's intention; nevertheless, his memorable description proved exceedingly ironic. Using George Dolby as a sort of John the Baptist to herald this second appearance, Dickens determined that the American public was familiar with his success performing in England and anxious to hear him bring to life characters and incidents from his own works. But instead of coming finally into his kingdom, the reader was penalized almost as severely as the pirated novelist had been. Figures in the next chapter will show that ticket speculators collectively—and one or two individually—realized bigger profits from some of the readings than Dickens did, even though he obtained the core of his estate from dollars made on the American continent. Thus it was an unusual second coming in which the Christ-figure turned out to be simple enough to fall victim again to the same kind of sharpness that had beaten him a quarter of a century earlier. American scalpers seem to have been just as proficient, indeed, far more inventive, than the pirates or "Paul Joneses"[1] when it came to taking advantage of Dickens.

The last three years of his life are critical for one's final opinion of the novelist and the man. But events during this period, for which the reading tour in America serves as both the inauguration and overall colorant, have been greatly distorted. Dickens did not start working himself to death in America, if indeed he ever overtaxed his bodily frame with self-destruction clearly in mind. A second coming that spelled the beginning of the end solely for the returning novelist would be *too* ironic. On the contrary, Dickens was fit enough for the awestruck wife of his American publisher to have fantasies about being the consort of so lively and fiery a genius, which meant enjoying pleasures physical as well as artistic and intellectual. In short, it was neither womanly affection nor personal well-being that Dickens had to forgo by returning to America in November 1867; he did not fail in *health* or at *love* nearly as much as he lost out financially, *money* being the only one of these three interconnected pursuits for which he has hitherto been awarded high grades.

Commentators on the reading tour usually sidestep the really interesting questions. For example: how much did Ticknor and Fields know about Ellen Ternan? (They were not only Dickens's official American publishers since April 1867 but promoters of the reading tour in general and sponsors of the all-important opening performances in Boston.) Little hard evidence exists to show that they were fully informed. This is the conclusion toward which the modern revaluator is driven after examining the existing correspondence between Dickens and James T. Fields and several little-known, long-unpublished passages from Fields's wife's voluminous diary.

This matter becomes particularly intriguing when taken up in connection with Annie Fields's almost immediate infatuation with Dickens. Her feelings must be examined in light of the legend that the fifty-five-year-old novelist expected his much younger mistress to join him in America, provided he found the moral climate sufficiently tolerant. Ignorance of Ellen on the part of Fields and his associates makes less likely any premeditated plan to bring her over; even if such planning did occur before Dickens left England, Annie's strong attraction to (and for) a man willing to present himself as wifeless and womanless rendered execution of so risky a design less compelling.

In "a very small pocket diary for the year 1867," Ada Nisbet discovered a code that Dickens had apparently agreed upon with W.H. Wills, his second-in-command at *All the Year Round*. If Dickens's cablegram from America read "all well," the diary said, then Ellen was to join him; if, however, he cabled "safe and well," which is what he did, she was not to come. Nisbet exclaimed: "Dickens had hoped to bring Nelly to America!" "No doubt," she then added more soberly, "there were many to advise against such action" (N, 54).

Diligently, one Dickensian after another has embellished Nisbet's inference. Thus Michael Slater states: "the plan" to have Ellen visit relatives in America while he toured "was abandoned, no doubt, because of the realization of the tremendous scandal that would ensue if his old enemy, the American press, should get hold of the story" (S, 210). Edgar Johnson's romantic embroidering is the worst: "Dickens could not bear to surrender his hope that [Ellen] might be able presently to come to him in America"; he longed to "have her speeding to him across the Atlantic" (J, 2:1076).

Dickens's mistress was closely involved with the novelist's second visit from its onset in the late 1850s as a recurring temptation: a "golden prospect" or the "golden campaigning ground." The idea of an American reading tour dates at the latest from 1859; friendship between Fields, one of Boston's most successful publishers, and Dickens, the world's most famous novelist, grew rapidly that year, the result of meetings both in London and at Gad's Hill (JA, 379). But Fields claimed he had begun pressing Dickens by mail well before he visited him, in fact "as long ago as the spring of 1858" (Y, 154). According to Dolby, who managed the world's first superstar throughout his American readings, Fields opened negotiations in 1857 upon hearing that Dickens had read *A Christmas Carol* profitably for the Jerrold Fund (D, 87-88). Whichever date one chooses—1857, 1858, or 1859—the possibility of a lucrative American tour unfolds with the breakup of Dickens's marriage and his involvement with Ellen Ternan as its backdrop.

Given the furor that separation from Catherine caused in 1858, six months in America may have seemed ideal as a retreat, not just a business proposition. Evidently, Dickens's growing attachment to Ellen soon created an obstacle, if it was not one immediately. By way of a letter in 1859 from Arthur Smith, then managing the public readings in England, Dickens told Fields of "a private reason rendering a long voyage and absence particularly painful" (A, 97). This was surely an allusion to Ellen, although it need not have meant that to the American; indeed, Dickens's vagueness (extramarital activity as "a private reason") might have been taken simply as a polite disavowal of interest.

Since war between the states broke out in 1860, Ellen Lawless Ternan is probably the main reason the reading tour became an event of the late 1860s. Ironically, an 1859 American engagement would have been medicinal, not debilitating, which is how the one in 1867-68 is frequently described: although the years 1858-59 were a period of tremendous personal upheaval for Dickens, his fatal stroke on 8 June 1870 was hardly in the offing. By 1867, with the Civil War over and Andrew Johnson in place of the assassinated Lincoln, Dickens's affair with Ellen was eight years old, a circumstance which may have caused a six-month absence to appear less painful—despite the "domestic reasons" for hesitating that Dickens was still vaguely citing in his letter to Fields a month before sailing (Y, 164).

Nevertheless, regardless of the evidence of the pocket diary, it would have been folly to send for Ellen. Dickensians have been foolish to believe that Dickens seriously intended to do so. A man who not only contemplated bringing his mistress to the New World but waited until Boston to make a final decision gives one's conception of the innocent abroad a new dimension. Inadvertently, Nisbet and Slater both suggest the implausibility of so naive a visitor by not supplying pertinent information: who were the "many" to advise Dickens against inviting Ellen and whose "the realization of the tremendous scandal that would ensue"? When was the advice tendered, the awareness of potential disaster achieved?

If both John Forster and Georgina Hogarth knew of the Ternan telegram code (A, 105), surely the former must immediately have counseled Dickens against taking Ellen. Dickens's literary adviser was the real stumbling block; he opposed the trip in its entirety and the readings themselves as a debasement for Dickens's talents. Flaunting one's mistress would have demoted to a misdemeanor what Forster already considered the grave impropriety of reading from one's work like a common actor.

Supposing Dickens overrode Forster's veto as well as Georgina's, could he have refrained from quizzing Dolby about America's attitude toward mistresses or rejected the negative tone certain to be audible in his manager's advice? Between 3 August 1867 and 11 September, Dolby had scouted America; traveling about with Fields's associate, James R. Osgood, he consulted prominent Bostonians and knowledgeable New Yorkers to determine whether Americans had forgiven Dickens for *American Notes* and would support the readings. According to Dolby's memoir, he interviewed civic leaders, appraised auditoriums, and estimated profits—all of which led to a preliminary

agreement with Ticknor and Fields (D, 93-129). In view of these elaborate precautions—such careful testing of the public's disposition and
the country's financial situation by a commissioned delegate and his
American adviser—it seems inconceivable that Dolby would have
tendered no opinion about bringing Ellen or that Dickens would have
insisted on waiting two months to gauge the moral climate for himself.

Slater's reference to the smoldering enmity of America's newspapers understates the danger. Dickens's old adversaries would gladly
have created a fatal uproar. In 1842, they had charged Dickens with
being hypocritical in coming as a guest and then asking for money (that
is, his royalties); most assuredly, they would have seized upon Ellen as
even stronger proof of his cupidity. How, editorials would have demanded, could he keep a mistress and still treat audiences as a virtual
congregation that laughter and tears were to uplift as gratifyingly as a
church service? "The knowledge that this most moral of novelists was
having an affair with a young actress," Sidney P. Moss concludes,
would have turned him "into a Pecksniff and the tour into a disaster"
(M, 254). Comparison of Dickens to *Chuzzlewit*'s celebrated poser,
Welsh's recipe for the first visit, would have been justified—and the
irony would have been colossal. Dickens could not have failed to fore-
see this outcome; nor could he have overlooked the immense satisfaction his being caught out would have given those Americans who still
resented the scorn shown for their manners and morals in *Chuzzlewit*'s
American chapters.

Yet Moss credits Dickens with these realizations only after the novelist was already in America: "No doubt he recognized that, as he
would henceforth be in the limelight, he would not be able to have Ellen come to him, no matter what ingenious plan he might devise for
concealing her presence" (M, 254). Hypothesizing such belated recognition for the obvious is even less generous than failing to specify
who perceived "a tremendous scandal" might develop if Ellen went to
America and when they said so.

More convincing is the description of an anxious Dolby getting
Dickens to his Boston hotel "quietly and without undue publicity until
they could ascertain just what the temper of the American public was
to be" (EP, 143). Only a few months earlier, James Gordon Bennett
had advised Dolby to have Dickens apologize to the American people
before returning; to make atonement seem necessary, his New York
Herald had then reprinted free for subscribers the entire text of Dickens's travel book (D, 123-24).[2] Dolby "feared that some crank, who
[thanks to Bennett] remembered 'American Notes,' might create a dis-

turbance which would get into the papers and work havoc with his roseate prospects and plans" (EP, 143). Clearly, the manager was determined not to aggravate old wounds, much less open new ones.

If Dickens actually arrived in America with the possibility of sending for Ellen still on his mind, the idea could never have survived the first night. Waiters in the Palmer House left open the door to Dickens's sitting room so that promenaders could "peep" in at him from the hall while he ate (D, 158-59). This "curiosity," Dolby recalled, did more than make "an unpleasant impression" on the visitor; it "caused him to regret that he had not adhered to his original determination never to visit America again." Dickens gradually rescinded his complaint that "these people have not in the least changed"; yet Nisbet and Slater require one to believe he left England expecting Americans not just to have improved "during the last five and twenty years" but to have become more open-minded about mistresses than his own countrymen were.

An article in the *Boston Post* (4 January 1868) reveals how ready the American press was to pounce: "Dickens does not live with his wife, it is said. This fact adds spice to this little story. (A lady well known in literary circles who suffers from an organ-ic disappointment, on the evening of the first readings sent Mr. Dickens a bouquet. The floral offering was returned with the thanks of the recipient and the announcement that a lady of London [the amateur actress Mary Boyle] supplied him with flowers for his buttonhole, not only in England but America.) Oh, Charles, at your age and with that bald head and that gray goatee!" (EP, 202). Besides the titillating allusion to a lady's "organ-ic disappointment," which may mean she lacked a man, one is struck by the loss of dignity in the transition from "Mr. Dickens" to "Oh, Charles"—precisely the form of insulting familiarity he had resented throughout his first visit. The writer commences with a bit of hearsay about Dickens's domestic arrangements in England; then he proceeds to put the reference to a London lady in the least favorable light: a man of Dickens's age, having given rise to scandal by separating from his wife, ought not to make matters worse by boasting of another woman's favors, even if they are only floral and yet plentiful enough to be showered upon him wherever he travels.

The example of Fanny Trollope, which Dickens knew well, militated against a married individual touring America with an unmarried person of the opposite sex. In addition to three of her children, a maid, and a manservant, Mrs. Trollope had been accompanied by a young

French artist, August Jean Hervieu, who had been living in the Trollope household as the children's drawing master. He was scheduled to
teach the slaves on Miss Wright's estate painting and French—a credible yet flimsy pretext for his presence, especially after the Nashoba
project collapsed.

"Although it is virtually certain that Mrs. Trollope's relations with
Hervieu were perfectly proper," Richard Mullen observes, "she realized that it would be best to keep his presence discretely quiet" (*DM*,
xiv). So the artist came aboard ship "separately and secretly"; and when
Mrs. Trollope wrote a book about America, he was never mentioned
in her text.[3] "Undoubtedly," Mullen admits, "this somewhat strange
travelling companion shocked many of Mrs. Trollope's American ac-
quaintances. It may have denied her invitations to better homes."

How, then, could Dickens have hoped to devise what Moss says he
needed: an "ingenious plan for concealing [Ellen's] presence"? It was
impossible to smuggle her into America as surreptitiously as the unknown Fanny Trollope brought along Hervieu. Nor could Ellen's subsequent presence have been kept from the army of ticket speculators
who followed Dickens from one tour stop to the next. Since Mrs. Trollope was denied access to so-called "better homes" despite the virtual
certainty that Hervieu was not her lover, Dickens must have recognized his improper relationship with Ellen as a greater social liability;
he could never have been royally entertained by James T. and Annie
Fields at their Charles Street salon, where the guest list of respectable
notables included Longfellow, Emerson, Oliver Wendell Holmes,
Professor Agassiz, and James Russell Lowell.

According to Edgar Johnson, who follows Nisbet's account unhesi-
tatingly in all other respects, "Ellen was going to Italy to stay for a while
with her sister Frances Eleanor and her brother-in-law Thomas Adolphus Trollope" (J, 2:1076). Had Dickens been intent on cabling for Ellen, she would have been better advised to remain at the ready in
England instead of proceeding to the Continent to be out of gossip's
range should the British press arouse its American counterpart by alluding to her.

In 1858-59, Dickens's correspondence after his break with Catherine revealed a man "seized by a panic" that "discovery" of a "skeleton
in his cupboard would destroy him" (N, 46). Having long since subdued his wife and her family, he nevertheless felt that to be truly "safe
and well" while reading in America, Ellen had best be dispatched to
a place of refuge, if only as a precaution. It was not enough to send her

to Florence; she had to be respectably housed there with a married sister, far away from the rooms Dickens apparently used an assumed name to rent for her in London.[4]

Finally, one may underscore the simplicity of the Ternan code itself. Dickens's memory, especially his grasp of practical detail, being prodigious, it seems odd that he would need to jot down the uncomplicated private meanings for such easily remembered phrases as "all well" and "safe and well." Having to record two short phrases seems as unusual as bringing Ellen to Boston via Italy would have been impractical. Conceivably, the code arrangement was concocted more for Ellen's emotional benefit than for Dickens's: to give the necessity for her Italian sojourn the appearance of a temporary expedient. The novelist may have gone to the extent of writing the code words down in her presence as proof of his abiding concern when he already knew before embarking—unless he was incredibly innocent—which message he would send.

Overly intrigued by Dickens's allegedly strong desire to have Ellen accompany him, Dickensians have lost sight of a larger problem facing the novelist: the tremendous obstacle to a second coming that John Forster represented. A previously unexamined letter from Dolby to Fields for 25 September 1867 sheds new light on the tour's troubled final planning stages and moves the question of what to do about Ellen out of the spotlight. In short, the mistress problem cannot be prolonged from spring 1867 through summer and into early fall. Contrary to Nisbet and Johnson, Dickens appears to have experienced less difficulty in persuading Ellen to remain behind than in securing Forster's permission to go.

Having found suitable halls in both Boston and New York, Dolby sailed on 11 September, reaching Liverpool on Saturday morning 21 September; passing through London, he continued straight to Gad's Hill and consulted with his employer until Monday 23 September. Then he brought Fields up to date in a letter from London on Wednesday, but it never mentioned "the result" of the Gad's Hill "deliberations," for nothing definite appears to have been decided, although it was just two months and seven days before Dickens's Boston opening. Dolby reported that he and Dickens went "full into the great American question & have a meeting on Monday to put the final touch to it and telegraph you the result" (FC, 1032). In other words, the matter was so debatable, so many last-minute difficulties unrelated to Ellen remaining, that even though the American publisher and his associates had already been kept waiting for thirteen days (indeed, since 1859, thanks to the Civil War), Dickens and Dolby agreed to postpone a final decision for another week.

Dickens was wavering, Dolby claimed, because he and his manager were unsure "of giving the requisite number of readings to produce the amount of money we require by the month of May, when Dickens would like to return to England" (FC, 1032). Dolby may have been gauging stamina: was Dickens strong enough to earn enough quickly enough? Yet Dickens had just scolded the London *Times* on 3 September for reporting that his rumored American trip was a medically prescribed cessation of labor (Y, 161-62). Also, since Dolby estimated profits from a projected eighty readings at less than Dickens realized from only seventy-six, the required amount must have seemed within easy reach. The real worry, the modern revaluator is apt to discover, was not explicitly mentioned on 25 September but proved formidable enough to account for an entire week's delay: Dickens and Dolby were not sure they could obtain Forster's approval, and until they persuaded him, they seem to have been unable to convince themselves completely.

A more discerning duo would have secured Forster's acquiescence ("the final touch") before opening negotiations with Fields or at least before sending Dolby to America to discuss dates. Each of these steps, especially the latter, was tantamount to going; yet Dickens unwisely saved what turned out to be the biggest hurdle for last, as if proceeding so far would compel Forster to add his assent. As a result of this miscalculation, Ticknor and Fields had been waiting two weeks for an affirmative reply when Forster was emphatically vetoing the very idea.

During their Gad's Hill conference, Dolby drew up a report regarding transatlantic prospects, which Dickens condensed to seven points, "the case in a nutshell" (D, 133-36). Not surprisingly, most of the arguments in America's favor appear to have been formulated with Forster's likely objections in mind. Since the demurring 25 September letter and this "case" were preludes to the marathon interview Dolby then had with Forster, one begins to comprehend the enormous diplomacy problem Dickens and his manager confronted. The adviser who thought public readings profaned an author's talents was being asked not to become mortally offended if Dickens went abroad to do a fresh series not just under a new counselor's supervision but upon his anti-Forster recommendations.

A hint of Forster-inspired uneasiness was already audible when Dolby's letter to Fields treated the upcoming interview with a touch of sarcasm. Having been deputized to enumerate Dickens's seven points, the manager observed: "I am looking forward to making the acquaintance of that *great* man" (FC, 1032). Although Forster's influence over Dickens supposedly waned in the late 1860s, the mixture of awe and disdain with which he still viewed his confidant seems to have rubbed off on Dolby. Equally marvelous is the strategy of pitting the newest adviser against one of the oldest—virtually an acid test to prepare Dolby for his buffer-like American role defending his employer from frustrated ticket seekers and avaricious speculators.

Instead of having to seek out Forster, Dolby only needed to return home after posting the 25 September letter. "The novelist's biographer," as he jealously dubbed Forster to distinguish him from *the public reader's biographer* (that is, himself), had taken rooms in the hotel at Ross; there he awaited consultation. This "odd coincidence," as Dolby called it, was later dismissed as a step the Londoner had taken "for the benefit of his health" (D, 136). The joke is rather pointed: since Dickens's fitness was at issue and the novelist generally referred to Ellen at this time as "the Patient" (because of her involvement with him in the Staplehurst railway mishap), Forster's concern is made to seem selfish. In fact, as Dolby's letter indicated, Dickens had instructed Forster to interview the manager. But subsequent mention of a "meeting to take place . . . in ten days after my arrival here" (D, 136) refers not to Ross but to the final decision-day conference with Dickens, set for Monday, 30 September—that is, for ten days after Dolby's return from America, a rather long deliberation period which it now becomes clear Dickens allocated not to conferring about Ellen but to overcoming Forster's opposition.

Dolby confessed to "considerable anxiety" because "much depended on the view Mr. Forster should take of the matter" (D, 136); nevertheless, the interview itself, as the irreverence implicit in "that *great* man" leads one to expect, is treated as an unmitigated farce: a four-page defamation of the novelist's biographer as a real-life Mr. Podsnap—too pompous, uninformed, and opinionated ever to have offered anyone sound advice. This most self-assured human being, Dolby recalled, had "made up *his* mind" against an American trip, and like Podsnap, a person only too well "acquainted with his own merit and importance" (*OMF*, 133), he assumed that settled it.

Just as Podsnap is always "flushing angrily" and declining to pursue topics he finds painful (*OMF*, 142, 147), Forster reportedly behaved in "the most unreasonable manner"; he carried on, Dolby claimed, "without any knowledge of the subject that I could see" (D, 136). As for the seven points, listing them was no different from "the meek man" reminding a complacent personage of "hideous solidity" that "some half-dozen people had lately died in the streets of starvation" (*OMF*, 136, 145): it amounted to waving "a red rag" at Forster-Podsnap, whom Dolby branded "more ferocious" than "a mad bull."

If the "case in a nutshell" was not designed with Forster's obstinacy in mind, Dolby mischievously tampered with cause and effect: he wrote down the points lucidly and then caricatured Forster's fulminations, making the points, in retrospect, more than equal to the objections and the objections ludicrous attempts at refuting the points. Thus Dickens had resolved that America was anxious to hear him, that he would restrict performances to "the great towns" (that is, Boston, New York, and "adjacent places"), and that he could expect full houses "on all occasions" with large profits in consequence. Indeed, points 3 and 6 both stressed the tour's metropolitan focus, while points 4, 5, and 7 emphasized the likelihood of financial success (D, 133-36). But Forster-Podsnap is depicted maintaining that America's "halls were not large enough" for Dickens's purposes; and "even if they were, there were not people enough" in the entire country to fill them (D, 137). "The oracle" announced that "there was no money in America, and, even if there were, Mr. Dickens would not get any of it; and if he *did*, the Irish . . . and the booksellers, between them, would break into the hotel and rob him of it" (D, 138). Furthermore, this model for Dickens's "eminently respectable man" (*OMF*, 134) is made to insist, illogically, that "a sea-voyage was the very worst thing in the world" for someone whose health had been shaken by "the Staplehurst [railway] accident" (D, 137).

Comical though these arguments sound, it took the better part of three days—26, 27, 28 September—to break down Forster's resistance. Dolby made little headway the first morning; Dickens, whom he summoned that afternoon as a reinforcement, fared just as dismally when he arrived next day. Forster informed Dolby that he would write to Dickens "by to-night's post" (on 26 September) to "tell him how fully I am opposed to the idea, and that he must give it up" (D, 138); this letter, along with Dolby's summons, brought Dickens to Ross. Although he spent the night of 27 September at Forster's hotel, matters did not improve until lunch on 28 September, when the besieged fort finally surrendered, but Forster told his opponents he only did so because "you have made up your minds" (D, 139).

By 27 September, therefore, Dickens and Dolby clearly wanted to go, yet the former apparently could not accept Fields's proposition without first obtaining Forster's permission—no matter if it had to be coerced. Arguably, Forster's vigorous support throughout the copyright controversy made the novelist reluctant to return without his old ally's benediction. He had most likely talked matters out with Ellen and had a safe place picked out for her. Still, if he encountered fresh difficulties abroad or accidentally reopened old wounds, he may have needed to be sure that Forster would again protect his reputation back home. September 29 being Sunday, "the word 'Yes' was cabled to Messrs. Ticknor and Fields" on Monday, 30 September—that is, only after Forster had been squared away.

Dickens acknowledged Ellen Ternan as "the gigantic difficulty" that must be "beaten" before he could recross the Atlantic; but this passage comes from a letter to W. H. Wills for 6 June 1867 (Huntington MS 18387)—long before Dolby went on his preliminary survey. The novelist may have been trying to be funny and certainly sounds hyperbolic, or else he recognized that Ellen's hold on him was now a greater obstacle than his need for her had been in 1859. Whatever the case, he would have written Wills differently on 25 September, by which time one presumes the mistress problem was less pressing because Forster had clearly replaced Ellen as the principal last-minute "difficulty."

The contest with Forster can be reconstructed virtually blow by blow if one combines the 25 September letter with relevant passages from *Charles Dickens As I Knew Him*, whereas the code messages "all well" and "safe and well" appear *undated* on a blank page at the back of a pocket diary for 1867. The code could have been worked out at any time during that year as a means of placating Ellen, thus meeting the "difficulty" described in the letter to Wills, and freeing Dolby to investigate American prospects seriously. Not passion for a young lady but continued regard for an old yet troublesome friend seems to have detained Dickens in England in the fall of 1867. And it would have been inexpedient to discuss Ellen with the Fieldses during that August-September because he and Dolby were preoccupied with Forster, on whose account the tour literally hung in the balance. Veiled references to this problem in the manager's letter suggest that Dickens did not want to disclose the Forster impediment, much less talk about his mistress. The 25 September missive would not reach Boston until *after* the decisive telegram of September 30, so Dolby may have mentioned Forster in case the cable answer was negative; then Fields could read between the lines of the follow-up letter and not blame Dickens.

Fred Kaplan believes that as late as a month prior to his departure, Dickens "still hoped to have Ellen join him" (K, 513-14). His argument rests on the second of two paragraphs in Dickens's letter to Dolby for 16 October:

> It will be a relief to you when you get this, to know that I am quite prepared for your great atlantic-cable-message being adverse. When you get this, the message will have been delivered and will have become a thing of the past, but in case it *should* be adverse the knowledge of my preparation that way may be agreeable to you. I think it likely that Fields may see shadows of danger which we in our hopeful encouragement of one another may have made light of. But I think the message far more likely to be No than Yes. I shall try to make up my mind to it, and to be myself when we meet.

Before quoting part of the above passage, Kaplan observed: "having charged Dolby on this second trip to consult with the Fieldses, both of whom knew about" Ellen, Dickens instructed the manager "to get his and their opinion about whether it would be safe to have her come."

But item 25 in a bound volume of Dickens letters in the Free Library of Philadelphia (DL/D686) does not support the inferences Kaplan has prefixed to it; it contains no mention of Ellen or Mrs. Fields and no commission to query one about the other. Nor does it assume prior knowledge of Ellen's importance on Annie's part or her husband's. Instead, the catalogue description relates the letter to "a lecture plan of James T. Fields," which suggests, as does the passage itself, that the issue was the gala New York opening Dickens and Dolby ardently desired, an idea the Boston publisher had probably vetoed. (This disagreement, recorded in Dolby's 30 September letter to Fields, is discussed in the next chapter.)

Dickens's first paragraph is quite specific regarding the cabin reservations he had just made for himself and Kelly, Dolby's assistant. Thus the second paragraph's failure to name names is disappointing. "We" could refer as easily to Dickens and Dolby as to Dickens and Ellen; "shadows of danger" is melodramatic but could be a weather report on renewed anti-Dickens sentiment in New York's newspapers. Such hostility, a problem with which Dickens and his manager were obsessed yet apparently wanted to discount, would have made an imperative of Fields's preference for a Boston commencement.

Inasmuch as cabin arrangements on the *Cuba* were already settled, Dickens's hopes of Ellen accompanying him must have been faint. Whatever its subject, the October letter's tone is noticeably resigned, its request almost pro forma. The man who sent it hardly expected an affirmative reply and could not have been promising his mistress one.

Dickens sounds relieved by the imminent "No" and has written expressly to spare Dolby anxiety; since a New York premiere for the tour was the manager's brainchild, such absolution makes sense. Although the resolve "to be myself again" could refer to affairs of the heart, its serio-comic stoicism is typically Dickensian, a mix of hyperbole and facetiousness that also colors the "great atlantic-cable-message."

If Kaplan's interpretation is correct, Dolby did not broach the mistress question during his August-September fact-finding visit. Raising it now, when he had come to supervise advance ticket sales, would surely have been awkward: more than two weeks had passed since he cabled the Chief's "Yes" to an American engagement. If the Fieldses "knew about" Ellen, would they not have asked Dolby sooner about provisions for her? Since Fields exercised little control over tour length and ticket prices (chapter 5 will show that his advice was disregarded), it seems improbable that Dickens would ask him to decide this critical matter. Still, if Kaplan is right, Dolby's position was unenviable: having survived the coercive interview with Forster, he now had to secure Fields's approval of his employer's mistress.

If the October letter empowered Dolby to inform Fields about Ellen, the publisher was probably hearing the full story for the first time—unless Dolby described her as Dickens's protégé just as Mrs. Trollope had called Hervieu her assistant. Even if the manager told all, Fields need not have transmitted the disclosures to Annie. Since no record of the "great atlantic-cable-message" has survived (Kaplan assumes it was "not determinative either way" [K, 514]), one surmises that it pertained to business just as Dolby's letters to Fields for 25 and 30 September had, and that Dolby was relieved to learn Dickens had not staked his happiness on the outcome of the upcoming interview. Kaplan's indeterminate cable, on the other hand, would mean that Ellen had to wait for *two* crucial cables in 1867, this one in mid-October and another from Dickens toward the end of November.

Additional arguments against Dolby conferring with the Fieldses come from Kaplan himself. Admitting that "no conclusive evidence has surfaced to determine whether or not their relationship was sexual," he treats "Dickens's intimacy with Ellen" as one of the era's "open secrets" but experiences great "difficulty" deciding "what any individual knew and when" (K, 410, 461). He estimates that only an "intimate circle of fifteen or so" perceived the truth during Dickens's lifetime (K, 461, 428), and one can supply the names of that many persons more familiar with Dickens or more essential to him between 1858 and 1867 than the Fieldses.

As it turned out, Dickens landed the afternoon of 19 November, and although the first reading was not scheduled until 2 December and he had scarcely as yet left his Boston hotel room, Wills received a cablegram with the negative words "Safe and well" on 22 November (J, 2:1078). Either it took Dickens two days at the most—20-21 November—to rule out Ellen's coming, or too much has been made of the code arrangement.

On the afternoon of 20 November, Longfellow called on Dickens, but it is hard to imagine so "benign and handsome" a figure, "with his white hair and long white beard" (J, 2:1078) being asked to cast the deciding vote on Ellen. On 21 November, however, something more momentous occurred: Dickens dined at the home of Mr. and Mrs. Fields. To his surprise, he found that the young fellow he had delighted at the Boston dinner in 1842 and had become friends with eight years earlier in London "was now a brown-bearded man of almost fifty" (J, 2:1078); even more surprising, Fields's wife Annie, whom he had only met a few times in 1859, was a vibrant thirty-three, just five years older than Ellen. Thus she was seventeen years younger than her husband, just as Ellen had been eighteen to Dickens's forty-five when they met in 1857 (an age differential of twenty-seven years).

Although Fred Kaplan has called Ellen "witty, playful," even "bold" (K, 411), her personality has left its mark on such difficult femmes fatales as Pip's cold-hearted, man-hating Estella (*Great Expectations*) and the fortune-hunting Bella Wilfer (*Our Mutual Friend*). In addition to being just as good-looking, Annie Fields was more intelligent than Dickens's mistress and much more susceptible to genius. Ellen can hardly be described as "a warm-hearted woman with the courage to glory in a permanent relationship" with a world-famous author, but Arthur Adrian's list of her shortcomings (A, 80) matches Annie's ministering abilities perfectly. She was very attentive and yet content to bask in Dickens's glory; that is, she willingly reflected its warmth back upon him, a sincere tribute to the novelist's talent and masculinity that one suspects was at least as invigorating to him at fifty-five as more palpable feminine services might have seemed.

For the possibility that Dickens "may have taken counsel with Fields" concerning Ellen during those "first three days in America" (A, 100), no tangible evidence has been found. Within forty-eight hours of landing, however, Dickens could easily have sensed in Annie Fields the attractions that subsequent events were to prove she possessed abundantly: a unique mixture of sisterly-daughterly regard and wifely-womanly sympathy that Dickens had been seeking since Mary Hogarth's death but had not always successfully obtained from Ellen Ternan upon separating from Catherine.

En route home in 1868, Dickens wrote warmly to James T. and Annie Fields in terms nearly as problematic for the modern revaluator as the coded telegram sent to Wills: "You will never know how I loved you both; or what you have been to me in America" (NL, 3:645).[5] If, however, neither had been told the whole story about Ellen, intimacy must have proceeded only so far. Subtract her from James's cognizance, and the publisher was unknowingly boasting falsely when he wrote of growing "so near" to Dickens that the latter "would reveal to me his joys and sorrows, and . . . the story of his life from his own lips" (Y, 128).

Whether or not Dickens was confiding such delicate matters as his traumatic stint at Warren's Blacking or his involvement with a young actress,[6] he and Fields sat for six months on a bombshell that could easily have exploded to smithereens their mutually profitable enterprise. Success of the second visit depended upon continued maintenance of a secret concerning a very live skeleton in Dickens's cupboard at home. In all likelihood, he and Dolby knew more about the chances they were taking than any of their American friends did, including Fields, who was running the same financial risks. These would have come into the open the moment Ellen followed Dickens to America.

Ironically, Dickens was guiltless of duplicity during the first visit, when roundly charged with it, but less so, although unaccused, during the second. Welsh's likening of the copyright seeker to the novelist's own Pecksniff is therefore sorely misplaced (AW, 33-36). In 1842, Dickens did not abuse the laws of hospitality by agitating for copyright protection; nor did he conspire with British publishing interests about such agitation before leaving England. When on 29 April Dickens urged C.C. Felton to distribute a petition that Forster had asked Bulwer, Carlyle, and others to sign, he claimed that "the British brotherhood," taking "fire at my being attacked because I spoke my mind . . . on the subject of international copyright," have "transmitted to me this small parcel of gauntlets for immediate casting down" (Y, 133). This statement in a letter Fields quotes in its entirety was close enough to the truth. Having spoken his colleagues' opinion by voicing his own, he was entitled to call a belated endorsement voluntary—its tardy arrival proved that there had been no conspiring.

In 1867, in contrast, Dickens was an innocent abroad mainly as an English performer insufficiently familiar with the audacity of American ticket speculators; when presenting himself to the public or to James T. and Annie Fields (particularly the latter), his innocence may well have depended on their ignorance. If he did not actually misrepresent himself, he never corrected the wrong impressions others, including Annie, had formed of his unhappy domestic circumstances. Since the prevailing idea of the readings as family entertainments would have been damaged by full disclosure of those circumstances,[7] Dickens arrived under false pretenses in 1867 rather than in 1842. Although he and Forster never conspired prior to the first visit, it is harder to acquit Dickens and Dolby before the second: the latter's scouting of the country in the fall of that year may have been intended to ascertain not only what Americans remembered from the copyright furor twenty-five years earlier but what they had heard about Dickens since the marriage breakup of 1858-59.

As late as 1867, Dickens's modern biographer opines, the novelist thought Frances Ternan Trollope and her husband were still unaware of the exact nature of his relationship with Ellen (J, 2:1060).[8] If he could keep her sister and brother-in-law in the dark for nearly a decade and use them to house his mistress respectably while he performed in America, surely he would not have instructed Dolby to mention Ellen to prospective associates in August 1867, nor would he himself have raised the subject after that November, when the readings were about to commence. By then, he and Fields were committed to a program promising splendid rewards, and Annie's admiration had made Ellen's presence less essential.

The modern revaluator may well decide that neither James T. nor Annie Fields knew all, if indeed they knew anything definite, about Ellen Ternan—at least not before most, if not all, of the readings had been given, probably not while Dickens was still in America, and possibly not even during his lifetime. The major reason for these conclusions, which are given in order of decreasing plausibility, is the frustration one experiences finding conclusive evidence to the contrary.

For the Fieldses' apparent ignorance of Dickens's true feelings for Ellen, on the other hand, no shortage of material exists from which to infer and conjecture. No letter, book, or diary entry by either husband or wife during Dickens's lifetime contains a clear-cut reference to his sexual involvement with Ellen. The American publisher and his spouse could, of course, have been part of the conspiracy of silence that Dickens was able to effect but surely not in Annie's private diary. Whenever she mused about filling up Dickens's emotional life or meeting his sexual needs, as she seems increasingly to have done, her thoughts turned to Georgina Hogarth. Dickens's sister-in-law repeatedly emerged as the likeliest candidate for Annie to envy, the person she most strongly suspected of taking the place in reality that she herself could occupy only in notebook fantasies.

As these multiply, settling upon literal meanings becomes problematic; still, it appears evident that Dickens was not averse to flirting with Mrs. Fields. She sounds convinced that he had not just solicited her regard but had given her to believe there were no serious rivals for his deepest affections. Dickens's conduct is less culpable if one grants that, although not inexperienced, he did not anticipate that Annie would respond to his requests for sympathy so ardently; not having read her diary, he may not have been fully aware of how ardently she had responded. Also, he may have been surprised to discover himself, a man with one mistress already, feeling the pull of an additional attachment—a pull that disclosed the limitations of his relationship with Ellen by revealing how lonely and unsatisfied he still was.

Thus one must take exception both to Philip Collins's suggestion that Dickens should not be blamed "for somewhat falling in love" with Annie (GC, vi) and with George Curry's conclusion that Annie herself was never "flirtatious" (GC, 59). Her diary does *not* indicate that even in its pages she never crossed the "delicate line between deep friendship and . . . [a] passionate intensity" at odds with "her wifely devotion and Christian principles." On the contrary, it was the one place the reader can be certain she made that transition, at first not without a struggle and often without admitting to herself—or at least trying to disguise—a yearning too strong and physical for Curry to euphemize as "utter fascination" (GC, 59). As will be shown, M.A. DeWolfe Howe, Mrs. Fields's literary executor and the first editor of her diaries, was very discreet when stating that Dickens "found in the Charles Street house of the Fieldses a second home" (MH, 137).

Previous assessments of the bond between Charles Dickens and Annie Fields run the gamut from the innocuous to the unintentionally insinuative to the ridiculous; they come from explicators unfamiliar with (or oblivious to) unpublished portions of the latter's diary, some of which Curry has made public. Annie is glowingly eulogized as "Dickens's greatest admirer and closest friend among the women that he knew in America" (EP, 141), a statement true enough yet incomplete; so, too, is the euphemistic judgment that she "had a great fondness for Dickens" (M, 251), or that she was "one of his Platonic favorites" (K, 509), merely "a close friend" (SN, 208). These misfires are less surprising in view of Annie's occasional propensity to be ambiguous, perhaps actually deceiving herself: "I feel, somehow, like one of his daughters," she informed her diary, "and as if I could not take too good care of him" (EP, 243), yet the second half of this compound declaration seems in danger of suborning the opening.

Less charitable is W.S. Tryon's dislike for the "cult of adoration" the otherwise "sober and sane" Fieldses allegedly established around Dickens, who thus fell victim to their "suffocating excesses" (T, 312), as if to the snares of an American Mr. and Mrs. Leo Hunter. The usually sensible J.W.T. Ley proffers the most laughable summation: at a time "when Dickens so needed friendship . . . during that tragic American tour . . . , Mr. and Mrs. James T. Fields . . . looked after him as though he were their only son,"[9] when he was fully five years older than his publisher and twenty-three years senior to Mrs. Fields. Angus Wilson's explanation supplies in tact and understatement what it lacks in disclosure: "Mrs. Fields, a lively, sympathetic American woman, gave [Dickens] just the understanding and slightly flirtatious companionship that he needed"[10]—except that her actions became increasingly serious, an important matter to her; that is, to her it was far more important than the unexpected but temporary blessing it seems to have remained for him.

Only the unscholarly Hebe Elsna insists vehemently that Dickens took Annie Fields thoroughly into his confidence: much to her delight, she "knew all about his worries over his sons, his affections for Georgy and his reliance on her, his liaison with his 'beautiful Nellie' " (E, 173). Indeed, continues Elsna, "Annie derived a vicarious excitement from hearing about this secret love affair" (E, 174). This is surely two parts fact and one part fancy, if not ultimately a lurid fiction; yet it usefully typifies the anachronistic lapses in most examinations of Dickens's last three years: the tendency, for example, to apply what is now known about Dickens's failing health in 1869-70 as if it had been apparent in 1867-68 or to enrich Dickens's affair with Ellen by assuming that Thomas Wright's *Life of Charles Dickens* (1935) appeared not only during the Inimitable's lifetime but prior to his second visit to America.

Elsna's instincts are sounder, however, than Ley's or Tryon's. She is correct about Dickens's sons and his regard for Georgina, and she speaks more truly than she realizes of a "vicarious" sexual excitement. It was not derived from Annie's putting herself in Ellen's place, however, but came, instead, from imagining what it would be like to be Miss Hogarth. Three days after Dickens left for home, Annie's musings about Georgina more than preclude her having learned about Ellen during his visit; they reveal, albeit indirectly, how pleasurable the challenge of tending to the wifeless Dickens had come to seem to her by spring 1868:

My respect for Miss Hogarth grows as I reflect upon Dickens. It is not an easy service in this world to live near such a man, to love him, to desire to do for him. He is swift, restless, impatient, with words of fire, but he is also and above all, tender, loving, strong, far-sighted, charitable and patient by moral force. Happy those who live and bear, and do and suffer and above all love him to the end—who love and labor with and for him. He *can* be, he *must* be, the whole world and the light of the future to them. Miss Hogarth has labored for him with remarkable success and for his children [five or six words scratched out] But even now he might be lonely, such is his nature. When I recall his lonely couch and lonely hours I feel he has had a strange lot. May his mistakes be expiated. [DAF, 25 April]

Miss Hogarth's position as an unmarried woman in charge of Dickens's household fascinated Annie. Despite the lip service her diary pays to convention by regretting the impropriety involved, she viewed what she elsewhere considered Georgy's "unnatural" and "anomalous" occupation (DAF, 25 February 1870) as a unique and enviable opportunity.[11] Disguised as an expression of "respect" for Dickens's sister-in-law, Annie's fantasies about taking care of genius could proceed apace. By the end of this increasingly unguarded passage, Annie's "I" has displaced both Miss Hogarth and the "happy" few whose continuing intimacy with Dickens, a chance to devote their lives to his welfare, the diarist seems to be imagining for her own. No woman aware of Dickens's relations with Ellen could have dwelt so long on his loneliness. If Annie had understood that he was steaming home to his mistress, she would not have meditated so affectingly on his temporarily empty bed, nor could she have regarded Georgina as a rival whom she nonetheless felt compelled to defend, as if to normalize her own strong feelings.

Annie Fields's lasting impressions of the recently departed Dickens depicted a vigorous, volatile individual apparently in his prime, not a burnt-out case with one foot in the grave after seventy-six grueling readings. She conceded that being helpmate to genius would seldom be "easy service," but even Dickens's faults, the product of an intense and virile energy, fueled her "desire to do for him." Swiftness, restlessness, and a tendency to use fiery language were aspects attractive to a woman confident she had also seen, and could easily bring out, his deceptively passive virtues: tenderness in spite of a "strong" sense of justice, and charitable patience that was actually a manifestation of great "moral force." Such force, in fact, that it "must" equal "the whole world" for those exerting themselves on its behalf. The insistence suggests an Annie who invokes the captivation others have experienced in order to justify her own yet wonders if they are as appreciative of the favor Dickens has granted them as she would be.

Reflections on Dickens's "strange lot" and the hope that his "mistakes" can be "expiated" could constitute veiled allusions to his connection with Ellen. So could an early diary entry—nearly six months earlier, in fact—in which Annie, already interested, notes how the newly arrived Dickens "appears often troubled by the lack of energy his children show, and has even allowed James to see how deep his unhappiness is in having so many children by a wife who was totally uncongenial. He seems to have the deepest sympathy for men who are unfitly married and has really taken an especial fancy, I think, to John Bigelow, our latest minister in Paris who is here, because his wife is such an incubus" (DAF, 28 November 1867).[12]

Significantly, this entry, like the one for 25 April, substantiates only two of Elsna's three points: Dickens confessed parental anxieties and alluded to marital unhappiness but did not mention a liaison with Nellie. Perhaps James was "allowed . . . to see" more than he told Annie, but the vague reference six months later in a personal diary to "mistakes" still seems to indicate a lack of precise knowledge concerning anything beyond an unfortunate marriage.

Annie Fields was obviously a perceptive woman whose understanding of Dickens's psychological and emotional state deepened steadily throughout the winter-spring of 1868. But the visiting novelist seems to have misled her from the start, which would have prevented her from fathoming his true condition. In November, she was analyzing an interesting stranger, whereas the April entry speculates rather intimately about a close friend's lack of a satisfactory love relationship. In both instances, however, Dickens is seen as the unhappily married man, a not uncommon phenomenon, as the reference to Bigelow proves;[13] he is never the admirer of a young girl no older than his daughters. That may well have been a social anomaly beyond the ken of a nineteenth-century Boston publisher's wife, who considered Georgina's presence at Gad's Hill sufficiently risqué.

Both diary entries—one from near the beginning of Dickens's visit and the other shortly after its end—indicate that he was not remiss in soliciting Annie's sympathy for his predicament as a wifeless parent—he was doing so in late November shortly after their initial meeting and by April had thoroughly ingratiated himself as an object for concern.

But Nellie disappears as a possible conversation topic between Dickens and Annie Fields if the modern revaluator, emphasizing her absence from *both* passages, uses each to illuminate the other and the latter to gauge progress since the former. The second passage probed deeper and considered Georgina but divulged nothing not implicit in the first. The novelist's "strange lot" thus meant that he was "unfitly married" and had separated from his wife; ironically, the person who could become "the whole world and the light of the future" to anyone who loved him, the novelist who championed hearth and home, was living under a cloud and had to rely for domestic comforts on his estranged wife's sister. In other words, Annie sincerely regretted that the man universally idolized, whom she elsewhere called "perhaps the greatest genius of our time" (*MH*, 190), had to risk scandal by living with Georgina but nevertheless was obliged to sleep alone.

The juxtaposed entries are as fascinating for what they tell about Annie as for their disclosures concerning Dickens. Everywhere in the diary when Dickens is the focus, she camouflages her feelings or comes to terms with them obliquely. The April entry shifts almost unconsciously from the desire simply to "live near" a man like Dickens to the indiscreet wish that his couch might become less solitary. In the November entry, James, not Annie herself, has been "allowed to see" Dickens's "deep disappointments," just as the ostensible object of scrutiny in the April passage is Georgina's situation rather than the diarist's state of mind. Annie seems overly emphatic, indeed pleased, when stressing how "totally uncongenial" Dickens had found Catherine, whom the diaries for 1867-68 never mention by name. The resoundingness of the rejection guaranteed Dickens would never go back, yet it also seems to have blinded Annie to the illogicality of not acting upon the discovery of a spouse's complete incompatibility until after twenty-two years of marriage.

If Dickens afforded James T. Fields glimpses of his unhappy personal life in November 1867, it follows that the publisher's prior knowledge could not have been extensive, either in 1859 when he first tried to set up an American tour or eight years later when he succeeded. Dickens was probably not appealing to Annie circuitously by confiding in her husband, but her conjectures about the novelist's fondness for Bigelow as a fellow marriage victim suggest that these overtures were not without impact (no matter how unintentional at first) and soon became less indirect. In addition, Dickens's emphasis on his children's "lack of energy" implied that his own surplus of it was difficult to sublimate, as if his excess resulted from their failure to burn up theirs.

Perhaps Dickens divulged everything to James in the late fall of

1867 and the latter withheld news of Ellen from his wife. If so, she appears none the wiser during their 1869 visit to Gad's Hill. Assigned to Dickens's bedroom, neither James nor Annie could sleep; it seemed as if Dickens's habitual wakefulness during much of the American tour had overtaken them. In a letter to her mother that Arthur Adrian quotes several times, Annie attributed Dickens's "sleepless nights" to his not having "a free heart" (A, 124, 126; 4 June 1869). Assuming she was referring her mother not to Dickens's entanglement with Ellen but to his separation from Catherine, a matter of public knowledge, one may take the passage to mean that he was weighed down by responsibilities and, even worse, still legally bound to an unwanted wife. Thus Annie characterized him as "a sad man," hardly the term for someone in love with a younger woman who had consented to become his mistress.

Despite having what she considered the jolliest time of her life during this visit to Dickens's England, Annie could still recall something ominous about it more than a year later, by which time Dickens was dead. Prompted by the anniversary of his demise, Annie remembered her sense of a "shadow" hanging over Gad's Hill (DAF, June 1871), but she seems to be in the dark as late as the summer after Dickens's death as to its exact nature, or else, in retrospect, she dampened the pleasure of her final time with Dickens because she realized that her sleepless host had then only a year and five days to live. That Annie would mention Georgina's compromising position and yet characterize Ellen only as a "shadow" also seems improbable.

This second visit to Dickens was of greater intimacy than the one the Fieldses had paid ten years earlier, for it built upon the many attentions the publisher and his wife had shown the visiting reader in Boston; their English host was anxious to reciprocate tenfold. He took rooms in London at the St. James Hotel for himself, his daughter Mamie, and Georgina Hogarth so that he could be near his American friends whenever James's business in town precluded parties at Gad's Hill. But Ellen must not have been included in any of the round-the-clock festivities Dickens staged, such as the outing to Canterbury or the churchyard picnic at Cooling (J, 2:1113). Neither Fields nor his wife appear to have been asked to play cards with Dickens and Ellen or to attend a musical evening in the apartments he allegedly maintained for her; yet several of Dickens's other friends—individuals such as Francesco Berger [musical director of *The Frozen Deep* (1858)], a man no closer to the novelist than Fields professed to be—have reported accepting invitations in the 1860s (N, 25-27).

"Happy those who live and bear, and do and suffer and above all love him to the end"—were a less scrupulous revaluator to cite this April 1868 benediction from Annie's diary as a virtual declaration of love, nothing in the Fieldses' subsequent visit to Gad's Hill or in letters about it would indicate that she changed her opinion or underwent any revulsion of feeling during the remainder of Dickens's lifetime. She was convinced that, in knowing him, she had feasted on honeydew and was right to attempt to envision what drinking the milk of paradise as part of her daily regimen might be like.

Arthur Adrian believes "there is evidence to suggest that the Fieldses knew of Nelly Ternan" in 1867-68 (A, 114); unfortunately, the tidbit is ambiguous and only appears in the diary subsequent to Dickens's departure. The day after he had reached Liverpool on his journey home, Annie Fields rhapsodized: "I cannot help rehearsing in my mind the intense joy of his beloved. It is too much to face, even in one's imagination—and too sacred. Yet I know today to be the day and these hours *his hours.* Tomorrow Gad's Hill" (DAF, 2 May).

Concurring with Adrian, George Curry writes: "This must surely lend credence to the supposition that when she wrote this entry, [Annie] knew something of Ellen Ternan" (GC, 27). But *what,* if anything, did she know? Having mused at length about Miss Hogarth's curious relationship to her brother-in-law, could she have accepted so rapturously the idea of Dickens having a *second* irregular household, this one run by his mistress instead of his sister-in-law? Curry suggests that Dickens may have misrepresented Ellen to Annie "as the great unrequited love of his life"—a daring ploy if her husband knew the real story, as Curry believes he did (GC, 59).[14]

For this entry to implicate Ellen, one must take "his beloved" to be single when it could as easily be plural, thus referring to Dickens's children and his sister-in-law; like the noun "beloved," used elsewhere for her husband, "sacred" would have to be accepted as Annie's unconventional adjective for an adulterous liaison; and hardest of all, the firsthand reportage of George Dolby, Dickens's traveling companion, and the reuse of it by Dickens's modern biographer (J, 2:1097) would have to be overturned.

All of Annie's other daydreams about Dickens's return to England envision his reception in the plural. Thus on the second day after he left, she reflected: "He goes to the English spring, to his own dear ones, to the tenderness of long tried love" (DAF, 24 April), all of which has familial connotations. In another entry for the same day, Annie revealed that she and her husband were so crushed by Dickens's departure that they could not bear to mention him or look at his photograph;

instead, they "furtively" ransacked newspapers for last mentions of their idol. She then quoted one such notice to the effect that Dickens "has gone home to his dear ones and to the splendor of England's summer"—adding simply that she has been repeating it "over and over" to herself (as the earlier use of "his beloved," proves) in an apparent effort to substitute his happiness for her increasing sense of loss.

One must interpret "beloved" as singular, Adrian assumed, because Annie's diary indicates that Georgina and her nieces and nephews had been requested not to meet Dickens at Liverpool but to await him at Gad's Hill; hence "the day" and "these hours" allegedly alluded to a tryst with Ellen, even if they could just as readily pertain to Dickens's anticipation of the next few days' events.

Actually, Annie's diary shows her behaving like a new widow, not a woman who has been abandoned for another. She anticipated Dickens's landing, describing it as "that day of joy to *them*" (that is, his relations; italics added). Then she added that "Dickens has given orders to have no one at Liverpool but I know of two or three hearts whose joy will be keen as pain" (DAF, 27 April). These hearts, one assumes, belonged to Dickens's children and Georgina, but their number most certainly included Annie's, with its commingled feelings of relief upon Dickens's safe arrival and mounting regret over his absence. Similarly, the subsequent entry in which she portrayed herself "rehearsing . . . the intense joy of his beloved" contrasted their state with hers: "today was *his* day of joy. It rains here!" (DAF, 2 May). In brief, Annie could not sufficiently underscore the contrast: happiness for Dickens and his family in the spring/summer of homecoming as opposed to bad weather in Boston as a projection of her dismal condition.

Annie's visualization of Dickens finally at home also manifests its share of ambiguity: "This morning," she began, "dear C.D. is at Gad's Hill," whereas "yesterday" she "felt sure C.D. was in London. What hours for him!! How can one be grateful enough for them" (DAF, 3 May). The wonderful "hours" Annie exclaimed over could be either the hypothetical London reunion with Ellen or the entire repatriation process. The only thing emerging for certain from Annie's diary between the end of April and early May 1868 is the herculean effort required to quell her own sorrow by imagining the "intense joy"—"It is too much"—of some sort of reunion, probably between Dickens and his family rather than with Ellen. To make things easier, she supposed herself present at it, if only in her "imagination," which had not just been thinking about such an event but "rehearsing" it again and again with a creativity surpassing Madame Bovary's.

George Dolby's version of the homecoming contradicts Adrian's inferences from Annie's ambiguous imaginings. He recorded that Dickens "deemed it inexpedient to travel to London the same night" after a "long and rough voyage," so the pair "were comfortably housed" in the Adelphi Hotel, "remaining quietly in Liverpool" until they could "continue [their] journey the following day" (D, 328-29). "By arrangement," Dolby continued, "there were no friends to meet us at the station [Euston Square] to give us welcome after our travels," so it was London, not Liverpool, as Annie thought, at which Dickens's family had been instructed not to wait for him, with a similar and therefore hardly eccentric interdiction covering Dolby's relations. Dickens and his manager then parted—"he for his home in Kent, and I," wrote the manager, "for my home in Herefordshire."

From the moment they left the deck of the *Russia* in Liverpool until Dickens turned away toward London's Charing Cross Station, Dolby implied that he and his charge were inseparable—more like close friends than employer and employee—just as they had been intimates throughout much of the American tour. Dolby's account leaves little time or room for the romantic interlude that Adrian reads into Mrs. Fields's musings, much less for the extravagant week-long dalliance that George Curry posits.

His contention that Dickens, despite a six-month absence, stayed in London with Ellen for the week of 2-9 May before continuing on to Gad's Hill to see his children rests solely on a notice in the *Chatham News and North Kent Spectator*: the issue dated 16 May states that the novelist returned "last Saturday."[15] By comparison with Dolby's detailed eye-witness report, a brief newspaper announcement—one not internally dated—is a slender thread from which to suspend a sensational argument. Even if the notice appeared promptly after being written (that is, when "last Saturday" was still 2 May) and the writer thought he had the date correct, it would still be insufficient evidence to discredit Dolby because it also contradicts Annie's timetable, which had Dickens at Gad's Hill by 3 May.

Dolby also recorded that the day after his separation from the homeward-bound Dickens being Sunday, "the bells" of Boz's "own church rang out a peal after the morning service in honour of his return." Surely better informed than a nameless journalist, Dolby ought to know for whom this bell tolled and when. Moreover, when the manager next saw his former charge in London "the following Thursday" (7 May), he attributed the Chief's returning health to good weather and "four days' rest at Gad's Hill" (D, 330-31), although according to Curry Dickens had not yet gone there.

The modern revaluator points again to the April diary passage expressing "respect" for Georgina Hogarth as a decisive preclusion. The blessings Annie conferred on those fortunate individuals who, unlike herself, would be able to "love [Dickens] to the end," cannot include Nellie because the novelist's sister-in-law is so uppermost in the diarist's ruminations. For "beloved" to encompass Ellen or refer to her instead of Georgina and her nieces and nephews, Annie would have to have learned about Miss Ternan sometime between the second or third day after Dickens left (24-25 April 1868) and the day after he landed at Liverpool (2 May). Even if one supposes this sudden increase in knowledge, proof that she knew of Ellen *during* Dickens's visit would still be lacking. If James, informed by Dickens at some earlier point, finally broke the news to soften her sense of loss and put her friend's regard for her back into proper perspective, Annie's diary evinces no shock or disappointment at hearing of another rival more serious than Georgina.

During the Fieldses' 1869 visit to England, Annie and Georgina "took to each other at once"; it marked what has been called the beginning of "a lifelong friendship based on their joint adoration of Dickens" (A, 124). Following the visit, Georgina wrote intimately and confidingly to the American woman who "had also come under Charles's magnetic spell" (A, 181); she timed her later epistles so that they would mark Dickens's birthday, the day of his death, and Christmas. But their tone did not grow increasingly warmer until after 9 June 1870, when Georgina needed sympathy from another idolater. Before that, she frequently sounded rather formal, writing to Mrs. Fields in Dickens's place—that is, in a semisecretarial capacity.[16] Thus one distrusts Curry's supposition that "the real substance of [Annie's] private talks with Miss Hogarth [in 1869] went unrecorded" in her diary (GC, 43), for none of the ninety-three letters Georgina sent Annie between 1869 and 1913 makes explicit mention of the woman whom the man they both venerated probably actually physically loved.

Consequently, the only genuinely sensational allusion to Ellen Ternan by either Mr. or Mrs. Fields occurs in Annie's diary for 6 December 1871, when Dickens had been dead over a year: I "heard quite accidentally to human eyes the other day of N.T. being in Rome. . . . I feel the bond there is between us. She must feel it too. I wonder if we shall ever meet." With this singular exception, the diary entries from the time Dickens left America until his death record Annie's struggle to accept her role as a temporary ministering angel to a man with many admirers whose professional and creative life, she sadly realized, would hereafter lie elsewhere.

Annie's discretion is amazing. If "N.T." indeed stands for Dickens's mistress (one might have expected the less familiar E.T.), the use of initials in a personal diary not likely to be seen in her lifetime by anyone except, possibly, her husband, seems unnecessarily elaborate. So, too, is the incompleteness of the entry, which omits the source of the information, leaving the reader to wonder what kind of accident Annie had experienced: did she read something not addressed to her or overhear remarks not intended for her ears?[17] Was information about Ellen kept from her out of consideration for her feelings? The most one can hazard is that by the winter of 1871, one year and six months after Dickens's death, Annie Fields may have known the full story about his mistress for some time, but the intensely private reflections to which the news of Nellie's whereabouts then gave rise resulted in an entry simultaneously revealing and enigmatic.

More astounding than Annie's discretion is her undaunted penchant for indulging in ludicrous fantasies. The Annie who had previously identified with Georgina now selected Nellie as an alter ego, the "bond" between them being their mutual attraction to Dickens. Just as she could imagine herself presiding over Dickens's household, Annie seems to have been willing to picture herself as being as closely tied to Dickens as his mistress was.

At precisely this point, remaining persuaded that Annie knew the whole truth about Ellen yet viewed her own relations with Dickens strictly in a spiritual light means accepting a contradiction. Curry's monograph, for example, cannot have it both ways. One must abandon either the notion that Annie's "worship" of Dickens was "a mystic bond" she felt Ellen might also have experienced or the argument that Annie had "positive evidence of Dickens's [sexual] interest in Ellen" (GC, 59-60). If Annie knew all about Ellen, she could not have described the tie both allegedly felt to Dickens *and to each other* as a spiritual one; if she felt the tie was spiritual, she probably did not know everything about Ellen.

That Nellie felt any tie to Annie seems preposterous; it assumes that Dickens talked glowingly to Ellen of the woman whose attentive adoration had made his desire for his mistress's presence in America less pressing. On the contrary, one surmises that Dickens would have experienced a double difficulty introducing his mistress and the visiting American woman to each other in London in 1869. Annie would have learned that she was far from being the novelist's closest female friend, while Ellen would have realized that she had been upstaged by her stand-in during the reading tour but without either woman's knowing it. Instead, Dickens wisely introduced Annie to Georgina, the unorthodox but respectable housekeeper she was expecting.

Annie's wonderings resemble Charles Bovary's absurd fascination with the first of his wife's lovers: meeting Rudolphe after Emma's death, the foolish husband wishes himself in the place of the man who displaced him.[18] But speculation as to whether she would "*ever* meet" (italics added) Ellen proves that Annie was not vouchsafed an encounter during the Fieldses' visit to England the summer before Dickens's death, which suggests that her husband was never introduced either—or that introductions were not followed by intimate conversations and full disclosure.

Kaplan has concluded that Ellen's "visits to Gad's Hill need not have revealed to those on the perimeter more than the impression that she was a friend of the family" (K, 500). This was how the Fieldses would have classified her if such a meeting took place. No conclusive evidence exists in Annie's diary for Kaplan's subsequent self-contradicting conjecture that in spring 1869 "Ellen came to visit at Gad's Hill, where probably she met the Fieldses" (K, 543). If Annie was wondering in December 1871 whether she and Ellen would "ever meet" *again,* perhaps she ought also to have added *now that I know all.*[19] In 1869, therefore, Dickens was willing to conduct Fields, Sol Eytinge (illustrator of the Diamond edition of Dickens's collected works for Ticknor and Fields) and Dolby "through the lowest criminal dives of the Ratcliffe Highway" (J, 2:1113), a tour performed under police protection; but he may never have taken the publisher and his wife totally into his confidence.

Of the numerous ways to chart Dickens's second American engagement—from city to city, in terms of receipts from successive readings, or as the medical history of the worsenings and abatements of a very bad cold—none is more engrossing than following his progress into Annie Fields's heart. She went from awe or hero-worship to a feeling that her liking for Dickens was reciprocated, to an acute sense of separation and loss. The pattern of increasing regard coupled with strong physical attraction led her to a sort of culminating fantasy on the morning of 27 April; except for Curry's monograph, which misreads it, this passage in her diary has never been quoted in print. It is one of several previously ignored entries indicating that Dickens transformed the period of Annie's life from 28 June 1859 through May 1868 into a Victorian love story never told outside her notebooks.

Ironically, the sense of growing endearment disclosed by their pages runs counter to both of the other patterns unfolding at the same time. As the impression Dickens made on Mrs. Fields strengthened, he was allegedly becoming physically weaker, his health breaking down. Also, the greater Dickens's profits when ticket sales soared for the farewell readings in Boston and New York, the severer Annie's impending loss began to appear as the departure day loomed. But the spell that the genius and vitality of a supposedly tired and ailing man cast over Annie remains of paramount interest; it was no less powerful and probably far more excusable than his hold had been on Mme. De la Rue, whom he called a "most affectionate and excellent little woman"; her "undesirable intimacy" (J, 1:541-42) with the novelist had annoyed Catherine dreadfully during the Dickens family's travels in Italy more than twenty years earlier.

A leaf from Annie's "English Diary 1859" shows that she met Dickens perhaps twice during that trip, but the warmth with which she described what appears to have been a first encounter is surprising: "Dickens came in the morning. Such kindliness as shines through that man's clay. We dine with him next week" (DAF, 28 June). Unfortunately, Annie was "too ill" to keep this engagement, so only James went to Gad's Hill with Dickens and Wilkie Collins (DAF, 6 July).

Mrs. Fields apparently did not dine with Dickens at Tavistock House until she and her husband returned from the Continent next spring, as evidenced by her entry for 6 May 1860. She goes on to observe that a "shadow has fallen" on Dickens's house, "making [him] seem rather the man of labor and of sorrowful thought than the soul of gaiety we find in all he writes." Since early May was a time when rumors about Dickens and Ellen could still have been circulating, Mrs. Fields's failure to be more specific even in the privacy of her diary is regrettable. Still, the separation from Catherine was already two years old, and the Hogarths (Kate's mother and sister, Helen) had long since retracted the gossip they had helped to start. Whatever the "shadow" was and whether or not Annie learned its exact nature or, more likely, was simply noticing that marital disappointment had caused Dickens's mood and appearance to belie the tone of his early novels, it did not deter her from looking forward to a "visit . . . at Gad's Hill bye and bye"—a visit one may suspect never took place or else went unrecorded.

Only one extended reference to Catherine appears in Annie's private musings but not until three years later, a signal nonetheless of her unflagging interest in Dickens's marital problems: "Mrs. Dempster called upon Mrs. Dickens as well as upon Dickens when in London. She found the former *living alone* and very sad. She desired to talk freely of her severe lot. She thinks they both suffer deeply because of their mistake. Her love for him is quite evident to all" (DAF, 12 September 1863). This is the closest Annie ever came to sympathizing with the unwanted wife. Five years later, in the entry for 25 April 1868 analyzed above, only Dickens's loneliness concerned her. But "lot" and "mistake" are the same words she applied to Dickens after he had sailed for home. Meditating upon his "strange lot" and hoping "his mistakes" could be expiated seems to establish that Annie still regarded him in 1868 the way she viewed Catherine in 1863: as a lonely individual with whom love and marriage had dealt unkindly.

Just after the midpoint of the reading tour, James brought home a newspaper containing what Annie called "the saddest of sad letters, written at the time the separation from his [that is, Dickens's] wife took place. The gentleman to whom he wrote it has died and the letter has stolen into print. I only hope the poor man may never see it" (DAF, 27 February 1868). The change is from curiosity about Mrs. Dickens in 1863 to an extremely personal regard for Dickens himself; it was already growing strong enough by late February for Annie to wish she could protect "the poor man" from his own past—yet another indication that the Fieldses knew little of Dickens's involvement with Ellen and had imperfect recollection of the "Violated Letter," of which this "saddest" missive is either the revival or a virtual twin.[20] Current news of Ellen, one realizes, would have raised more eyebrows and done more damage than a ten-year-old letter, one that maintained Annie's dominant image of Dickens as a man separated from his wife for a decade but forever being painfully reminded of that fact.

The biggest news the spring after Mrs. Dempster's call on Mrs. Dickens was Hawthorne's death (DAF, 19 May 1864); although James T. Fields had consulted a doctor about him, it had been too late, and Ticknor and Fields was minus its headliner. Possibly, Fields had long been considering Dickens as an eventual replacement, hence the bid to bring the novelist to America on a reading tour as early as 1859. Two years after Hawthorne died, when Annie jotted down Oliver Wendell Holmes's remark, during breakfast with the Fieldses, that Dickens is "a greater genius than Thackeray" (DAF, November 1866), the major figure to be wooed by the publishing firm had surely been determined. By the following August, Dolby had come to survey prospects for a reading tour to be hosted in Boston by Ticknor and Fields, now Dickens's authorized American publishers, and in November, Annie was recording her husband's account of Dickens's arrival "in grand health" (DAF, 19 November).

Initially, entries in Annie's diary pertaining to Dickens's visit are all business; she wrote down any observations that the great man ventured if they were literary in nature. She noted, for example, his opinion that "Mr. and Mrs. Lewes" were "both exceedingly homely" but that George Eliot was "very interesting with her shy manner of saying brilliant things" (DAF, 29 November).[21] One wonders who—Dickens or Mrs. Fields—decided to refer to George Eliot and G.H. Lewes as a married couple; such propriety, if it originated with Dickens, further militates against an immediate frankness about Ellen.

From an undated entry (sometime between 22 and 28 November), one learns that a certain "Mrs. Bigg" was forbidden to enter Dickens's rooms in future because she jealously assaulted a widow to whom the novelist had granted an interview. Whether or not this harridan was John Bigelow's wife, whom Annie earlier called "an incubus," the focus in this passage has already changed from professional to personal; also, despite the omission of illuminating details for what was probably a comic incident, Annie's awareness of the interest other women express in Dickens is unmistakable. By spring, when the same "Mrs. Bigg" apparently went after Dickens again, he would be saved by Annie (DAF, 12 April).

Even by Christmas, however, after the Fieldses went to New York for the first set of readings there in early December, one finds indications of deeper affection: Annie reported that she and James "cannot help loving [Dickens] as all must do who have the privilege of coming near him and seeing him as he is" (DAF, 24 December)—an encomium in such beatific terms that it sounds as if the subject must be almost divine and yet a deity whose manliness also appealed to her. As the new year commenced and Dickens arrived not just for dinner but to stay through the readings of 6-7 January, Annie referred to her guest at 148 Charles Street as "the dear chief" (DAF, 4 January); thereafter, his name seldom appears without some term of endearment. Thus although De Wolfe Howe's *Memories of a Hostess* (1922) was rightly subtitled "A Chronicle of Eminent Friendships Drawn Chiefly from the Diaries of Mrs. James T. Fields," no other celebrity in those diaries is mentioned so lovingly throughout.

How important an addition Dickens had made to Annie's emotional life—and all within the space of two months—became clearer after that short visit in early January. From then until late February, when Dickens was on tour through New York, Philadelphia, Baltimore, Washington, Hartford, and Providence, Annie missed him greatly; he was seldom absent from her mind or her diary. It is not inconceivable that, without wishing to say so even in her private notebook—indeed, without being fully aware of it—Annie was already half in love with Dickens, perhaps passionately in love or on the brink of it for the first time in her life. During his forty-six-day absence, whenever she thought of him, she confessed that she grew elated; so much so, in fact, that she continually looked around for someone to help, for a good deed she could do, to use up these astonishing surges of charitable energy.

"How the month slips away," Annie exclaimed, perhaps somewhat wishfully, four days after their visitor left for his New York engagements: "We think of Dickens a great deal & find ourselves talking of him in a kind of unconscious way to each other, wondering what he is doing *now* or startling ourselves and each other with some reminiscence from the Reading. I don't think anybody ever gave more pleasure during a little visit than he, in this, to us" (DAF, 11 January). Curiously but doubtless as a semiintentional form of self-deception, Annie attributed to herself and her husband James a joint emotional life and a common nervous system, as if neither could think or feel startled without the other's reacting in kind. But one may ponder whether James *and* Annie or *just* Annie spent the entire month "wondering" from one moment to the next what Dickens was doing, reliving the Boston readings, and savoring over and over the "pleasure" of his recent visit.

In mid-February, Annie interrupted her reading of *A Tale of Two Cities* to anticipate "the next two or three weeks," which were to be "connected" exclusively with Dickens, all other plans having been put aside (DAF, 15 February). Three days later, as self-appointed guardian of the novelist's reputation, she wrote: "Whatever unpleasant is said of Charles Dickens I take almost as if said against myself. It is so hard to help this when you love a friend" (DAF, 18 February). The nature of the unpleasantness went unexplained, but one doubts it pertained to Ellen Ternan.[22] Earlier, Annie had concluded that people were jealous of Dickens because "he had excited more love than most men" (DAF, 26 January), a tribute to his powers that may have been offered on the basis of personal experience.

As things turned out, Annie and James T. saw Dickens before he returned to Boston: they traveled to Providence to hear him read

"Marigold" on Friday 21 February (M, 332), although Annie's entry for 22 February, the morning after, says "Sunday," not Saturday. She discloses that she "lay awake from pure pleasure after such a treat. Hearing 'Marigold' and having supper afterward with the dear great man. We played a game at cards which was most curious—indeed, something more—so much more that I have forgotten to be afraid of him" (DAF, 22 February).[23]

From this passage it seems reasonable to assume that Mrs. Fields believed the distance between herself and the awe-inspiring Dickens was narrowing; she felt her relationship with "the dear great man" was now one of mutual regard, no longer simply a woman's infatuation with a celebrated entertainer or a case of that entertainer patronizing an ardent admirer. Although Dickens was still "great," Annie could moderate the stature keeping him out of reach with a sense that he was also (and wanted to be) a "dear" one; he was closer to her now insofar as he appreciated the fondness she felt for him, which he had somehow acknowledged wanting and inspiring.

Dickens had often taken the lead when he, Dolby, and other guests at the Fieldses' James Street residence indulged in parlor games that December and January, but this February card game in Providence was apparently of a different order: if Annie's cryptic entry is trustworthy, the game brought into full consciousness feelings she had not dared to confront in her diary, much less to suppose Dickens might reciprocate. From Providence on, the appellative regularly conferred on the visiting reader became "Dear C.D." (DAF, 24 February).[24]

Four readings scheduled in Boston for the first week of March were canceled because of impeachment proceedings against Andrew Johnson (the vote to impeach had been taken on 25 February). Dickens amused himself by overseeing the "Great International Walking Match" between Osgood and Dolby, in which Mrs. Fields's involvement is too well known to need additional corroboration from her diary and letters.[25] The point to remember is not the unfair assistance she tendered the winner, Osgood, by feeding him pieces of bread soaked in brandy, which kept up his strength in the closing stages of a thirteen-mile walk through snow in frigid weather; rather, her interference designates her the only woman ever to have participated so significantly in Dickensian highjinks, those inherently mock-heroic larks contrived to stave off boredom and burn up the Inimitable's excess energy. He usually regarded them as an all-male preserve.

During Dickens's second extended absence from Boston (6-30 March), James T. and Annie Fields exchanged letters with him; she tracked his progress through upstate New York and New England, noting, for example, his stop at Niagara (DAF, 14 March) and counting the days until his return. One entry preserved her husband's expression of enthusiasm for Dickens's "many sided intellect and the large heart and the noble spirit we call Charles Dickens" (DAF, 12 March); another reported how she and her husband "laughed till we cried" over one of Dickens's letters (DAF, 20 March); a third disclosed that she had "finished 'Our Mutual Friend' "—she judged it "one of Dickens' finest books" (DAF, 22 March).

Thus, throughout March of 1868, having "forgotten to be afraid" and considering their relationship as "something more" than hostess to guest, Annie thought about Dickens unceasingly. She talked about him, wrote to and received letters from him, and read his latest novel—all ways of staying in contact. With month's end only eight days off, she anxiously awaited not just Dickens's return and the final Boston performances but the "flight to New York" that she and James had planned in order to attend the farewell readings there as well (DAF, 23 March).

Only as March concluded and April began did Annie voice serious concern about Dickens's health. One must remember that he had been out of her sight for weeks at a time, so that some of his difficulties were invisible to her, and that she had referred to the subject previously; even so, her prognosis at the end of Dickens's fourth month in America was positive. When the Fieldses dined with Boz at the Parker House, Annie "found him in the best of spirits because his travelling is all over and he is within eleven readings of home. His catarrh still clings to him but he is better and will feel quite well if he can sleep—but he has no talent *that* way with all his gifts" (DAF, 31 March).

In other words, to a person becoming greatly absorbed in Dickens's well-being, there appeared to be no cause for alarm as late as 31 March, with sixty-five of the eventual seventy-six readings completed. Dickens could see ahead to the end of his labors; he still had a cold but was mainly troubled by insomnia. Typically for Dickens's contemporaries but contrary to his modern biographers, Annie beheld no suicidal workaholic in the spring of 1868; as the American tour neared its end, her "dear great man" seemed in better condition than posterity has been willing to allow.

Judging from Annie's diary, one may conclude that Dickens's biggest health problems did not assail him until early April, when, oddly enough, he had ceased traveling. It is as if the pressures he had been under—hurrying, for example, from Syracuse to Rochester to Buffalo to Rochester to Albany and thence to Springfield, Worcester, New Haven, Hartford, New Bedford, and Portland, or eleven cities and thirteen readings within twenty-one days (9-30 March)—finally caught up with him the instant he slowed down.[26] Such a rigorous schedule, however, reflected poor planning by Dickens and Dolby jointly, not some sort of self-destructive compulsion on the performer's part.[27]

According to one of Annie's entries for early April, Dickens was "too ill" to visit her: he was "in a wretched state of health" and yet that night, she marveled, he "read . . . magnificently." Not until Dickens had just seven performances to go did Annie mention the possibility of cancellations—"we beseech him not to finish the readings" (DAF, 7 April)—but the point was to spare him further stress, not to lengthen a life perceived as gravely endangered.

In the same entry that entreated Dickens to desist, Annie talked self-revealingly about the toll the readings took on audience and performer alike: "we all agree that it is very exhausting to go to the Readings. We become excited, sleep is almost an impossibility until morning—this, added to prolonged attention in listening and our feeling for the Reader himself makes this great pleasure one of the most absorbing we have ever experienced" (DAF, 7 April). An excited, exhausted, sleepless Annie exhibited all of Dickens's postperformance problems except for his catarrh. She makes the "great pleasure" of listening to the "Carol" or the "Trial" from *Pickwick* sound like a unique form of torture, a pleasurable ordeal with enduring aftereffects. Either one must redefine the kind of popular entertainment Dickens gave as something too stimulating for anyone's good, an emotional exercise more enervating than the American camp-meetings Mrs. Trollope reviled (*DM*, 144), or else look past Annie's use of "We" and "our" to an intense personal preoccupation with "the Reader himself," an absorption peculiarly hers. If the strain of giving readings caused Dickens's sleeplessness, he caused hers.

Dickens's health, Annie reported, obliged him to forgo the Boston farewell dinner, at which Longfellow was to have presided (DAF, 8 April). But the visiting reader's approaching departure, not his temporary indisposition, remained paramount in her thoughts as April progressed: "I felt how deeply we had learned to love him . . . for us to part" (DAF, 10 April).

Similar anxieties seemed to overtake Dickens at about the same time, or so Mrs. Fields's entry for a Sunday in New York (two days later) leads one to believe. She and Dickens began innocently enough by talking of Lemaitre, the French actor, and about the difference in the taste of fish in England and America; but Annie was agitated all the while by "the feeling of his presence, the flashing eye which loses nothing, the kind strong hand, the face so worn by all the fires of the spirit" (DAF, 12 April). These "fires," she encourages one to believe, were not so much creative energies as pent-up passions, unspoken declarations. The modern revaluator must remind himself that this heat and warmth was radiating toward Annie apparently by design from a glowing Dickens allegedly too ill just four days earlier to attend a public banquet.

After French actors and fish, Dickens and Annie spoke of Mrs. Galverston, an unfortunate woman (either separated from her husband or divorced) "who had come to us in Boston to ask if she could succeed as a reader there" (DAF, 12 April). At this point, Dickens's role in the conversation and in Annie's diary changes dramatically; the change is noted more explicitly than the one that occurred previously during the Providence card game. Dickens seems to step out of the diarist's fantasies in order to make an almost overt appeal for a larger helping of the wifely-sisterly combination of admiration and compassion she had long wanted to bestow more openly. Dickens, wrote Mrs. Fields, "then said how much wrong on both sides there had been in that case and most others—speaking somehow with a consciousness of his own position underlying the words . . . yet with a firm and even eager manner. Though he was addressing me I could not look at him and when I raised my eyes *at last* as he ceased speaking I saw a look of suffering about his face which showed as neither his voice nor words had done how painfully [sic] the subject was upon which he had found himself launched."

Of course, Annie may have misinterpreted Dickens's intentions or read into them what pleased her—the use of "somehow" to define his method of alluding to himself is as vague and subjective as the analysis of his facial expression. Her inability to "look at" Dickens while he spoke and the effort required "at last" to raise her eyes to his compare with countless episodes in Victorian fiction in which the embarrassed but extremely pleased heroine shyly listens to the hero's marriage offer.

To someone already overwhelmed by Dickens's "flashing eye" and "fires of the spirit," such a solicitation must have been well nigh irresistible. Mrs. Fields's agitation is therefore excusable: Dickens's declaration of personal unhappiness, containing an implicit request for solace and understanding, could be considered a performance that outstripped his reading of "Marigold," which had already caused her a sleepless night. Recalling how polished and moving an actor Dickens was in public, one may wonder whether he exercised similar skills on this private occasion. Had he "found himself launched" on the subject of personal misery or had he broached it intentionally? If the former, he had to be phenomenally innocent, too full of self-pity to calculate the tremendous impact he was having. If the latter, he seems a bit caddish to play so heavily on a woman's sympathies, especially when she was the wife of his American publisher. But it was definitely not the sort of appeal he could have attempted with a woman who knew he had a mistress.

Although Annie wrote down her regret that Dickens had been taken "lame" the night before the New York press dinner (DAF, 19 April), the sleepless night she spent prior to his departure distressed her more (DAF, 21 April). A lengthy entry for the day of separation, perhaps forever, features a telltale shift from the plural ("we") to the singular ("I") that always signals the breaking out of Annie's strongest feelings:

Rose at six this morning sleep being out of the question—I must confess to sitting down in my night-dress in a flood of tears. When I remember all Dickens has been, has become to us in these short short months and that I can never see him again under the same conditions, even if we should ever meet at all in this world it seems more than I can bear. Jamie feels this too but he will go to the steamer and will always have a more [word unclear] -full connection than is possible on earth between men and women. In the numbers of people who have lavished everything upon Charles Dickens, the beautiful, the inspired, what to him can be the tenderness of one woman like myself—I say this and then I remember how precious beyond all gifts is the gift of love and I feel instinctively that what is everything to us *must* in Heaven's goodness be something to him. Mary Dickens' letter has not reached us unhappily! [DAF, 22 April][28]

The "flood of tears," the lament that she will never again see Dickens under such favorable circumstances (that is, as guest of honor in her home), and a complaint that relationships between men enjoy advantages denied to those between men and women—cumulatively, these constitute a major outburst of grief at impending loss. Annie Fields would not even be able to see Dickens steam away. For her he had become "the beautiful, the inspired," expressions of an extraordinary nature, surely, if not the actual realization of being deeply in love; for Dickens, however, in contrast, she was just one caring woman in a world anxious to shower "everything" upon him.

Annie seems to have tormented herself with her own sense of insignificance. Not mistakenly, however, she already foresaw her contribution to the reading tour subsiding into a passing phase in Dickens's life, whereas he had become the focus of hers. For consolation, she could only assume that a woman's "tenderness," the "gift of love" that is "precious beyond all gifts," had to mean a lot to Dickens because it has always meant "everything" to "us," that is, to women generally and to her in particular. This assumption would have seemed even truer if, as appears likely, Dickens had appealed to Annie for sympathy.

Complaining about an overdue letter from one of Dickens's daughters sounds anticlimactic in this context but is not: convinced she was to be denied the kind of shipboard parting scene she deserved, Annie considered maintaining a direct line to Gad's Hill extremely important if she was to avoid losing all connection with Dickens.[29]

Between 22 April, a Wednesday, and the climactic entry the following Monday that is the diary's Dickensian high point, entries build steadily in emotional energy as if forming a crescendo. On Saturday, three days after Dickens had gone, Annie wrote: "we count the days when letters will come from him but with a sadness nothing can heal for his presence" (DAF, 25 April). In addition, she recalled "the hours we have sat with him watching the kindling of his sad eyes, their swift flashes, their frequent merriment! That skull so delicately yet so strongly defined, the whole glowing presence! We can think of nobody but Shakespeare as ever having been like him." Allowing for Annie's infatuation, one can still accept as factual a fifty-six-year-old Dickens who flashed, glowed, and kindled despite his bad cold and long schedule, a man whose creative effervescence gave him so singular and inspiring a vitality that few holy men possess its equivalent and only the immortal Bard, among writers, may have surpassed him.

Having penned the passage about her "respect" for Miss Hogarth, an entry discussed earlier, Annie adopted a penitent, self-sacrificing tone, hoping she would soon get past her sorrows: "I know it is wrong to give up to this and when the skies clear I shall try to work for others and forget not *him* but myself" (DAF, 25 April). This, too, could originate from a Victorian novel, whose heroine had just been either jilted or widowed. Self-abnegation would begin once Annie's tears stopped.

Mrs. Fields then added that she was reading Crabbe's "The Lovers' Journey," which Dickens had suggested. Since this poem is mediocre and lifeless, one wonders why the departing Dickens steered her toward it. Crabbe's John (Orlando) rides to see Susan (Laura) but learns that she has forsaken the appointment to visit another. As the hero pursues her, a landscape that seemed idyllic moments before turns ugly and hateful. Alternative endings seem to follow: in the first, Laura apologizes and promises to return next day with Orlando; in the second, he returns despairing and alone. Crabbe's point was that nature shines gloriously "When minds are joyful"; but when "they sicken," they "Cast their own dull and melancholy hue" upon everything.[30] Was Dickens flattering Annie by suggesting that his own journey home to a springtime England, a journey toward which he had been eagerly working, would be less pleasant for leaving their association behind?

On Sunday, Annie refused to believe it was merely four days since Dickens had said goodbye: "It seems ages, long years" (DAF, 26 April). In a tone one might expect from Coleridge's "Dejection: an Ode" or from a downcast Byronic hero facing exile, she groaned: "the thread of life will be difficult to take up and our fires will smoulder as if nothing could awake a flame again." This was not Dickensian hyperbole; Annie sounds sincerely convinced that she would never be able to resume her former existence. Furthermore, reference to "fires" now doomed to "smoulder" is quite sexual, regardless of the "our."

Next morning, however, something did "awake a flame again." Although not all of the words are written legibly enough to be unmistakable, the vividness of the experience recorded is like Tennyson's at a critical point of *In Memoriam* when the deceased Hallam's "living soul was flash'd on" the poet's:[31] "By night as we lie down we pray for him and in the morning I awake dreaming that he [Dickens] has just come to say 'goodbye'—I see that sharp painful look dart up his brow like a lightning of grief. I feel his parting kiss on my cheek and see my arms stretched out to hold him—vanished. It was but one dreadful moment, yet now that it is over the pain of it lasts—lasts. We both of us tried to avoid it but it was inevitable" (DAF, 27 April).

Teeming with enticing ambiguities, this climactic entry teases the would-be revaluator of Dickens's American engagements into thought and beyond. To "awake dreaming" could mean that Annie had just awakened from a dream and was unsure whether she was awake or asleep or that, paradoxically, she experienced the dream, the illusion of Dickens's presence, upon waking—as if prayers recited the evening before had summoned him. Is the scene that follows her fantasy or a replay of the actual parting? Is the "dreadful moment" that actual parting or this apparent reliving of it? What does the "it" refer to that they both "tried to avoid" but that Annie mentions five times? Was it Dickens's "sharp painful look," a taxing parting scene, some inadvertent declaration of strong mutual attachment during that scene when his kiss triggered her unpremeditated detaining embrace, the mutual attachment itself, or, although most unlikely, some engagement between them even more improper and inexpressible? Could "us" simply indicate Annie and James, who may have resolved not to dwell so obsessively on their loss of an admired and beloved companion?

The "sharp painful look," which Annie renders so convincingly, resembles the one Dickens trained on her in New York on 12 April. Perhaps Annie's dream is a conflux of more than one scene. Nevertheless, using the present tense adds to the impressiveness and immediacy of the writing: the "feel" of a "parting kiss" and the sight of her "arms stretched out to hold" the vanishing, miragelike Dickens suggest an abnormal intensity of feeling; it goes well beyond what a wife ought to have felt for her husband's most valued addition to his publishing list, no matter how much their friendship had ripened in the space of five short months.

De Wolfe Howe deliberately omitted this fascinating passage on grounds that Mrs. Fields expressed her grief "and the genuine sorrow of . . . her husband at parting from a friend who had so completely absorbed their affection . . . in terms which the diarist herself would have been the first to regard as more suitable for manuscript than for print. The pages that contain them throw more light upon Mrs. Fields . . . than upon Dickens" (*MH*, 187). Such discretion was commendable yet ultimately unpardonable because a similar bowdlerization also befell many of the passages quoted earlier in this chapter, such as the conversation on French acting and American fish that led to Dickens's disclosure of his unhappy "position." Also, the assertion in the last sentence is debatable: throughout Annie's diary, new light is thrown on Dickens, too, especially if one tries to deduce what actions on his part may have prompted her entries.

Following the waking dream of Monday 27 April, Annie imagined Dickens's return to Gad's Hill via Liverpool and tried to share in the joys of his homecoming. In light of the dream, however, Adrian's surmise that on 2 May Annie was generously relishing Dickens's reunion with Ellen becomes even more implausible; he never discusses the waking dream passage.

It was more than two weeks before Annie could exclaim: "First letter from dear Dickens!!!" (*DAF*, 14 May), and she waited more than three weeks again until 11 June for a second.[32] In between, she jotted down her determination "to be patient now and expect nothing" from a man whose "work presses on every hand" so that he "must let his friendship keep in his heart" (*DAF*, 21 May). It sounds as if Annie, feeling neglected, tried to invent excuses for Dickens, as happened again when she attributed the lack of letters to his being in Paris (DAF, 23 May).

But a note of petulant disappointment eventually modified the excusatory tone: "A whole month has gone since Dickens left us! We have had but a short note *since* his arrival. He is overwhelmed with business but is not too much occupied to forget some little things he was to send us: the very smallness of them proving his attention all the greater" (DAF, 31 May). The neatly turned phrase after the colon could be an attempt at self-reassurance; his execution of small favors proved she had not been completely forgotten. On the other hand, it is difficult to separate excuse-making from resignation and personal regret in a subsequent entry (DAF, 7 June): Annie reminded herself "how strong Dickens's power to attract is and often times what a burden really to him when he cannot give a satisfactory response to the feeling he has excited."

Intense though one finds the waking dream of 27 April, descriptions of its recurrence inadvertently tend toward the comic. Annie's entry for 7 June is sensible enough: she reported that she continued to dream of Dickens at night and to talk about him with James all day. After Dickens, she grieved, "other men, many others, seem so dull and inapprehensive," a lament that one thinks ought to have perturbed her husband. By the end of the month, pleasures of the preceding April-May were still so ever-present, Annie wrote, that "I suppose we cannot wonder, one night he [James] dreams of Longfellow, I, the next, perhaps of Dickens" (DAF, 29 June). Poor James, it appears, was obliged to perpetuate Annie's regret for her experience of a lifetime now over, but he was not permitted to dream about Dickens, not even on alternate nights when his mind was clear of Longfellow and the subject of Dickens became available.

Gradually, something of the gleam must have faded. The unadorned entry stating "I dreamed we had letters from Dickens last night" (DAF, 5 July) seems typical of this subsidence. Nevertheless, when letters did come on 20 July, Annie rejoiced—"We live with Dickens for days after his long letters come" (DAF, 21 July)—yet nothing actually in the missives surviving from this period suggests that they should have affected her so strongly or that news of their arrival merited capital letters ("A LONG LETTER from Charles Dickens" [DAF, 31 December]). Dickens wrote steadily but at greater intervals (26 April, 14 and 25 May, 7 July, 30 October, 16 December).

On 27 August, Annie was pleased to have received a letter from Mary Dickens, but only a month and a half later, when she ascertained that Dickens was about to start his readings again, she sounds sorry to have to hear of him mostly "from the papers" (DAF, 19 October). Thus she read the account of his November triumph with a preview performance of the murder of Nancy in the London *Times* (DAF, 2 December). Later, in 1869, she made herself reread the terrible scene from *Oliver Twist* and dreamed both of it and Dickens all night. But the Fieldses were not destined to experience "The Murder" firsthand; the final tour for Chappell's was postponed for health reasons in late April, shortly before James and Annie stepped across the pond in May.

As late as 15 February, when the Fieldses wrote to announce this trip, Dickens foresaw no insuperable health problems; he wrote back exhorting his American friends to "arrive before the Farewells were over." To be certain they did, he supplied dates for "the Final Course of Four Readings in a week" (7, 8, 10, 11 June), adding that besides "the London nights," he would do "3 morning murders . . . not yet announced" (FC, 1226). Unfortunately, Annie never got to record her impressions of "dear C.D." as Bill Sikes striking down Nancy—possibly murdering Catherine by proxy. One can only wonder whether the spectacle would have altered her predominant image of him as a "sad man" whose good spirits had been dampened by marital misfortune, an image of Dickens as victim.

In spring and early summer 1869, when the Fieldses saw Dickens constantly in England, Annie's entries indicate that she had brought her emotions firmly under control. Besides recording a burgeoning friendship with Miss Hogarth as a way of sublimating her regard, Annie adds virtually nothing to accounts of the visit in her husband's *Yesterdays with Authors*, which are recapitulated in Edgar Johnson's biography. Until the reference to "N.T." in Italy examined earlier, there are few post-1869 intimate allusions to Dickens. "Our dear friend Charles Dickens died last night" is the way Annie's diary noted the expiration of one of its principal figures (DAF, 10 June 1870). Thereafter, she never failed to remind herself of this anniversary, just as she regularly commemorated Dickens's birthday.[33] His "lightness of heart" forever remained her standard of measurement, as when a party afforded her "more jollity" than any other "except at Dickens's" (DAF, 28 June 1871).

News of his sudden death reached 124 Tremont Street, the Boston offices of Ticknor and Fields, on Friday 10 June. The note James immediately sent his wife commenced "O my dear Annie"—at once a salutation and cry of woe; it revealed his shock and grief in the face of unexpected catastrophe:

A telegram has just come from England to the associated press, and they have sent word to us, saying that our dear, dear friend Dickens died this morning. God grant there may be some mistake in the dispatch, but I have deep and dreadful fears. I am here and must remain here to watch for more intelligence over the wires. If any better tidings come you shall hear at once, but if you don't hear, you will know I have got nothing further. I am terribly shocked by this blow, and know not how to believe the report. God help us all if it be true. A world without Dickens! It is hard to think of such a calamity & I won't believe the report till it is further confirmed.[34]

Fields undoubtedly credited the fatal telegram as soon as he received it; hoping twice in seven sentences that the news might be a "mistake" and promising to write again if it was—these were ploys to soften a disaster's finality. "Deep and dreadful fears" more accurately expressed his lugubrious state of mind. To the publisher's credit, his note only bemoaned the demise of a "dear, dear friend," although he had also sustained a serious financial reversal: he would never issue the second half of *The Mystery of Edwin Drood*. Ironically, the only American publisher with whom the world's foremost novelist ever came to profit-sharing terms would never print a Dickens novel that was both new and complete, although he had sought this privilege for over a decade. Despite being dazed and flustered, however, he recognized that Annie had to be informed as quickly as possible because her loss would be even greater than his own.

Annie's diary entry seems oddly subdued, but its matter-of-factness is misleading. She took her husband's bulletin bravely because she already knew what a world without Dickens was like; for her it had begun the moment he sailed for home and she started schooling herself to accept the end of the most invigorating intimacy she had ever enjoyed. Annie had less reason to question the authenticity of the dispatch because the brand new calamity unexpectedly overtaking James would not remove Dickens from the publisher's ken more drastically than he had distanced himself from hers; death only "further confirmed" the wrench of separation she had suffered, which no subsequent visit to Gad's Hill could have repaired.

Hence the similarity in tone between her husband's note and a funereal passage in Annie's diary two days after Dickens's departure: "My memory goes back again and again to the last scene, the last embrace the look of pain; the bitter bitter sobs after he had fairly gone. . . . He leaves us only the memory of our joy and the knowledge that we can see him no more as we have done. Never again the old familiar intercourse, the care for him, his singleness of vigour for us—" (DAF, 24 April). Although Annie relates how both she and James cried over the absent Dickens, the lines appear chiefly to describe her reactions; it sounds as if she has been in attendance at a deathbed or has just returned from a graveside service. In short, Annie's bereavement commenced two years before her idol died, and she did not let go the disappointment or overcome her sense of loss until the 1871 meditation on Ellen Ternan, which can be read as a cathartic reassessment that finally laid Dickens to rest and brought a kind of acceptance, if not peace.

The context in which Annie mentioned "N.T." as being in Rome is therefore more complex than has been realized. The entry began when memories of Dickens returned, "not only thoughts of him" but a "rising of his presence" so lifelike that the diarist wrote: "I see his eyes looking into mine" (DAF, 6 December 1871), details Curry fails to emphasize. It was Dickens who now seemed to be haunting and beseeching her, not just she who was still obsessed with him. Only then did Annie bring herself to incorporate "N.T." and speculate on the "bond" between them. Did Annie imagine she saw in Dickens's gaze a plea for additional understanding now that he knew that she knew that he had captivated her only while on leave from Ellen? Was his looking her in the face a hallucination or equivalent to an apology for having let their friendship subside, perhaps even an admission that she was the woman better suited to him? The latter might explain the belated elegiac turn that the entry then took: "Where is Dickens what is his life what is his relation to this scene of his hearty loving labor for those 56 [sic] long long years so full of joy and grief." Through this eulogy's mixture of resignation and regret, Annie fully acknowledged to herself that knowing Dickens had been the emotional high point of her existence. For her, more so than for James, his death was a painful reminder that life consists of partings and endings. The date 6 December 1871 came long after her no less strongly affected but more practical husband had learned to cope with a Dickens-less world.[35]

Not surprisingly, the Fieldses devoured Forster's *Life of Charles Dickens*, which is initially described as a "great treat" capable of bringing "his dear presence back to us" (DAF, 21 November 1872).[36] But Annie subsequently reported with approval Mrs. Agassiz's opinion that the biography was "much too personal" (DAF, 31 March 1874) even though it effectively censored the Ternan affair. The Fieldses never commented on Forster's glaring omission, but Annie seems to have been sensitive to the implications of the first provision in Dickens's will, a document that appeared in the London *Times* for 22 July 1870. After reading of the bequest of "£1000 free of legacy duty to Miss Ellen Ternan" (F, 2:522) when the will was reprinted in the *New York Times* for 3 August, she noted: "J told Longfellow, as was quite right about E.L.T." (DAF, 12 August).

This reference to Ellen by three initials is nearly as startling as mention of "N.T." the following December but hardly self-explanatory. George Curry contends it "showed that more was known at Charles Street about 'Nelly' than would ever be committed to paper" (GC, 58). Yet one may suspect an argument that claims to become truer the more a lack of evidence for it accumulates (that is, the less that was put down on paper, the greater the amount known). What did Fields tell the sixty-three-year-old poet? Possibilities range from a correction of the *Times*'s misprint in both London and New York ("Ellen Lawless Fernan") to a simple statement of E.L.T.'s good fortune to full disclosure of whatever the Fieldses knew or else by now surmised from the prominent gift in the published will. They need only have put two and two together: a young woman Dickens had spoken of admiringly and the unconventional bequest.[37] Why was it "quite right" for James to speak? No scandal was about to break, and Longfellow was no more protective of Dickens's good name than the Fieldses were.

Conceivably, James's action, if instigated by Annie, was more rebuke than favor. Six months earlier, Annie had been offended when Longfellow and the visiting English actor, Charles Fechter, talked about Dickens's problems with his children but scrupulously avoided referring to Georgina. "Poor Miss Hogarth," Annie silently fumed, "spends her life hoping to comfort and care for him. I have never felt more keenly her anomalous and unnatural position in his household. Not one mentioned her name. They could not dare, I suppose (lest they might do her a wrong)" (DAF, 25 February 1870; A, 131).

Mrs. Fields attributed the omission to a despicable mixture of propriety and cowardice, the result being an implicit slander. Thus it may have been "quite right," merely an act of justice to her friend, to inform Longfellow of the new prime candidate for one's suspicions.[38] As late as February of 1870, Annie was still preoccupied with Georgina whenever she pondered Dickens's private life. Had she benefited from his total confidence in 1868, had she known everything there was to know by early 1870, she would surely have incriminated E.L.T. in her diary in order to exonerate Miss Hogarth. Even if she had refrained from defending one woman aloud at another's expense, Longfellow's conversation with Fechter would have affected her differently.

If James enlightened Longfellow in August 1870, the poet could not have been consulted about sending for Ellen when he visited Dickens on 20 November 1867. Unfortunately, no account of this postwill eye-opening process survives; and Longfellow, like Annie herself, not only seemed unruffled after supposedly learning the shocking truth, but remained as loyal to Dickens as ever. No alteration in tone colors his subsequent letters to either James or Annie.

Fields's notes to Longfellow in the summer months following Dickens's death indicate that the pair had not met regularly for some time, possibly not since 29 June.[39] On 21 July, the poet invited the Fieldses to his Nahant retreat, but this was a standing invitation; as the end of August approached, he was still expecting them.[40] In the invitation letter, Longfellow also wrote: "I have read your Dickens Paper with great interest and satisfaction. It is very good, neither overdone nor underdone." This essay was probably Fields's "Some Memories of Charles Dickens," which appeared in the *Atlantic* in August 1870. Like every other reminiscence of Dickens that Fields would publish, this commemorative piece did not include Ellen Ternan. It would surely have been ironic, indeed, mutually painful, for Fields to hurl a thunderbolt into Longfellow's life by disclosing Dickens's sexual entanglement so shortly after the poet had praised the Dickens paper's perfect balance and moderate tone.[41]

Although no modern revaluator can ever be certain, Mrs. Fields's knowledge of Dickens's private life was probably less complete than either Thomas Wright's or K.M. Longley's.[42] Whatever Annie did learn probably reached her secondhand; it almost certainly did not come from Dickens himself and possibly not from James—Annie never mentioned either man telling her about "E.L.T." the way her husband allegedly spoke to Longfellow. It seems likely, therefore, that (1) Annie never knew the whole truth, at least not during Dickens's 1867-68 visit; (2) she experienced a strong attraction to him before hearing about Miss Ternan; and (3) she persisted in thinking about him intensely even after Ellen may have replaced Georgina as the woman with whom ardent admirers of Dickens's talents and person might want to trade places.

Three dates are especially critical: 25 February 1870, when Annie simmered while Fechter and Longfellow conversed; 12 August 1870, by which point she had read Dickens's will; and 6 December 1871, when she felt bonded to "N.T." Only on the last two occasions, both *after* Dickens's death, does full cognizance of Ellen's sexual importance seem plausible. The disapproval one would have expected either of Dickens the mistress-taker or of the mistress herself is strikingly absent even then because Annie had felt personally the strength of his "power to attract" (DAF, 7 June 1868).

From one point of view, the perspective perpetuated by De Wolfe Howe's *Memories of a Hostess*, the winter-spring of which Annie spent so much in Dickens's company was chiefly a literary event involving a fascinating person, hence obligatory for a "Journal of literary events and glimpses of interesting people," as she titled her sixty-one volumes (1859-74). From another viewpoint, namely that of George Curry, Annie's strong feelings for Dickens, her sense of his fiery, overpowering presence, was either "an innocent devotion" or, when the entries became increasingly fervid, a tremendous spiritual experience (GC, 60). But from the perspective furnished by the unexpurgated diaries themselves, Dickens's second visit supplies material for a love story that Annie could never discuss publicly and which she frequently tried to disguise even from herself. In *Yesterdays with Authors*, Dickens is but one of the famous figures about whom James T. Fields reminisced, but neither in the voluminous diary nor in the subsequent record Annie kept in 1907-12 did anyone begin to rival "dear C.D." in fascination for her.

Annie confessed that her concern for Dickens could "never be spoken of except with my beloved [that is, James], and it is for his sake as well as my own comfort that I make this little record that if we both live as years roll on our mutual joys and pains knitting us more closely together we may refer to points where memory fails us" (DAF, 24 April 1868). This curious passage of self-justification, written two days after Dickens left, occurs about midway between 10 April 1868, when the Fieldses joined Dickens in New York for the final readings, and early May, after he had reached Gad's Hill; during that stretch of time, Annie's diary corruscates with entries that were surely indiscreet, no matter how ambiguous. The passage addressed to James suggests that a married Victorian woman could not confide her strongest feelings to paper and thus to herself without some excuse besides the need for outlet and release. Annie, one feels, was being defensive—self-deceptive, yes, but not hypocritical. An aid to memory, a favor to her spouse—such were the guises under which she indulged her otherwise inexpressible, perhaps inadmissible, thoughts and imaginings.[43]

Of all Dickens's American engagements—with the press and book pirates in 1842 or with scalpers and the American winter in 1867-68—none surpasses in interest or excitement his encounter with Annie Adams Fields, if only because the fifty-six-year-old novelist steps forth from her diary ebullient enough to enthrall an attractive, intelligent thirty-three-year-old woman with his charm, genius, and, above all, *energy*. This glowing, vibrant presence—"Charles Dickens the beautiful, the inspired" (DAF, 22 April)—contradicts Kaplan's presentation of a steadily declining, unlikeable Dickens who left for America "a sickly, elderly man" (K, 513), having aged prematurely by the 1860s: ruined complexion, wrinkled skin, thinning hair, straggly beard, even "middle-aged" eye-sockets to detract from his brilliant eyes (K, 294).

After 1858, a rapidly deteriorating Dickens allegedly "had a close relationship with no other woman besides Ellen"; his "friendship" for her grew so "emotionally satisfying" that he "ceased his characteristic flirtations" (K, 410), that long series of comically serious expressions of amorous regard for, among others, Frances Colden, Christiana Weller, Augusta de la Rue, and even the young Queen Victoria. It is as if the ever-weaker but increasingly contented novelist-reader, who spent long, unexplained absences from London with Ellen in a hideaway at Condette south of Boulogne, had finally found compensation for an unloving mother, an untrustworthy father, and an unhappy marriage—in short, the perfect soulmate, "the one friend and companion" (NL: 2,621) he had long regretted never having met. But this twofold rule of satisfaction producing restraint, which controls the latter portion of Kaplan's biography, can stand only if Annie Fields is recognized as the exception that proves it.

Regrettably, the modern revaluator can never expect to measure the exact degree to which Dickens either solicited Annie's affectionate regard or responded warmly to it. Still, Mrs. Fields's diary has been unwisely neglected as a biographical source for at least three reasons: (1) her concern for Dickens and his apparent relishing of it make one wonder how much he regretted being unable to send for Ellen Ternan; (2) it repudiates suggestions that Dickens was already tired and ailing in 1867-68, intent on using himself up; and (3) it describes one of Dickens's emotional attachments from the woman's side, whereas Ellen continues to elude his biographers, none of whom bring the affair alive from her point of view—what it meant to her.

Dickens's conquest of Annie Fields proved a hollow triumph, however. Despite the initial elation, she was left with a sense of frustration and disappointment,[44] the very handicaps an unhappy Dickens had arrived with and complained of. For him it was an ironic second coming in that he discovered that someone of Mary Hogarth's caliber could never truly materialize a second time; he could never expect to find intelligent sympathy, physical attractiveness, and domestic virtues combined and waiting for him in a single person. Ultimately, Mrs. Fields was a reminder of what would never be: she was as illusory a promise of fulfillment in 1868 as America had been of his ideal republic in 1842. The realization that Mary Hogarth was unlikely to appear reincarnated can be said to jeopardize the efficacy of second comings in every respect; for example, by returning to America as the public reader, Dickens could not recoup monies that the lack of an international copyright had already cost the novelist.

5

Health and Money

Dickens's health is reported to have declined steadily in the winter-spring of 1867-68; it has continued to do so even more rapidly in scholarly accounts of the reading tour. The process began with Forster, who "never" saw Dickens during the summer of 1868 "without the impression that America had told heavily upon him. There was manifest abatement of his natural force, the elasticity of bearing was impaired, and the wonderful brightness of eye was dimmed at times" (F, 2:441).

One should pause here to italicize the phrase "at times"; or to suggest that Forster, observing Dickens after a five-month absence, was only noticing that the Inimitable was aging; or to remember how opposed the biographer had been to the American tour and public readings generally as a comedown for the artist and thus how foresighted he became by blaming them for Dickens's death; or to point out that Boz did not actually break down until 22 April 1869, when the remainder of the last English tour had to be canceled.

But to question Forster's anachronistic application of Dickens's 1869 condition to the winter of 1868, the revaluator need only cite Edgar Johnson's melodramatic embellishments: by the end of the American tour, "the mechanism of [Dickens's] body . . . was disastrously weakened." Although "in some miraculous way the vessel had not been dashed to pieces . . . and sunk, all its fabric was twisted and broken with the dreadful strain" (J, 2:1094). When one learns from yet another source that Dickens "undertook a gruelling [American] tour . . . at a time when his health was deteriorating rapidly" (SN, ix), the decline seems to precede the second visit and to welcome it as an ally. Kaplan's pretour Dickens is the sickliest yet: a "grizzled-looking veteran," prematurely "aged," worried about cardiac illness, and exhausted to the point of "general weariness" (K, 507-8). Such a decrepit figure, one may object, was in no condition to perform at home or abroad and ought to have died in America, if not on the way there.

If giving public readings, not just those in America, killed Dickens, his demise was accomplished slowly: he turned professional in 1858 at age forty-six and died twelve years and 423 performances later (D, 450).[1] All told, the number of readings is surprisingly small for so long a period of time—smaller, for example, than the run in modern times of many successful shows in London or New York.

At home or abroad, the rigors of constant traveling probably did as much, possibly more, to decimate Dickens than the strain of the readings themselves. Dickens and Dolby innocently underestimated distances in America and the perils of going by train; they also failed to anticipate how easily bad weather could increase both. On 30 March, with only a dozen readings to go, Dickens complained to Forster: "I am nearly used up. Climate, distance, catarrh, travelling, and hard work, have begun . . . to tell heavily upon me" (F, 2:432). Provided one takes "catarrh" as the product of "climate" and "travelling," the actual readings—"hard work"—ranked fifth out of Dickens's five reasons for feeling "used up."

Winning the right to represent Dickens in America was a coup for Ticknor and Fields only if one agrees that the novelist-turned-reader did not have a virtual death wish; indeed, he looked healthier to his contemporaries than to modern critics who push back into 1867-68 problems that first surfaced seriously in 1869. Having labored for a decade to become Dickens's official American publisher, James T. Fields had no reason to believe that his prize catch had less than three years to live, nor should he have suspected Dickens would write only one more novel and an incomplete one at that. Since 1837, he had authored fourteen novels within thirty years, although the later ones came at greater intervals. Conservatively, Fields could have anticipated another three, perhaps four, if the world's best-known novelist reached seventy. The situation compares favorably with Cadell's expectations, earlier in the century, from an old and ill Sir Walter Scott.[2] To describe Fields capturing "the splendor of a sunset after the sun had gone" (T, 319)[3] is to savor the irony of the anticlimactic Dickens-Fields arrangements at the risk of sounding as anachronous as Forster and Johnson.

Before Dickens left for the United States, his health had become a question mark but was never "deteriorating rapidly," a circumstance that may make one skeptical of subsequent bulletins with an alarmist tone. On 3 September 1867, Dickens told Fields how an American visitor had expressed surprise that the author was not in the "critical state" the New York papers had reported (Y, 161-62). Invited to dine at Gad's Hill, Mr. Fisk was allegedly "staggered" to see Dickens up and around and "in sporting training." The novelist also informed Fields that he had written the London *Times* to contradict rumors of his being sent abroad as a "cessation from literary labors." Such "nonsense," Dickens hoped, had not reached the American press, where it could dampen prospects for the impending tour.

The September letter to Fields concluded with some heavy-handed jocularity: Dickens related how his current guests, fellow novelists Wilkie Collins and Charles Reade, both feigning panic, would continually feel his pulse at table. Amusing though the episode was, it now reads like a preview of the close watch Dolby kept on Dickens during the last stage of the American tour, not to mention the readings for Chappell's back home in 1869-70.

Actually, Dickens's difficulties with his health date back to mid-May of 1866, not to the fall a year later; in Glasgow he "was attacked by a severe cold, and it was with difficulty that he could get through the Reading; indeed," Dolby recalled, "but for the fact that all the tickets had been sold, . . . he would have postponed it" (D, 37). Similar inconveniences beset Dickens in Scotland in February 1867, causing Dolby to yearn for England, "where the climate was less severe" (D, 71). After Glasgow's cold weather, a trip down the Clyde by steamer restored Dickens just as the sea journey home from America would later. But at the time Dolby left for America, Dickens was "suffering from erysipelas in the foot" to the extent that he was obliged "to walk with a stick" (D, 95), a predicament also duplicated in the New World. In short, virtually every health problem associated with the American tour had afflicted Dickens previously, usually under circumstances that ironically and unluckily would recur in capital letters and probably ought to have been anticipated.

When Dolby arrived to go over the ground, Annie Fields recorded the manager's description of his chief's condition: "Dickens has lamed one of his feet with too much walking of late" (DAF, 14 August 1867). This explanation of what seems to have been an early warning of eventual stroke would be invoked several times before 8 June 1870; here it was surely an attempt to downplay the fitness issue. Mid-August was less than a month after Dickens had asked the *Times* for a clean bill of health.

Three points need underscoring: (1) Dickens's medical problems, if real rather than trumped up, may have antedated the American reading tour but were by-products of performances in places like Glasgow (too much travel in cold weather); (2) Dickens and Dolby may have been less than candid in the repeated assurances they offered Fields, to whom, not unexpectedly, Dickens directed nearly all of his comments on his physical condition; (3) assuming Dickens was anxious not to perturb the key figure sponsoring the Boston readings, one must label the state of his health during the spring of 1867 a more clouded issue than whether James T. and Annie Fields had been told all about Ellen Ternan.

Fields was clearly concerned. Otherwise, he would not have addressed the problem so directly in a letter to Longfellow the day after the novelist's boat docked: "Dickens is in fine health and spirits and longs to see you" (FC, Wednesday, 20 November 1867). A less worried correspondent would have put the message to Longfellow first and the news with which he himself was pleased last. Perhaps Fields and Longfellow had been uncertain enough to speculate about the shape Dickens would arrive in. Behind Fields's observation: "I thought he never looked in better health" (Y, 166), one detects a sigh of relief.

Throughout his stay, however, especially when he was performing, impartial observers—not just Fields—were uniformly awed by Dickens's vitality. "Mr. Dickens' Readings," a report in March 1868 for a North Carolina periodical, is typical: Thomas Cooper DeLeon, the correspondent, wrote as if Dickens had discovered the fountain of youth; he praised the reader's "springiness and elasticity of muscle that—as much as his florid skin—shows a high physical condition. For despite the immense brain-labor . . . , despite his hard struggles in early life and his domestic ones in later, years still set lightly on his head."[4] This assessment, made well after Dickens had contracted his "American catarrh," merely confirms an earlier estimate on 29 November: the Boston *Morning Post*'s admiration for Dickens's "vigorous health" (EP, 179).

Just four days later, as December began, the Boston *Daily Journal* added its tribute: "Though time has laid a frosting upon the well-kept and trimly-shaped beard, and thinned the locks that cover his head, Mr. Dickens has still the air and port of a young man" (M, 271).[5] This is the well-preserved Dickens, the athletic marathon walker of whom Fields wrote: "when in America, scarcely a day passed, no matter what the weather, that he did not accomplish his eight or ten miles" (Y, 234).

Such eyewitness reporting on Dickens's robustness, his capacity for strenuous physical activity, glaringly contradicts modern appraisals too strongly colored by the breakdowns of 1869-70, such as Monod's virtual epitaph: "The final years in Dickens's life were a painful sequence of illnesses, about the seriousness of which he would have liked to deceive himself."[6] If there was deception in 1867-68, it was not by a novelist who knew deep down that he was dying, perhaps killing himself; instead, Dickens and Dolby may have kept Fields and the American press misinformed. They were protecting their business interests, of course, but seem to have been confident that they could honor their commitments.

Nevertheless, one cannot simply conclude that the fifty-six-year-old Dickens looked more zestful to his contemporaries than modern critics admit. Nor is it sufficient to deny that America got even for *American Notes* and *Martin Chuzzlewit* by driving the first nails into Dickens's coffin. If we chart the state of his health by using the day-to-day observations of his associates (George Dolby in particular), we see a pattern totally unlike the steady inroads he made into Annie Fields's heart. Instead of an uninterrupted worsening somehow satisfying to Dickens's subconscious desire for self-destruction—that is, instead of an irreversible deterioration of his general health—a fascinating muddle emerges: a series of ups and downs unlike the dangerous declivity that Dickens did not plunge down until the reading at Preston was called off a year to the day after his departure from New York. Dolby and Fields were often frightened by Dickens's fluctuations—he seems variously to have taken a bad cold or possibly influenza in consequence of one of the worst winters ever[7]—but their concern rose and fell as the Chief got better or relapsed, both of which he did repeatedly.

Accounts differ as to where and when Dickens caught his famous cold. Forster says it happened after "half of his first New York readings"; that is, the problem developed in mid-December: returning to Boston after finishing in New York, Dickens "found himself at the close of his journey with a cold and cough that never again left him until he had quitted the country" (F, 2:402). But Edward F. Payne adds nine days to Dickens's sufferings: on Friday 6 December, having read "Dombey and Son" and "The Trial" from *Pickwick*, Dickens went off to New York, contracting his cold en route (EP, 203). This is the version one can cite Dolby to sanction, somewhat vaguely at first but then with precision, giving exact time of day: "Dickens had caught a severe cold early in the proceedings"; reaching New York at 6:00 P.M. on 7 December, he was "very tired" after the nine-hour train ride from Boston, and his cold was "showing signs of taking an influenza turn" (D, 179-81).

By the first New York reading, Dolby had promoted Dickens's cold into "an attack of influenza"; thus he did all of the New York readings "under the burden of an influenza cold" (D, 182, 184). On 9 December, following a snowfall of sixteen inches, Dickens was "literally streaming at the eyes and nose from the effects of his influenza" (D, 188). As would happen over and over, however, he rebounded from this low point; "two weeks in New York, without the inconvenience of travelling, had a most beneficial effect on Mr. Dickens's influenza," which was "much better" on 18 December (D, 195-96), not long after Forster said it began.

Three days later, Dolby downgraded Dickens's ailment to a "cold" but mentioned ominously the first of his Chief's "many sleepless nights" (D, 198). At the end of the month, although it was influenza again, the vacation between 27 December and 2 January helped to off-set "the severity of the climate and the discomfort of the travelling" (D, 199). The Christmas-day departure from Boston for New York was complicated by "the return of the influenza," yet a few days' rest "had a most beneficial effect on Mr. Dickens's cold" (D, 202, 205). In the modern world, the plane trip from Boston to New York requires little more than an hour, and dosing Dickens with antibiotics would have cured him quickly. (But Johnson [J, 2:1083] has Dickens giving a "Christmas night's reading" in New York, and Moss [M, 330] adds performances on 28, 30, and 31 December; these last three are essential for my total of 76.)

Midway through January en route to Philadelphia, Dickens brought on "a fresh attack of influenza" by standing on the platform outside his car to avoid the noxious air within; in Brooklyn (16 January), he first jokingly "dignified" his "head" cold as the "American catarrh" (D, 212, 214).[8] But back in Philadelphia (23-24 January), Dickens had to adopt the regimen he hoped would enable him to complete his schedule: rising at noon (often after a sleepless night), no breakfast, dining at three, no additional food until after the evening's performance "and then only something very light," and "an egg beaten up in sherry" to refresh himself between a given program's first and second readings (D, 218-19).

Influenza is a viral disease characterized by inflammation of the respiratory tract, fever, muscular pain, and irritation in the intestinal tract. Although not usually considered life-threatening, it could prove fatal to an actor's hopes of finishing a successful run. It explains not just Dickens's difficulty eating and sleeping but why he found travel uncomfortable generally and smoke-filled, overheated railway cars particularly unbearable. He was the victim of a vicious circle: it was impossible to recover under circumstances exacerbating his problems.

Although a short month, February had its share of medical ups and downs. In Washington when these began, Dickens was "completely prostrate with his cold," and Dolby uses the word "anxiety" for the first time in describing his concern for the Chief's health (D, 230-31). Yet as the readings in the nation's capital progressed, "Mr. Dickens. . . . partially recovered from the effects of his cold" (D, 232), so another apparent breaking point was followed by still another rebound. This, however, proved short-lived in that by 7 February "the 'catarrh' was worse than ever" (D, 238).

Several times in his day-to-day account, Dolby praised Dickens's "indomitable character," his power of "coming up to time" when most observers thought he would be unable to do the night's work. The last Washington performance was no exception: just "five minutes before" Dickens had to begin, "his powers returned to him, and he went through his evening's task as if he had been in the most robust health" (D, 239). Such resiliency, such a reserve of adrenaline, is worth underlining because it "saved" Dickens and Dolby "a great deal of anxiety"; with forty-one of the eventual seventy-six readings completed, it proved that Dickens's "general health was not affected by the 'catarrh.' " In other words, he was miserable and obviously struggling but to reach only the end of the tour, not the grave.

Between 28 February and 9 March, a fortuitous hiatus was created when Dickens canceled four Boston readings; he feared the country's absorption in the impeachment proceedings against Andrew Johnson would ruin attendance. Despite Dickens's involvement in the Great International Walking Match, held outdoors in Boston in the worst possible weather,[9] Dolby expected that "during the rest Mr. Dickens would have got rid of his catarrh" (D, 259).

Innocently or otherwise, both the performer and his manager spent most of the tour anticipating the former's recovery, which often seemed about to transpire yet never did. Thus in early March, on the last day in Boston before the swing through upstate New York, "the catarrh showed signs of leaving the patient," and Dickens set out "in the best of spirits" (D, 272). This sequence of one-night stands has been branded a "killing odyssey" (J, 2:1091), but in Buffalo on 12 March, with just twenty-one performances remaining, Dolby told an inquiring sheriff's officer that "Mr. Dickens's cold has nearly left him, and he is in excellent voice" (D, 281).

What the Walking Match failed to cause, a pleasure trip to Niagara did: the "return of the old malady in [Dickens's] foot," not just in the left, as formerly, but in the right foot also, which "caused him to be lame for the remainder of the time he was in America" (D, 286). Still, despite an arduous journey through snow to Albany for the 18 March reading, Dolby concluded that Dickens was not "any the worse for the extra exertion and inconvenience he had undergone" (D, 291). Then snowstorms and a cruel frost "brought a return of the 'true American' "; by 24 March in New Haven, pain in Dickens's swollen foot "rendered walking almost an impossibility" (D, 293-94). Only at this juncture, with just the farewell series still to come in Boston and New York, did Dolby express worry that the tour might have to be halted.

Between 24 March and month's end, Dickens went downhill faster than at any previous time, but the pattern of the sharpest rallies following the steepest declines continued. Returning to Boston from supervising ticket sales in New York, Dolby was "shocked" at the deterioration in Dickens since he had last seen him in New England. For the Boston farewells, a regimen more Spartan than the one adopted in Philadelphia had to be introduced: a wineglass of champagne after the reading "to give action to [Dickens's] heart," then soup or beef tea at the hotel.[10] Even so, Dickens had to lie down in his dressing room for thirty minutes "in a state of the greatest exhaustion" before he could leave the performance hall (D, 294).

Only Dickens's "extraordinary powers of recuperation" pulled him through the third of six Boston farewells (3 April). Dolby identifies this performance as his charge's "nearest approach to an actual collapse," the "turning-point of the 'true American,' " which was no longer switching back and forth from cold to influenza but threatening "lasting injury" to Dickens's lungs (D, 296). Paradoxically, James Edward Root, attending the 3 April performance ("Marigold" and "Mrs. Gamp"), considered Dickens to be in "better spirits and in more perfect sympathy with his audience" than had been the case at the reading he witnessed three months earlier.[11]

Furthermore, the last farewell in Boston, just five days later, was the most successful of the entire tour; "the first Reading in America," when Dickens was perfectly fit, ranked "as nothing compared with this final one." Grossing $3,456, it brought in the largest receipts from a single performance (D, 300-1). On the day of the final Boston farewell, Dickens's friends concluded he was "greatly improved and in fine spirits," whereas two days earlier Dolby reportedly sat at the side of the speaker's platform out of concern for the Chief's poor health (EP, 258, 254). Similarly, Dickens's swollen foot, diagnosed as erysipelas by Dr. Fordyce Barker, made attendance at the New York press dinner an ordeal, but he was "sufficiently well," sitting instead of standing to do the "Carol" and the "Trial" for the final New York reading (20 April), which produced $3,298, the tour's second largest receipts (D, 310, 319).

The most astounding rebound was yet to come. Sailing homeward less than a month after flirting with "actual collapse," Dickens "had not been at sea three days before there was an evident improvement in the state of [his] health. . . . on the fourth day he was enabled to get a boot on his right foot and to take some exercise. The sea air brought a return of appetite, and with this came a return of health" (D, 328). To Fields on 26 April Dickens wrote: "I am greatly better, I hope. I have got on my right boot to-day for the first time; the 'true American' seems to be turning faithless at last; and I made a Gad's Hill breakfast this morning" (NL, 3:644-45). Instead of evincing a death wish in this and other passages in the same vein, Dickens exuberantly—but perhaps naively—enumerated each piece of evidence pointing to a quick recovery; comebacks of this kind may have given him a false sense of immortality.

Besides corroborating Dickens's letter to Fields, Dolby corrects Forster's impression of a Dickens whose constitution was permanently affected by the American reading tour. When he visited the chief on the Thursday following his Saturday return to Gad's Hill, the manager "was surprised to find all traces of his late fatigues and ill-health had disappeared, and, to quote the words of his own medical man, he was looking 'seven years younger.' The sea air, and the four days' rest at Gad's Hill, favoured by beautiful weather, had brightened him so that he looked as if he had never had a day's illness in his life" (D, 330-31).[12]

Admittedly, as Dickens complained to Forster, it may have been "impossible to make Dolby understand" how close he had sometimes come to collapsing because the manager was overly impressed by what Boz himself called a "return of force when it is wanted" (F, 2:423). Yet Dickens, too, was impressed. His letters home show him undecided which to emphasize: his plight or his pluck; lamentations and self-pity rub shoulders with the pride he took—one could say the delight—in being able to carry on and astound others by doing so. If one part of Dickens wished they would "understand," another part was interested in amazing them. For instance, in a letter dated 1 April, he told Georgina Hogarth that he felt "far from strong" and had "no appetite," these and other distressing details creating a predominantly pathetic picture, but, he added at one point in a changed tone, "to see me at my little table at night, you would think me the freshest of the fresh. And this is the marvel of Fields' life" (NL, 3:642).

Despite the Chief's reservations, Dolby seems to have made the proper allowances: "it was only by a most careful observation," he conceded, "that any one could form any idea of the extent of [Dickens's] sufferings" (D, 226-27). Or again: "Our men though, and those who were not as much with him as I was (even Fields), could scarcely be made to understand the real state of the case with regard to his health, as they only saw him at his best" (D, 295).[13] Consequently, the modern revaluator suggests that Dolby recognized his charge's miseries better than Fields did and nearly as accurately as the somewhat deceptive public reader himself. It seems advisable to credit Dolby's chartings of the comings and goings of an influenza cold over both Forster's less disinterested account and Edgar Johnson's sensationalism.[14]

The nautical metaphor that the modern biographer invented in summing up the American trip—Dickens is a "vessel" not quite "sunk" or "dashed to pieces" but "twisted and broken" nonetheless—was inspired by the novelist himself, who told Forster of dreading he might "sink altogether" under the strain (F, 2:423). But he did not mean death, merely incapacitation, an onslaught from his catarrh so definitive that the performer's voice and throat would be vanquished. Insofar as Dickens recovered health and buoyancy *aboard ship* on the return voyage, Johnson's shipwreck metaphor seems unintentionally ironic, hence inappropriate.

"A week after [Dickens's] return," Dolby insisted, "no traces of his American sufferings were discernible—those best acquainted with him declaring that he looked better than ever" (D, 335). In effect, the lowest point healthwise on the tour was followed immediately by the biggest recovery, a tribute to Dickens's inimitable recuperative powers. "Perhaps," Edgar Johnson speculated, "if he had given up all further public readings his extraordinary vitality might even now have restored his strength" (J, 2:1096); indeed, as early as mid-May 1868, it apparently had.

If Dickens hankered after self-destruction, he did not do so *during* the American reading tour. Delighted with Annie Fields but plagued by a wretched cold whose waxings and wanings were closely monitored, he was not at the mercy of that "restless and resistless energy" to which Forster made him a slave and of which Johnson says he became the victim. Throughout the winter-spring of 1867-68, Dickens used that energy literally to glow in Mrs. Fields's presence and to subdue his influenza whenever performance time arrived. Dickens's health problems in 1869-70 attest to the truth of these conclusions in that they eclipsed their predecessors; moreover, they date not from the resumption of the readings but from the introduction of the "Sikes and Nancy" piece.

The demands that this "powerful novelty" (D, 345) placed upon the performer were unprecedented, nor should one overlook the resurgence of post-*Chuzzlewit* pessimism signified by the introduction of this darker piece: its terror seized control of a reading schedule previously dominated by selections meant to generate either tears or laughter. The murderous murder was an intrusion into his popular entertainments of the bleaker view of life Dickens first began acquiring in earnest during the 1842 visit, and so it can be said that America both did and did not kill him. Although "Sikes and Nancy" was excerpted from an early serial, the scene, when isolated for presentation by an otherwise beaming popular entertainer, had an affinity of tone and mood with the Manichean theme of the double or split personality so dominant in Dickens's last novel.

Only with his absorption in dramatizing the killing of Nancy did serious health problems resume. The novelist wanted a sensational addition to his stock, a new reading to draw bigger-than-ever crowds to the English tour, but in the same paragraphs describing the search for it, Dolby observed that his Chief's health began to assume "the old American form" (D, 345-46). The new piece that Dickens had started rehearsing before the readings for Chappell's commenced (D, 352) was more taxing than the actual performances he gave of older material when the tour opened.

Specifically, Dolby regretted two successful tryouts of the murder reading in Dublin right after the New Year, "for otherwise Mr. Dickens would have been saved an enormity of labour and extra fatigue which he was ill prepared to endure, and which, in my opinion, and in the opinion of those who knew him the best, did more to hasten his end and to aggravate his sufferings than he himself would admit" (D, 352). Here Dolby sounds like Edgar Johnson—except that he insisted it was not the idea of reading for profit, not America or even the final English reading tour per se that proved fatal but the enormous effort and "extra fatigue" accompanying the introduction of its highlight and eventual centerpiece.

In New York, at the conclusion of the American tour, Mrs. Fields had found the postperformance Dickens "a perfect picture of prostration, his head thrown back without support on the couch, the blood suffusing his throat and temples where he had been very white a few minutes before" (*MH*, 181). Now, from its inception, "Sikes and

Nancy" could reduce Dickens to a state worse than what America's aw-
ful winter and seventy-three readings had brought him to by mid-April
1868.[15] During the final London farewells in March 1870, Dickens's
pulse rose from 72 to 112 and 118, respectively, for the last two renditions of the "Murder" (D, 444).

Once the "Sikes and Nancy" reading had been incorporated, Dolby grew alarmed and stayed that way. There were no ups
and downs for Dickens's health after 5 January 1869, the new piece's
London debut; instead the pattern is downhill precipitously, every decrease in Dickens's stamina accompanied by an increase in performances for the culprit reading. Dickens soon experienced pains in his
foot again, "and occasionally his old enemy, the American catarrh,
would assert itself" (D, 360).

The same Dolby who once marveled at Dickens's resilience was
now preoccupied with "dangerous symptoms" and the inadvisability of
"running risks" (D, 362, 380). On 16 February, roughly a month after
the debut of the "Murder," Dickens had "the worst attack" yet, "not
excepting the American experiences" (D, 381). By 13 April, he was also
hampered by "a return of the sleepless nights he had experienced in
America" (D, 401). The New World killed Dickens in the sense that he
seems to have relived the six-month second visit all over again, cruelly
telescoped this time, during the first three months or so of 1869.
America became and thereafter remained Dolby's standard of comparison for Dickens's health problems; these were more disconcerting
in England in 1869, he constantly alleges, than at any time on the
American tour.

The manager, if not the Chief, seems to have been less innocent
medically in 1869-70. Although unconcerned in America about the
"general state" of Dickens's health, Dolby now warned his charge that
"a too-frequent repetition of [the 'Murder'] would seriously and permanently affect his constitution" (D, 361). On 22 April, having reported a sense of deadness in his left side and crippling foot problems,
Dickens was told he had a "a disposition to paralysis"; it sounds as if he
had already weathered several minor strokes, harbingers of what
Dolby called his "fatal apoplectic fit" (D, 465). Not surprisingly, Dickens's doctors compelled him to suspend the tour.

In early June 1869, however, a "much sunburnt" Dickens astonished Dolby as "the picture of health" (D, 421). It must have seemed
as if the major rebound that had helped Dickens to look "better than
ever" upon quitting America for Gad's Hill in spring 1868 would be repeated. Unfortunately, this failed to happen. Dickens's condition dur-

ing the few London readings his doctors allowed, the farewell forever series of early 1870, was poor from the start . It was only then that Dolby, sounding like Forster in the summer of 1868, "noticed a slow but steady change working in [Dickens]" (D, 440); formerly confident that his Chief would withstand seventy-six American performances, the manager now doubted that he could finish an English dozen.

Like Edgar Johnson, Dolby accused Dickens of hastening his own end but not until January 1869, after "Sikes and Nancy" was added to the reader's repertoire. Also, he attributed to the London farewells of March 1870 the "manifest abatement" of Dickens's brightness and elasticity that Forster claimed to have detected nearly two years earlier. If one opts for Dolby's firsthand daily knowledge in preference to the views of Forster and Johnson, the latter pair seem to have pushed back developments of 1869-70 into 1867-68. From a storyteller's viewpoint, this had the advantage of lumping *all* of Dickens's readings together as part of the same debilitating process; it made his last three years (1868-70) a tragedian's dream: one uninterrupted march toward a foreseeable fall that could be attributed, in large part, to some self-destructive internal drive.

Paul Schlicke contends that Dickens's readings did more than consume "the greater portion of his energy in the later years of his life"; they "so drained his strength and affected his health that he can quite literally be said to have killed himself in the effort" (PS, 227). At first, this blurring together of the American and British tours seems to vindicate Johnson's insistence upon Dickens's pathological search for professional stimulation, whether from a need to sublimate sexual energy left over from an unhappy marriage or to cement author-reader bonding at a time when creative juices were flowing slowly and rival novelists thought to overshadow him. But for Schlicke, Dickens's motives were "altruistic," not "obsessive" (PS, 246); he was not an addict whose "emotional needs the readings relieved with a drugged excitement" (J, 2:1096). On the contrary, they marked the "culmination of his lifetime dedication to the cause of popular entertainment" (PS, 227), to which he thus became civilization's first and only martyr.

This view of Dickens the showman rejects any notion of the readings as "an unhealthy, even suicidal manifestation of dark obsessions. . . . Dickens devoted himself to reading not because he was driven by unconscious forces to find some distraction for the turmoil seething inside him, but because he saw forces outside, in society, which required urgent attention" (PS, 245). Unfortunately, having overexternalized these ominous-sounding forces, Schlicke reduces them to the loss of wholesome popular amusements: the vanishing, in urban-industrial centers, of older forms of entertainment that encouraged extensive emotional and physical participation rather than passive viewing. Dickens, therefore, solicited audience involvement; he relished giving listeners an emotional workout.

But the "Murder" reading of 1869-70 cannot be explained as a reprieve for wholesome amusement; it was mainly a reminder that *Oliver Twist* (1837-39) had shown an underside to life contrary to both Mr. Brownlow's comfortable urban existence and Rose and Harry Maylie's idyllic country surroundings. The new reading drew upon the starkest episode from Dickens's pre-America fiction, in which the worst in Sikes's nature struck down the best in Nancy's. Sudden devotion to this piece suggests that the increasingly satirical post-*Chuzzlewit* novelist could not be prevented indefinitely from encroaching upon any attempt to recapture Dickens's youthful manner. Despite a darkening social vision throughout the 1850s, Dickens had contained his Swiftian streak since *Our Mutual Friend* (1864-65)—indeed, since the start of his professional reading career. In 1863, he had experimented by himself with "the Oliver Twist murder" but found it too "horrible" (NL, 3:353) for public consumption. During this period, public readings greatly outnumbered new novels, and Dickens was often his early self again onstage and his later self only occasionally in print.

The "Sikes and Nancy" piece did not spell the end of the readings as a period of escapism just for Dickens himself; the compulsion to introduce and emphasize it also meant a retraction of the monumental sop the readings had offered to critics and book buyers who lamented his departures (especially in *Bleak House* and *Little Dorrit*) from the Pickwickian mode. In short, the dark side of Dickens, the antiperfectibilitarian, anti-utopian social critic increasingly dominant in his personality after 1842, finally came forward to compete with his earlier, sunnier self, just as Fagin's underworld snatched Oliver from the Brownlow-Maylie milieu and just as the lustful murderer was to erupt from within Cloisterham's respectable choirmaster in *The Mystery of Edwin Drood* (1870). Dickens was not obeying some obsessive psychotic urge, not succumbing to a secret criminal drive peculiar to him. Instead, the sensational-psychological realist within the public reader felt obliged to impersonate the dark side of human nature (Sikes)—just as, in *Oliver Twist*, the budding satirical novelist within the successful comic serialist had exposed London's dark side.

As Philip Collins has noted, Dickens's dramatizations were "not drawn from the later and more socially critical novels"; more than half came from his Christmas books and stories (SN, xii). From these he deleted the stronger passages of social criticism—Scrooge's vision of the terrible children Ignorance and Want, for example, or Will Fern's social-protest speeches. Dickens was content at first—indeed, determined—to appear as the early, pre-America Dickens all over again, a master of the comic and sentimental, of laughter and pathos, an artist primarily interested in touching hearts and tickling ribs.

After the second visit to America, the readings darkened, just as the novels from *Chuzzlewit* on did after the first. Dickens had not been traumatically disillusioned a second time, however; instead, the creative impetus toward greater realism and sharper social awareness, which had led him from *Pickwick Papers* and *The Old Curiosity Shop* through *Chuzzlewit* to *Bleak House* and *Our Mutual Friend*, simply took over the readings. At work since the early 1840s, this impetus had forced Dickens toward greater acknowledgment of society's persistent ills as proof of evil's interiority, its ineradicable presence in forms both perennial and new, not only within men but enshrined in their unsatisfactory institutions.

No unspeakable "obsessions," no perverse inclinations, one must reiterate, were involved in what Dickens jokingly called his "murderous instincts" (D, 386). Perhaps he was vicariously murdering Catherine, his estranged wife, much as he may have been eliminating his former protégé and current rival, Wilkie Collins, by having John Jasper kill the younger Edwin Drood. The attraction of allowing Nancy's assailant to emerge from the outwardly benevolent public entertainer was not unlike that of drawing forth a second self, a Mr. Hyde figure, from Cloisterham's choirmaster. But the spellbinding sensationalist in Dickens resembled a moralist-philosopher rather than a compulsive suicide purposely overexerting himself to release the would-be murderer within. The oral performance becomes, in retrospect, a kind of research and rehearsal for the later written one; the point in both cases was to scare the Victorian community into a more honest conception of itself—that is, a greater realization of civilization's shortcomings and of man's capacity for evil deeds.

Society not only produces desperadoes, devilish outcasts like Sikes; pressures from its sense of propriety, its cultivation of seemingly necessary social strictures, generate lives of quiet desperation among the so-called better classes. Eventually, a secret sharer, a white-collar criminal every bit as violent as Sikes, develops internally in someone like Jasper and determines to revolt. These were the discomforting propositions Dickens was turning over in his mind when he prepared "Sikes and Nancy" in the autumn of 1868 and then conceived of *Drood* no later than the following summer. "Sikes and Nancy" and *The Mys-*

tery of Edwin Drood were a two-part response to evolutionary humanists who foresaw no serious obstacles to the gradual betterment of society and human nature. The short interval between suspension of the reading tour (22 April 1869) and the inception of Dickens's final novel (summer 1869) makes sense: he began the latter when the other outlet was no longer available, even though that outlet had initially furnished an escape from the darkening novels.

Dickens was an innocent abroad in 1867-68 to the extent that he came to America while still on holiday from the sterner satirist he had been throughout the 1850s and 1860s, the essentially satirical novelist he had started to become in earnest during his first disappointing visit. But he could not maintain the illusion of a second coming—the idea that he was his earlier and more congenial artistic self again—any more than he was able permanently to find another Mary Hogarth in Annie Fields.

Dolby demanded to know why three out of the four readings every week had to be "Murders" (D, 387). Several times he advised Dickens to "reserve" the "Sikes and Nancy" piece for larger towns "just to keep [his] hand in," instead of "tearing [himself] to pieces every night." A year later, in January 1870, Dickens "confessed" to his manager "that it was madness ever to have given the 'Murder' " (D, 442). Nevertheless, it was a creative madness, not a suicidal one. Just as Dickens the novelist had to anatomize Chancery, Utilitarianism, and the Circumlocution Office, Dickens the reader could not let audiences off with "The Trial" from *Pickwick* or "The Carol"; he had to adhere to the pattern that he saw built into the life process since the creation story: art was obliged to bring evil to bear upon good, to bring Sikes to Nancy in the readings the way Quilp was visited on Little Nell in the novels or Jasper upon Cloisterham and Drood.

From one point of view, neither America nor the readings given on her soil contributed to Dickens's death, but fourteen months of "Sikes and Nancy," a short period at the end of twelve years of reading publicly, may have done so. If such was the case, the later or less sanguine Dickens can be said to have overtaken the early humorist, who had been resurrected to perform on stage. The murderer of Dickens and Nancy in 1869-70 was one and the same: an outbreak of the dire pessimist—the *real* Dickens to most moderns. From a second point of view, however, America assumes greater responsibility because Dickens's essentially satirical social vision, his deepest reservations about progress, fresh starts, and human nature in general, began to mature there: as the counterpoint involving America and England developed in *Martin Chuzzlewit*, the former inspired and the latter completed

Dickens's dystopian, anti-Victorian view that barbaric new societies and hypocritical older ones constitute the beginning and end point in any mapping of man's attempts at civilization.

"I think myself that [Dickens's] lust for money made him unconsciously a suicide"—so wrote John Bigelow, who knew the Inimitable both in London in the 1850s and later in America. His opinion, stated in *Retrospectives of an Active Life*,[16] is the sort that surely influenced Edgar Johnson's biography and other commentaries before and after it, some of which exaggerate Dickens's health problems during the reading tour *and* his covetousness, as if each were an extension of the other.

Despite "bleeding hemorrhoids" and "crippling attacks" on his foot, a mercenary Dickens, says his most unsympathetic observer, was still bent on "milking the American market": he simply "could not bear to turn off the spigot that was pouring out so much money" (M, 261, 286). In the same vein but fifty-six years earlier, Ralph Straus added "fainting fits" and a drug dependency[17] to Dickens's American tribulations before concluding that the opportunistic novelist returned home "an exhausted, but wealthy, old man." Straus and Moss to the contrary, Dickens was neither over the hill nor burnt out, as Annie Fields's diary and Dolby's reminiscences reveal. It remains to be shown that he was not wealthy either, not if one measures the money actually made against the profits that might have been.

A thirty-year-old Dickens was too inexperienced to have planned in advance—that is, before leaving England—a campaign against piratical publishers; at fifty-five, however, the public reader had come again to reap the full reward from his popularity as a novelist. He still had to put on a good show, of course, but no other performer in the world was so respected, indeed, revered; none could have anticipated audiences so familiar with his work or so predisposed to be entertained.[18] Nevertheless, wiser planning and more flexible on-the-spot decisionmaking would have yielded greater gains. Dickens deserved better luck in 1867-68, but poor financial judgment on his part and gross mismanagement by Dolby and his staff, often acting in obedience to the Chief's instructions, hurt profits more than inclement weather or a bad cold did.

Dolby's letter to Fields on 25 September 1867 (on the Gad's Hill deliberations discussed in chapter four) revealed the reader and his manager still undecided about America; but another heretofore little-known communication to be examined shortly, a letter addressed to the publisher just five days later (FC, 1033), announced *three* pretour decisions in quick succession, all of them unwise: on ticket prices, length of stay, and selection of an assistant ticket seller. The reading tour was characterized throughout by premature resolutions seemingly carved in stone and last-second maneuvering that was generally ill advised—whether or not the changes considered were actually implemented. Since Dickens surely wanted to avoid the pitfalls of his 1842 visit, the second trip exhibits unusual economic innocence: persistent gullibility in the midst of extensive planning, hence an abundance of inadequate safeguards. This is surprising at so late a date for a professional author who had contended with—in fact, had often bested—the publishers Macrone, Bentley, Chapman and Hall, and Bradbury and Evans.

For an example of premature resolution: by exchanging his American receipts for gold out of mistrust for the post-Civil War dollar, Dickens lost nearly 40 percent (39 1/2 percent plus 0.25 percent banker's commission) of his profit. Dickens and Dolby determined upon this course in England, months *before* the tour began (D, 136)—a fact, incidentally, that renders the argument that they waited until *after* arriving to decide about Ellen Ternan even more implausible. Instead of clearing more than £38,000 ($266,000) as he would have done if gold had been at par (D, 332) or if he had invested, as advised, in American securities until the currency rebounded, he realized only about £20,000, or $140,000 (J,2:1096), all of which figuring is based on Dickens's tabulation of gains in terms of "7 Dollars to the pound" (NL, 3:579; D,136). This was a considerable amount, if not a "magnificent sum," in 1868 (RF, 141);[19] but the £16,480($115,360), forfeited through conversion and by not investing at 6 percent, more than doubled the £8,000 ($56,000) which Chappell's guaranteed for 100 readings that Dickens subsequently could not finish back home.[20]

That Dickens had committed a grievous financial blunder became self-evident long before *Charles Dickens As I Knew Him* (1885) appeared. "Sagacious business friends in America," the manager confessed, not only "strongly" warned against trading greenbacks for gold but recommended buying bonds at 6 percent and awaiting better days to come, "as they undoubtedly would, and did" (D, 133). If Dickens had listened, even Dolby's lower calculation of the receipts—namely, $228,000, accepted hereafter as gospel, regardless of expenses—would have grown at least another $13,680 at 6 percent annually by 1869, or almost four times his best box office $3,456 at the final Boston reading—that is, with little additional effort, he could have nearly quadrupled the proceeds from his finest American night within a year.

The decision to appear again for Chappell's was reached while Dickens was still in America, possibly early in December before the first week of Boston readings had ended (J, 2: 1096), although Kaplan chooses 8 November 1867, before Dickens left England (K, 515). Eventually, in light of the large conversion loss, it may have seemed prudent to tour England again, one bad resolution having led to another; but if Dickens was driven to the final English series by responsibilities to his large family of "many sons" (F, 2:440) and by his proverbial "fear of want" (J, 2:1096), he need only have exercised patience. Instead, he agreed to 100 performances in England—24 more than the entire American tour—for less than half the money.

For once at least, the satiric author of *American Notes* and *Martin Chuzzlewit* was wrong to sell America short. At the New York press dinner, he declared that his "English heart" was "stirred by the fluttering of those Stars and Stripes, as it is stirred by no other flag that flies except its own" (J, 2:1094); unhappily, he was not similarly stimulated by the country's fluctuating money market. On 9 July 1859, when the American proposal was first in the works, Dickens confided to Forster that he felt "much stirred . . . by the golden prospect [America] held before [him]," but things did not turn out as aureate as they might have because the conversion decision in effect refunded the price of admission for forty out of every hundred people—that is, two of every five—who had paid two dollars apiece to hear Dickens read.[21]

Collectively, Dickens's reading tours were hailed as "the most brilliantly successful enterprises of their kind that were ever undertaken" (D, vii), which was true. But with "greater ruthlessness," Philip Collins contends, Dickens "could indeed have made far more in America. His takings could have been greater: he charged $2.00 a seat throughout the house, which many thought rather steep, but as the black-market price for tickets rose to $26.00 he might well have set a higher top price. 'Why doesn't Mr. Dickens charge five dollars a seat,' remarked the *New York Tribune* (13 December 1867), 'and have no reserved seats and no sales until the hall opens? If the money is to be paid to him, no one will murmur. It goes to speculators, however, who probably make more out of Mr. Dickens than he does himself.' "[22] For "ruthlessness" one should substitute "business acumen." By never charging anywhere near what the market would bear, Dickens penalized only himself; a decision to stop doing so ought not to be confused with callousness. In all other respects, however, the above passage is an understatement. Instead of making "far more," which sounds vague, Dickens could have realized *three* or *four* times as much without offending customers.

Their animus, incited by the newspapers, fell on Dolby anyway because of the latter's futile efforts to frustrate ticket speculators; his clumsy preventive measures proved as costly to the public and the reading tour as they now seem comic and foolish. Dolby, in turn, faulted the public for paying extortionate prices; actually, it had little choice: if neither he nor Dickens could outsmart the scalpers, ticket purchasers were unlikely to do so. Pitted against shrewd, conniving, well-organized speculators and hampered by their refusal to raise prices, the two Englishmen were babes in the woods trying to secure fair play—"a fair and straightforward" method of ticket distribution (D, 146)—in a contest being played without rules.

Genuine heartlessness belonged exclusively to the speculators: as a group and in some cases individually, they *actually* (not "probably") earned more from some of Dickens's readings, if not from the entire tour, than he did. They had only a fraction of his expenses (these came to $39,000) and no conversion losses awaiting them. Frequently, a single speculator controlled fifty or sixty tickets to a given performance and could charge five to ten times the legitimate price.

Dickens's receipts could have been more substantial had he elected to take better advantage of the American market in any of the following ways and then been well enough to follow through: (1) giving all of the readings originally planned instead of cutting back by eliminating potentially lucrative stops such as Chicago; (2) extending the tour in light of popular demand; (3) charging realistic admission prices; (4) foiling "the noble army of speculators" (D, 216); and (5) not converting dollars into gold. A hypothetical scenario benefiting from all five of these suggestions results in astronomical profits. They would not just have made the Chappell's tour inexpedient; the outcome would have constituted a genuine financial blockbuster—one capable of atoning for a considerable portion of the American royalties of which Dickens had been robbed throughout his career. (Computations rely on Dolby's figure of $3,000 as the average box-office handle per reading [D, 331-32].)

Had Dickens not reduced the 100 readings Dolby initially recommended to 80 (M, 234), a "reduction of twenty per cent . . . at a blow" (D, 134), he could have earned another $60,000. In any case, four Boston performances canceled because of President Johnson's impeachment cost him $12,000. Having arrived with two weeks to spare before the 2 December opening, Dickens fretted at the delay (D, 160-61); had he done four (or eight) readings right away, instead of wasting ten days becoming "acclimatized," the additional profit would have been another $12,000 (or $24,000) before the real acclimatizer, his cold, set in.

One reading that Dolby had to cancel for mid-February may have been more costly than the ten days Dickens wasted in late November. Riots broke out in New Haven after one of Dolby's deputies, bowing to pressure, sold speculators tickets for the first eight rows before commencing the public sale. Although this performance was rescheduled and later given successfully, Dickens lost more than the £300 ($2,100) Dolby immediately refunded (RF, 130; D, 251, says $2,600). The manager's refusal to allow the tainted reading to proceed was a matter of principle but no blow to the speculators and thus totally quixotic; it angered ticket holders who had paid scalpers' prices but were entitled to only a two dollar refund. Newspapers up and down the eastern seaboard regaled readers on 10 February with charges that Dickens was defrauding the public.[23] Thus the real but incalculable loss came in terms of the bad publicity and ill will generated by this incident.

Controversy revolved around Dolby's man Kelly, who not only took bribes from speculators but dabbled in their trade himself (J, 2:1087). Having followed the manager's deputy to New Haven en masse while Dolby was busy with Dickens and arrangements in Baltimore, the New York speculators "plied him with Bourbon whiskey" until he turned over the tickets, an act of dishonesty that "became apparent" the moment sales commenced, triggering a riot the police had to quell (D, 248). Inasmuch as scalpers were Dolby's biggest headache, discovering one of the enemy in his employ was embarrassing professionally as well as financially.

The Kelly affair—Dolby "instantly dismissed" the assistant and he was sent home in disgrace (D, 254)—affords a sorry commentary on Dickens's business acumen; it reveals the extraordinary gullibility of which he and his manager were equally capable, their joint failure to anticipate that someone they personally engaged, a fellow Britisher moreover, would listen to an American speculator's overtures. The incident can stand in miniature not just for several shortenings of schedule but for all the negative consequences from premature decisions that came back to haunt Dickens and Dolby in America.

Dolby's letter to Fields on 30 September 1867, besides elaborating on Dickens's willingness to come, disclosed that the publisher had advised hiring an American assistant—indeed, Fields had apparently written to say a suitable person had been found, someone the firm may actually have interviewed during Dolby's fact-finding days in Boston. But Dolby declined to act on this suggestion; he explained that he and Dickens had determined on "bringing with us our man Kelly, who is a first rate man both outside and inside the establishment" (FC, 1033). Dolby was wrong on both counts. Since Kelly came over with Dickens on the *Cuba*, he, too, had failed to gauge the man's character, although he later claimed always to have disliked him (J, 2:1087). Mid-February or one and a half months into the tour was a late date for performer and manager to discover that their assistant ticket agent was dishonest. For the next two and a half months Dolby had to assume Kelly's duties in addition to his own; even with James Osgood filling in as Dickens's traveling companion, the manager was overburdened and never totally regained the public's confidence.

Throughout his recollections of the American tour, Dolby solicited reader sympathy for his recurrent ineffectiveness by describing the speculators sarcastically as a noble "army" (D, 216), an unscrupulous force that obviously outnumbered him. He recounted the admittedly comical New Haven fiasco with the same mixture of levity and moral indignation it will be seen that he also used for other victories the scalpers achieved at Dickens's expense. (One reason for accepting Dolby's assessment of Dickens's health over Edgar Johnson's is his cheerful candor on this and other subjects. In short, the gap one discovers between the manager's satisfaction and a more objective assessment of the tour's success can be used to disclose that no comparable discrepancy exists between his opinion of Dickens's health and his actual condition.) No matter how many compromising anecdotes Dolby told about himself, however, he never mentioned in print his glowing but expensive testimonial for "our man Kelly."

Supposing Dickens had adhered to the plan of including such "smaller cities" as Pittsburgh, Cincinnati, and St. Louis, not to mention a potential gold mine like Chicago? One performance in each place at half the average receipts would have grossed $6,000.[24] Also, Dickens need not have ruled out the entire South—everywhere below Washington and Baltimore—on grounds that its postwar finances "were in a very troubled state" (D, 114). Using just the figures in this and the last few paragraphs, the revaluator finds that at least $94,100 escaped Dickens from readings that were planned or else plausible yet never given: this is the "large harvest" that Dolby realized "would be left unreaped" (D, 134). By concentrating on Boston and New York, Dickens drew audiences to him as only such a magnetic figure could have, but probably not very many persons from the West and Southwest and then only those who could afford the fare and take time for the journey. Since ticket sales were held well in advance of performances, out-of-town spectators would have had to arrive early or delegate someone to secure their seats or, most likely, patronize speculators.

James T. Fields "regretted extremely" that Dickens "felt obliged to give up visiting the West" (Y, 185). He did not make this sacrifice definite until February when, due to his cold, "not only were Chicago and the West abandoned, but also the Readings in Canada and those in Nova Scotia," so that "the tour list had again to be changed, and . . . the number of Readings had to be considerably reduced" (D, 220).[25] In short, although the public came in throngs and tickets grew ever scarcer, Dickens crossed off too many places while the tour was still in its planning stages and then, once in America, had to cut back his schedule several more times.

An expanded itinerary of the sort Fields imagined would have required better health and a much longer stay; Dickens soon lacked the former and always objected vehemently to the latter. Still, had Dickens not contracted his catarrh or, as Fields put it, "if his strength had been equal to his will," the acclaimed performer "could have stayed in America another year, and occupied every night of it with his wonderful impersonations" (Y, 185). For instance: he could have spent the summer in Canada, performing there on the lightest of schedules or just recuperating from the first tour and marshaling his faculties for a second the following winter.

This proposition is not as ridiculous as it first sounds. On 1 January 1868, the Boston *Transcript* had a similar inspiration: Dickens could "spend two years in America and not fulfill half the [invitations for] engagements" pouring in from other cities and towns besides Boston and New York (M, 283). But Dickens seems to have been impervious to suggestions like the *Transcript*'s not because of his cold, which still seemed manageable in early January, but from the same rigidity, the same lack of imagination, that blindly trusted Kelly and proscribed raising ticket prices to meet escalating demands.

Fields did not just imagine an expanded itinerary or regret the shortness of the eventual tour; his original proposals were actually premised on a much longer stay, and he clashed with Dolby over them. Although both *Yesterdays with Authors* and *Charles Dickens As I Knew Him* suppress the disagreement, Ticknor and Fields persisted in expecting a formidable Dickensian invasion—at least until Dolby's 30 September letter arrived. It settled the duration question by quashing what the manager called Fields's "hope that Mr Dickens is packing his trunk for a three years cruise in America" (FC, 1033). Despite the lighthearted rephrasing, this statement evidently describes the publisher's ideal tour; he must have discussed it with Dolby in Boston because he then pressed Dickens himself in a communication dated 7 September—that is, shortly before the manager completed his American reconnoitering.

Referring to Fields's letter by date, Dolby replied: "I am sorry to say that his [Dickens's] residence in that country will be but limited as he must be home here in the month of May. Consequently I am in hopes that he will not have much travelling and that the greater portion of the Readings will be confined to New York, Boston and the other large cities." Speaking authoritatively for Dickens, Dolby set down ground rules about time and places that Fields would have to abide by whether or not he considered himself an equal partner in the upcoming venture; the manager put his own "hopes" before Fields's "hope" and New York before Boston on the list of major cities.

Nevertheless, an extended tour sounds ridiculous primarily because Dickens encountered health problems that a longer stay might have prevented. If bad weather and constant traveling weakened him, a more casual program could have lessened, possibly eliminated, these dangers without becoming less lucrative. Granted, the circuit Dickens followed would have had to be widened to include prosperous cities such as Chicago, but whether reading or just resting, Dickens could have tarried longer in larger urban centers instead of commuting back and forth, going to Philadelphia, for example, on *four* separate occasions between 13 January and 14 February. He could also have given fewer performances a week, perhaps reading only on Wednesday, Friday, and Saturday, with one of these a matinee.

That crowds would come to Dickens in selected metropolises proved a sound prediction—but not the wisest or most profitable course. A more sensible itinerary could have covered more ground overall at a greatly relaxed pace, demanding fewer hours a week on the road by substituting longer trips on occasion for the rigors of incessant travel—above all, by requiring less retracing of steps. Knowledge that Dickens would be remaining in key locations for more than just four or eight performances at a time and then making encore appearances the following spring might have tempered the irrational demand for tickets; this kept growing after sellouts were announced, and only the speculators benefited. Dickens ought to have risked smaller nightly turnouts for the likelihood of mining the campaigning ground more thoroughly—that is, reaching a larger total audience eventually.

A less rigid, less repetitious "cruise," even if made twice over a two-year span, would have been preferable to the commando raid of seventy-six readings within five months followed by the 100 Dickens then tried to do for Chappell's. This hypothetically revised and expanded travelogue might have taken Dickens from a long stay in Boston to several weeks in New York via stops in Springfield, Hartford, and New Haven; then from Philadelphia (a dozen appearances) to briefer stints in Baltimore and Washington; then west through Pittsburgh, Cincinnati, and Louisville to St. Louis, before turning north again through Columbus, Cleveland, Chicago (long stop), and Buffalo; from there he could have headed back to New York City and New England via stopovers in Syracuse and Albany—in short, an itinerary less like the English tours necessarily predicated on frequent comings and goings through London and closer to the one Dickens followed on his 1842 sightseeing visit. Ironically, instead of contributing to the popular explanation for Dickens's rapid decline in 1867-70, a longer, better-managed American tour could have prolonged his life.

Unfortunately, curtailing Fields's expectations became the dominant theme in Dolby's 30 September letter. It appears as if the manager dreaded the possibility that a single theatergoer might postpone hearing Dickens instead of seizing the earliest chance; Dolby forbade procrastination by insisting that his star would be less accessible than lesser phenomena such as Tom Thumb and Jenny Lind. In a firm postscript, Dolby urged Ticknor and Fields to structure publicity around the tour's irreversible brevity. They were not just to understand that the engagement "cannot be prolonged" beyond the end of April; they had to make certain that the public was acutely aware of this too. Breaking up twenty-two New York performances into four separate blocks or eighteen in Boston into five also seems to have been designed to create the impression of a whirlwind, so that each reading would seem a rare event.

No accurate price tag can be put on Dickens's hypothetical American engagements—the larger, longer tour of the West, the South, and Canada for which there was more than just a polite clamoring. But Dickens had realized only £150 ($1,050) per reading in England, or one-third his American average, so that, in effect, he had to give three performances at home for every one he could have given in America had he stayed on. The $228,000 in receipts Dickens accumulated, it follows, could surely have been increased by at least half (to $342,000), if not doubled (to $456,000) in America in 1868-69. Three performance years—fall 1867 through spring 1870, if one takes Fields literally—could have meant as much as $684,000, or more than £97,000, a sum by itself in excess of Dickens's total worth as of 9 June 1870. Personal preference, not bad health or good business, remains the strongest reason Dolby initially chose an April deadline and then stuck to it. This self-imposed limitation was forgivable in a performer with loved ones at home; but if the tour was undertaken with their financial security uppermost in mind, it is ironic that they should have prevented its maximum success.

A Dickens less adamant about charging higher prices might easily have asked five, seven or even ten dollars a ticket without appearing to gouge the public.[26] As the *New York Times* commented when news of a possible tour first broke: "there are tens of thousands who would make a large sacrifice to see and hear the man who has made happy so many homes" (D, 125). At $5 a seat, the price the *Tribune* recommended, receipts would have risen two and a half times to $570,000; at $7, or three and one half times more, the outcome amounts to $798,000, all else being equal.

When Dolby interviewed New York newspaper editors in August-September 1867 about prospects for a tour, James Gordon Bennett astounded him by advising Dickens "not to charge a cent less than ten dollars (!) a ticket" (D, 124). In retrospect, Dolby's exclamation point accentuates his naiveté, not the disapproval of Bennett that it was meant to convey. Not at all exorbitant in light of the $26 some scalpers later demanded, this $10 figure would have brought in five times as much, for a total in excess of one million ($1,140,000).

No matter, therefore, how satisfied Dickens was with the fruit of his labors, he marketed himself too cheaply in America. Just as he initially had no conception of his value as a serial novelist when contracting for *Pickwick Papers*, he seems to have been ignorant of his transatlantic worth as the phenomenon an Irish journalist once called "the greatest reader of the greatest writer of the age" (*SN*, xv). This phenomenon, after all, was making a one-time-only tour of only eighteen American cities, so that the difference between supply and demand was bound to be enormous. Even where he gave more than one series of readings (twenty-two New York appearances, for example, or eight in Philadelphia), he never ceased to be a novelty or overstayed his welcome.

Dickens did not walk into an ambush in 1867-68. "Sharp practice in the sale of the tickets," which Horace Greeley decried in the *Tribune* (M, 258), was not something encountered unexpectedly; it differed in this regard from the newspaper conspiracy of 1842, which caught Dickens unprepared. When he informed Fields of Dolby's coming to reconnoiter, he insisted that the mission be kept secret lest "every kind of speculator . . . set on foot unheard-of devices for buying up the tickets" if the news "oozed out" (D, 84). Before the first Boston sale, Dolby heard "rumours . . . the speculators, not only of Boston, but of

New York, were making their plans to purchase all the tickets they could get, in the hope of selling them at a premium" (D, 145). Sure enough, these rumors, like the fears expressed to Fields, proved well founded: "one of the earliest purchasers" for the course of the first Boston readings "turned out to be one of the advance guard of the New York speculating brigade" (D, 148), yet neither rumors nor the initial materialization of all they portended scared Dolby into implementing effective preventive measures.

Nor were speculators indigenous to America: at Peterborough, prior to the better-known performance at Birmingham, Dickens gave a benefit reading for the Mechanics' Institute, setting prices at from sixpence to two shillings, but "guineas and half-guineas were paid for front-row seats" (KF, 26-27). Given this British foretaste, the forewarning to Fields, and the rumors circulating around Dolby, the tour ought to have fared better in its struggles with scalpers, if only by raising prices. But having settled "arbitrarily" (EP, 173-74) on $2 for reserved seats and $1.50 for general admission if tickets remained unsold at performance time, Dickens refused to budge.

Was it because of his "commitment" to inexpensive popular entertainment that he deprived himself of extra income and "left ticket sales prey to speculators, who made fortunes by scalping tickets" (PS, 233)? Possibly, yet it seems quixotic to stick to the two dollar price as if it would be sacrilegious to charge more: although Dickens lived up to his ideals and kept his conscience clear, the public still paid outrageous prices.

Consequently, Dickens's old nemesis, the American press, blamed "pudding-headed Dolby"[27] for virtually licensing speculation. As early as 19 November, Bennett's New York *Herald* deplored Dolby's failure "to profit from our recent suggestion—that the price for [tickets] . . . might safely be put at a higher figure" inasmuch as speculators in "possession of no inconsiderable number" were "selling them at twenty dollars apiece" (M, 253)—that is, for exactly twice as much as Bennett had advised Dolby to charge.

At first, remembering 1842, Dickens is reported to have been "greatly annoyed and somewhat frightened at the uproar" (EP, 174), the possibility arising that stories about "speculators would prejudice the success of the tour" (RF, 115) by causing a resentful public to stay away. After a while, when sold-out houses continued, he allegedly grew resigned to "the speculating mania" as "an evil that could not be corrected" (EP, 174). Rather feebly, he consoled himself with the "gratuitous advertisement" given him by an irate press (D, 170). This, however, reflects poorly on his concern for popular amusement; furthermore, free publicity could not really boost sales, since the number of those desiring seats exceeded from the start the number of tickets available.

It is unclear whether the Chief or his much-maligned manager was more intractable about raising prices. One must hold them jointly responsible, each serving as the villain at a different point. Dolby's businessman's manner has been described as "dictatorial," and "stringent laws laid down by him" were supposedly observed "too faithfully by the great author" (EP, 139). But Dickens's compliance seems voluntary; he never upbraided Dolby or disciplined him during the tour, being content to employ the manager as a buffer between himself and the press, the public, and the speculators. Greatly to Dickens's amusement, Dolby became the "best abused man in America" (D, 168). If Dickens was subservient to Dolby's directions, the spectacle of the latter trying to obtain the former's permission to charge five dollars a seat for the Washington readings becomes an ironist's delight. Limited space in Carroll Hall mandated such an increase in order to garner the usual receipts; reluctantly, Dickens agreed to three dollars a ticket and held the line there despite Dolby's urgings (RF, 127).

Yet the manager called the $2 ticket his own idea, a "medium course" between one authority's opinion that $0.75 (the price Thackeray had charged for a lecture) would be sufficient and Bennett's $10. But this figure is much closer to the lowest estimate than to the highest; it appears to have been set unrealistically, perhaps in conformity with Dickens's English resolution to keep seats within reach of the working man. "If on any occasion I consulted him in times of difficulty," Dolby recalled, "his frequent reply was, 'Do as you like, and don't bother me' " (D, 230).[28] But many of the supposedly "stringent" regulations Dolby imposed were mutually conceived when the second visit was still in its planning stage. In America, therefore, Dolby was in a bind: free to do as he chose in meeting the scalping crisis but with no leeway to adjust prices.

In the 30 September letter, Dolby credited the $2 price to himself and Dickens jointly but proclaimed it as a fait accompli, not a topic for negotiation. "We have fully discussed the matter of prices of admission," the manager wrote, "& have decided on $1.50 [for tickets unsold at performance time and for standing room] and $2.00 [for reserved seating]" (FC, 1033). His imperiousness seems ironic in light of the speculators' subsequent success at putting Dickens to work as much for their advantage as for his own. The $1.50 tickets to which Dolby gave first mention were a needless precaution: few ever came into play because seats were generally obtainable at curtain time only from speculators.

That Fields's opinions counted no more than Forster's becomes clearer when hubris is compared with modesty—that is, when the manager's regal tone is measured against Eyre Crowe's deferential manner in a letter to Fields from New York on 2 December 1852: "Mr. Thackeray wishes me to ask you whether it would not be advisable to fix the figure of single-tickets at Boston, at the same price at that [which] was commanded here; namely 75 cents. He, however, gladly leaves the matter in your hands, knowing that whatever you determine on will be for the best" (FC, 4278). The author of *Vanity Fair* was lecturing on England's comic writers, not giving dramatic readings from his own work; hence the short price. The point to emphasize, however, is that Fields had supervised touring English novelists before; yet in 1867 Dickens and Dolby frequently relied on their English touring experience rather than solicit the American publisher's advice.

Four observations seem called for: (1) ticket speculation was not an incurable evil inasmuch as several practical suggestions were offered gratis by the American press; (2) speculators did not resort to the "unheard-of devices" Dickens worried about but acted brazenly; (3) neither Dickens nor Dolby ever grew indifferent to scalping, for as the former confessed to Georgina Hogarth, they were "at [their] wits' end how to keep tickets out of the hands of speculators" (F, 2:397); (4) admittedly outnumbered, Dolby and his assistants lost out to speculators because they were regularly outsmarted and outmaneuvered.

The New York *Tribune*'s suggestion that "reserved seats" be abolished had merit, as did the call to discontinue advance sales. Speculators' men were always first in line when tickets were sold starting from the theater's front rows and moving back. Thus scalpers generally obtained the best seats in the house and had several days to resell them at an inflated figure. News of a sellout within hours of the advance sale immediately enhanced a ticket's value. A policy of "no reserved seats" and "no sales until the hall opens" would have meant first come, first served, with little or no interval between time of purchase and the start of a reading. Also, no two dollar seat would be worth more than another because of its location: any ticket would be good for any empty seat. Since only those desirous of actually attending would be in the queue, gaining control of as many as fifty or sixty tickets would be impossible, indeed, reckless: they would have to be resold almost immediately, with only the disappointed purchasers already on line at the sold-out theater as potential takers.

Unfortunately, many would-be purchasers would be unsure of getting in until showtime; they might not succeed even then unless they were willing to stand in a long line in winter weather, possibly for several hours prior to the start of the night's sale. One cannot imagine the country's notables or a major city's carriage trade welcoming this prospect, although such a procedure would have been truly democratic, more in accord with genuine regard for popular amusement. Those who could afford it naturally preferred to pay four and five times a ticket's face value for the privilege of being certain that they could attend the performance of their choice without camping out overnight to forestall speculators' agents (RF, 121).

Dickens and Dolby tried to appear magnanimous by maintaining the two dollar ticket but were conservative capitalists, not egalitarians; in reality, they chose lower overall profits and tacitly sanctioned speculation in return for guaranteed sellouts and steady, predictable receipts. The system to which they cleaved caused havoc outside the box office but brought those behind its doors a security invaluable despite its costliness. Even if the resale price of a ticket soared throughout the spring as one successful performance followed another, the burden of supplying ever greater demand was shifted to the speculators, while Dickens continued to earn what Dolby had promised. Once the advance sale was over and all seats taken, weather on performance nights ceased to be a concern. News of a sellout in one city swelled competition for tickets during the advance sale at the tour's next stop. Conversely, reports of customers being turned away night after night under the *Tribune*'s rubric might have hurt the turnout on subsequent evenings.

Several New York papers supported a public auctioning of tickets in lieu of advance sales (M, 258), but Dickens rejected the idea outright, although "he might have doubled his profits if he had" agreed (RS, 306). Technically, he could have surpassed a doubling if bids reached the $26 a ticket some speculators were asking: at $20 apiece, for example, Dickens stood to realize $2,280,000, or ten times his actual receipts.

Here, however, one may detect the dedicated popular entertainer declining to play a politer version of the speculators' game. Even the *Tribune*'s assurance that "no one" would "murmur" if Dickens benefited instead of the scalpers failed to move him. In truth, reports of feverish bidders with Dickens selling his talents to the highest might have angered the public more than news about speculators' successes. Dickens seems to have believed that it was better business to be exploited than to give the appearance of cutting himself in on the exploiters' profits, a lesson he may have learned in 1842 when he was called money hungry for demanding the dollars that went to book pirates. He could consider himself blameless for scalping excesses as long as he avoided hoisting prices; that is, as long as he avoided doing directly the very thing his intransigence indirectly permitted. Had he set prices at five or seven dollars, he would still have been powerless to prevent speculators from setting them even higher.

Dolby's war with "the speculating brigade" (D, 148) constitutes the third pattern traceable from the second visit's beginning to its end. Unlike the charts of Dickens's steadily increasing hold on Annie Fields's regard and the puzzling ups and downs of his influenza cold, this one must be drawn in red ink. On rare occasions, Dickens and Dolby hit upon a useful stratagem only to be outwitted by their opponents' countermeasures—the result being that speculators, emulating the piratical reprint houses of the 1840s, literally made more money from Dickens's exertions than he did. This point can be established first from several documented instances, representative pitched battles that show scalpers outearning Dickens as a group, if not individually, and then by mapping out a hypothetical campaign for a fictional Mr. Speculator operating parallel to Dolby from the first reading through the last.

When Dickens's manager wanted to charge $5 a ticket, he appealed to common sense with an argument resembling the *Tribune*'s: his point was that, "thanks to speculators, the audiences in Boston, New York, Philadelphia, and Brooklyn had all paid an average of five dollars a ticket"(RF, 127). In Washington, therefore, nothing would change if the asking price rose except the recipient of the extra $3 per seat. As has already been noted, Dickens demurred. A scorecard for the thirty-one readings just mentioned—the ones from Boston through Brooklyn and again figuring at $3,000 a night—would show Dickens grossing $93,000 between 2 December 1867 and 21 January 1868. Speculators by comparison took in at least one and one half times that amount, or $139,500, which was $46,500 more than Dickens received and mostly clear profit.

Before Dickens reached Halifax on the *Cuba*, ticket sales had begun, and on 18 November some Bostonians were buying from scalpers at "twenty-five dollars" per ticket. The New York *Evening Post* gave credence to a rumor that "*a single speculator* [italics added] . . . made $3,000" from such ticket transactions, probably before Dickens had set foot on American soil (M, 252). At that rate—$750 clear profit for each of the first four Boston readings at Tremont Temple—the same entrepeneur, immortalized as Mr. Speculator, could have banked $57,000 from the entire tour.

Bennett's *Herald*'s estimate of the eventual price of a scalper's ticket at "one hundred dollars or more" (M, 253) sounds preposterous. Nevertheless, using such a figure, a speculator need have resold 2,280 tickets between December 1867 and April 1868 to match Dickens's gross receipts from 114,000 admissions to 76 readings; even at fifty dollars per ticket, the number of required resellings jumps to only 4,560 and to just 9,120 at twenty-five dollars.

One speculator had twenty men in line to secure "a large share of the tickets" for the first four New York readings. From an allotment of four tickets per man per reading, he thus could have gained possession of a total of 320 tickets (EP, 180). Their gross worth to Dickens was only $640; if resold at $5 apiece, this speculator could have earned $1,600, or $3,200 at $10. By selling at the price Bennett had instructed Dolby to charge, therefore, one speculator could readily have made from four readings a sum greater than the performer himself averaged from each—in short, it would be virtually as if Dickens had given a fifth New York reading exclusively for this individual's financial benefit.

Dickens and Dolby were such easy prey that purchasers often became instant speculators. It was not just the professional scalper who resold tickets "at enormous premiums" (M, 258); private individuals—"Wall street brokers, merchants, lawyers"(D, 168)—followed suit, unable to resist a quick profit. One New Yorker, who could attend only the first reading, sold his other three tickets for that performance and two for the second, third, and fourth for $50—that is, he disposed of nine of his sixteen tickets at about $5.50 apiece (D, 167-68). Thus he walked away from the advance sale with more cash than he had paid out plus, in effect, a free ticket to the first reading and six tickets to the later ones (two for each). Having invested $32, he had $50 in bills and $14 worth of tickets at face value) for a total of $64, an amount double his own money and double what Dickens stood to make from the sixteen tickets sold. If the neophyte speculator used the ticket to the first reading and later took $5 each for the rest, he ended with $94, a profit of $62 simply for being early enough in line.

Since the queue in front of New York's Steinway Hall began forming at 10:00 P.M. on 28 November, the night before the sale, lining up early was not a simple matter. Places at the front were soon worth "as much as twenty dollars," or ten times the price of a single ticket (M, 257). Given the tremendous resale value of sixteen tickets—they were worth $160 at $10 each—paying $20 to get to the front did not prevent one from turning speculator and emerging $140 to the good.

Supposedly, Dolby was "in no mood" to be outsmarted in New York as he had been in Boston, where, in "a roaring trade," two dollar tickets "in a good position near the platform were immediately bought for as much as twenty-six dollars each" (RF, 112; or D, 150). But the manager's preventive measure was to change only slightly the method of distribution; instead of six, he proposed selling no more than four tickets to a man (M, 258). This precaution merely cut down the speculators' profit margin without improving Dickens's. Moreover, if Dolby was better prepared in New York than he had been in Boston, so too were his tormentors, who quickly increased the number of their agents so that forty-five of the first fifty persons in line were speculators' representatives (D, 165).

With a limit of four tickets apiece (one per reading), scalpers still garnered 180, worth $1,800 at $10 each; if their men bought four apiece for each reading, which is presumably Dolby's meaning (a reduction from six), their total was more than 700, valued at $7,000. And some of the purchasers after the fiftieth were doubtless also speculating. No wonder an indignant Kate Field branded the New York speculators "vampires" for reselling the best seats in the house for the first reading at "ten or twenty dollars a ticket" (KF, 17).

Dolby failed to learn much from the Boston fiasco, no matter what mood it had left him in. Prior to the opening New York sale, "the most prominent" of that city's speculators "were desirous to know what [his] plan of action was to be"; they plied him with drinks and interrogated him at length. But his self-satisfaction at proving "not communicative" must be balanced against the admission that "he had no fixed plan" (D, 164-65). Besides reducing sales from six to four tickets a man, he held back 400 tickets for each reading, a suppression of 1,600 tickets that he later admitted only "assisted the speculators' trade immensely" (D, 167) by curtailing supply even further below demand. Meant to be held in reserve for nonspeculators among the general public, these retained tickets greatly increased the value of those already sold.

Astonishment is the key theme punctuating Dolby's accounts of incessant ticket scalping. Over and over during the antispeculation campaign, the manager and his Chief registered surprise at the enemy's number, tenacity, and, as a consequence, success,[29] the extent of which neither Dickens nor Dolby may have fully understood. Indeed, beneath the latter's efforts to treat speculation with contempt or with a dismissive sense of its "humorous side" (D, 211), one detects grudging admiration: one example is the manager's depiction of scalpers' agents camping out in Brooklyn from 10:00 P.M. until 8:00 A.M. next morning in bitter January cold. Dolby carefully described their mattresses for open-air sleeping, suppers of bread and meat, and potations of bourbon whiskey so that the hardihood of this mock-heroic expeditionary force almost sounds Homeric; but he never dared to calculate precisely how much money he and his employer were losing.

"One of the biggest [speculators] could put fifty men in a queue at any time and so get three hundred tickets into his own hands" (RF, 120). This happened, Dickens moaned, "any place we go" (F, 2:399). Actually, if each scalper's deputy bought four tickets, the total would only be 200, whereas with each man buying sixteen tickets or four per night for the performances in New York, for instance, it would reach 800. Taking the figure given, however, this candidate for Mr. Speculator could resell at $5 a seat, for $1,500; at $10, for $3,000; or at $25, for $7,500. The plausible gross of $3,000 from just 300 tickets at $10 apiece is eye-catching: Dickens's best house of the entire tour, one must repeat, came to $3,456 for the final Boston reading (D, 300-1).

The speculator who could place fifty men in line at a moment's notice is probably the New Yorker whom Dolby credited with mustering fifty agents to buy tickets at the second Boston sale: he secured 300 tickets each for the performances on 23 December and Christmas Eve before scurrying back to New York to supervise the sale of "an equally large stock" for the second set of New York readings the following week (D, 190-91). In short, this Mr. Speculator had quickly become a painful parody, a sort of auxiliary manager as much in charge of Dickens's ticket operations as Dolby was and apparently far more efficient. Between 23 December and 3 January, Mr. New York Speculator handled a minimum of 600 tickets in Boston and possibly as many as 2,100 in New York (at 300 for each if there were seven readings), or 2,700 in all. This figure is astounding in light of the earlier calculation that a scalper need only have sold 9,120 tickets at twenty-five dollars to match Dickens's total receipts from the American tour;[30] in just one week, this speculator progressed nearly a third of the way toward that goal.

Like the experienced parasites they were, several speculators traveled with Dickens's entourage, sticking so close as to seem part of it. These opportunists caught the same trains Dickens and Dolby rode and stayed in the same hotels, where they could keep watch over the golden goose who was laying eggs as much for their benefit as for his own. Dolby called these businesslike gentlemen "the principal speculating firms" (D, 190) to distinguish them from less organized loners and upstarts. Indeed, speculation enterprises were so tremendously successful, thanks to Dickens, that the New York scalpers and even the speculators from out of town moved off their sidewalk perches and opened "temporary offices . . . for the disposal of their tickets at handsome premiums" (D, 184). Suddenly converted into semirespectable promoters of culture, these hardened souls must have been amazed at their good fortune: to them had come the world's most popular showman with a manager who would not (or could not) raise prices and who also failed to find a method for equitable ticket distribution that clever speculators could not circumvent.

By the second New York sale, having scented a sure thing, "speculators were in greater force than ever, the New York brigade being augmented by contingents from Brooklyn, Philadelphia, and Jersey City" (D, 184). It is no exaggeration to surmise that for long stretches during the tour, few tickets reached a theatergoer's hands without first passing through a speculator's, at least not when front row seats were at stake.

Several times Dolby was shocked to see the same faces in one city after another. Dickens had hoped he would shake off the scalpers upon departing from Boston and New York, or else that less vigilant varieties of the species would be less annoying in the smaller cities; but he soon began to recognize the easily mobilized army of speculators as if it consisted of old friends: these bothersome men were as loyal in their fashion as his "true American" catarrh. Thus in Philadelphia on 5 January where places near the head of the queue sold for five to ten dollars (F, 2:399), the New York speculators, clearly the most dogged, turned up "in a body." Except for brief apostasies in Washington and Baltimore, which they unwisely bypassed as poor propositions, they never left Dickens unattended thereafter.

If the modern revaluator hypothesizes a scenario in which Mr. Speculator, a composite of the shrewdest examples of the breed mentioned so far, followed Dickens from place to place, his operations would virtually constitute a second or shadow tour: he would match the reader's earnings without having to give a single performance or bear similar expenses. Had such a person controlled 200 tickets for every reading on the schedule, the resale of 15,200 seats at $5 apiece would have given him $76,000; at $10 each, he would have grossed $152,000. For 300 tickets a performance, a figure Dolby did not consider unrealistic for Boston and New York, the profits at $5 and $10 for 22,800 tickets grow to $114,000 and $228,000, respectively, this last figure *equaling to the penny* Dickens's gross receipts from five months of arduous effort in bad weather in less than the best of health.

Two additional observations may be made: (1) even if Mr. Speculator acquired fewer than 300 tickets per performance and passed some up completely, he could still have amassed nearly as much as Dickens by asking $20 or $26 a ticket both in larger cities and in those where Dickens read for only one or two nights; (2) if one speculator could hypothetically have rivaled Dickens's gains, collectively the speculating fraternity must surely have surpassed him.

At no point in the war against speculation did Dickens and Dolby enjoy an impressive victory, although they dealt their persecutors a few minor setbacks. For example: Dolby handed over to the New York police an individual caught forging thousands of tickets (D, 163), but this happened only because speculators tipped him off; they considered the forger as serious a threat to their incomes as to Dickens's.[31] Also, Ticknor and Fields rapidly issued cheaply priced texts of the readings, thereby superseding pirates who were planning on sending shorthand writers to transcribe Dickens's words (D, 177).

In the latter incident, however, Dolby simply took Fields's suggestion. The manager's 30 September letter acknowledged the publisher's wisdom in being forewarned; he promised to bring Fields the materials his printers would need to prepare texts before 2 December (FC, 1033). Thus the manager was not being strictly accurate when he subsequently wrote: "before the announcement of the Readings in Boston, an intimation had reached me that the 'pirates' had decided . . . to 'take them down' " (D, 177). This passage gives the impression that a vigilant Dolby alerted Ticknor and Fields, who then marketed "small volumes" no act of piracy could undersell.

Occasionally, providence came to the manager's rescue. At daybreak before the advance sale in Brooklyn, for instance, police attacked speculators' men whose "enormous bonfire in the street" counteracted the subzero January cold but endangered the neighborhood's wooden houses (D, 210). These determined would-be purchasers put up a "terrific" fight to preserve their source of warmth, only to be defeated by their own greed: whenever those nearest the sales door were routed or left their posts to support allies in another part of the fray, others ceased battling in order to rush into their places (RF, 126).

Similarly, a "tremendous snowfall" before the start of the first reading in the second New York series caused some speculators to panic. Afraid prospective buyers would be kept away, they started selling out "at considerable reductions" (D, 189). But the public came despite adverse weather, and patient scalpers who stood fast until fifteen minutes before the performance realized "handsome profits" of "as much as ten or twelve dollars for a ticket." Speculators also sustained minor losses from the farewell reading in Philadelphia's Concert Hall (14 February) but only because the public refused to believe that Dickens would not be returning again before the tour ended (D, 253).

In general, however, Dolby's more ambitious offensives proved ineffective, sometimes ludicrously so. He seems to have thought that he could "frustrate" the speculators' designs merely by being present to superintend sales in each city, as if speculation were an impropriety that could go on only behind his back (D, 206). Whenever he acted, he was injudicious, thereby adding ineptitude to what deserves to be called a comedy of errors; indeed, some of the sales could be described as scenes from a Mack Sennett movie.

Consider the circuslike mixup at the sale for the first series of New York readings, the occasion on which forty-five of the first fifty in line allegedly were speculators' agents. A panic-stricken Dolby acted on the advice of Harry Palmer, owner of Niblo's Gardens, who was said to be "very knowledgeable about the ways of speculators" (RF, 115; D, 166): since most of the scalpers' representatives wore caps, the manager decided to sell tickets only to men wearing hats. Nothing more childish or futile could have been devised, for a meleé of sorts ensued as the speculators' deputies collected hats, buying, renting, or just taking them from waiters and customers in nearby restaurants as well as from shopkeepers and passers-by. Despite the chapeau ploy, ticket speculators took possession "of most of the first seven or eight rows in the hall" and resold their tickets for these choice locations "at enormous profits" (RF, 115).

Almost as absurd were Dolby's "desperate" instructions to his clerks on 11 December, prior to the sale for the set of four New York readings slated for 16-20 December (the second week of the first New York appearances). He ordered selling to commence at the tenth row of seats; after satisfying the first fifty persons in the queue, his men were to start selling at the first row (RF, 119-20). Dolby hoped to keep the best tickets out of the speculators' grasp, thereby allowing the general public to obtain them directly at least once. In the event, some of the scalpers' men must simply have drifted back in line: the people's excitement at such good luck turned to outrage when it was discovered they were first on line for rear-seat tickets (D, 185; M, 258).

Dolby's only significant maneuvers to confound "the speculating fraternity" (D, 162) occurred early in the tour and were comic as well as ineffective. Although Dickens would perform through April of the following spring, the winners of the antispeculation war—namely, the speculators themselves—had already been determined by late December or early January. Routed on both of his major forays, Dolby seems to have lost much of his initiative; for the remaining four months, the bulk of the tour, his campaign can be called mostly defensive—he conceded the scalpers their large premiums and concentrated on trying to appease the general public, thereby protecting the core of Dickens's profits, his sellouts at the box office, from a decline in interest that might have been fatal to performer and speculator alike.

When combined, the refusal to raise ticket prices and the losing battle to forestall speculators dispel the myth that Dickens began destroying himself in America out of greed or that the tour was a financial phenomenon that made him a Victorian Croesus. The same factors go some distance toward tarnishing one's image of Dickens as an eminently resourceful, practical man of letters: he was too inflexible and his manager too blundering for either to be called grasping.

Although the post-1842 novels teem with exploitative and parasitical creatures, Dickens was still the fair-minded Britisher abroad in 1867-68, prone to demand British standards in American situations. Despite the modest ticket scalping witnessed earlier at Peterborough, he found speculation distinctly un-English; to the very end of the tour he included speculators prominently among the "many obstacles . . . thrown in an Englishman's way" (F, 2:409). This profiteering was not illegal but it seemed unfair, certainly undignified. One may ask whether Kaplan is correct in saying that Dolby "deserved his reputation for efficiency, competence, and insensitive toughness" (K, 509). The chapter the manager called one of the "brightest" in his life (D, viii) loses some of its luster when money that got away from his Chief is subtracted from dollars made, leaving a deficit. That Dickens's profits from readings at home and abroad in the late 1860s may have been "the equivalent of at least £1 million" today (K, 527) would be more impressive if such large amounts had not been lost in 1867-68. Ironically, Dickens hauled off only a fraction of the just deserts America was finally willing to give him.[32]

The dubiety of one other monetary myth connected with the American reading tour remains to be exposed: belief in an exceptionally "handsome" publishing agreement binding Dickens to Ticknor and Fields (T, 305). Actually, neither party granted favors. Despite Fields's professions of eternal friendship, Dickens's gratitude to his erstwhile sponsor and host, and a mutual reluctance to discuss dollars and cents in their correspondence, neither of these good Victorians allowed the warmth of a close personal relationship to cloud his business sense. On the contrary, they dealt more rigorously with each other than Dolby ever did with speculators. Just as the reader and his manager dictated ticket prices and the length of the reading tour, the publisher was fair but scarcely munificent about profit-sharing. Indeed, the royalty percentage he offered Dickens was not as substantial as the figures quoted in some of his dealings with other English Victorians. In addition, author and publisher almost quarreled over serial rights to *The Mystery of Edwin Drood*, the only novel on which Dickens worked after naming Fields his "only authorized" American publisher.[33] When retirement from the stage necessitated a return to the writer's desk, Dickens offered to sell Harper's early sheets (proofs) of installments for his last novel; he either exercised a prerogative he thought he had retained or else tried to find a lucrative loophole in a contract he had signed mainly with the American tour in mind.

One ought not to fault Dickens for reneging on his threat not to sell advance sheets of his novels to the highest American bidder. Within a decade of uttering it, he negotiated with Harper and Brothers for *Bleak House* (£400) and, subsequently, for *Little Dorrit* (£250), *A Tale of Two Cities* (£1,000), *Great Expectations* (£1,250), and *Our Mutual Friend* (£1,000) (M, 111). Having failed to secure copyright protection in 1842, Dickens would have been spiting only himself: withholding early proofs would have allowed *all* the pirates free play when his work appeared, whereas some reprint houses were willing to pay moderate sums in order to get a head start at pirating him, which is essentially what purchasing early sheets meant.

Although Dickens can be said to have collaborated with his enemies in the 1850s and 1860s, no great principle was at stake; copyright came no nearer to enactment after the first visit whether or not Dickens assuaged his damaged pride by declining American monies entirely. Indeed, the resuming of negotiations could be taken as a reinstating of his claim to royalties: he was reminding American publishers that they were stealing his property, and their willingness to acknowledge as much by spending up to £1,250 for the privilege indicates how profitable the robberies were.

Granted, Dickens received small payments periodically from such American publishers as Carey, Lea and Blanchard, T.B. Peterson and Brothers (both of Philadelphia), and Harper's of New York. But this was more like guilt money than royalties; it was sent in the guise of a courtesy but never in amounts close to his rightful share. Can one doubt that profits from *Bleak House* alone were sufficient to pay for advance sheets of all the other novels just listed? *Harper's Monthly Magazine's* circulation rose to 118,000 per issue during *Bleak House's* serial run, and in one form or another 250,000 copies of the novel were sold (KP, 12). At just twopence for every copy over 5,000, and with 120 twopences to the pound and even allowing for a fifty-fifty split with his English publisher (as per the subsequent agreement with Ticknor and Fields), the novelist would have been richer by at least £1,000, or more than twice the cost of advance sheets. Moreover, the novels mentioned above were not simply novels but some of the best works of the world's best-known novelist—the entire maturity of Dickens, so called, for under £4,000, a bargain unprecedented in the history of printed literature.

On 16 April 1867, the spring prior to the reading tour, Dickens wrote Fields: "in America, the occupation of my life for thirty years is, unless it bears your imprint, utterly worthless and profitless."[34] American commentators such as Kappel and Patten have demonstrated that this statement was scarcely accurate ("more pique than truth" [P, 343]); still if one were to balance the sums actually received at intervals from Carey, Peterson, and Harper's against fair compensation, the discrepancy would surpass the one that can be posited between real and possible earnings from the American reading tour.

The remarks to Fields are cast in Dickens's habitual comic-ironic hyperbole. And yet, if not strictly "profitless," his royalty surrogates became so when divided by thirty and imagined to be the living he had earned at his chosen occupation, the point being that he would have starved long ago if survival had depended on the charity of his transatlantic publishers. Even if Dickens did receive nearly £10,000 from American firms between 1837 and 1867 (P, 342), he averaged only £333 a year. His rights were "utterly worthless" in that, legally, he could not insist upon them; they had no certified or stipulated value.

Dickens was neither unscrupulous nor unfair in contracting with Ticknor and Fields over objections from Carey, Peterson, and Harper's. Fields's aspiration to represent Dickens in America and the latter's desire to have a recognized publisher instead of three unauthorized ones cannot be called "an attempt to corner the market on Dickens' work" (M, 214). Cornering the market on one's own productions is a contradiction in terms; it treats retention of rights as monopolization. The New York *Tribune* correctly distinguished Fields's organization as the only firm eager to pay Dickens "a share of the profits on the sale of his works in America"; other publishers paid for "a service"—that is, for a copy of his books to be sent them sooner than to anyone else (M, 221). Technically, therefore, in the American sphere, Dickens's occupation had been "profitless" insofar as he had participated in none of the actual profit making.

Instead of the once-only lump sum for advance sheets (Harper's unvarying proposal), Ticknor and Fields agreed to pay both the novelist and his English publisher a percentage of the retail price for every Dickens volume sold bearing the American firm's imprint (M, 213-14). This supposedly put an unfair end to "trade courtesy" (T, 306-7)—a euphemism for the practice whereby reputable competitors refrained from pirating the American publisher who had made the best offer to an English writer for advance copy (JA, 376). Neither Dickens nor Ticknor and Fields behaved reprehensibly in stifling what was actually another tacit press conspiracy: "trade courtesy" afforded publishers a modicum of copyright protection from each other while denying it to the author.

Dickens's 1867 agreement with Fields and the reading tour so soon afterward constituted a virtual package deal no other firm thought to provide. Fields's method of enlisting famous authors stressed the advantages of sealing the publishing contract with a lecture tour. Sign on, the implicit argument ran, and he would sponsor an American visit guaranteed to generate additional book sales beneficial to all parties. The pitch failed with Wordsworth and De Quincey but the reading lure worked with Thackeray (T, 301), who prophesied: "I shall carry back sacks full of shekels" (JW, pt. 1:2). Similarly, Dickens told W.H. Wills: "I believe that an immense impulse would be given to the Charles Dickens Edition by my going out" (NL, 3:530).

He was not alone in this opinion. Dickens's presence in America, Dolby reasoned, "was calculated to give an additional value to his works, the only authorized edition of which was published by Messrs. Ticknor and Fields" (D, 107). "The American sales of Dickens's last edition," Kappel and Patten conclude, "were unquestionably stimulated by his visit, so that he profited both from the readings themselves and from the additional books the readings sold" (KP, 8). In preparation for Dickens's second coming, Ticknor and Fields took from Chapman and Hall 5,700 volumes of the unillustrated Library edition of Dickens's works and 6,750 of the illustrated edition prior to 1867 and then another 52,000 volumes of the latter (2,000 complete sets) during the tour (KP, 14). The American firm also began issuing its own collected edition—the so-called Diamond edition—in anticipation of the sales increase from Dickens's arrival, and it announced publication jointly with Chapman and Hall of the Charles Dickens edition, destined to be the "last" in his lifetime.

Promising though all these American orders appear, it is difficult to determine precisely how sharply Dickens's visit spurred his American sales. Such a set of figures would greatly influence the final estimate of the tour. Did frustrating many of the pirates by coming to terms with a single American publisher offset losses to ticket speculators? Did the ardent advocate of copyright in 1842 finally win that battle—for himself personally but not for the English writing fraternity—and so experience less regret as speculators grew rich?

Relying on Kappel and Patten's compilations, one sees that as many as 64,450 volumes of Dickens's collected works from Chapman and Hall may have been sold during the 1860s by April 1868, not to mention copies of the Diamond edition and sets of Dickens's collected works previously ordered from England by American publishers other than Ticknor and Fields. But a casual survey of the publishing records of Dickens's American firm indicates few dramatic upswings during the touring period or immediately thereafter.[35] Recorded sales of *Our Mutual Friend*, for example, show no meteoric rise in the records for 1867, 1868, or 1869-70.

The modern revaluator may suspect that nothing to match the runaway sales of *American Notes* and *Martin Chuzzlewit* after Dickens's first visit took place for his collected works following his second—the important difference being that he shared in profits from the latter. No new novel from Dickens appeared in 1868 or 1869, so the tour could only prompt those who lacked complete sets of his work to remedy the deficiency by choosing one or by acquiring the volumes they were missing.

According to the agreement that Fields's junior partner, James R. Osgood, signed with Dickens and Frederick Chapman in London on 15 April 1867, the novelist stood to benefit almost immediately in at least three ways: first, he would earn money from Chapman and Hall for his share in the sale to Fields of 1,000 copies (twenty-six volumes in each set) of the illustrated Library edition; second, he and Chapman would receive "a Royalty of Twopence Sterling per Volume" of the forthcoming Charles Dickens edition; third, the same royalty would be paid on every copy beyond 5,000 of the Diamond edition then being marketed in America (CD-TF, 37-38). Osgood gave Dickens £200 as his share from the sale of this edition so far, a goodwill gesture that the 15 April contract did not call for.[36]

Dickens and his English publishers both received royalties from the Diamond edition, plain and illustrated, for which Chapman and Hall bore none of the expense, and Dickens would get royalties both from Chapman and Hall and from Ticknor and Fields on sales of the upcoming Charles Dickens edition. In return, Ticknor and Fields purchased the "exclusive right of publishing the said Works of the said Charles Dickens in the United States of America and the British Provinces in North America." For five years, Dickens and Chapman and Hall were not to sell anyone else "any Copies of any Edition of said Works collectively or of any individual Work" without the consent of Ticknor and Fields (CD-TF, 36).

How sweet the surprisingly short 15 April agreement was remains arguable. Compared to the modest sums publishers had sent Dickens previously and nonpayment from blatant piracies, the new situation was a vast improvement. For example, Dickens thought he had sold *Bleak House* forever for £400 when Harper's bought advance sheets because he stood to earn nothing else from serialization or American hardcover editions, but Ticknor and Fields's Diamond edition of the collected works, *Bleak House* included, netted him £200 right away and would go on earning. On the other hand, twopence is a less than staggering amount, as in the proverbial disparagement "Not worth a twopence." It fell far short of "fifty cents or a dollar on every copy of his books sold in this country"; in December 1867, that was still the New York *Herald*'s conception of Dickens's aspirations in 1842 (KP, 23).

The modern revaluator may conclude that the contract with Ticknor and Fields was satisfactory monetarily but had greater value psychologically as it belatedly brought America to terms and constituted a recognition by one of its foremost firms that the novelist had always been entitled to more than he would ever receive. Accordingly, the contract was retrospective, emphasizing the extant body of his work and thus finally allowing him to profit from it in America: having been denied royalties as each new novel appeared, he would garner them now when his writings reappeared in collected editions. That the readings Dickens had perfected for delivery in America were taken largely from his earlier, less embittered self tied in nicely with the prevailing aura of retroactivity.

The readings enhanced the contract for Ticknor and Fields by generating additional sales of the Diamond edition. The firm found the tour a persuasive drawing card for a publishing arrangement that both Harper's and Peterson would envy; prior to 1867, indeed since the 1850s, Harper's had been unofficially the publisher of Dickens's serials, while Peterson's considered itself the leading publisher of his work in volumes (KP, 12-13). From Dickens's standpoint, however, any royalty agreement obtained as late as 1867 had to be secondary: it possessed value mainly as a sort of entry visa, a semiofficial invitation to return to America and perform there, from which course of action the real money was to be expected. Coming to terms with Fields was sound business: a virtual peace treaty with American publishing interests (newspapers and journals included) that cleared the path for the public reader. Dickens could never have recovered the £2,000 he and Chapman deserved for *Bleak House* or made £20,000 in five months from Ticknor and Fields; within six months of the royalty agreement, however, Dolby was predicting £15,000 from America's theater audiences—that is, one and a half times the sum American firms had sent him in voluntary royalties over the previous thirty years.

That the 1867 contract did not enrich Dickens is a matter of simple mathematics—a case of too little too late. At twopence a volume, for example, the 1,000 sets or 26,000 volumes Fields accepted of the Library edition upon signing would have earned Dickens and Chapman only £216, a royalty of $1,512 if it could be turned into gold without any conversion loss; $1,512 was about half the average receipts Dickens would get from a single reading in America. These 26,000 volumes were *not* included in the royalty provision, however. The 2,000 sets, or 52,000 volumes, ordered during the tour could have brought Dickens royalties in excess of £433 ($3,031), better than the average nightly receipts but still less than Dickens's best night in Boston or New York. News that the Diamond edition sold a high of 12,000 copies of *Pickwick Papers* and never fewer than 2,000 of any other title (KP, 28) is not very sensational; the royalty Fields owed Dickens and Chapman for reissuing the former's first novel was only about £100.

Prior to 1867, Ticknor and Fields reportedly took a total of 12,450 volumes (the illustrated and unillustrated editions combined). Had it been 12,450 *sets* and had the contract Osgood negotiated been in effect throughout that period, Dickens and his English publishers would have divided £2,698—that is, roughly £1,344 apiece, or $9,408, which is only slightly more than Dickens realized from his first three readings. Had an agreement with Fields been in place since 1842 and had it covered each work published serially and then in volume format and in collected editions, so that the novelist received a substantial percentage of Ticknor and Fields's profits in addition to royalties on whatever his English publishers sold to the American firm, Dickens's American engagements might be a shorter story. Benefits from such a long-standing arrangement could have precluded reading tours of any kind, British or American, but by 1867, income from belated royalties could not rival the quick gains Dickens and Dolby foresaw from a single foray of five months' duration.

Maintaining that Dickens achieved "indirectly through the sale of his collected works several thousand additional pounds" thanks to the reading tour is, therefore, no understatement and possibly an exaggeration (KP, 33). Sadly, he did not long outlive publication of either the Diamond or the Charles Dickens edition. Irrecoverable royalties, monies he ought to have had from serialization in American magazines selling 100,000 copies a month, make "several thousand additional pounds" seem paltry. These lost royalties, one must repeat, exceed those he eventually obtained more drastically than possible profits from the reading tour outweighed actual receipts.

In 1855, Fields offered Robert Browning "10 pr. cent on the retail price" of each copy of *Men and Women* sold, or £30 outright." The poet replied that his new poems in two volumes should count double, and the publisher acquiesced.[37] Similarly, in October of that year, Charles Reade informed Ticknor and Fields: "I am quite satisfied with your offer of ten per cent on each copy sold and paid and am ready on these conditions to hold myself engaged to you with respect to 'Susan Merton' and future works."[38] Five years later, however, Reade, like Browning, opted for a flat sum—£250 for a story—because he had found "the percentage system . . . unsatisfactory."[39] When Fields sounded out Anthony Trollope during the latter's stay in New York, the novelist replied that Lippincott in Philadelphia already gave him "12 1/2 per cent on the retail price of all copies to be sold above 2,000."[40]

Measured against the above, nothing in Dickens's 1867 royalty arrangement at first seems munificent enough to be called "handsome." The difference lies not in the promised percentages, which actually favor Browning and Reade,[41] but in the quantities in which Dickens's business was to be transacted: in complete sets (as many as twenty-six volumes a set), such as the 1,000 sets of the Library edition to be ordered from Chapman and Hall, or the expected sale beyond 5,000 not just cumulatively for the Diamond edition but for some of its individual novels. Browning grasped at £60 straightaway, and Reade preferred

£250 to a percentage because, unlike Dickens, neither man anticipated a phenomenal sale. Lippincott's liberality toward Trollope was also premised on the unlikelihood of a sale much beyond 2,000 copies, a fact of life Trollope's letter to Fields went on to discuss.

On one hand, Ticknor and Fields were buying not a new work from Dickens, as they had from Reade, but a series of works, the initial sale for each of which could never be recaptured, hence the lower royalty offered. On the other hand, Dickens's reprinted novels could still be counted on to sell better in America than Reade's did originally or than some of Trollope's (remember that no volume in just the Diamond edition sold less than 2,000). In other words, any generosity in Fields's proposal was matched by Dickens's established strengths, on which it can be said to have capitalized: his best-seller's ability to extract the fullest advantage from quantitative terms.

In one sense, Fields gave Chapman and Hall a formal share in the American market by agreeing to sell the Library edition; in another, Dickens, along with Chapman, legitimatized the Diamond edition, making it, at least for Americans, as respectable a purchase as the Library edition. This give-and-take was confirmed by the willingness of both firms to cooperate on the Charles Dickens edition. But adjectives such as "handsome" seem exaggerated for a serviceable agreement from which all three parties derived some benefit. Moreover, this mutual advantageousness did not prevent a disagreement from breaking out almost immediately, a heretofore unexamined battle of the wills that surpasses the better-known dispute over ownership of *The Mystery of Edwin Drood.*

After returning from the telegraph office on 30 September, the day yes to an American tour was cabled to Boston, Dolby used *All the Year Round* stationery to enlarge upon this "favorable" reply; he wrote that he expected Fields would be reading the good news even as this follow-up letter was being composed (FC, 1033). But it must have checked jubilation sparked by the telegram, for although he had accepted a Bostonian's offer, including the guaranteed profit of £10,000 put up by Fields and associates, Dickens suddenly insisted upon opening in New York. "I have submitted to Mr. Dickens," said Dolby,

the advisability of commencing the Readings in Boston, and on considering the matter with him, we are of opinion that it will be as well to commence in New York. Having this in view I have written by this mail to Harrison of Irving Hall asking him if he can let us have the Hall for *one* evening in the week from the 25th to the 30th November. This will not interfere with the dates on the list as arranged with Osgood, but will merely be an *extra* reading. After which we will go on at Steinway Hall. Commencing there on the 9th December—If possible I would prefer Friday the 29th November for the Irving Hall night. This would give us Saturday the 30th for travelling to Boston, and Sunday for rest.

Lafayette Harrison was among the New York entrepeneurs Dolby had questioned about a successful American tour, but Irving Hall was not engaged in August 1867 because it was "too small" (D, 126). By the end of September, however, Dickens thought enough of the eastern metropolis's importance (vis-à-vis Boston) to plan a one-night gala opening there—the Victorian equivalent of a modern Hollywood premiere. Evidently, he and Dolby were still very concerned about the former's old antagonist, the American press. Irving Hall's compactness meant that this special event would attract a first-rate first night audience, just as the initial copyright speech had been recited to a dinner gathering of elite Bostonians a quarter of a century earlier. The appeal to a select group at the outset of the first visit may have backfired, but Dickens and Dolby still felt that a predictably favorable response from New York City's finest would curb press hostility—in 1842, attacks in the New York papers had been climactic, if not also more virulent and prolonged than in Boston's; thus a triumph in Gotham virtually ensured excellent reviews and future sellouts.

To palliate the blow to Boston's reputation as the nation's cultural hub, Dolby insisted that the New York opening would "merely be an *extra* reading"—just "*one* evening"—after which the tour would revert to the schedule hammered out with Fields's lieutenant: four Boston readings the first week of December, followed by eight over the next two weeks in New York's Steinway Hall. If the New World premiere were held "in the week from the 25th to the 30th November," preferably on the twenty-ninth, Dolby reasoned, Dickens could travel to Boston with a whole day to spare "for rest," and so he would be at his best for the *second* opening night. In short, the manager strove to convince Fields that a New York opener would not "interfere with" the arrangements they had discussed in America; on the contrary, it would add something, as if addition in one place were not subtraction elsewhere.

Nevertheless, the proposal was not being submitted for Fields's consideration. In keeping with the letter's dictatorial tone, Dolby stated that he had already written to Harrison. The 25 September letter, reporting Dickens's postponement of a final decision on America until the thirtieth, contained no hint that the reader and his manager were thinking about "commencing" in New York; yet they must have discussed it by then, unless it was an afterthought on Sunday the twenty-ninth—that is, subsequent to the three-day interview with Forster.

Why Dickens ultimately opened in Boston's Tremont Temple on Monday, 2 December, remains unclear. Perhaps the New York hall was unavailable the week of 25-30 November or on the coveted twenty-ninth. More likely, Ticknor and Fields refused to countenance an affront to Boston. In either case, a significant difference of opinion impeded the beginning of Dickens's business relationship with Fields, just as it will be seen that sparring over control of the American serial rights to *Drood* marred its ending.

Although Dolby said "we are of opinion" that New York should take precedence over Boston, it was *he*, not Dickens, who "submitted" the "advisability" of a Knickerbocker premiere. Here the modern revaluator finds additional evidence, beyond the Dolby-Forster clash on 26-28 September, for promoting the manager; he was the individual who had most to say about Dickens's doings and whereabouts from the time he began supervising the readings (from 1867 at the latest) until the final London farewell performance in mid-March 1870. Dolby's proximity to Dickens and the amount of authority he was permitted to wield, even if not always successfully, designate him the most knowledgeable narrator of the 1867-68 visit—more reliable, in effect, than Forster or subsequent biographers.

In 1842, Dickens had celebrated "the intellectual refinement and superiority of Boston" over New York, the latter "by no means so clean a city"—indeed, it was comparable in places to "Seven Dials, or any other part of famed St. Giles's" (*AN*, 77, 127-28). But Dolby, whose impressions were more recent, clearly championed New York as the world's new crossroads (not just the New World's). He was greatly impressed by Central Park and "the *élite* of New York society" disporting themselves thereabouts—this myriad of potential theatergoers imparted to the scene an "animation and vivacity far exceeding anything of the kind either in the Bois de Boulogne, in Paris, or in Hyde Park" (D, 121-22).

New York, Dolby later recalled, had been "regarded as the test place" for determining how much resentment lingered from *American Notes* and *Martin Chuzzlewit* (D, 122). The enthusiasm of Ticknor and Fields spoke well for success in Boston, sanctioning the tour with the firm's respectability, but in August 1867, Dolby had done most of his poll taking in New York. Besides consulting prominent showmen on

Dickens's behalf (P.T. Barnum, Harry Palmer, and "Colonel" Bateman), he interviewed makers and repositories of public opinion: the newspaper proprietors Horace Greeley, William Cullen Bryant, and, in particular, one of Dickens's meanest adversaries from copyright-seeking days, James Gordon Bennett of the New York *Herald*, whom the manager described in a letter for 23 August as "that wicked old ruffian" (FC, 1030). Logically, the locale used to ascertain the feasibility of a reading tour seemed to deserve first rights to it—if only because an inaugural triumph in New York would validate Dolby's American findings right away.

Turning to secondary matters, Dolby's 30 September letter struck out two matinees scheduled for 14 and 21 December in favor of just one on the twenty-eighth of that month; the first two dates stayed open, while Dickens performed "Copperfield" and "Boots" in New York for the tour's only matinee on the third (M, 331). The craving for a New York opening imbued these rescheduling proposals. Thus instead of Philadelphia for 6-7 January, Dolby inserted a return to Boston with a promise Dickens would do " 'Marigold' *for the first time* there." The switch from Philadelphia to Boston was doubtless an attempt at appeasement for planning a New York start.

On 6-7 January, Dickens would appear in Fields's city for a *third* time—that is, for a third series of performances—before branching out to places besides Boston which, jointly with New York, would monopolize the first twenty-five readings. Furthermore, this early January show would be a premiere of sorts, the debut of the "Marigold" reading. The change of venue stood, but "Marigold" was not given in Boston until 24 February, perhaps because the need for a trade-off disappeared after Dickens began the tour as originally designed. In any case, Dolby's "there" could have referred only to a local Boston premiere, since Dickens introduced "Marigold" to America on 2 January in New York.[42]

Fields's success in becoming "exclusive publisher of the foremost living writer in the English language" has been called an experience tantamount to "entering the promised land" (T, 301). His recollection of being summoned to the Gad's Hill library one Sunday in October 1869 to hear "from the author's lips the first chapters of Edwin Drood" (Y, 228-29) reminds one of Moses on Mount Sinai. Unfortunately, Dickens used the occasion to disclose that he was accepting £2,000 from Harper's for advance sheets of the monthly parts (P, 317). (Dickens had evidently asked during the American tour if Harper's was interested in early copy of any new work). Either Gad's Hill lay outside the promised land or Fields was wrong to assume exclusiveness. No matter which statement better explains the situation, the result is a curious splitting or doubling, variant forms of which pervade Dickens's last years: for example, just as Dickens and Dolby argued for *two* American opening nights at the start of the Dickens-Fields relationship, there were *two* novels at the end of it, the serial and the potential addition to the collected edition.

The *Drood* incident has been dismissed as a "needless controversy" (P, 317) or an all-too-convenient "forgetting" on the novelist's part (M, 225); on the contrary, it brought Dickens's second visit and his engagements with America to an ironic conclusion. Having been pirated and scalped, his talents virtually divided into so many pieces by total strangers, Dickens seems to have resolved to subdivide himself for his own benefit. Selling the serial Dickens to one publisher and leaving the collected Dickens in the hands of another confirmed the American status quo the day the agreement of 15 April 1867 was signed—only now Harper's and Fields (the latter replacing Peterson) were in an involuntary partnership, whereas in the earlier situation two publishers had tacitly divided Dickens between them without his consent.

No one knows "what words were exchanged" (M, 225) in Dickens's library or whether the parties grew heated, since Fields's account in *Yesterdays with Authors* ignored what could have been a serious rift. Patten states that Fields, having returned to America, consulted his old agreements "and found one specifically committing Dickens to his house for any new serial" (P, 318). If so, it would have to have been the April 1867 contract, since there does not appear to have been more than one. Moss erroneously reports that Dickens and Fields "reached a compromise": *Harper's Weekly* got the serial rights and Ticknor and Fields "the book rights" (M, 225), which would have been exactly what Dickens wanted. Actually, the novelist backed down; he must have accepted Fields's interpretation of their 1867 contract because he told Harper's he had made a mistake in contacting them. Nevertheless, one can side with Dickens and argue that the "book rights" were all Ticknor and Fields ever purchased.

The semantics of the situation are on Dickens's side. His letter of 2 April 1867, reprinted in the New York *Tribune* for 18 May, identified Ticknor and Fields as "the only authorized representatives in America *of the whole series of my books*" [italics added] (KP, 15). In the 1 June 1867 issue of *Publisher's Circular*, the American firm claimed to have become "the only authorized publishers of [Dickens's] works in

America" (KP, 19). Its 1868 catalogue carried word for word the endorsement from Dickens publicized in the *Tribune*.[43] Dolby, one recalls, used virtually the same formula: Dickens's second visit gave "additional value to his works, the only authorized American edition of which was published by Messrs. Ticknor and Fields" (D, 107).

Clearly, "the whole series of my books," like the many similar phrasings of it in the above paragraph, is a synonym for Dickens's collected works, not a title to any subsequent serial. The 1867 contract forbade Chapman and Hall to sell anyone else "Copies of any Edition of the said Works collectively or of any individual Work"; but until Fields set him straight, Dickens must have assumed that the latter part of this provision meant "any individual Work" already serialized and either in the collected editions at that time, or about to be, an interpretation which the context supports.

No matter how intensive the tutoring in America by shrewd pirates and conniving speculators, Dickens had not become two-faced in 1869; he did not display to Fields the duplicity of a Zephaniah Scadder, each of whose profiles "had a distinct expression" (*MC*, 352). Instead, the serial novelist tried to separate from the author of collected works, just as the lover of Ellen Ternan had become in America the womanless object of Annie Fields's adoration or just as the powerful public performer had repeatedly replaced the prostrated victim of an influenza cold. Thus it seems almost inevitable that a Dickens so concerned with different aspects of himself should also have been engaged in darker explorations of doubling through self-division: not just as the murderous performer of "Sikes and Nancy" challenging the jovial reader of "The Trial" and "The Carol" but as the melodramatic psychological realist probing John Jasper's dual personality.

Dickens doubtless believed "that publishing rights for a new serial might be split between two firms" (P, 317). Strictly speaking, however, it was not rights that he split but himself. He had not attempted to divide one item two ways or to sell *Drood* twice in America; on the contrary, he saw his new novel as different things: first a serial and then an addition to the collected works, whose only certified publisher he agreed was Fields. Either Dickens considered the disposing of serial rights an option he had retained or else he thought he had found a weakness in the 1867 contract, probably the former, since the approach to Harper's and subsequent declaration to Fields seem forthright—except that they might better have been made in reverse order.

Harper's motives in responding to Dickens's overtures were surely mischievous as well as mercenary: the firm still smarted from Fields's coup in having himself recognized as Dickens's "authorized" representative. But Dickens's motivation is obscure by comparison. He seems to have enjoyed using Fields as a club with which to lambaste other American firms yet was not averse to perturbing Fields as well. If several publishers had previously reprinted his writings without his assent, why should he not have more than one publisher now that the arrangement with Fields gave him some leverage to play one against another? Dickens may have considered his contract with Fields insufficiently lucrative by 1869 when a new novel was imminent, but if he sincerely believed that future serials had not been on anyone's mind back in 1867, he was naive to think Fields had courted him so diligently and helped to organize the reading tour just to secure an imprimatur for the Diamond edition.

Later, Harper's learned that Dickens would allow no part of *Drood* to appear from Ticknor and Fields before it was published in England and that Fields was as annoyed by the refusal as Dickens was by the request; the New York firm quickly renewed its offer. Whenever there was a fifth Saturday in a month preceding the last day of that month, Fields, publishing *Drood* weekly in *Every Saturday*, could come out before the next monthly part appeared in England (P, 318-19). This time, however, the publisher backed down because Dickens insisted that prepublication in America would endanger his copyright at home[44] and Harper's was disappointed again.

Even after the contract with Fields, therefore, some intrigue and a good deal of maneuvering continued; many hard feelings persisted not just between competing American firms but between all of them and Dickens. Neither he nor they were willing to forget how much more profitable printing Dickens had been prior to 1867: publishers tried both to justify their former misconduct and to weaken the Dickens-Fields alliance that prevented full-scale resumption of it. Thanks to the surety of the arrangement with Fields, Dickens was apparently willing to play in this game when it was to his advantage—that is, whenever he innocently supposed he could hold fast to hard-earned gains while also extracting additional vendibles from them.

No matter how much Fields gave Dickens for *Drood* in order to keep all of his prize author's talents under one roof—apparently it was only half of what Harper's offered (P, 318-19) plus the eventual twopence per hardcover volume—the ironic outcome of the so-called "handsome" 1867 contract remains unchanged: it put an end to trade courtesy but not to the purchasing of early sheets which such courtesy had originally made feasible. Thus although Fields in effect paid for early sheets and published each monthly part in smaller weekly portions, Harper's simply ran its aggregate copy of those portions in monthly supplements to *Harper's Weekly Magazine*, thereby reprinting Dickens and Fields without having to compensate either. The greater irony is that Dickens died before the first "individual Work" not yet in the Library or Diamond editions was finished. By 9 June, the results of having split himself in half amounted to half a serial and half a novel, with no new work forthcoming.

On 10 June 1870, when America learned of Dickens's death, Edward Everett Hale wrote Fields a letter of condolence. Recalling how Scott "died abandoned—when his American readers could have paid his debts" (as Dickens had observed in 1842), the author of *A Man Without a Country* (1863) voiced his "sense of satisfaction in remembering that Dickens had no reason for bitterness against us here." Thanks to Fields "personally," Dickens had "outlived the sharpness of his early resentments against America" (FC, 2453). Yet one must keep in mind the distress the speculators caused Dickens, their roguery a new case of "sharpness," and then underline his struggle to control the serial rights to *Drood*, in which instance he and Fields had no choice but to become reconciled—not to mention how "early resentments" (that is, disappointments) sharpened the satire in Dickens's later novels. Hale's sincere but starry-eyed "satisfaction" previewed posterity's overly positive verdict on the business aspects of the Dickens-Fields relationship.

Dickens's inspiration to subdivide himself into serial novelist and author of the collected works was latent in the idea of a second coming: he had returned to America as a reader in order to earn again money that should have been his royalties as a novelist in the first place. So many unauthorized persons had taken a piece of his profits both before and after 1842 (but in such plain sight in 1867-68) that he must have felt entitled to sell himself one part at a time. In 1866, George Eliot borrowed characters and situations from *Bleak House* to rewrite Dickens's masterwork as *Felix Holt*, and with *The Moonstone* in 1868, Wilkie Collins did his best to outdo his former mentor's melodramatic realism.[45] Thus two major attempts to supplant Dickens, by either negating or superseding him, bracketed the scalping he received from American ticket speculators. To someone so greatly harassed, these incidents must have seemed like a flurry of cannibalizations. Numerous difficulties the second time in America and the disagreement over *Drood* thus shed light on Dickens's eagerness to "tear himself to pieces," as Dolby put it (D, 387), by reading "Sikes and Nancy" several times a week. Whatever else its fascination, this selection must have had a perverse "charm" (D, 362): it became a symbolic frontal assault, unfortunately fatal, on all the dismemberment processes he had hitherto survived.

6

Last Words

"How unchanging national characteristics are! I have been re-reading *Martin Chuzzlewit* and the letters from America reprinted in the *Life of Dickens*; the people—at any rate to judge from the specimens one meets here and from what they write—are just the same; the same interminable canting balderdash about high moral principles and ideals, couched in the same verbose, pseudo-philosophic, sham-scientific, meaningless language, the same pretentiousness then as now." Thus in 1925 Aldous Huxley summarized for his brother Julian the handful of Americans he had met in Europe.[1]

No American going to Europe ever primed himself by reading Twain's *Innocents Abroad*. More than three-quarters of a century after Dickens's first visit, however, the modern era's most intellectual novelist prepared for his first glimpse of the New World by reexamining *Chuzzlewit* and the letters on which *American Notes* was based, as though, together, they equaled a Baedeker.[2] From this the modern revaluator can proclaim Dickens the ultimate victor in the battle of the Victorian travel books. His was the lasting view of nineteenth-century America formed not just by a plenitude of Victorians but by subsequent Englishmen like Huxley who applied that view to America's posterity.[3]

When Chollop dubbed his countrymen "the intellect and virtue of the airth, the cream Of human natur, and the flower Of moral force" (*MC*, 523), he was speaking "balderdash," but his mixture of hypocrisy with conceit, as clumsily poetic as it is fallacious, inspired the Dickens of the later novels (and the Huxley of 1925) with dystopian fears: both came to suspect that the worst aspects of human nature, not just "national characteristics," remain "unchanging." Were it not for the reference to Forster's biography, Huxley's denunciation could almost pass as Dickens's; the problem would lie in assigning a date. It sounds like an echo of the Victorian novelist's first impressions the second time around. When promenaders continually tried to "peep" into his hotel room, Dickens complained angrily to Dolby: "These people have not in the least changed during the last five and twenty years" (D, 158-59).[4]

A nagging question, therefore, remains: how efficacious were Dickens's reconciliatory parting words at the New York public dinner on 18 April 1868, just four days before he sailed for home? These were the basis for remarks the novelist vowed would stand henceforth as the conclusion to all editions of *Martin Chuzzlewit* and *American Notes*. If Dickens was naive enough to hope that his presence could stimulate demand for a copyright agreement, was he less innocent a quarter of a century later in thinking a "Postscript" (*AN*, 295-96) citing positive "changes," improvements in manners all across America, could palliate the harsh judgments to which they were affixed?

American Notes already had a postscript: the final three paragraphs in chapter 18, although none of the declarations in them is the least bit ingratiating. "I have written the Truth," Dickens asserted, without stooping "to court . . . the popular applause" (*AN*, 292). No "friend on the other side of the Atlantic, who is . . . deserving of the name," he then stipulated, can say otherwise. Finally, he insisted that he had not allowed his "reception" in America—the many personal kindnesses received—to "influence" him an iota. In tone these "Concluding Remarks" not only sound defensive but seem calculated to cause additional resentment; Dickens told his American readers that they could either recognize themselves in his travel book and stand condemned or go to the devil.

When the official "Postscript" underscored improvements in "amenities" and "in the Press, without whose advancement no advancement can take place anywhere," Dickens actually reaffirmed the importance previously attached to these interrelated phenomena: civility and honest reporting were the two things he still felt he had most sorely missed in 1842. He went on to chide newsmen for detailing "the vigour and perseverance with which" he had "for some months past been collecting materials for . . . a new book on America" (*AN*, 295). Even as he assured the public that "no consideration on earth would induce [him] to write" a sequel to *Martin Chuzzlewit*, he gently remonstrated with the press for its tendency to be "sometimes mistaken or misinformed."

Adding this "Postscript" to both *American Notes* and *Martin Chuzzlewit* in perpetuity, Dickens maintained, would "express [his] high and grateful sense of [his] second reception in America"; it was his "duty" as a good Victorian to perform this "act of plain justice and honour" with "the greatest earnestness." Implicit in such an act, however, is a good deal of regret that it could not be executed the first time. It was possible in 1868, Michael Slater has argued, because America had demonstrated its maturity by becoming more like England (S, 64). If the New York speech was to "form a part" of Dickens's American engagements, to be forever "inseparable from [his] experiences and impressions of America," it could only help to keep earlier disgruntlements fresh, both by referring to them directly and by subtly restating them.

Huxley's acceptance of the satire in *Chuzzlewit* as gospel came fifty years after Dickens's pacifying observations at Delmonico's; therefore, it was absurd to expect that the novelist could make amends to his hosts or they to him, regardless of their admiration for the readings or his overestimate of the tour's financial success. The New York speech was the final gesture of an Englishman always an innocent abroad in America; Dickens's pacification effort naively relied on his skill as an after-dinner speaker and the simple inclusion of parts of his farewell speech in an apologetic appendix. Even if he sincerely believed he had compensated Americans for unforgettably abusing them, the 1868 "Postscript" overlooked long-term consequences of the 1842 disillusionment: the irreparable damage America had done to his worldview. A steady interrogating of man's capacity for self-betterment is a major dystopian motif throughout the post-*Chuzzlewit* novels.

In other words, Dickens had discovered a sad truth since learned many times over by would-be utopians: no place at home or abroad can succeed in illustrating the perfectibility of the species without a prior improvement in human nature. Yet that was the very thing some Victorians thought would automatically spring from a new environment or from revamped institutions, while others, equally deluded, conceived of it as the natural product of societal evolution. Out of the 1842 disappointments came much of the impetus for Dickens's deceptively simple call for personal, inward transformation as a prerequisite for lasting change. It is against such a call that one must measure his initial dismay upon finding Americans unaltered after a quarter of a century; his last words in New York merely indicated a slight softening of this anti-utopian stance.

Ironically, the final speech to "two hundred representatives" of the United States press resembles in tone and spirit the 1842 postprandial at Papanti's, in which the young novelist had hailed copyright as a foreseeable goal. Whether being welcomed in Boston or saying goodbye forever in New York, Dickens invariably sounded good-natured, even when prodding his listeners. Yet both speeches must be classified as exercises in futility, the last nearly as quixotic as the first in that neither changed anything. One can only wonder whether Dickens ever paused to consider fully how different his later masterworks might have been if his first American speech had been as politely reported as his final words have been less deservingly acclaimed.

Post-America manifestations of Dickens's lifelong restlessness, not to mention the visits themselves, were as much the product of ideological frustration as of personal unhappiness—although together these made an unpleasant combination. The resolute Englishman he became after 1842 continued to abhor the Utilitarian *present* but could not countenance Romantic nonsense about recapturing an idyllic *past*. Least of all could he tolerate visionary projections of society's movement into the *future* as the working out of a slow but unstopping amelioration.

Using *Martin Chuzzlewit* as the linchpin, one can construe much of Dickens's subsequent writing as a prolonged elaboration of his 1842 discoveries. Once "Self, Self, Self, dilated on the scene" (*MC*, 525) as the common failing of individuals and societies in New World and Old, he had few affirmative options. Utopianism—the perfectibility implicitly the goal of evolutionary humanism, also known as gradualism—became as untenable as enlightened self-interest, itself an oxymoron. Consequently, Dickens's post-America novels follow logically from each other; his satiric exposures of interrelated aberrations and their side effects converge, in retrospect, as prescribed stages in a genuinely inevitable unfoldment: it resumes with Dombey's ice-cold pride and extends to Chancery's self-perpetuating litigation and the selfishness in both Utilitarianism and laissez-faire economics, a self-centeredness epitomized by Gradgrind's disdain for the sympathetic imagination as a vehicle for self-transcendence; it excoriates the relentless pursuit of status and wealth as the only viable forms of salvation in a mercenary world at once irresponsible and repressive; and it castigates the superficial proprieties that preserve appearances, concealing temporarily what cannot be controlled and thus guaranteeing that the darker energies in John Jasper's repressed self percolate toward disaster.

Branding Dickens Pecksniffian as an undercover agent for the British publishers he always distrusted renders the latter half of the Dickens canon suspect at its root, when it is the root of things, man's selfish nature as reflected in society's heartless institutions, that he grew steadily better at delineating—the sense of something grievously wrong at the core, not just stemming from a personal sense of duplicity.

Revaluators for whom the reading tour was an expedition to the "Golden Campaigning Ground" (M, 231) cannot have the final word either; Dickens did not plunder El Dorado in 1867 any more than he traveled to Altruria in 1842. Despite "the golden lure of America" (J, 2:1070), the second visit was not an adequate recompense for the first; instead, one must follow Huxley's clue about "unchanging" characteristics and draw parallels between the two. For example: the second visit mirrors the first in that one ended with bad feelings, while the other began that way. To Forster's resentment at home and the jealousy he and Dolby felt for each other, one must add the displeasure of Ticknor and Fields when the firm was informed of the shortness of Dickens's projected stay and his preference for a New York opening.

No matter how profitable America proved to be in dollars and cents, Dickens never discovered how to take maximum advantage of its opportunities, just as he had been baffled previously in his pursuit of copyright. He tried to be better prepared in 1867-68 than his inexperienced younger self had been for the 1842 press conspiracy; yet both the reader and his manager were still amazingly gullible, easy prey for unprincipled ticket speculators. Idealistic notions of democracy and fair play made the thirty-year-old novelist vulnerable; ironically, a parallel kind of innocence, the conviction that inflexibility would keep them unbeatable, hampered Dickens and Dolby. Despite considerable last-minute tinkering, including reductions in the number of performances, the tour suffered from excessive ordination as disastrous in its way as mentioning copyright in a virtual afterthought to the 1842 after-dinner speech at Papanti's.

If a lack of elasticity turned out to be as detrimental as a sensibility too easily bruised by the absence of "humanizing conventionalities" (MC, 278), Dickens's Englishness was decisive both times. The eventual author of *American Notes* and *Martin Chuzzlewit* imagined he would find a democratic republic exalting the noble savagery idealized by Rousseau but with the good manners that civilizations such as England's acquire only over centuries. Similarly Procrustean, the public reader and his manager expected to impose on a New England winter, the great distances between American cities, and a horde of indefatigable scalpers the same sort of timetable, itinerary, and rudimentary business precautions that had worked on tours of England and Scotland. Still, the verdict is that Dickens, given his dues, should not have suffered lifelong monetary anxieties; he ought to have been relieved of these several times over, hence spared some of the oblique self-incrimination in *Great Expectations* for being so money-minded.

The last word on Dickens in America must be sought in his private dreams, not in public speeches. "I very often dream I am in America again," Dickens wrote C.C. Felton; "I am always endeavoring to get home in disguise, and have a dreary sense of the distance."⁵ This 1843 letter is far more revealing than the subsequent New York speech and makes a better epitaph for both of Dickens's American engagements.

Throughout his life, the novelist was obliged to relive his traumas in recurring nightmares. Thus he confessed to dreaming about Mary Hogarth "every night for many months" after her sudden demise (J, 1:200), and his returns in sleep to Warren's Blacking continued into the 1850s. "Even now, famous and caressed and happy," Dickens confided to Forster, "I often forget in my dreams that I have a dear wife and children; . . . and wander desolately back to that time of my life" (F, 1:27). Dickens's initial encounter with America resulted in a persistent nightmare because, like Mary's death and his stint in the warehouse, it altered his conception of himself by darkening his impression of the nature of things.

Interpretations of Dickens's recurring American dream should emphasize his sense of being disguised and his failure, regardless of persistent endeavor, to decrease the miles between himself and home. Dickens probably took these Kafkaesque circumstances to mean that he could never forget how hot an anticopyright America had become; to a visitor more maligned in the press than a notorious criminal, the New World seemed light years away not just from the the utopian republic he expected to find but from the civilities even a problem-laden society like Great Britain's could afford. But only in nightmares did Dickens fully intuit that he would *never* get home again after 1842 because the world suddenly looked so very different—that is, far less hospitable; he had to move warily but with little hope of safe arrival. America was more difficult to escape from than Warren's because it was the key to all places. Despite having discovered his fundamental Englishness, indeed because of this twofold process of self-discovery, on the one hand, through alienation from the land of promise, on the other, Dickens was now truly himself and yet no longer the same person.

Notes

1. DICKENS DISCOVERS DICKENS

1. On 13 September 1841, Dickens wrote Forster that he was "haunted by visions of America, night and day," but "Kate cries dismally" whenever he mentions the subject (F, 1:192).

2. Dickens's favorite novel is less of a departure if one sees it as accentuating the difficulty of reordering past events; it is about David's realization of the distance he has traveled and the need for additional earnestness and is not simply an instance of revitalization through recall. See Alan Shelston, "Past and Present in *David Copperfield*," *Critical Quarterly* 27 (Autumn 1985), 17-33. Conceivably, coming to terms with the first visit prompted a larger stocktaking that made it easier to drop hints to Forster in 1847 about the Autobiographical Fragment, the basis subsequently for *Copperfield* (1849-50).

3. See the preface to vol. 3, 1842-43 (PL, vii).

4. David Paroissien agrees that America shook Dickens's assumptions that a society with fewer controls promoted greater civility, but he rightly credits the nation's interest in educating her people and caring for the poor with sparking Dickens's reform efforts throughout the 1840s (i.e., the Ragged School in Field Lane, the rehabilitation of prostitutes at Urania Cottage); see *Selected Letters of Charles Dickens* (Boston: Twayne, 1985), 180. To Macready for 22 March Dickens confessed: "In every respect but that of National Education, the Country disappoints me" (PL, 3:156).

5. Admittedly, Dickens never forgot the pleasure he originally took, even if mistakenly, in so much unexpected acclaim: the canceled preface to the Cheap Edition of *American Notes* (1850) fondly referred to "that spontaneous effusion of affection and generosity of heart" (*AN*, 298) but also reemphasized the justness of his 1842 critique.

6. Michael Slater gave traditional prominence to international copyright and slavery in his otherwise excellent introduction to *Dickens on America and Americans* (S, 18). He agreed with the Pilgrim editors (PL, 3:x) that Dickens's attitude changed during 15-17 February, when illness confined him to his hotel room and he read with chagrin newspaper editorials criticizing his outspoken interest in a copyright law. Angus Wilson blamed the copyright question for the "first rifts" be-

tween Dickens and America; see *The World of Charles Dickens* (London: Secker and Warburg, 1970), 164. Edgar Johnson (J, 1:443) acknowledged the importance of slavery and copyright but attributed Dickens's negative reactions to the incomplete view of America he was given; his views were distorted by the "furore" accompanying his progress (J, 1:444-45). Sylvère Monod explained Dickens's disillusionment and the so-called excesses of *Chuzzlewit's* American chapters by citing the novelist's weariness from overwork at home and the rigors of riverboat travel abroad; see SM, 38-39.

7. Dickens invited comparison with Swift when Mr. Bevan tells Martin: "I believe no satirist could breathe this air. If another Juvenal or Swift could rise up among us to-morrow, he would be hunted down" (*MC*, 276). For the view that Dickens employed material from his travel book unfairly in the novel, see Harry Stone, "Dickens' Use of His American Experiences in *Martin Chuzzlewit*," *PMLA* 72 (1957), 464-78.

8. In a letter to Forster (PL, 3:67), Dickens wryly observed: "As every man [in America] looks on to being a member of Congress, every man prepares himself for it."

9. Rousseau's *The Social Contract* (1762), with its thesis that happiness belonged to man in the state of nature, that is, before the growth of civilization corrupted his natural goodness and increased the inequality between men, seems to be the chief culprit; see Maurice Cranston's translation (Harmondsworth, Eng.: Penguin, 1968) of what he calls an "intensely republican book" (23).

10. Virgil Grillo explored this paradox but accused Dickens of being unable to make up his mind about what constitutes man's natural—that is, his best—state; see *Charles Dickens' Sketches by Boz* (Boulder: Colorado Associated Univ. Press, 1974), 188-206.

11. Yet Peter Conrad argued that Dickens disliked America for claiming to be able to alter human nature because he preferred mankind's "chronically heroic refusal to correct itself"; see *Imagining America* (New York: Oxford Univ. Press, 1974), 49.

12. Sylvère Monod ("Mr. Bevan," *Dickens Studies Annual* 15 [New York: AMS, 1986], 23-40) accused the American doctor of being "ill-informed and improvident"; he is not the only good American in *Martin Chuzzlewit* but "a man who has dangerous friends." Monod's article denied that Martin is an innocent abroad: from the moment he lands, he is burdened with "boiling indignation" (29) from experiences Dickens had already had. Similarly, other commentators have argued that Martin, a nobody, should not be lionized to the extent that Dickens was. But whereas the latter found his early days in Boston pleasant, Martin registers disgust from the outset because the novelist's first impressions were wrong and his character's are not. In 1876-77, Anthony Trollope's Senator Gotobed observed that "every Englishman of distinction was received in the States as a demigod, and that some who were not very great in their own land had been converted into heroes in his" (*The American Senator*, ed. John Halperin, [Oxford: Oxford Univ. Press, 1986], 349). Surely Dickens belongs to the first category and Martin to the second.

13. Dickens gave a resounding no to James Fenimore Cooper's question as to whether a model Christian could weather the moral compromises necessary for survival in the wilderness; the Victorian novelist knew an English gentleman could not. See Ivan Melada, "'Poor Little Talkative Christianity': James Fenimore Cooper and the Dilemma of the Christian on the Frontier," *Studies in the Novel* 18 (Fall 1986), 225-26.

14. Kate's clumsiness must be added to the carnivals, junketings, balls, and

dinners that Boston's *Morning Post* said were virtually designed "to make an ass of the lion," giving the entire visit a "serio-comic opera aspect" (NP, 91, 86).

15. Slater (S, 67) called the novelist "a natural American," but the adjective is not suitable.

16. Yet Angus Wilson (*The World of Dickens*, 164) theorized that Americans considered Dickens ungentlemanly for talking about money in public, a trumped-up charge that I reexamine in detail in the next chapter.

17. Thomas Carlyle, "Shooting Niagara: And After?" in *Victorian Prose*, ed. Frederick William Roe (New York: Ronald Press, 1947), 70-85; Carlyle advocated an alliance for power between the worthy among England's "Titular Aristocracy" and her "Aristocracy by Nature," to whom God has granted wisdom, talent, nobility, and courage.

18. Jackson pinned Dickens's near lapse on his failure to realize that a certain amount of pandemonium was a "normal" consequence of the political emancipation desired (TAJ, 47); actually, Dickens seems to have recognized this rather well.

19. The absence of counterproposals prompted writers who agreed with Dickens's satirical vision of Victorian England to supply the missing utopian alternative; Aldous Huxley merely borrowed from *Our Mutual Friend* for *Brave New World*, but William Morris, in *News from Nowhere*, attempted to create the obverse of the predatory London he found in Dickens's last completed novel. See Jerome Meckier, "Boffin and Podsnap in Utopia," *Dickensian* 77 (Autumn 1981), 154-62.

20. Dickens was more disappointed than Alexis de Tocqueville, often an avowedly "hostile" critic; the novelist came down harder on the deleterious effects of equalitarianism, as chapter 3 of this book will show. See *DA*, 12, 53.

21. See Jerome Meckier, "Dickens and the Dystopian Novel: From *Hard Times* to *Lady Chatterley's Lover*," in *The Novel and Its Changing Form*, ed. Philip G. Collins (Winnipeg, Can.: Univ. of Manitoba Press, 1972), 51-58.

22. Mary Rosner ("Reading the Beasts of *Martin Chuzzlewit*," *Dickens Quarterly* 4 [Sept. 1987], 131-41) argues that Dickens's sixth novel encouraged "readers to recognize the animal within," the "beasts behind the civilized masks of nearly every character," American or British. As a "griffin," for example, Jonas Chuzzlewit unites an eagle's head and wings with a lion's hindquarters—the two animal symbols for America and England.

23. Dickensians need scarcely be reminded that sixteen years later Dickens apparently chose a young mistress over his wife.

24. Two delegates pursued Dickens about the deck in hopes of conversionary conversation. One of these depressed him as "perhaps the most intolerable bore on this vast continent"; the other, besides being a temperance fanatic, was a phrenologist, thereby combining in Dickens's eyes two unspeakable aberrations (PL, 3:179). The Broadway Hotel in Cincinnati overflowed with the temperance convention. Having heard several of the speeches, Dickens could not resist observing that he had never met with "drier speaking" (PL, 3:193); for his description of Judge Walker's party, see PL, 3:194. William Glyde Wilkins located the Galt House incident in the Louisville *Courier* for 1870 (W, 207). Wilkins also reports the encounter with Porter (W, 210), while Dickens records his dislike for the Ohio (*AN*, 215).

25. According to *Lloyd's Steamboat Directory* (1856), Cairo was "advantageously situated" at the confluence of the Ohio and Mississippi rivers, where it was allegedly destined to become a leading commercial metropolis. The Directory discounted as "minor inconveniences" the low banks of the Ohio, which sometimes

kept the city under water, and the marshy soil, which contributed to regular outbreaks of fever; see W, 218-19.

26. Wilkins repeated this unfounded story (W, 210-11); Gerald Grubb dismissed it as a fairy tale but wrongly concluded that the Cairo episode is unimportant: see "Dickens's Western Tour and the Cairo Legend," *Studies in Philology* 48 (1951), 87-97.

27. Whitley and Goldman posited this "collapse" (*AN*, 35) in their introduction without pinpointing its occurrence. But see John S. Whitley, "The Two Hells of *Martin Chuzzlewit*," *Papers of the Michigan Academy of Science, Arts, and Letters* 50 (1965), 589-97.

28. After being thrown out by Pecksniff, young Martin stops at an inn where discolored "scripture pictures on the walls" show "how the Prodigal Son came home in red rags to a purple father, and already feasted his imagination on a sea-green calf" (*MC*, 255); when Martin and Mark get back from America, Pecksniff greets the latter as "the Prodigal returned" (*MC*, 661). One should ignore the technicality that Martin is a prodigal grandson, as Cynthia Sulfridge did in "*Martin Chuzzlewit*: Dickens's Prodigal and the Myth of the Wandering Son," *Studies in the Novel* 11 (1979), 318-25. Thackeray reused the Prodigal Son theme in *The Virginians* (1857-59) for both Henry and George Warrington, American brothers abroad in London.

29. Joseph Gold rightly asks: "Did Dickens have in mind the Book of Jonah when writing *Martin Chuzzlewit*, or can the Biblical story throw any light on the Dickens novel?" See *Charles Dickens: Radical Moralist* (Toronto, Can.: Copp Publishing, 1972), 130. As Mrs. Gamp watches Jonas's attempt to escape from Tigg by the Antwerp packet, she wishes the ship "was in Jonadge's belly" (*MC*, 624).

30. The same chapter that first alludes to life as a "wale" also contributes to the novel's satiric tone by referring jocularly to "the curse pronounced on Adam" (*MC*, 311).

31. David Parker thinks the new country showed Dickens anxieties within himself that he "did not wish to come to terms with"; if so, devoting one-seventh of *Martin Chuzzlewit* to American adventures seems a curious stratagem; see "Dickens and America: The Unflattering Glass," in *Dickens Studies Annual* 15 (New York: AMS, 1986), 55-63.

32. See *HD*, 71.

33. For parallels between Martin and Mark's journey to Eden, Marlow's up the Congo to Kurtz, and Tony Last's with Dr. Messenger to the Brazilian jungle, consult Jerome Meckier, "Why the Man Who Liked Dickens Reads Dickens Instead of Conrad: Waugh's *A Handful of Dust*," *Novel* 13 (Winter 1980), 171-87.

34. Emphasis on Jonas's blackness—"dark shade," "darker and darker," "black night"—lends support to the thesis that Jasper, described as a "dark man," need not be so in a racial sense (not partially Egyptian, for example); see *The Mystery of Edwin Drood*, ed. Arthur J. Cox (Harmondsworth, Eng.: Penguin, 1974), 43. Dickens would later argue that evil is not foreign, foreign not evil—that is, the problem is not external but inside all men, as the confirmation of Martin's American epiphany by Jonas's London metamorphosis seems to suggest.

35. The young James T. Fields's lighthearted sobriquet for a newly arrived, soon-to-become-disenchanted novelist also gives title to Fred Kaplan's chapter on the critical years 1842-44 in *Dickens: A Biography* (K, 122, 126). This chapter's tone, however, seems more indebted to my essay in the *Modern Language Review* (see n. 40 below) than to either Forster's or Johnson's biography. Cairo receives only a single mention, but the new life is predicated on Dickens's "genius for trans-

forming personal loss," including the loss of republican principles, "into aesthetic wealth" (137, 439-40).

36. This seems to be John Hildebidle's main point in "Hail Columbia: Martin Chuzzlewit in America," in *Dickens Studies Annual* 15 (New York: AMS, 1986), 41-63.

37. See Myron Magnet, *Dickens and the Social Order* (Philadelphia: Univ. of Pennsylvania Press, 1985), 176. For a fuller account of my reservations, including the charge that Magnet's views of Dickens on society would be better applied to George Eliot, consult "Recent Dickens Studies: 1985," in *Dickens Studies Annual* 16 (New York: AMS, 1988), 362-65.

38. Magnet cites Dickens's fascination with Laura Bridgeman, a blind deaf-mute successfully educated at the Perkins Institution and Massachusetts Asylum for the Blind (*AN*, 82-94), as proof that socialization generates the soul (see pp. 176-78, 183). Actually, like Helen Keller subsequently, Bridgeman was redeemed not by society, not by the everyday "humanizing conventionalities of manner and social custom," as Magnet claims, but through the good offices of a gifted specialist, in this case Dr. Howe, whom Dickens exalted (*AN*, 90).

39. Stuart Curran ("The Lost Paradises of *Martin Chuzzlewit*," *Nineteenth-Century Fiction* 25 [1971], 51-68) noted Dickens's many variations on the themes of downfall and collapse. Their abundance, one might add, reflects the novelist's heightened post-1842 awareness of devastating loss and deprivation.

40. That Dickens became Victoria's grateful subject was the punch line in an earlier version of this essay in the *Modern Language Review* 79 (April 1984), 266-77.

41. See George Eliot, *Felix Holt*, ed. Peter Coveney (Harmondsworth, Eng.: Penguin, 1977), 616.

42. For an account of the parodic revisions Dickens's competitors did of his allegedly overly negative novels, see Jerome Meckier, *Hidden Rivalries in Victorian Fiction: Dickens, Realism, and Revaluation* (Lexington: Univ. Press of Kentucky, 1987); although written and published subsequently, the present book can be considered a kind of delayed prelude to *Hidden Rivalries*, which it both clarifies and depends upon.

2. THE NEWSPAPER CONSPIRACY OF 1842

1. According to Robert B. Heilman, Dickens's dislike for "smartness," a mixture of greed and cunning, pervades his critique of America. Pride taken in sharp practice—Dickens called it "the national vanity" (F, 1:289)—revealed that individual hypocrisy and the country's materialism were interconnected; see "The New World in Charles Dickens's Writings (Part Two)," *Trollopian* 1 (March 1947), 19.

2. At the New York dinner, for instance, Cornelius Matthews, of whom more later, spoke for twenty minutes, deploring piracy as a recurring setback for American authors (W, 239).

3. Paul B. Davis has concluded that the newspapers were "divided" on copyright yet virtually unanimous in saying that Dickens's embroilment was vulgar and tactless (PD, 69); the issues were inseparable, however, since some papers realized that they could avoid opposing copyright directly by accusing Dickens of poor taste.

4. Dickens told Forster he had been called "no gentleman" (PL, 3:83); James Gordon Bennett, editor of the New York *Herald*, coined the other epithets (M, 40).

5. The example of Scott persuaded Dickens that a trip to America was an "imperative necessity" (F, 1:197): Lockhart's *Life of Scott* revealed a worn-out man journeying through Italy, which Dickens took as a warning to travel young and in "plenitude of power" (J, 1:358).

6. Colonel Webb made the claim on 8 February (M, 10).

7. For Cooper's letter, see James Franklin Beard, ed., *Letters and Journals of James Fenimore Cooper* (Cambridge: Harvard Univ. Press, 1960-68), 4:302-5.

8. A commonplace during the first visit, this accusation was reiterated by Colonel Webb in the *Courier and Enquirer* as late as 24 October 1843 (M, 43). Concurring, Moss states that Dickens was unable to remove "the stigma of self-interest" from his efforts on behalf of copyright (M, 7).

9. See chapter 15 of *The Warden* (1855).

10. Information about different editions of *American Notes*, the cost of each, and number of copies sold has been compiled from Moss (M, 37-38) and Robert L. Patten, *Charles Dickens and His Publishers* (P, 131-32). Edgar Johnson talks of proof sheets that were stolen from Bradbury and Evans, Dickens's printers, by a "smart American journalist" and used for "cheap editions" that "flooded" this country "at six cents a copy" (J, 1:441). Since Dickens put the price of a ticket to Papanti's at "three pounds sterling" (PL, 3:34) and Johnson says "fifteen dollars" (J, 1:374), one can compute the conversion rate in 1842 at five dollars to the pound sterling.

11. See Dickens to Forster on the pride a novelist should take in being liked in America: "The Americans read him; the free, enlightened, independent Americans; and what more *would* he have? Here's reward enough for any man" (J, 1:421); this statement roundly retracted Dickens's preference in his Boston speech for America's good opinion over gold mines.

12. Edward J. Evans, "The Established Self: The American Chapters of *Martin Chuzzlewit*," in *Dickens Studies Annual* 5 (Carbondale: Southern Illinois Univ. Press, 1975), 62-63. Discussing Thackeray, Samuel C. Chew (*A Literary History of England*, ed. Albert C. Baugh [New York: Appleton-Century-Crofts, 1948], 1359) argued that *The Virginians* "suffered, as does Dickens' *Chuzzlewit*, from the shifting of scenes between England and America"; but a comparison of these novels is one way of demonstrating the effectiveness of Dickensian counterpoint.

13. Ada Nisbet, "The Mystery of *Martin Chuzzlewit*," in *Essays Literary and Historical Dedicated to Lily B. Campbell by Members of the Department of English, University of California* (Berkeley: Univ. of California Press, 1950), 204-5.

14. Norman Page, *A Dickens Companion* (London: Macmillan, 1984), 136.

15. Publication of *The Chimes*, on which Dickens began working in October, was still six months away.

16. Forster estimated its sales to be less than those of only *Pickwick Papers* and *David Copperfield* (F, 1:328).

17. Forster insisted that this provision was never meant to be invoked, which makes its inclusion inexplicable (F, 1:328).

18. Contrary to Forster and Ford and more improbably, Alexander Welsh has turned the time between *Chuzzlewit* and *Dombey* into an Eriksonian "moratorium" (AW, 10): a sort of second emergence from adolescence (between the ages of thirty and thirty-four)—an emergence not contingent upon prior events but with a resultant search for new beginnings. Unfortunately, this approach leaves Dickens's change of tone and direction *within* his sixth novel (not *after* it) insufficiently

motivated. Like the rejection of trauma as a shaping experience, the failure to provide motivation—indeed, a refusal to study events of the early 1840s in search of
it—compromises Welsh's treatment of identity formation. This is clear from the
only rationale given for the first visit: "having no other plans" in 1842, Dickens
"decided to go to America" (AW, 9).

19. Edmund Wilson decreed that *Chuzzlewit* "marks the transition from the
early to the middle Dickens"; see *The Wound and the Bow* (New York: Oxford
Univ. Press, 1965), 27. Oddly, Sylvère Monod stressed Dickens's "desire to revert" to the leisurely style of *Pickwick Papers*; he contended that *Chuzzlewit* "does
not show much progress since the days of *Oliver Twist*." But his subsequent view
of Dickens's sixth novel as a final attempt to solve things comically suggests a breaking point, not a digression (SM, 142, 170). For additional comments on Monod's
Chuzzlewit monograph, see Meckier, "Recent Dickens Studies: 1985," 308-10.

20. Chesterton referred to Dickens's "great quarrel" but insisted that the
novelist "did not go to America with any ideas of discussing copyright laws," a statement Moss omits. See *CD*, 128-29, 138.

21. Webb, who also called Dickens "an upstart foreigner," makes Colonel
Diver of the *New York Rowdy Journal* seem docile: although "still recovering from
a bullet wound he had recently sustained in a duel and facing a mandatory two-year
prison sentence for engaging in the duel," he was "moved" to respond vigorously
to articles in the *Foreign Quarterly*; Moss's description, just quoted, indicates that
he admires Webb's pluck (M, 41).

22. Welsh quotes the retraction (AW, 38-39), which one can also read in the
Edinburgh Review 76 (1843), 500-1.

23. Welsh's inspiration may have been Michael Steig, who saw Dickens "unconsciously revealing *himself*" as the novel's "supreme confidence man"; see
"*Martin Chuzzlewit*: Pinch and Pecksniff," *Studies in the Novel* 1 (1969), 187. The
seriousness of Welsh's charge—that Dickens was Pecksniff in ways that Molière
was never Tartuffe—jars against his other judgments: such as the Chestertonian
misreading of Pecksniff as lovable because so laughable or the idea that Dickens
was attracted to the "amoral appeal of hypocrisy" (AW, 25).

24. Forster reported Dickens's anger at "the injustice done by his entertain-
ers to their guest by ascribing such advocacy [of copyright reform] to selfishness"
(F, 1:235).

25. Dickens had been in his grave "twenty-one years," Johnson marveled,
before England and America signed a copyright agreement in 1891 (J, 1:421).

26. An earlier version of this chapter appeared as a two-part essay for the
Dickens Quarterly, largely in response to Moss's book; see "Part One," vol. 5
(March 1988), 3-17; and "Part Two," vol. 5 (June 1988), 51-64. Like most commentators on the first visit, Moss and Welsh fail to mention that Dickens looked
hopefully to America as a result of reforms at home; the 1842 Copyright Acts permitted successful writers, who did not need to sell their copyrights outright, to
keep a lifetime interest in their work.

3. THE BATTLE OF THE TRAVEL BOOKS

1. See Marryat, *Diary in America* (1839); Fidler, *Observations on Professions, Literature, Manners, and Emigration in the United States, Made During a
Residence There in 1833*; and Hall, *Travels in North America in the Years 1827-
1828*.

2. Seymour Martin Lipset (*SA*, 10) awarded Miss Martineau's study this distinction.

3. The description comes from Richard Mullen's introduction to Mrs. Trollope (*DM*, ix).

4. Such a road, Dickens explained, "is made by throwing trunks of trees into a marsh, and leaving them to settle there," forcing carriages to jolt "from log to log" (*AN*, 236-37); see repeated objections to such roads catalogued in Max Berger, *The British Traveller in America, 1836-1860* (New York: Columbia Univ. Press, 1943), 45.

5. According to Percy G. Adams, travel writers have always been quarrelsome and self-serving: "often travelers themselves, both the truthful and untruthful ones, ironically contributed to the bad reputation of their fraternity by attacking the credibility of all travelers, or just those who preceded them to a particular spot, in order to claim uniqueness as dependable reporters"; see *Travel Literature and the Evolution of the Novel* (Lexington: Univ. Press of Kentucky, 1983), 87.

6. Heilman ("The New World in Charles Dickens's Writings [Part One]," *Trollopian* 1 [Sept. 1946], 29) likened Mrs. Trollope's disillusionment to Dickens's.

7. Mullen rightly called attention to the connection (*DM*, xviii-xix).

8. Lipset (*SA*, 5) used this phrase to express nineteenth-century Europe's conception of the United States.

9. This observation about "faith" having turned into "distrust," taken from the preface to the Cheap Edition (1850), reveals the poignancy Dickens's American disappointments continued to have for him as he moved toward his bleakest fictions. By comparison, Harriet Martineau's open-mindedness seems partisan: "I went with a mind . . . as nearly as possible unprejudiced about America, with a strong disposition to admire democratic institutions" (*SA*, 50).

10. Mrs. Trollope merely sounded petulant when deploring the "violent intimacy" and "most vexatious interruptions" forced upon her by people "whom I have often never seen, and whose names still oftener were unknown to me" (*DM*, 83).

11. See Paul Fussell, *The Great War and Modern Memory* (London: Oxford Univ. Press, 1975), 8, 169.

12. By comparison with Dickens, Miss Martineau was less imaginative when she simply echoed Tocqueville on conformity: "It seems, at first sight, as if all the minds of the Americans were formed on one model, so accurately do they follow the same route" (*SA*, 23).

13. Writing to Forster from Niagara Falls, Dickens equated "the national love of 'doing' a man in any bargain or matter of business" with "the national vanity"; he was surely alluding to Tocqueville, who began a section by proposing to explain "Why the National Vanity of the Americans is More Restless and Captious Than That of the English" (*DA*, 252).

14. Sidney P. Moss thinks Dickens was rash to expect copyright protection when "the state legislatures of Mississippi, Louisiana, Maryland, Indiana, Illinois, Michigan, and Pennsylvania had repudiated their obligations to foreign investors by voting to default on state bonds," a matter of "about forty millions sterling" (M, 83).

15. Conditioned by depictions of European scenery in Romantic poetry, Victorian travelers often sounded comic when searching in vain for the beautiful and the sublime. Dickens, Miss Martineau, and Mrs. Trollope understandably ad-

mired Niagara Falls, and Mrs. Trollope relished the "glory" of a transatlantic thunderstorm (*DM*, 246), but Dickens found no "sublimity" in a prairie and seconded Basil Hall's depreciation of American scenery's "general character," which fell below "even the tamest portions of Scotland and Wales" (F, 1:279); similarly, Mrs. Trollope considered the Ohio "perfect" except for the lack of an occasional "ruined abbey, or feudal castle" (*DM*, 27).

16. Curiously, Mullen has stated that few of Mrs. Trollope's illusions about America "survived the voyage" out (*DM*, xiii-xiv).

17. On another occasion, Mrs. Trollope referred to "the grim tinge of the hateful tobacco" on " 'many yet unrazored lips' "; given such self-conscious artificiality, one may question Mullen's decision that Mrs. Trollope remains "readable today" because "she often used words that the growing puritanism of the nineteenth-century found 'vulgar' " (*DM*, 300,xxi). Mrs. Trollope was capable of both invoking propriety and scorning its strictures. Dickens's imagination was inspired by vulgarity: he told Forster that "flashes of saliva" flew "so perpetually" from the gentlemen's railway car "that it looked as though they were ripping open featherbeds inside, and letting the wind dispose of the feathers"; the stone floor of every barroom and hotel-passage was so stained with tobaccospit that it looked "as if it were paved with open oysters" (F, 1:238-39).

18. Actually, a particularly repulsive dinner table sequence takes place in *American Notes* just a few paragraphs before Dickens passed Cairo, but these events are shrewdly transposed in *Martin Chuzzlewit*. The traveling novelist chastised his "fellow-animals," each busy at "his Yahoo's trough," for satisfying their "natural cravings" in "funeral feasts" that parodied the "social sacraments" (*AN*, 214-15). To Forster, Dickens wrote: "Indeed the Americans when they are travelling, as Miss Martineau seems disposed to admit, are exceedingly negligent: not to say dirty" (F, 1:265; *AN*, 203); thus the climactic debate in *Chuzzlewit*'s American chapters, besides outdoing Mrs. Trollope, shows Dickens improving not only on *Society in America* but on himself. The jibe at Miss Martineau is that even a starry-eyed optimist can recognize dirtiness provided it is "exceedingly" dirty.

19. Dickens also appropriated one of Mrs. Trollope's observations about the gentlemen in this scene—"we heard them nearly all addressed by the titles of general, colonel, and major" (*DM*, 15)—and had Martin elaborate upon it when surveying the diners at Mrs. Pawkins's (*MC*, 273).

20. Michael Sadleir, *Trollope: A Commentary* (London: Constable, 1927), 63-64.

21. Helen Heineman (*Mrs. Trollope: The Triumphant Female in the Nineteenth Century* [Athens: Ohio Univ. Press, 1979], 209) concurred with Edgar Johnson's statement.

22. Even when Miss Martineau mentioned "the use of tobacco and the consequent spitting," she quickly added: "I am ready to acknowledge that the American manners please me, on the whole, better than any that I have seen" (*SA*, 279). Throughout, she appended apologies to her criticisms: only an aristocracy of wealth was possible in America, that of birth having been ruled out; still, the pursuit of rank through riches was "the only kind of vulgarity I saw in the United States" (*SA*, 259).

23. See "I am shown Two Interesting Penitents" (*DC*, chap. 61).

24. According to Gillian Thomas (*Harriet Martineau* [Boston: Twayne, 1985], 34), Miss Martineau held, "from the outset, a buoyantly optimistic view of the New World"; she "had already tested her theories of political economy against the ex-

amples of British social institutions she saw around her, and it was logical to want firsthand experience of a country whose institutions had been deliberately designed in contrast to those of the Old World" (p. 15).

25. Throughout the early scenes, Faust portrays himself as a lowly "worm," a prisoner of the "moth world," whose fettered, molelike soul, "burrowing upwards," wishes for wings. At the conclusion, when Goethe's hero is conveyed to celestial spheres, his immortal part is a "Chrysalid entity" whose "cocoon" must be stripped away so that it can take wing; see Louis MacNiece's translation of *Goethe's Faust* (New York: Oxford Univ. Press, 1959), 28, 12, 299.

26. Inexplicably, in Dickens's opinion, Miss Martineau thought America's "infinite diversities" were not yet "blended into" a "national character" (*SA*, 325), unless, of course, she meant that it was still unfolding, as George Eliot's characters subsequently do, and would improve in the process. See n. 28 below.

27. An attack on *Society in America*, Dickens realized, would make good Captain Marryat's failure to thrash Miss Martineau, democracy's utilitarian champion; the captain's prejudiced, often ill-informed account of his eighteen-month tour had chiefly disclosed the personal deficiencies of a rabid Tory. See Captain Marryat, *A Diary in America*, ed. Sidney Jackman (New York: Knopf, 1962).

28. For more about the evolutionary energy George Eliot's characters possess, an inner force that urges them to realize their potential through interaction, see Jerome Meckier, " 'That Arduous Invention': *Middlemarch* versus the Modern Satirical Novel," *Ariel* 9 (Oct. 1978), 31-63. That "the great scroll of nature has been steadily unfolding to reveal a constantly richer harmony of forms and successively higher grades of being," however, was precisely the sort of future vision against which H.G. Wells reacted in "Zoological Regression" (1891); the passage sounds like Dickens rebuking Harriet Martineau in ways that subsequently upset George Eliot; see Robert M. Philmus and David Y. Hughes, eds., *H.G. Wells: Early Writings in Science and Science Fiction* (Berkeley: Univ. of California Press, 1975), 158. Unlike Wells, Dickens never subscribed to "cosmic pessimism," the theory that survival of the most ethical was incommensurate with survival of the fittest. But Wells had Dickens's awareness that the beast in man is liable to break out at any moment, a position that the pupil of T.H. Huxley adopted contrary to the air of cosmic optimism he felt evolution had created among the general public. Thus it is not too great an oversimplification to pit the school of thought that included Harriet Martineau and the evolutionary humanism later espoused by George Eliot, who drew ammunition from Darwin, against a less enthusiastic group diverse enough to encompass not only Dickens but Wells's embellishments upon T.H. Huxley.

29. This pejorative is Lipset's (*SA*, 10). When Miss Martineau's fervor was aroused, her outpourings exceeded Mrs. Trollope's attempts at being literary in the face of vulgar material. Visiting Mammoth Cave in Kentucky (*SA*, 133-35), for example, Miss Martineau struggled "in vain to describe a cave"; her "impressions . . . may be recalled in those who have wandered in caves, but can never be communicated to those who have not." Nevertheless, instead of bringing the place to life, as Dickens could have, she likened the bundled-up ladies in the party to "the witches in Macbeth," the "light on the drips of water" to a "Rembrandt," and "the unseen canopy" overhead to a dark "roof" only "Milton's lake of fire might have brought . . . into view."

30. William Lloyd Garrison complained of "stubbornly incredulous" readers unwilling to believe the cruelties slavery inflicts on its victims; for them, one must

describe "cruel scourgings, . . . mutilations and brandings" or else be accused of libeling southern planters. See *NFD*, 40.

31. Louise H. Johnson showed that Dickens borrowed many of these examples from *American Slavery As It Is*, a contemporary pamphlet; see "The Source of the Chapter on Slavery in Dickens' *American Notes*," *American Literature* 14 (Jan. 1943), 422-30. But Johnson's findings no more invalidate Dickens's artistry than the discovery that Jo in *Bleak House* was based on George Ruby, a fourteen-year-old crossing sweep whose condition had been described in Dickens's *Household Narrative* in 1850. The most curious naming of names, however, is a case of someone named not by Dickens but after him. In a letter to James T. Fields for 29 January 1869, Cyrus Augustus Bartol reported encountering in Jacksonville, Florida, "a black man 'Boz'—named, when a slave, 'Charles Dickens'—but bearing the great author's self-nickname now to all mankind. Would it not please Mr. Dickens," Bartol mused, "to know how his influence, so long ago, penetrated into the barbarism of that very slavery among us he hated, with such a flavor of the humor which is the organ & outlet of his own humanity as to give him this double name-sake." See FC, 242.

32. Berger (*The British Traveller*, 122) stated that this argument had currency. Brahma Chaudhuri ("Dickens and the Question of Slavery," *Dickens Quarterly* 6 [1989], 3-9) contends that after 1850 Dickens "demonstrated . . . a modified and softening attitude" toward slavery. Also see Arthur A. Adrian, "Dickens on American Slavery," *PMLA* 67 (1952), 315-29.

33. Mrs. Trollope appeared to better advantage when she nursed an eight-year-old female slave who had eaten a poisoned biscuit set out for rats; she records the consternation of the white family upon seeing that she was "really sympathizing in the sufferings" of one of their slaves (*DM*, 210-11). But Thackeray's failure in 1852-53 to perceive slavery as a serious problem is to his everlasting discredit: "The Negroes don't shock me or excite my compassionate feelings at all; they are so grotesque and happy that I can't cry over them"; he referred to "little black imps" and "well fed and happy" slaves. Admittedly, Thackeray witnessed slavery mostly in the towns, but his disdain for *Uncle Tom's Cabin* and the "tirades of the Abolitionists" seems irresponsible (JW, pt. 1:131, 145-46).

34. Charles Dickens, *Hard Times*, ed. George Ford and Sylvère Monod (New York: Norton, 1966), 84.

35. The fracas took place in 1854-55. Harriet Martineau accused *Household Words* of "unscrupulous statements, insolence, arrogance, and cant" in its treatment of the frequency of factory accidents. Dickens's reply, written under his supervision by Henry Morley, smashed every argument she had used to defend the National Association of Manufacturers, which subsidized her attack. Although "impeccably polite," Dickens's rejoinder was not without satirical "bite" (J, 2:854-55).

36. Edgar Johnson's introduction to his edition of *Martin Chuzzlewit* (New York: Dell, 1965), 26, stigmatized Pecksniff in these terms.

37. Surprisingly, Johnson's prefatory enumeration of the vices stemming from selfishness does not emphasize self-pity; see p. 27.

38. Magnet (*Dickens and Social Order*, 205-12) misinterprets Dickens's use of Monboddo and Blumenbach but explicates their views admirably. Most Dickensians forget that Boz first mentioned "spontaneous combustion" in chapter 11 of *Chuzzlewit*. Dickens referred to Bianchini in his preface (*BH*, 828).

39. According to Lipset (*SA*, 18), Miss Martineau could be described as "a left-wing English woman" throughout her career.

40. Thomas (*Harriet Martineau*, 82) also reported Dickens's unfavorable opinion.

41. Twain avoided having to reconsider travel-book material in a subsequent novel by going straight to the latter; it was based on fifty letters he contracted to write for the *Alta California* and the New York *Tribune*.

42. John Lauber has cited Twain's "habit of evaluating everything in American terms." See L, 257. Also useful is Dewey Ganzel, *Mark Twain Abroad: The Cruise of the Quaker City* (Chicago: Univ. of Chicago Press, 1968).

43. This is Leslie A. Fiedler's term from his afterword to the novel (*IA*, 481).

44. Richard Mullen included Twain's comments on Mrs. Trollope in his edition of *Domestic Manners* (p. 369); since these annotations date from 1883 or thereabouts, one must rely on the texts themselves to show he knew Victorian travel literature well in 1869.

45. In the more interesting one, Dickens is said to have "made facile mockery" of religious iconography in Italy much "as Mark Twain was later to do in *The Innocents Abroad*" (J:1, 561).

46. The idea that Twain was defining the American identity is Fiedler's (*IA*, 478).

47. Henry James did not begin exploring his international theme—the pitting of American innocence against European experience—until *The American* (1877) and *The Europeans* (1878).

48. Anthony Trollope's two-volume commentary on *North America* (London: Chapman and Hall, 1862) predated Twain's travel book but has been omitted from discussion because it was not part of the 1830s' cluster of Victorian peregrinations, nor did it look back on them in a revising manner. Trollope claimed that he hoped to "mitigate the soreness" previous travelogues had created, but it was a different country to which he came, an America with what he called "intestine troubles" (that is, the Civil War). Interestingly, he labeled his mother's *Domestic Manners* "essentially a woman's book" (p. 2), just as Dickens had charged. The North would win, Trollope decided, but secession, a division into two countries, would take place inevitably anyway. Chapter 6 in volume 2, "Cairo and Camp Wood," corroborated everything he had read in Dickens: "I do not think that I shall ever forget Cairo," Trollope moaned; its "wet blanket of thick, moist, glutinous dirt" and the fact that "fever and ague universally prevail" made it "of all towns in America the most desolate." Trollope thought Dickens was right to model his inverted Eden on this city in Illinois; his own efforts to emulate Mark Tapley and be happy there failed miserably, he confessed.

4. AN IRONIC SECOND COMING

1. Dickens coined this expression in a letter to James T. Fields, which the latter reprinted in *Yesterdays with Authors* (Y, 144).

2. According to Peter Bracher, Dolby exaggerated: in both 1842 and 1867, Bennett simply published "racy extracts"; see "The New York *Herald* and *American Notes*," *Dickens Studies* 5 (1969), 81-85. But the *Herald* for 7 November 1842 claimed to include "the cream of the book," all of its "principal portions," and six columns of extracts in 1867 gave what the paper termed "a very fair notion of the volume." On both occasions, *extract* and *reprint* become relative words. Bracher questioned Dolby's credibility, but, besides his grievous yet comic inability to comprehend and overcome ticket speculators, I have found only three peccadil-

loes: (1) the exaggeration of Bennett's misuse of *American Notes*; (2) a reluctance to take responsibility for his assistant, Kelly; and (3) the impression that Dolby, not Fields, prevented the pirating of Dickens's reading texts. Items 2 and 3 are discussed in chapter 5.

3. Hervieu proved a valuable asset: he produced twenty-four drawings for the first edition of *Domestic Manners*. But in the pirated New York reprint of 1832, the "editor" hinted that the illustrator's contributions had not been strictly aesthetic: Mrs. Trollope, he wrote, "pretends to have a husband," yet "whom she travelled with" in America "or why she travelled at all is an inscrutable mystery . . . she must have had a protector" (*DM*, xxi).

4. Michael Slater, *Dickens and Women* (Stanford, Cal.: Stanford Univ. Press, 1983), 377. On the other hand, Edward Wagenknecht seconded Gerald Grubb's caution ("Dickens and Ellen Ternan," *Dickensian* 49 [1953], 121-28) that the diary code is susceptible to a variety of interpretations and remained skeptical concerning the entire Dickens-Ternan affair; see EW, 33. Although one tends to believe that the relationship was not Platonic and that its sexual aspect began well before 1864-65 (the date Wagenknecht reluctantly proposed), this witty rebuttal of the so-called scandalmongers retains its pungency. It exposed the eagerness of Thomas Wright (*Life of Charles Dickens*, 1935), Hugh Kingsmill (*The Sentimental Journey*, 1935), Gladys Storey (*Dickens and Daughter*, 1939), and especially Ada Nisbet (*Dickens and Ellen Ternan*, 1952) and Felix Aylmer (*Dickens Incognito*, 1959) to accept as fact the likelihood that Ellen became Dickens's mistress.

5. Dickens's sense of epistolary propriety never wavered; when he wrote to one of the Fieldses, he always sent his love to the other—except that expressions of fondness for Annie in letters directed to James are sometimes uneasily playful, Dickens self-consciously exploiting the embarrassment of having to declare affection for another man's wife through the man himself. See, for example, the letter for 3 February 1868 (FC, 1204); Dickens fairly salivated describing Annie to James as a "charming creature," sympathetic and delightful, but he attributed these compliments to a letter he had just received from Georgina Hogarth and Mamie Dickens, who were responding to his praise of Mrs. Fields.

6. George Curry has assumed that the "confidences" Dickens "doubtless" was "sharing" with Annie's husband extended to his involvement with Ellen, but since the Fieldses seem to have known nothing about Warren's, reticence concerning Ellen would not have been Dickens's only exception to total candor. See GC, 9.

7. Paul Schlicke (PS, 227) says the readings were "self-professedly intended to fill the highest aspirations for popular entertainment"; they gave Dickens a chance to present his most cherished works to a live audience.

8. Even in 1858-59 when the scandal nearly broke wide open, misinformation prevailed: Dickens was said to have separated from Catherine because of a love affair with Georgina Hogarth, a rumor Thackeray clumsily contradicted by saying "it's with an actress" (J, 2:922). An entry in John Bigelow's London diary for 10 March 1860 indicated that he had heard something of Ellen as "a Miss Teman" (N, 23), but there is no follow-up. This friend of the Fieldses could have informed them but appears not to have done so; if he had, that fact would explain some of James's cryptic moral judgments, for example that Dickens "was human, very human" (Y, 172).

9. J.W.T. Ley, *The Dickens Circle* (New York: Dutton, n.d.), 203.

10. Angus Wilson, *The World of Charles Dickens* (London: Martin Secker and Warburg, 1970), 288.

11. Elsna to the contrary, Annie must have heard rumors concerning Dickens and Georgina but none pertaining to Ellen; Adrian quoted most of the 25 April passage and all of the February one, about which more later (A, 113-14, 131). Whenever critics such as Michael Slater (*Dickens and Women*, 427) have agreed with Elsna that Annie was a full confidante, their "clear evidence" is never forthcoming. The most plausible suggestion in Elsna's book is that since bearing ten children took its toll on Catherine's figure, Dickens's marriage might "have prospered had contraceptives been then available as they are today" (E, 18).

12. Ada Nisbet (N, 53) and Philip Collins both quoted part of this entry, but the latter dated it 24 November 1867, just five days after Dickens's arrival; see *Dickens: Interviews and Recollections* (Totowa, N.J.: Barnes and Noble, 1981), 2:317.

13. For Bigelow, see n. 8 above. Could Dickens have been so friendly in hopes that the minister would not mention what he had heard in London in 1860, or was Dickens's fondness mostly in Annie's mind?

14. Similarly, Curry cites Annie's ejaculation "Ah! What a mystery these ties of love are" (DAF, 19 April) to suggest she knew Dickens's "personal situation" by the time of the New York farewell dinner (GC, 21), but the reference was to Dickens's alarm lest reports of his ill health, reprinted in the British press, distress his family. Also, like other lines in the diary, this one seems to have been added later, possibly during a rereading after Dickens's death. He allegedly wrote to Ellen from America at least thirteen times, roughly twice monthly; see Curry's note 42 (GC, 64) for dates.

15. See the *Chatham News and North Kent Spectator* (16 May 1868), 4.

16. The ninety-three letters form part of the Huntington's Fields Collection (FC, 2694-2786). Only five were written prior to Dickens's death, eighty-seven afterward. In the black-bordered sixth for 4 July 1870 (FC, 2779), "My Dear Mrs. Fields" first became "Dearest Friend." Later, one finds scattered references to visiting Margate where Adrian believes Georgina and Mamie sometimes saw Ellen and her clergyman husband, George W. Robinson, at the school he ran; see, for example, the letter to Annie for 17 August 1883 (FC, 2756). Initially, Georgina rebuffed Annie's curiosity about Mrs. Dickens but subsequently kept her American friend informed about "poor Catherine's" slow death from cancer; see letters for 18 June 1872, 19 September 1878, and 13 October 1878 (FC, 2707, 2740, 2734).

17. Since Annie says she "heard quite accidentally to human ears," the source could have been some comment in or about a missive to Fields from Thomas Adolphus Trollope, brother of the novelist and Ellen's brother-in-law; periodically, he had business dealings with Ticknor and Fields, and several letters from him, sent between 1869-73, are in the Huntington's collection. The Trollopes (Thomas and Frances Eleanor) moved to Rome in 1872, when he accepted a position as political correspondent for a London newspaper, but Ellen went to them in Florence shortly after Dickens's death (N, 53). Curry suggests the informant was John Rollin Tilton, a New England painter whose Rome studio was frequented by visitors from New England (GC, 60). The Fieldses met Thomas Adolphus in Florence (DAF, 5 February 1860) and dined with him and Anthony in England (DAF, 12 May 1860), but the former's marriage to Frances Eleanor Ternan did not take place until 1866.

18. See Gustave Flaubert, *Madame Bovary*, ed. Francis Steegmuller (New York: Modern Library, 1957), 395.

19. One can discount as harmless the diary's only mention of Ellen by name, not by initials. Annie's entry for 8 June 1869 reads: "C.D. told J. that when he was ill in his reading only Nelly observed that he staggered and his eye failed, only she

dared to tell him." Curry concludes "that Miss Ternan had been in a position to observe Dickens closely" during the 1869 British reading tour that had ended in April with his "forced retirement" at Preston (GC, 42). Clearly, the Fieldses knew by 1869 that Dickens knew an Ellen Ternan, whose professional opinion and nerve he valued.

20. Significantly, Miss Hogarth was the only person besides Catherine mentioned by name when the so-called "Violated Letter," Dickens's defense of his conduct in separating from his wife, appeared without his permission in the New York *Tribune* for 16 August 1858; it portrayed Georgina as the household's mainstay and de facto mother of his children; see J, 2:923-24. Rumors reaching America along with the letter accused Dickens and his sister-in-law of engaging in criminal intercourse (that is, incest, according to British statutes).

21. James T. and Annie Fields remain prime candidates for the Gad's Hill notetaker; see Jerome Meckier, "Some Household Words: Two New Accounts of Dickens's Conversation," *Dickensian* 71 (Jan. 1975), 5-20.

22. According to Curry, Mrs. Fields was upset by criticism in the press of Dickens's alleged vanity and covetousness (GC, 14).

23. Cf. De Wolfe Howe, 157. Like Howe, Curry steadfastly refuses to address entries of this sort; his historian's chronological approach also prohibits comparisons between earlier and later passages.

24. See, for instance, DAF for 11 and 12 March.

25. Accounts of this match: J, 2:1088-89; D, 261-70; *MH*, 161-62 (with Annie's comments). Since Georgina Hogarth told Annie that she considered recollection of this event by the *Atlantic Monthly* unseemly (A, 228), one can imagine how tight-lipped she must have been regarding Ellen.

26. See Moss's invaluable appendix C (M, 331-33).

27. The next chapter contains a fuller assessment of Dickens's health.

28. Curry supplies "reposeful" for the word difficult to unscramble; if so, it seems to have been meant to distinguish male intellectual friendship from more problematic (i.e., intellectual *and* physical) male-female encounters. Reading this outburst as a sign of Annie's "fervent commitment" to Dickens's genius, proof that she "saw a religious significance in her gift of love to him" (GC, 23), amounts to imposing one's preferences.

29. Similarly, in August 1868, Annie would be pleased with the visiting Harriet Stephen, Thackeray's younger daughter and best friend of Dickens's daughter "Katie." (But neither in August nor that Christmas when she enjoyed a visit from Richard W. Spofford, Jr., a Massachusetts lawyer related to the Ternans through his mother, does the diary say anything about Ellen.)

30. See F.L. Lucas, ed., *George Crabbe: An Anthology* (Cambridge: Cambridge Univ. Press, 1933), 103-15.

31. See line 36 in number 95, in Douglas Bush, ed., *Selected Poetry of Tennyson* (New York: Modern Library, 1951), 210.

32. According to Annie's diary, the 14 May letter merely announced that "he was better and full of love to us both."

33. Annie's entry for 7 February 1875, written in New York, begins: "Dickens's birthday."

34. "Particulars" of the sort the Fieldses wanted concerning Dickens's last hours stayed scarce, however; Annie and James waited for letters from Gad's Hill beyond the end of the month (DAF, 30 June 1870). This entry reveals that Dickens last wrote the Fieldses on 5 June, three days before his fatal stroke. James's note survives in Box 12 (envelope 7) of Addenda to the Huntington's Fields Collection.

Undated, in purple ink, on a scrap of paper without letterhead, this sheet has escaped notice because it is not a letter to Fields and thus not officially part of the 5,438 items mostly of that nature in fifty-seven boxes. Instead, it is mixed in with more than fifty other letters from James to Annie on inconsequential domestic matters. Dickens died at "ten minutes past six" (ten after one in Boston) on the evening of 9 June, "just four months and two days past his fifty-eighth birthday" (J, 2:1154). The handwritten date of 10 June—not in Fields's hand but penciled in at the bottom of the note—suggests a certain delay either in cabling across the Atlantic or in sending word to 124 Tremont Street. Equally disconcerting is the inscription on the reverse side, again in pencil and presumably by the same executory hand that added the date: "Letters from Mr. Fields to be destroyed."

35. W.S. Tryon has pictured the fifty-three-year-old Fields perturbed by forebodings of his own demise: that his partner, Ticknor, had died at precisely his age became "a disturbing thought and it was not bettered by the dreadful news from London which told him of the sudden death of his beloved Charles Dickens" (T, 386). Fields resigned the editorship of the *Atlantic* in December 1870, citing health problems; given the selfless sincerity of the 10 June note, however, Dickens's death could only have become a memento mori to him subsequently.

36. Forster's biography was "the last book" her husband "laid down" before his death; see Annie's *James T. Fields: Biographical Notes and Personal Sketches* (Boston: Houghton Mifflin, 1881), 273.

37. Wagenknecht, however, considered £1,000 out of a £93,000 estate "a pleasant legacy" for "a dear young friend" but "very niggardly" if intended for a woman who, without being able to demand marriage, "had given an older man her youth" (EW, 45).

38. In the spring of 1858, Longfellow had been upset by reports of Dickens's domestic difficulties. Wagenknecht noted ("Dickens in Longfellow's Letters and Journals" [EW, 86]) that he complained to Charles Sumner (3 June) and Mary Mackintosh (22 June) about "a fair reputation" being "eagerly . . . dragged through the mire," but the poet never specified what he had heard or how much of it he believed.

39. See the letter for 28 June 1870 (FC, 5010), in which Longfellow plans to visit Fields next day.

40. See the letter for 21 July (FC, 495) and 22 August 1870 in Andrew Hilen, ed., *The Letters of Henry Wadsworth Longfellow* (Cambridge: Harvard Univ. Press, 1982), 5:370.

41. On 9 November 1871, Longfellow sent Fields a letter from Cambridge containing a twenty-five dollar check as his "Gad's Hill contribution" (Letters, 5:469); Hilen suggests the publisher was collecting "either for the purchase of Gad's Hill . . . or for the maintenance of Dickens's family there," but the charity was Georgina Hogarth's fund for a former maid (A, 202). After two paragraphs about the check, Longfellow writes in his third: "I have missed seeing you for a long time, not having been able to go to town. But I want to see you very much. I am still a 'doubting Thomas,' about some things." This, says Hilen, refers to the next paragraph about proofs to *The Divine Tragedy*, but it could more easily relate to the first two paragraphs and the Ternan affair. If so, Fields may not have discussed Ellen with the poet until late in 1871 (not 1870); that is, not until shortly before 6 December 1871 when Annie, perhaps fully apprised, speculated about her bond with "N.T." Longfellow (Journal, 30 August 1871) persuaded Fields "to suppress certain things" in the essay that became the Dickens chapter in *Yesterdays with Authors* (EW, 87).

42. See Katherine M. Longley, "The Real Ellen Ternan," *Dickensian* 81 (Spring 1985), 27-44.

43. The relationship between James T. Fields and Annie Adams, his second wife, may not have been a mutually passionate attachment, a possibility perhaps implied in Annie's pious hope that their joys and pains would continue to knit them closer together. James wed Annie in 1854, four years after the death of Eliza Willard, his first wife, who was Annie's cousin. Fields's biographer, however, tells a romantic story: "Annie worshipped her famous and popular husband and James in turn cherished deeply, almost paternally, this child who had entrusted her life to him" (T, 211). The diaries do not preclude the judgment that Annie and Dickens may inadvertently have made each other aware that each was missing something.

44. Hence the unintentional irony first in Harriet Beecher Stowe's letter for 21 November 1867, just after Dickens's arrival, and then in John Greenleaf Whittier's for 17 December 1868, a year later. "I suppose," Mrs. Stowe wrote, "the Dickens has got possession of you all before this—May he bring you back when he is done with you" (FC, 3969). "And how pleasant it must be to thee," Whittier noted, "to know that his winter here was made happier by thy friendship!" See John B. Pickard, ed., *The Letters of John Greenleaf Whittier* (Cambridge: Harvard Univ. Press, 1975), 3:186.

5. HEALTH AND MONEY

1. Philip Collins computed 472 readings, of which 27 were for charity (SN, x); but his figure of 75 American performances is one more than Raymund Fitzsimons counted (RF, 140) and one short of the total documented by Sidney P. Moss (M, 331-33). Annie Fields also noted that Dickens had read 76 times and added: "It seems like a dream" (DAF, 18 April 1868); but on 18 April Dickens still had one more performance to go. He last did a reading publicly on 15 March 1870, almost three months before his stroke.

2. Between 1825, when financial disaster began to overtake Scott at age fifty-four, and his death in 1832, the ailing prose artist turned out more than half a dozen works although seldom at his best; see Edgar Johnson, *Sir Walter Scott: The Great Unknown* (London: Hamish Hamilton, 1970), 2:941-71.

3. Securing Dickens, Tryon added, was "the last great satisfaction" of Fields's life.

4. See *Land We Love* 4 (1868), 421-33.

5. Similarly, on 2 December 1867, Charles H. Taylor, the New York *Tribune*'s Boston correspondent, described Dickens at the opening reading as a "radiant spirit" who was "full of life" (EP, 188-89).

6. Sylvère Monod, *Dickens the Novelist* (Norman: Univ. of Oklahoma Press, 1967), 382.

7. It was "an exceptionally hard winter," one of "unexampled severity" (D, 151, 179).

8. Dickens's sobriquet for his cold—"the true American"—may have been a facetious allusion to Cassius Marcellus Clay's unpopular antislavery paper. No true American, it argued, could countenance slavery; ironically, Dickens's faithful ailment would not set him free. See the "Appeal of Cassius M. Clay to Kentucky and the World" (Boston: Macomber, Pratt, 1845); the title could be Pogram's.

9. Dickens was too indisposed to leave his room on 25 February; next day, however, he and Fields stepped off the course for the match, doing four miles per

hour for one and a half hours each way—a total of twelve miles. On 29 February, the day of the contest, Dickens did it again, but how he "could go through such a race, evidently outwalking both contestants (Osgood and Dolby) on the way to the turn at least, when so ill with a cold that he could scarcely appear for his readings," one analyst has decided, "must forever remain a mystery" (EP, 231).

10. One critic has maintained that Dickens's letters for the 1860s "contradict" Edgar Johnson's notion of a self-destructive performer: "despite the hectic pace, . . . Dickens did his best to take care of himself"; he adopted "Spartan principles" not because he had squandered his resources but to prevent them from being depleted. See Paroissien's edition of the *Letters*, 15. Analyzing the breakdown that later caused the cancellation of the Chappell's tour at Preston ("Dickens's Last Provincial Reading," *Dickensian* 83 [Summer 1987], 79-87), R.D. Butterworth showed that Dickens carefully monitored his health in mid-April 1869 and concealed his anxiety from the public.

11. Edward F. Payne reprinted this entry from Root's diary (EP, 248-49); in addition, Root gave his wife's opinion that Dickens "never was in better form."

12. On 25 May, Dickens wrote his Boston friends that he was, in Forster's paraphrase, "brown beyond belief" from his ocean voyage "and causing the greatest disappointment in all quarters by looking so well" (F, 2:439). Dickens added: "My doctor was quite broken down in spirits on seeing me for the first time last Saturday. *Good lord! seven years younger!* said the doctor recoiling."

13. Fields was either taken in or, like Dickens, eager to accentuate the reader's courage: his "spirit was wonderful, and, although he lost all appetite and could partake of very little food, he was always cheerful and ready for his work when the evening came round" (Y, 167).

14. Johnson never rejected Dolby's narrative outright: the manager *mistakenly* "believed in America that his Chief's illness was mainly due to fatigue and the true American" (J, 2:1103). The thesis for Johnson's biography stems from Forster's comment on the American reading tour: "the sadness" (illness) "underlying his triumph makes it all very tragical" (F, 2:422).

15. Annie's diary entry is for 15 April 1868; presumably, it referred to the previous evening's performance, because Dickens did not read that night.

16. Moss quotes Bigelow (p. 269).

17. RS, 308, 322. Dickens allegedly could not perform in America "without the aid of the strongest stimulants, not excluding drugs" (318).

18. Horace Greeley's New York *Tribune* called Dickens's "fame" the "capital stock" in the reading enterprise, although it had never yet "yielded him anything particularly munificent in America" (F, 2:396).

19. Thackeray, by comparison, made $12,000 in 1852-53, according to Philip Collins, " 'Agglomerating Dollars with Prodigious Rapidity': British Pioneers on the American Lecture Circuit," *Victorian Literature and Society*, ed. James R. Kincaid and Albert J. Kuhn (Columbus: Ohio State Univ. Press, 1984), 8; from the lecture tours of 1852-53 and 1855-56 combined, Thackeray realized £9,500 (JW, pt. 2:13).

20. Despite accepting Dolby's estimate of total receipts at $228,000 (D, 331), another source stated that Dickens got to keep only $95,000 after deducting expenses and conversion costs (EP, 250). Even so, the £13,571 into which this sum translates exceeds Chappell's offer but would have been less than the £15,500 profit Dolby had predicted; according to the manager, Dickens realized £19,000, or $126,000 (D, 322). Dickens later told the Fieldses he paid the 40 percent con-

version cost on the advice of Coutts', his London bankers (DAF, 10 October 1869).

21. Dolby's subsequent outrage in late April at New York customs agents who tried to block Dickens's departure seems ridiculous (as does their greed); Dickens was obviously not liable for an American income tax and had been specifically exempted. In light of the massive conversion loss, however, an uneasy Dickens could ill afford further depletion of his profits by an estimated $12,000 (M, 296).

22. Philip Collins, ed., *Charles Dickens: The Public Readings* (Oxford: Clarendon Press, 1975), xxix. Oddly, Collins elsewhere terms Dickens's financial "reward" for the American tour "splendid," an "enormous sum for four [*sic*] months' work" (*SN*, ix-x).

23. "Riot at the Sale of Charles Dickens's Tickets at New Haven!" was typical of the headlines; another read: "Dickens's Agent and New York Speculators Arrested!" See D, 247.

24. Forster stated that in February the plan was still to accomplish eighty-two readings but that six were dropped due to political excitement; eliminating places like Chicago and Cincinnati, he added, enabled Dickens "to get home nearly a month earlier" (F, 2:416-17).

25. Dolby's resolve "to induce the public to come to Mr. Dickens rather than that he should go to them" (D, 179) is a combination of hindsight and virtue made out of necessity: it does not explain why the manager started for the Midwest *three times* only to be recalled on each occasion.

26. If Dolby's prospecting report included profit calculations based on various prices of admission (M, 234), Dickens must have ignored it.

27. The New York *World* gave Dolby this moniker (RF, 115).

28. Dolby was hired by Messrs. Chappell in 1866 so that Dickens "might be relieved of all business cares in connection with the Readings" (D, 2); similarly, in America Dickens "did not wish to be embarrassed with the details of money matters" (D, 140).

29. Dolby's boast that Dickens's second largest receipts ($3,298 at the final New York reading) were "exclusive of the premiums obtained by the ticket speculators, which, on that occasion, as on all others, must have been enormous" (D, 319), betrayed an ignorance of the precise sums involved; receipts may have been smaller than premiums.

30. Given $228,000 total receipts, Dickens and Dolby sold about 114,000 tickets; 9,120 resold would amount to only 8 percent.

31. Less plausible is Dolby's contention that newspaper articles criticizing his management were "instigated by the speculators themselves" (D, 168), even though it would have been to their advantage to keep the public incensed at him instead of them.

32. The list of persons besides Dickens who profited legitimately from his talents is extensive. Ticknor and Fields, at whose bookstore the first Boston ticket sale was held, received a "commission" of £1,000 ($7,000) (PL, 3:644), plus "5 percent of the Boston gross receipts" (T, 319); thus the firm may have made more than $10,000, or a 14 percent profit on the £10,000 it had put up as guaranteed minimum earnings for Dickens if he came to America (the normal interest rate was 6 percent). Dolby's commission came to £3,000.

33. The contract, which can be found in the Pierpont Morgan Library, has been printed in full at the end of Sidney P. Moss, "Charles Dickens and Frederick Chapman's Agreement with Ticknor and Fields," CD-TF, 35-38.

34. This letter appeared on page 6 of the New York *Tribune* for 18 May 1867.

35. Houghton Mifflin has deposited the records of its predecessor, Ticknor and Fields, in Harvard's Houghton Library, where the cost books can be examined.

36. Kappel and Patten speculated that by early April 1867 "Dickens may . . . have signed some kind of contract" (p. 15), but they seem to have been unaware of the actual document and its provisions.

37. See Browning's letters to Fields, especially the one for 6 September 1855 (FC, 330-36); it is quoted by Ian Jack, "Browning on *Sordello* and *Men and Women*: Unpublished Letters to James T. Fields," *Huntington Library Quarterly* 45 (Summer 1982), 186.

38. See the letter to Fields for 4 October 1855 (FC, 3678); "Susan Merton" appeared in 1856 as *It's Never Too Late to Mend*.

39. See the letter to Fields for 23 July 1860 (FC, 3620). Eventually, Reade was so distressed by the "small return" from *It's Never Too Late to Mend*—only 4,000 copies had been sold—that he questioned Fields's accounting; see the letter for 12 March 1857 (FC, 3673).

40. See Trollope to Fields, 11 March 1862 (FC, 5283).

41. Were one to accept Tryon's statement that Dickens was "offered . . . a royalty of 10 per cent on the retail price of every volume sold" (T, 305), his share would still have been no higher than Reade's; but the 1867 contract contained no such provision for old work or new.

42. Surprisingly, James T. and Annie Fields took a special trip to Providence to hear "Marigold" on 21 February (DAF, 22 February), just days before it was first performed in Boston; the only reading, therefore, to debut in Boston after 6 December was "Gamp" on 3 April, which gave novelty to the tour's final weeks.

43. Several catalogues put out by Ticknor and Fields during the 1860s survive in the Massachusetts Historical Society, including one for 1868.

44. Technically, Dickens had jeopardized his English copyright when *Great Expectations* ran in *Harper's Weekly*; from 24 November 1860 through the end of January 1861, the American periodical was one week ahead of *All the Year Round*. Thereafter they coincided because the ocean steamer did not bring advance sheets for 26 January 1861, thus allowing the British magazine to catch up.

45. See chapters 1 and 5 in Meckier, *Hidden Rivalries*.

6. LAST WORDS

1. See the letter for 25 January in *Letters of Aldous Huxley*, ed. Grover Smith (London: Chatto and Windus, 1969), 241.

2. Ironically, Huxley's round-the-world journey, described in *Jesting Pilate*, first brought him to the country that later became his home; he arrived for good in 1937 to avoid the oncoming war. Earlier, his ideas of modern America and Victorian England were strongly influenced by Dickens's sixth novel. The latter period he damned in another letter as "the Pecksniffian epoch" (278); in June 1925, a visiting American scientist, "talking in that loose pretentious meaningless American way," struck Aldous as "a sort of scientific Jefferson Brick" (250). Not surprisingly, besides borrowing ideas from Henry Ford and J.B. Watson for *Brave New World*, Huxley sent Bernard Marx and Lenina to America in chapters 7-8; their estimate of natural, primitive man on the Malpais reservation deflates Lawrence's atavistic Romanticism as effectively as Dickens disparaged Rousseau.

3. Given Dickens's use of America's vulgarity and England's subtler hypoc-

risy first to compare and then to discredit both places, Thackeray's program in *The Virginians* seems simplistic; he aimed at "contrasting the vitality of the emergent country with the decadence of the autocratic society across the sea," which is Robert A. Colby's description in *Thackeray's Canvas of Humanity: An Author and His Public* (Columbus: Ohio State Univ. Press, 1979), 401. Thackeray showed Americans an image closer to the one they held of themselves.

4. Unchanging characteristics were the recurring theme when Theodore Roosevelt commented on *Chuzzlewit* in letters to his children. To Ted on 20 May 1906 he wrote: "Jefferson Brick and Elijah Pogram and Hannibal Chollop are all real personifications of certain bad tendencies in American life, and I am continually thinking of or alluding to some newspaper editor or Senator or Homicidal rowdy by one of these three names." He told Kermit on 29 February 1908 that Dickens, being no gentleman, was "utterly incapable of seeing the high purpose and real greatness which (in spite of the presence also of much that was bad and vile) could have been visible all around him here in America to any man whose vision was both keen and lofty"; nevertheless, the novelist "was in his element in describing with bitter truthfulness Scadder and Jefferson Brick, and Elijah Pogram, and Hannibal Chollop, and Mrs. Hominy and the various other characters, great and small, that have always made me enjoy *Martin Chuzzlewit*. Most of these characters we still have with us," testimonials to Dickens's lasting words. See the *Dickensian* 82 (Summer 1986), 118-20.

5. James T. Fields quoted this letter in its entirety (*Y*, 150-51); also see Georgina Hogarth and Mamie Dickens, eds., *The Letters of Charles Dickens* (London: Macmillan, 1893), 97.

Index

Gaskell, Elizabeth Cleghorn, 10, 37, 61, 73, 78, 108-9, 122
Godwin, William, 108, 109
Goethe, J.W. von, 105
Gold, Joseph, 246 n 29
government: theories of, 105, 106
gradualism, 78, 85, 86, 240
Great Expectations (Dickens), 18, 22, 221, 241 "Great International Walking Match," 166, 189
greed: of book publishers, 41, 56; as "first principle," 92, 110. *See also* selfishness, theme of
Greeley, Horace, 47, 57, 208, 231
Grillo, Virgil, 244 n 10

Hale, Edward Everett, 235
Hall, Basil, 69, 75, 100, 101
Hard Times (Dickens), 18
Harper and Brothers publishers, 53, 221, 222, 225, 226, 235; negotiations with Dickens, 231, 232, 233-34
Harper's Monthly Magazine, 222
Harper's Weekly Magazine, 232, 235
Harrison, Lafayette, 229
Hartford: copyright speech in, 41, 43, 44, 45
Hawthorne, Nathaniel, 66, 163
Heart of Darkness (Conrad), 27, 28, 36-37
Heilman, Robert B., 247 n 1
Hervieu, August Jean, 139, 146, 255 n 3
Hogarth, Georgina, 16, 157, 191, 211, 258 n 41 knowledge of Ellen, 136; Annie's fascination with, 149-50, 152-53, 154, 155, 171, 178-79; friendship with Annie, 159, 175
Hogarth, Mary, 1, 5, 147-48, 182, 198, 242
Holmes, Oliver Wendell, 139, 163
Holt, Felix, 36
home: theme of returning home, 27, 62
Hood, Thomas, 51
House, Madeline, 3
Household Words, 68
Howe, M.A. DeWolfe, 150, 164, 173, 180
Hume, David, 11

Huxley, Aldous, 20-21, 237, 239, 241, 245 n 19, 262 n 2
Huxley Julian, 237
Huxley, T.H., 252 n 28
hypocrisy, 19, 20, 24, 55; of Dickens, 70, 71, 137

imagination, 18
"individualism," 87
influenza, 187, 188
"Inimitable, The," 82, 84
In Memoriam (Tennyson), 107, 172
innocence, 8, 10, 63, 81; in *Martin Chuzzlewit,* 26, 28-31; of Dickens, 43, 76, 148-49, 200
Innocents Abroad or The New Pilgrims Progress (Twain), 65, 237
irony, 12, 33
Irving, Washington, 14, 48, 49, 66

Jackson, T.A., 15-16, 38
Jeffrey, Francis, 62
Jerrold Fund, 135
Jesting Pilate (Huxley), 21
Johnson, Andrew, 136, 166, 189, 202
Johnson, Edgar, 3, 23, 45, 72, 244 n 6; on Ellen Ternan, 139, 140; on Dickens's health, 183, 192, 193, 195, 199, 204
Johnson Louise H., 253 n 31
Jonah and the whale 26, 27, 61-62

Kaplan, Fred, 161, 181, 201, 220; on Ellen Ternan, 144-45, 146, 147; on Dickens's health, 183-84
Kappel, Andrew J., 223, 224
Keats, John, 26
Kelly (Dolby's assistant), 203, 204, 205

Lea and Blanchard publishers, 53, 221
Lemaitre (actor), 168
Lewes, G.H., 164
Ley, J.W.T., 151
liberalism to Toryism, 95-96, 97
Library edition of Dickens's work, 226
Life of Charles Dickens (Forster), 177
Life of Charles Dickens (Wright), 151
Lind, Jenny, 207
Lippincott publishers, 227, 228
Little Dorrit (Dickens), 18, 20, 27, 37, 46, 221

reading tour in America (*Cont'd*)
203, 208, 209-14; success of, 201;
poor business arrangements for, 202-
3, 206-7; problems with scalpers,
213-15; antispeculation campaign,
215-16; tickets forged, 218; aids book
sales, 223, 224, 226, 227, 233; gala
opening, 228-30, 232. *See also*
Dolby, George; Ticknor and Fields
publishers
reading tour in England, 135, 183,
193, 200-201, 230; profits from 202,
221
realism, 235
rebirth, 108. *See also* death/rebirth
Reform Bill of 1832, 78, 86
religion, 76, 100
"reprint houses," 53
republicanism, 16, 28, 76, 85, 94, 96,
108
Retrospectives of an Active Life (Bigelow), 199
robbery imagery, 47
Romanticism, 18, 22, 108, 109
Roosevelt, Theodore, 263 n 4
Root, James Edward, 190
Rosner, Mary, 245 n 22
Rousseau, Jean Jacques, 2, 10, 11, 18,
19, 24, 36, 107, 241
Ruskin, John, 66

Sadleir, Michael, 102
satire in Dickens, 2, 4, 46, 56; in *Martin Chuzzlewit*, 11, 15, 61-62, 101,
239; themes for, 18-19, 46, 53; after
first American trip, 63, 80
scalpers, 39, 208, 213-15. *See also*
ticket speculators
Schlicke, Paul, 195-96, 255 n 7
Scott, Sir Walter, 43-44, 184, 259 n2
second trip to America. *See* reading
tour in America
secular humanism, 122, 123
self-assertion, 56, 57
self-awareness, 32, 36, 80
self-forgetfulness, 32-33
"Self-ishness," 87
selfishness, theme of, 17, 19, 28, 32-
33
serial novels, 57-58, 61, 62, 225, 226,
235; selling of rights to, 232, 233

"Sikes and Nancy" piece, 193-94, 196-
98, 236; Dickens's purpose for, 195-
96
Slater, Michael, 135, 136, 137, 138,
239, 243 n 6
slavery: Dickens on, 68; Martineau
on, 76, 102, 110, 111, 112-13; travel
writers compared, 76, 113-18. *See
also* abolition
Smith, Adam, 11
Smith, Arthur, 135
Social Contract, The (Rousseau), 244
n 9
social evolutionists, 78
social issues in Dickens, 77, 197
socialization, process of, 34
Society in America (Martineau), 16,
76, 83, 92, 105, 108; importance of,
110; Dickens's view of, 112, 114
solitary confinement, 26, 27, 103, 104,
110
Southey, Robert, 108, 109
Spedding, James, 70
Staplehurst railway mishap, 142
Straus, Ralph, 199
swamp imagery, 86

T.B. Peterson and Brothers publishers, 221, 222, 226
Tale of Two Cities, A (Dickens), 18,
109, 165, 221
Tartuffe (Molière), 4
technological revolution, 18
temperance convention, 23
Tennyson, Alfred, 51, 107, 172
Ternan, Ellen Lawless (Nelly), 74,
162, 165, 181, 256 n 17; during reading tour, 134-40, 200; coded telegram regarding, 135, 136, 140, 144,
146, 255 n 4; "the Patient," 142; as
difficulty for Dickens, 144, 145; limitations of relationship with Dickens,
147, 148, 150, 155; Annie's knowledge of, 151, 152, 153, 154, 156,
164, 256 n 14; after Dickens's return
home, 155, 157, 161, 173; "bond"
between Annie and Ellen, 160-61,
180; eludes biographers, 181
Thackeray, William Makepeace, 59,
73, 82, 211, 223, 253